On Feminist Ethics and Politics

FEMINIST ETHICS

On Feminist
Ethics and Politics

EDITED BY CLAUDIA CARD

 UNIVERSITY PRESS OF KANSAS

Published by the University Press of Kansas (Lawrence, Kansas 66049), which was
organized by the Kansas Board of Regents and is operated and funded by
Emporia State University, Fort Hays State University, Kansas State University,
Pittsburg State University, the University of Kansas, and Wichita State University

Library of Congress Cataloging-in-Publication Data

On feminist ethics and politics / edited by Claudia Card.
     p.   cm. — (Feminist ethics)
   Includes bibliographical references and index.
   ISBN 0-7006-0967-9 (alk. paper). — ISBN 0-7006-0968-7 (pbk. :
alk. paper)
    1. Sex discrimination against women.   2. Feminism—Moral and
ethical aspects.   I. Card, Claudia.   II. Series.
HQ1237.05   1999
305.42—dc21   99-11259

British Library Cataloguing in Publication Data is available.

Printed in the United States of America

10 9 8 7 6 5 4 3 2 1

In Memory of
Genevieve C. Card Samp (1909–1987)
and Adaline Ellen Johnson (1918–1996)

Contents

Introduction

1 / *Groping Through Gray Zones*

CLAUDIA CARD

An important early task of feminist ethics was to address undeserved negative judgments of women's character and behavior. Slander helps to lock women, in a deeply misogynist society, into positions of powerlessness. Yet another task has been to identify and then overcome the real damage oppression has wrought in us, including character damage. Oppressive social structures are an unfavorable context for flourishing or developing good character, whether we are favored or disfavored by those structures. Authors in this volume are sensitive to this situation.

What follows is in two parts. The first presents "gray zones," a term I borrow from Primo Levi for certain areas inhabited by agents who are at once victims of oppression and involved in perpetrating oppression on others. The second previews this book's essays, noting overlapping or connecting ideas among them and raising questions suggested by Levi's concept. In Levi's gray zones, agents confront real choices between horrifying options created by unspeakable oppression. This book's essays do not discuss the kinds of evil found in Levi's gray zones. Yet, I introduce the concept here, both because I think feminist ethics must take it seriously and because many contributors' essays do discuss problems shared by Levi's gray zones. These are problems of moral ambiguity, moral compromise, and complicity, under stress, in perpetrating oppression.

GRAY ZONES

One of the greatest evils threatening victims of oppression is the danger of becoming evil oneself, becoming complicit in evils perpetrated against others. Not everyone becomes or remains so complicit. Nor among those who do is everyone equally so. But avoiding or ceasing complicity can require alertness, loss of innocence, sensitivity to risks, and then moral imagination and creativity. Most of us face this challenge to some degree. But for some, the challenge is acute.

In the 1970s feminists identified women's complicity in misogynist oppression in the "Athena" syndrome (being born again from Daddy's head) and in "harem politics" (a power hierarchy among female slaves, some charged to discipline others). In both cases, women are drawn, by hope of favor and privilege, into being men's instruments of oppression. "Favor and privilege" may sound like superfluous goods. In reality, they are often no more than reprieve from abuse. To resist being "divided and conquered," some women who refuse such favors still stand in solidarity with those who do not. At any rate, some refuse to judge women who give in. Yet, refusing to evaluate the choices would expose us to being manipulated and worse.

I take the occasion of this introduction to reflect, from a commitment to female development and flourishing, on women's involvement in perpetrating evils in a social context of misogyny. I do so not because I find most women basically lacking in integrity or hostile, even toward other women. Contrary to patriarchal myth, I have found most women's strongest bonds to be with other women, despite the double binds of patriarchy that do so much to pit us against one another. Yet people who are bonded to others can also be abusive to them. The realization of women's capacity to compromise with evil can be disillusioning. Yet its undeniable history requires us to take it seriously and reflect on its implications. If initially an appreciation of female involvement in evil threatens feminist solidarity, ignoring the complexities of female relationships to evil produces a superficial feminism. The main reasons to take seriously women's capacity for evil are to move beyond myths of female innocence in our relationships with each other and to confront our responsibilities for past and potential damage to victims.

My concern is not with milder misconduct, such as hurtful or insensitive remarks, but with involvement in the real evils of oppression. The seriousness of these evils is hinted at in metaphors Marilyn Frye identified as embedded in the concept of oppression—reducing, molding, immobilizing.[1] That seriousness is made more concrete by

Iris Young's analysis of "faces" of oppression: violence, powerlessness, marginalization, exploitation, cultural imperialism.[2] Evils are losses or deprivations of what is basic to a tolerable existence, when those losses are produced, aided, or abetted by wrongdoing. Many things are disappointing, undesirable, even bad, without being evil. Evils command our attention. As Nietzsche saw, it is natural to hate what we find evil.[3] There is even danger of becoming obsessed with it, whereas we are not likely to become overinvolved with what we find merely poor or inferior.

Evildoing need not be sadistic. It can be negligent, callous, or simply lacking in scruple. These are more common, more banal sources of evil than sadism.[4] Yet, however banal the motive, the result is often far from banal.

Misogyny is an evil. Although "misogyny" means "woman hating," feminists use it to refer to practices, behaviors, and socially created environments that are hostile to women and girls. Hostility here is not identical (albeit compatible) with the emotion of hatred. Hostility refers here to hindrance of female health and development. Misogynist environments are hostile to women as polluted ground and water are hostile to plants. To regard misogynist environments as evil, ethically, is to find them also the result of wrongdoing.

It has long been observed that misogynous environments are routinely maintained by women. There are many degrees of (in)voluntariness in this participation. Many who appear to participate voluntarily would only do so in an oppressive situation already created by others. Women run whorehouses, sometimes with pride. Mothers socialize daughters into aspects of femininity that endanger their health and safety. Sometimes they ostracize lesbian daughters. Women who do patriarchy's dirty work occupy positions of trust and responsibility. Some not only accept but actively seek such positions. Their tasks draw on female initiative, energy, imagination, creativity, intelligence, and skill. In other cases, such as child abuse, oppressive behavior may be an outlet for cruelty, or the result of demoralization, produced by oppression.

Consider Hedda Nussbaum. She was nearly as battered by Joel Steinberg, with whom she had lived since 1976, as was his illegally adopted daughter, Lisa, who died from his abuse at the age of six in 1987. Hedda Nussbaum's life with Steinberg was a living death. She did not deserve the abuse; no one does. But neither did she, apparently, seek help (such as dialing 911) for Lisa, who was even more helpless and had no one else to help her. Years of battery and prior compromises thoroughly demoralized Hedda Nussbaum. Andrea Dworkin, survivor of domestic battery, writes: "I don't think Hedda Nussbaum is 'innocent.' I don't know any innocent adult women. Life is harder than that for everyone. But adult women who have been battered are especially not innocent. Battery is a forced descent into hell and you don't get by in hell by moral goodness."[5] But she continues, "I am upset by the phony mourning for Lisa Steinberg—the hypocritical sentimentality of a society that would not really mind her being beaten to death once she was an adult," and she notes, "There was a little boy, too, Mitchell, seventeen months old, tied up and covered in feces. And the only way to have spared him was to rescue Hedda. Now he has been tortured and he did not die. What kind of man will he grow up to be?" (1997, 53–54).

The issues these phenomena present take us into what we might recognize, following Primo Levi, as a "gray zone, poorly defined, where the two camps of masters and servants both diverge and converge."[6] "Gray zone" was the term he used to describe the moral area occupied by *Kapos* (captains) and other prisoners of Nazi concentration camps and ghettos who held positions of responsibility and administration.

Gray zones "confuse our need to judge" (Levi 1989, 42). They are inhabited by people who are implicated, through their choices, in perpetrating on others the evil that also threatens or engulfs themselves. Levi does not define gray zones specifically. He conveys the idea mainly by examples, noting that such zones are varied, ambiguous, and have multiple roots. Among these roots are the oppressors' need for "external auxiliaries" and realization that the best way to bind them is "to burden them with guilt, cover them with blood, compromise them as much as possible, thus establishing a bond of complicity so that they can no longer turn back" (Levi 1989, 43).

"Gray zone" is a problematic term if it presupposes that "dark" or "black" represents evil. Such usage may unwittingly reinforce racism. It may do so today, even if the metaphor of dark as evil originated historically in references to the night in a society where nights are dangerous or difficult (because it is hard for the visually dependent to make their way). For that reason I hope to find an alternative metaphor.[7] Meanwhile, I use Levi's term "gray zone" and acknowledge that if its use instantiates what it names, "gray zone" is itself a gray term.

In his chapter "The Gray Zone" in *The Drowned and the Saved*, Levi wrote about prisoners whose labors were used to carry out the Nazi oppression and genocide. Some were drafted; others sought such positions. Some did clerical work or were officers' domestic servants; some became camp doctors. Some ghetto prisoners were members of Ghetto Councils, eventually charged with deportation tasks.[8] Others became ghetto police, charged with rounding up prisoners for deportation.[9] In death camps, prisoners were chosen for the *Sonderkommando*, charged with cremation detail. Almost all *Sonderkommando* prisoners were murdered within months or weeks.[10] Some prisoners became *Kapos*, with power over other prisoners, in exchange for food or additional privileges (Levi 1989, 36–69). Levi notes that although a minimum of harshness was expected of *Kapos*, there was no upper limit to the cruelty they could inflict with impunity.

Prisoners who occupied such positions lost their innocence.[11] Loss of innocence, even when it involves "dirty hands," is not the same as loss of virtue.[12] Yet it carries moral risk. We lose innocence in becoming responsible for others' suffering, even when we make the best decision under the circumstances. When we fail to live up to that responsibility, or lack the means to live up to it, our integrity may be compromised. We risk losing self-respect and moral motivation. Once we feel we have crossed the line of participating in the infliction of evil, we may have less to restrain us from more and worse in the future.

Privileged prisoners, Levi observed, were a minority of the camp populations. But he also claimed that "they represent a majority among survivors" (1989, 40). How such a realization should affect the attitude of survivors toward themselves and toward other survivors were questions that troubled him profoundly and led him to draw distinctions. Regarding members of the *Sonderkommando* who did not kill with their own hands, he wrote, "I believe that no one is authorized to judge them, not those who lived through the experience of the Lager [camp] and even less those who did not" (1989, 59). Yet he did not refrain from all judgments of gray zone inhabitants, noting that "they are the rightful owners of a quota of guilt" (1989, 49) but also that, were it up to him, he "would lightheartedly absolve all those whose concurrence in the guilt was minimal and for whom coercion was of the highest degree" (1989, 54).

Gray zones, areas whose inhabitants are both victims and perpetrators of oppression, develop wherever the evils of oppression are severe, widespread, and persistent. The labor of the oppressed in the daily workings of maintaining oppressive power structures frees the energies of those on top for the joyous pursuits of cultural development. Their insulated positions enable them to avoid confronting dirt on their own hands, offering them the illusion of innocence.

Women have suffered the evils of oppression globally and for millennia. And women have been implicated in perpetrating evils not only of misogyny but of slavery, racism, anti-Semitism, classism, hatred of sexual diversity, and hatred and fear of the poor.[13] Women can inhabit gray zones in relation to children and in paying male protection rackets for protection against violence.[14] We are not always sensitive to the grayness of zones we inhabit. But feminists have been aware of the problem at least since the lesbian / straight battles of the 1970s.

In her struggle to envision a way out, Joyce Trebilcot came close to using the gray zone metaphor: "My life is like a muddy lake with some clear pools and rivulets—wimmin's spaces—but many areas thick, in one degree or another, with the silt and poisons of patriarchy."[15] Although she was describing her life, she did not want to count as a "wimmin's space" those portions of it marked by oppressive practices. Yet counting only ideal spaces as women's suggests, however unintentionally, that women interacting with women are better at resisting compromise with evil. History neither supports the view that we are nor yet sustains the hope that we might be. In women's spaces, too, we need to confront the ethical challenges of living with gray zones.

In appropriating Levi's term "gray zone" there is risk of misappropriating the experiences of Holocaust victims.[16] I do not wish to trade on the horrors of the camps or ghettos to get attention to the evils of misogyny. I do wish to explore the significance of the concept Levi identified for other contexts than those he had in mind. It is a concept that complicates our understandings of choices people make in oppressive circumstances, our assessments of the moral positions of victims of oppression, and the responsibilities such victims may have to and for one another. The choices facing many victims of misogyny bear no comparison with those of camp or ghetto prisoners. Most women are not Hedda Nussbaum (although more are than is commonly acknowledged). My point, however, is not to compare suffering or degrees of evil but to note patterns in the moral complexity of choices and judgments of responsibility. Evil is essential to what makes gray zones gray. But the kind of evil and one's relationship to it vary considerably. Helpful comparisons lie, rather, in the complexities of our assessments of responsibility and our relationships to evils that we would and should resist.

Levi's gray zones have three striking features. First, their inhabitants are victims of evil. Second, these inhabitants are implicated through their choices in perpetrating some of the same or similar evils on others who are already victims like themselves. And third, they act under extraordinary stress. Many have lost everything and everyone and face the threat of imminent and horrible death. It may seem at first that grayness is conveyed by the first two features alone: being both a victim of evil and being implicated in the perpetration of that evil on others. These two features already can be enough to "confuse our need to judge" (Levi 1989, 42). But the third feature—the extraordinary stress of extreme loss and the threat of imminent and horrible death—makes judgment even more problematic, given the frailty of human nature. Something like this third feature is important for distinguishing gray zones from other mixtures of good and evil. I understand the basic idea of a "gray zone" in such a way that the third feature is satisfied when agents must choose under conditions of major stress, such as intense or prolonged fear for one's life or for the lives of one's children. Misogyny's gray zones seldom, if ever, reach the extremity of death camp conditions. (Perhaps they did so in the case of the rape / death camps in Bosnia-Herzegovina, if there were targeted women who became complicit in that atrocity.) Yet major stress and the motive of survival or fear for one's basic security are present often enough.

The grayness of a gray zone has multiple sources. One is the presence of a mixture of evil and innocence. Victims of oppression undergo suffering they did nothing to deserve. They are in that sense innocent. Yet services they perform with some degree of voluntariness implicate them in perpetrating evil on others who also did not deserve to suffer it and who may not be similarly implicated themselves. The involvements of gray zone inhabitants are not of the same order or extensiveness as that of perpetrators who are not victims. Gray zone inhabitants lack the same discretion and power to walk away. One often would not readily describe as "murderers" prisoners who did not kill with their own hands. At the same time, it can be difficult to draw the kind of line that "kill with their own hands" suggests. Gray zone inhabitants are both innocent and not innocent—in other words, "gray."

Yet another source of grayness is ambiguity. Levi calls gray persons ambiguous and "ready to compromise." He goes on to describe the moral status of prisoners in the gray zone as somewhere between that of victims and custodians. The readiness to compromise, however, also suggests an ambiguity in the positions that external auxiliaries occupy. To function effectively, auxiliary functionaries must have some power and some discretion regarding its use. This presents the seductive thought that one may be able to use such a position for sabotage. Some did. Of those involved in secret defense organizations, such as Eugen Kogon in Buchenwald and Herman Langbein in Auschwitz, Levi says they were only apparently collaborators but that in reality they were camouflaged opponents (1989, 45–46). Even as opponents of the Nazis, however, they may have had to acquiesce in the infliction on others of undeserved suffering or death in order to further their resistance efforts. It can be argued that the risks were in the interests of even those victims, who almost certainly would have been killed anyway, as some of our interests outlive us. Yet even such activity carries the moral risks of dirty hands.

There is a greater likelihood that those who accept a position of privilege will be able to do nothing significant to resist, that all they will manage to do is become implicated in the perpetration of evil. There is danger of using the bare possibility of sabotage as a rationalization for saving one's skin or gaining reprieve from suffering. Levi notes that the power wielded by Kogon and Langbein was counterbalanced by the greater risks they ran in belonging to secret defense organizations.[17] The power wielded by many others, however, simply reduced their own risks or benefited a few friends without sabotaging the operation or any significant part of it.

Gray zone choices defy ordinary moral judgment. Whether we think the choosers chose well or poorly (often choices have to be made fast), their choices implicate them in the machinery of evil, with consequences for who suffers what. Further, circumstances under which choices are made frequently suggest unclarity of motive or intention. Choices made by some may appear the best anyone could do. Yet even these can carry great moral risk and a price. Some choices may appear shameful. Yet who could escape shame in such a context? Many appear to fall somewhere between, and yet others remain totally ambiguous.

Thus, "gray" can mean many things. Sometimes it evokes a complex judgment whose elements are mixed although clear enough individually. There may be no simple way to do justice to the case with an overall summary such as "good on the whole" or "bad on the whole." At other times, "gray" evokes a deed whose moral elements are genuinely unclear or ambiguous.

La Malinche, or Malinztin (a.k.a. Dona Martina), is an ambiguous figure in the history of the conquest of Mexico.[18] She appears to me to have lived in a gray zone after she was presented to Hernán Cortés to serve as his lover, translator, and tactical adviser. Refusal might have cost her life and perhaps the lives of others, although records left by Cortés's biographer and by one of his soldiers suggest that she served willingly and with pride.[19] (Should we trust them?) Did she prevent Cortés from doing even worse damage than he did? Did she significantly facilitate the Spanish conquest? Did she do both? How much did she know? What had she seen?

And what of Sacajawea (a.k.a. Sacagawea), who traveled with and translated for Lewis and Clark? Lewis and Clark were not Cortés. But Sacajawea, like La Malinche, was a slave. She was enrolled as one of his "wives" by a French Canadian, Toussaint Charbonneau, who also traveled as a translator on the expedition. He had won her in a bet with, or purchased her from, the Hidatsa raiding party, who had stolen her from the Shoshone, or Snake, people four years previously when she was ten or eleven years old.[20] We do not know a lot about her contributions to the Lewis and Clark expedition. Her main role, it appears, was to translate from the Shoshone so Lewis and Clark could purchase horses from them. Historians say it is an exaggeration to call her a guide.[21] But there is documentation in Lewis's journal of her having rescued important materials from a capsized boat. Considering how the "Lewis and Clark" explorations were subsequently used by white people and the effects on Native peoples of this "opening of the American West," as historian Stephen Ambrose calls it, Sacajawea's agency is morally unclear.

Sacajawea gave birth to a son shortly before the expedition began and carried him on her back for the journey. Escape, had she been so inclined, would probably have risked his life. She may not have wished to escape, as she wanted to see her people, the Shoshone, which the expedition enabled her to do. On the other hand, she left Charbonneau later in life because he beat her cruelly. What did she know of European-Native relations when she was fifteen? What could she have foreseen? Was she able to do anything for Native peoples? Was she able to engage in sabotage? Had she any interest in doing so? We have primarily in her case not only the testimony of white men but also the researches in 1924 of Charles Eastman, who was a Sioux Indian. He researched her life and death at the request of the Commissioner of Indian Affairs, interviewing people who had known her. White children in the United States, who learn that she was brave and resourceful (but not that she was a slave), idolize Sacajawea. The Girl Scout camp of my childhood in Wisconsin was named Camp Sacajawea. But she must be an ambiguous figure from the points of view of Native American interests.

Also gray but less ambiguous were the wives of slave owners in the United States who held responsibility for managing house slaves, especially wives who did not resist the system of slavery (as some did, covertly).[22] As with *Kapos*, there was, effectively, no limit to the cruelty they could inflict with impunity. To some extent, their functions were analogous to those of overseer slaves. Both might count as what Levi calls "external auxiliary functionaries," although slave overseers were more "external" than white women, who were not vulnerable to being sold away. Nor were slave owners' wives generally under a death threat. Marriage was not totally involuntary. Separation was an option for some. Marriage saved upper- and middle-class white women from the social death of spinsterhood and the outcast status of prostitution or poverty. These could be wretched alternatives, albeit far more endurable than many slaves' fates (although some prostitutes were slaves). Such a set of options is surely itself an evil. But that way of escaping the worst alternatives implicated white women in running the institution of slavery, which imposed not only social death but also terrible, premature biological death on slaves.

A white woman caught (or suspected) of a sexual liaison with a black man could be threatened by white men with battery or worse if she refused to accuse her lover of rape. The woman who gave in and accused him confronted a gray zone at the intersection of sexism and racism. She might reason that if she didn't do it, others would, or that some other excuse would be found to lynch the man. But if all white women refused to cooperate in lynching black men, public support for the practice might have been less. It might not have lasted so long or spread so far—as some might be tempted to say that the Nazi killing machine might have operated less efficiently had *Sonderkommando* (and other) prisoners generally and immediately refused their assignment (which at least one group did).

It can legitimately be objected that such a comparison is unfair, even outrageous, and perhaps also, for some similar reasons, comparing *Kapos* with members of the *Sonderkommando*. Such comparisons ignore differences in the level of control that gray zone agents had over their choices' consequences. *Sonderkommando* prisoners faced certain death, whatever they chose; they had so little to lose by resisting (as compared with not resisting) that their not resisting seems more an indication of the power of terror and the frailty of human nature than of any character corruption. Nor was their position one of "responsibility and administration," except in the most minimal sense. They had no discretion or decision-making power. *Kapos* had more discretion. But slave owners' wives (and administrators serving other oppressors) have often had considerable discretionary power. Incrementally and over time, they could sometimes raise the stakes so that although they had little to lose at first, later they had a great deal to lose by ceasing to cooperate (and much to gain by continuing).[23] Such a pattern does raise questions about character deterioration, and it suggests greater complicity.

Confronted with gray zone choices, it is tempting to reason, "If I can just stay alive, there is a chance I can help, but there is no chance I can be any good to anyone dead." Similarly, one may reason, "If I can get a little power, I may be able to help, but I can do no good as long as I acquiesce in my own impotence." Yet it is not true, as some of these cases show, that as long as one is alive, there is any real chance that one can help, or that as long as one has more power, one is in a better position to help. One may have no control over how one's life or one's power is used. Being no good to anyone is not the worst thing. Being an instrument of evil is worse.

Vulnerability to evils of misogyny has had a role in white women's becoming instruments of racism. But the evils threatening white

women seem different from those in which they become implicated;
sexism threatens them, whereas they become implicated in racism.
That distinction, however, may be ethically less important than similarities between the evils. Some camp prisoners became implicated
as *Kapos* in the evils of gay-bashing to gain reprieve from the evils of
political hatred against themselves. Tortures varied. Yet prison conditions alone might kill any of the prisoners. Levi did not treat such
distinctions in sources of evil as important in his reflections on the
gray zone. He wrote not only about Jewish prisoners but about camp
prisoners more generally. Likewise, women's gray zones do not always
implicate us in misogyny. Sometimes they implicate us in racism,
child abuse, or the torture of animals.

If the idea of a gray zone is understood to comprehend all who are
both victims and perpetrators of evil, it will be too wide. It will include those who survive to take revenge, for example, by doing to
former torturers—or to persons suspected of being former torturers—
some of what was done to them, even though the revenge-takers are
no longer in danger of suffering torture themselves.[24] It will include
those who wrong others when doing so saves them from no wrong
at the hands of still others and when the wrongs they perpetrate bear
no particular relation to the wrongs they suffer. Such deeds are not
"gray" in the senses discussed above. They are not ambiguous. They
are not even morally difficult or complex, although we may have
mixed emotional responses to them. The fact that a person's life as
a whole evokes in us a mixed emotional response—sympathy insofar as they are wrongly victimized by others but also anger insofar as
they wrong others—does not imply that any of their choices possessed the moral complexity or ambiguity of a gray zone. Probably
most people's lives taken as a whole would evoke mixed emotional
responses. When the gray zone is understood this broadly, it threatens to encompass the entire world, for evil appears to be part of the
human condition, and who besides young children (and perhaps most
animals) is entirely innocent?[25]

Like Levi, I understand gray zones more specifically to result from
choices that are neither gratuitously nor willfully evil but nevertheless implicate choosers in perpetrating, sustaining, or aggravating
evils (paradigmatically, evils that also endanger the choosers themselves). Like Levi, I resist the idea that we are all murderers or oppressors, even when we benefit from murder and oppression by others.

"I do not know," Levi wrote, "and it does not much interest me to know, whether in my depths there lurks a murderer, but I do know that I was a guiltless victim and that I was not a murderer" (1989, 48). To confuse murderers with their victims, he wrote, is "a moral disease or an aesthetic affectation or a sinister sign of complicity . . . service rendered (intentionally or not) to the negators of truth" (1989, 48–49). I agree. Yet, I find gray zones not only where agents acted under the extraordinary stress of the Nazi death camps. Conditions less extreme can be severe enough to produce the ambiguities and complexities of grayness. Misogyny's evils are not always imminent or looming in the form of well-defined events. They often take shape gradually and are less readily noticed or identified. They may inflict social rather than biological death, or permanent deformation, disability, or unremitting pain. Or they may produce undeserved self-hatred.

Two decades ago Mary Daly wrote in *Gyn / Ecology: The Metaethics of Radical Feminism* about mothers binding daughters' feet and mothers participating in daughters' genital mutilation.[26] Mothers who did so were not in imminent danger of a horrible death. Nor did they act under stress comparable to that of death camps. No spectacular events precipitated their action. Rather, their whole lives prepared them for it. They acted for their daughters' marriageability, not to advance their own personal standing. Still, that choice implicated them in the evils of marriage systems that deformed and immobilized women, including themselves.

Like Levi in commenting on many prisoners in the camps, Mary Daly refused to judge mothers who did these things. She called them "token torturers." I take her, like Levi, to have backed off from judging the agents, finding it inappropriate. Yet there are also complicit women who are not well described as "token torturers." Mary Daly could have used a concept like that of the gray zone to distinguish complicit mothers from Nazi women, who she also, unfortunately, wanted to call "token torturers." Such Nazi women as Irma Griese and Ilse Koch (Daly 1978, 301–2) were no more in gray zones than the Indiana women (Blee 1991) who joined the Ku Klux Klan as a way to socialize in the 1920s.

Mary Daly and Primo Levi reflected on others' past choices, choices with irreversible consequences. Thinking in a forward-looking and first-personal mode, rather than a retrospective and observer mode, changes one's position as a potential evaluator. In the forward-looking first-personal mode, a refusal to judge is apt to seem too quick an abdication of responsibility.

Contributors to this volume tend to think first-personally and to look forward as they grope through difficult, often ambiguous zones to find ways to take responsibility for harms we do and to find ways to do better in the future. Although they do not take up the kinds of stress under which agents in Levi's gray zones had to make their choices, many of their essays do discuss or touch on ethically important themes shared by gray zones: moral ambiguity, moral compromise, and complicity, under stress, in perpetrating oppression.

As in *Feminist Ethics* of 1991, many contributors refer in the text to women, as I do, by both given names and surnames, even after the first occurrence, to avoid identifying them only by patronyms. One contributor follows the same practice for men also.

In previewing for you these fifteen creative and thought-provoking essays, I sometimes raise questions about ideas suggested by one essay because of something in another, or I note comparisons between essays. I also raise questions regarding possible gray zone themes. My questions are not rhetorical. They are genuine expressions of wonder.

Sandra Bartky revisits the idea of the "guilty liberal," a pejorative concept of the Left from the sixties. She argues that, in fact, many of us (liberal or not) *are* guilty. It is not necessarily that we are blameworthy for anything we have done. But we are guilty through our relationships to wrongdoing. For example, we may have profited without protest from (others') wrongdoing, even if we did not perpetrate it ourselves. Guilt is etymologically connected, as Nietzsche noticed, with debt (Nietzsche 1969, 62–63). It does not always refer to feelings but often, rather, to what we owe, a relatively objective fact, or, as Sandra Bartky puts it, an existential condition. It is to some extent luck, which becomes our moral luck, whether we are so connected to wrongdoing that we become guilty (indebted).

The question naturally arises whether we can get rid of this guilt. Sandra Bartky argues that in some cases we can but that in others we probably cannot. Thinking about what we can do leads easily to general issues regarding character. It is our moral luck to have been formed under often oppressive institutions. Whether we profit or pay under those institutions, our characters are likely to emerge mal-formed, compromised, inconsistent. Can we become better? Can we become good? Marilyn Frye asked many years ago in pondering her relationship as a white woman to racism, "Does being white make it impossible for me to be a good person?" (1983, 113).

Marcia Homiak addresses the questions whether under oppressive institutions we can still improve our characters. She argues that even under oppressive social structures most of us have what it takes to become better. For "what it takes" she draws upon Aristotle, noting his apparent ambivalence on the subject, and she delves into passages that suggest a relatively optimistic view. What it takes, she argues, is not simply the capacity for rationality but certain nonrational psy-chological capacities, which most of us have. Although she finds that most of us can become *better*, she does not pretend that it is either easy or equally demanding for everyone; we may be lucky or unlucky there. She is less optimistic about our prospects for becoming *good*, as what it takes to become good (not just better) outruns our indi-vidual psychological equipment.

Suppose that we are of relatively good character but systematically misperceived and thus misunderstood. Suppose we are misrepresented in our societies as irrational fanatics, as perverts who celebrate per-versity, or as vengeful man-haters devoted to bringing successful men down and making them suffer what we have suffered. (What feminist activist has not been represented or perceived as any of these?) Some-times we attempt to reclaim stigmata ("bitch," "witch," "butch," "dyke") used, historically, to put us down and turn those stigmata into badges. We may unearth original meanings or peel away false stereotypes. Among ourselves, we often succeed. But because we do not live only among feminists, our reclamations risk profound mis-communication, both to friends (who do not always share our poli-tics) and to strangers to whom we may never have meant to commu-nicate anything. Cheshire Calhoun investigates such systematic misreadings as a kind of moral failure in the lives of revolutionaries who are often morally ahead of their times. Like most of the guilt dis-cussed by Sandy Bartky, this failure need not make us worthy of blame. Nonetheless, it makes a life fall short of an important moral ideal. It is luck whether we live in a society able to give us the moral uptake we deserve. If we do not get that uptake, what then? If we compromise ideals to maintain relationships with family, friends, or coworkers who would otherwise misunderstand us, do we risk complicity in oppression? Are the lives of moral revolutionaries necessarily morally compromised?

The questions these three philosophers explore lead us naturally to politics. For the conditions under which we can become good (without qualification), avoid guilt, or avoid moral failure include favorable political environments, social structures that are not oppressive but allow for the expression and perception of good character and are conducive to its development. There is no consensus on how to answer the question of which social structures will do these things. Philosophers in the second section of this book investigate aspects of this question, considering how race, class, and sexual orientation complicate it.

Iris Young argues for a social democracy that is inclusive in that its decision-making debates address publicly all who will be affected by their outcomes. Public address is what she calls "greeting." We greet people when we acknowledge their particular, individual presence and our accountability to them. Greeting encompasses everything from "hello" to highly ritualized customs of international diplomacy. It precedes discussion of substantive issues, setting a context for discussion to proceed with mutual respect and trust. Failure of public address is a form of "internal exclusion." It makes democracies less democratic than they could and should be. She applies this concept to the 1993–1996 American welfare debates, arguing that those debates exhibited a profound failure to address publicly (greet) lower income, single mothers, who stood to be most affected by the outcome. Those women were thus excluded from the debates. Iris Young presents public address (greeting) as an aspect of justice too often ignored. I note, also, that it shares with care ethics a concern for the particular individual.

Thinking about "greeting" and "moral failure" might also lead one to ask whether some failures of communication that Cheshire Calhoun discusses might have roots in failures, or refusals, of address (greeting) among the parties in question.

Amber Katherine takes up the idea of inclusiveness in another context. She revisits Mary Daly's radical feminist philosophy, inviting white feminists to (re)read Mary Daly as not simply the outsider to patriarchy that she felt herself to be in writing *Gyn / Ecology: The*

Metaethics of Radical Feminism (1978) but also as an insider to race privilege. That awareness complicates Mary Daly's project of developing a metaethics of radical feminist politics global in its perspectives. It reveals a complicity in racism of (paradoxically) a relatively unself-conscious radical feminist politics. Using Iris Young's concept, one might say that although *Gyn / Ecology* addressed the texts of white men, it failed, however inadvertently, to address women of color.

Audre Lorde's 1979 open letter to Mary Daly protested that in *Gyn / Ecology* only white European women were presented as agents (even as ancient goddesses) and not simply as victims. In contrast, African women (one might add, Indian and Chinese women) were presented only "as victims and preyers-upon each other."[27] "Where is Afrekete?" asked Audre Lorde; where are the African (Indian, Chinese) goddesses? What would be a good response to Audre Lorde's letter, if one wished to continue to learn from Mary Daly's project and build on it? This question inspired Amber Katherine's dissertation. Her essay here builds on a chapter from it.

One response is to redo *Gyn / Ecology*'s project more inclusively. Instead, Amber Katherine favors (re)reading that book to become aware of the global and temporal positions from which it was written and of the influence of European-American foresisters whose work inspired it. She explores relevant connections with *Woman, Church, and State* by late nineteenth-century radical feminist Matilda Joslyn Gage and with Virginia Woolf's *Three Guineas*, her most radical feminist work, as well as with Virginia Woolf's essay "A Sketch of the Past."

Jacqueline Anderson argues that in order to escape the inevitable complicity of reformism, a revolutionary community needs a radically feminist ethic. Without a moral revolution, she fears, things will not become substantially better for most women. We need a feminist ethic to decide such basic issues as who may even rightly be counted as a member of the community. How should a lesbian community respond to transgendered people who wish to participate in its projects? (Should it greet them?) Such questions have torn apart radical feminist communities that had rejected assimilationist politics in favor of forming separate organizations to start over (rather than try to reform existing practices). Where do "trans" people fit in relation to revolutionary feminist politics? Multiple-gender identities complicate feminist politics in ways that call for ethical decisions. Jacqueline Anderson suggests that three principles put forward by Joyce Trebilcot offer a promising basis for a moral revolution that could preserve the spirit of radical feminism. They do not tell us what to do; they offer models for negotiating differences. Jacqueline Anderson notes that these principles may not yield a stable community, but she finds that that may be all right.

Anna Stubblefield rejects both pluralist and assimilationist visions of what the politically good society would be like with regard to gender. She examines Iris Young's culturally pluralist urban ideal (in *Justice and the Politics of Difference*), in which diverse groups interact but maintain their separate group identities, and she sets out to compare and contrast that ideal with Richard Wasserstrom's ("assimilationist") gender-free society, in which everyone's political identity is just that of a human being, or citizen. Working within the social constructivist tradition, she offers a new account of what it means to be a woman in a sexist society. Her account distinguishes, in a way that promises to be helpful in many contexts, between being a woman and being feminine. Cultural pluralism, she allows, might be workable for ethnic groups. But, she argues, it would not yield a stable social structure with respect to gendered groups on a constructivist understanding of gender. Instead, she finds, it would evolve toward Wasserstrom's ideal of a gender-free society. That ideal, however, she finds unhelpful as a political model for policy today, as it does not address issues that arise in a society in which people's social places have been determined by histories of oppression based on gender.

One might go on to wonder whether assimilationists who favor affirmative action in misogynist societies might also find themselves compromised morally if their policies tend to affirm the very gender distinctions that they would ideally like to abolish.

"Discrimination" is one of the least pejorative terms to describe what misogynist societies do to women and girls. Unjust discrimination is wrong but not necessarily evil. Whether it is evil depends also on the nature, duration, extent, and severity of its consequences and whether they are irreversible or irreparable. In law, discrimination can be a harm in itself. But in life, we sometimes survive discrimination undamaged. Targets of misogyny suffer not only discrimination but profound harm, often violently inflicted. In Part Three, four essays reflect on violence and harm to women in misogynist environments.

Robin Schott focuses on sexual violence in her essay, reflecting on the mass war rapes perpetrated during the civil war in the former Yugoslavia. Taking sexual violence as a reference point raises issues about morality, she finds, that may not otherwise be evident. She examines the views on evil of Julia Kristeva (who draws on anthropologist Mary Douglas), Ervin Staub (who offers a psychological analysis of how people become capable of perpetrating evil), and Hannah Arendt (who analyzes failure of judgment in a civil society where moral standards have collapsed) to see what insight they might offer into war rape. She finds that although each offers important ideas, each also has limitations with respect to war rape, which has not been among the paradigms of evil that moral theorists have reflected upon. She concludes that the kind of moral theorizing to emerge from reflection upon war rape will move away from purely cognitive or rational accounts of morality to incorporate bodily elements of judgment and that it will be nonhegemonic and, like all moral theory, inevitably incomplete.

Susan Brison reflects on both ethical and epistemological uses of narrative in the processes of understanding, recovery, self-reconstruction, and restoration of trust that become necessary after suffering severe trauma, such as that of the violent rape and attempted murder that she survived herself. Philosophers have downplayed first person accounts as not of sufficiently general interest to play an important role in philosophical thinking. Arguing against this view, Susan Brison's essay picks up a theme also in Robin Schott's reflections on the kind of moral theory that we can expect to emerge from reflection on the violence of rape: the importance of the concrete particular and the inevitability of incompleteness. First-person narratives connect us with the experience of others in ways that enhance our understanding of trauma. (It is tempting to add that they also address—greet—the reader in a way that abstract reasoning does not.)

In exploring this idea, Susan Brison also takes up pitfalls of reliance upon first-person narratives—dangers of becoming complicit in what we hope to resist—suggesting ways to avoid such pitfalls. But trauma narratives function not only as epistemological tools. They also help the survivor reconstitute herself as a subject by retelling the story in ways that make her not just an object and not helpless. Making oneself not helpless risks, of course, the self-blame that comes from thinking one could have done something to prevent the trauma. In discussing the dilemma of helplessness or self-blame, Susan Brison considers how learning self-defense can help one become angry and place blame for assaults where it belongs—on the perpetrators.

Lynne Tirrell and Joan Callahan look at speech that subordinates women. Lynne Tirrell focuses on pornography and how it silences women. Joan Callahan focuses on antilesbian derogatory speech. She considers how such speech legitimates the practice of depriving the (surviving) lesbian parent of social security death benefits (and other economic benefits that currently require married status) and how it leaves lesbian parents and their children unprotected against violent assault. Both philosophers employ narratives in arguing that the speech they write about is genuinely harmful (not "merely offensive"), that it actually subordinates its targets. Lynne Tirrell offers the case of Sylvia Bowman, who lost the election in Massachusetts for president of her union when her coworker David Heller circulated photocopies of her face pasted onto a body cut out of a pornographic magazine. Joan Callahan frames her essay with examples from her life. She opens with a letter from the Social Security Administration detailing death benefits to which (in the event of her death) her surviving partner would be entitled, were they married. She closes with harassment experienced by their son at school for having two female parents. She defends, against many objections, a proposal to make speech that subordinates actionable in civil courts.

Lynne Tirrell's critique of Catharine MacKinnon's theorizing about pornography resonates with Anna Stubblefield's critique of Catharine MacKinnon on what it means to be a woman in a profoundly sexist society. Both find Catharine MacKinnon's work unable to accommodate the (admitted) fact that women can, and do, resist and reject sexist norms and that we can and do develop alternative meanings. We sometimes learn to hear each other, even in profoundly sexist environments. If we are eventually able to implement Joan Callahan's proposal, it may be only because we are not completely silenced, even as feminists.

The essays in Part Four address the balancing of two fundamental values of feminist relationship and agency: the values of love and respect. Chris Cuomo's essay insists on the importance in sexuality of both justice and joy, in rethinking aspects of the feminist "sex wars" over such issues as pornography and sadomasochism. On one hand, she acknowledges the vital importance of norms. She rejects the extreme libertarianism that disdains morality, rules, and judging as necessarily limiting in a harmful way. On the other hand, she insists on the importance of flourishing, creative brilliance, and joy. Here, she finds, we should allow room for great diversity. Philosophers have attended more to justice than to joy. Chris Cuomo's narratives, accordingly, focus more on joy. Like Robin Schott, she urges us to give up the idea that ethics is a purely rational, conscious matter.

As Chris Cuomo acknowledges, justice limits our legitimate sources of joy. What if those limits threaten to leave us, in some contexts, with a joyless existence? Do we risk complicity in oppression, then—I cannot help wondering—if we insist on joy anyway, perhaps even as necessary to motivate our continued search for justice?

Virginia Held examines and rejects several objections of liberal political theory to the idea of carrying care ethics into the public world of markets and governments. She finds that ethics based simply on impartiality in our treatment of individual agents is insufficient, and she proposes that we look also to the model of ideal parenting for values in public life. Her idea is not to reject liberalism and its valuing of justice. Her idea is, rather, to add to its values others that she finds equally important and necessary for a good society. Just as Chris Cuomo finds joy no less important a value than justice in our sexual lives, Virginia Held finds care a value no less important than justice in our more public lives. She argues that liberal theory does not handle well the question of which activities should be subject to market values. Health care, human reproduction, and environmental concern are examples where justice is clearly not the only fundamental value.

Reflection on balancing caring with justice invites the difficult question of how we can have caring without favoritism. The retreat to impartiality certainly avoids favoritism, but at a high price if it rides on our not becoming emotionally involved. Yet, I often wonder, if we allow ourselves the emotional engagement of caring, how are we to avoid the morally compromising behavior of favoritism?

Returning to the personal, which is, of course, also political (if not public), Sharon Bishop defends objectivity in the ethics of personal relationships, such as that of intimate partners who may confront the question of whether to try to rescue their relationship or to leave it. In Ibsen's play *A Doll's House*, Nora confronts her husband with the complaint that they have never seriously tried "to get to the bottom of anything." Sharon Bishop argues that "getting to the bottom of things" involves recognizing values that are objective, even if they do not determine what everyone ought to do under the circumstances. Objective values do determine the difference between what is permissible and what is not, although they may leave us a choice among permissible options. Nora might have decided to stay and work it out. But in deciding to leave, she appealed to values not reducible to her personal tastes as legitimating her decision, such as the value of being treated as a whole person, not just somebody's toy. The case of Nora shows that personal relationships without respect are not saved simply by attachment. On the contrary, attachment can make it difficult to develop the requisite insight for being moved to rectify the situation or to seek something better. Sharon Bishop's essay also traces Nora's character growth and speculates on what would have to take place in her husband for his to grow comparably. Nora is an interesting case for applying Marcia Homiak's ideas about the malleability of character. A crisis in Nora's life stimulates a kind of reflectiveness in her that was absent before.

Jean Rumsey reflects on ways of thinking about dying in a culture (the United States) that often emphasizes individuality at the expense of relationships. We "pay our respects" when someone dies. She argues that it is equally important to attend to the relationships that death disrupts (or changes) and not simply to regard survivors, or the dying person, as individuals with needs that are their own. Like Robin Schott, Jean Rumsey turns to anthropology in her reflections. She cites a range of folklore, song, and poetry in support of her plea for greater attention to relationships and to how they (and therefore, we) become transformed by the deaths of those who have played meaningful roles in our lives. Even though someone has died, we may find that, to use Iris Young's concept, we continue to greet them (if only in dreams or reveries).

NOTES

I thank Paula Gottlieb and contributors to this volume for reading an earlier draft of this chapter and for valuable comments. I bear responsibility, however, for the views expressed herein.
1. Marilyn Frye, "Oppression," in *The Politics of Reality: Essays in Feminist Theory* (Trumansburg, N.Y.: Crossing Press, 1983).

2. Iris Young, *Justice and the Politics of Difference* (Princeton, N.J.: Princeton University Press, 1990).

3. Friedrich Nietzsche, *On the Genealogy of Morals,* trans. Walter Kaufmann and R. J. Hollingdale (New York: Vintage, 1969), pp. 15–56.

4. Cf. John Kekes, *Facing Evil* (Princeton, N.J.: Princeton University Press, 1990), chaps. 4–5.

5. Andrea Dworkin, *Life and Death* (New York: Free Press, 1997), pp. 51–52.

6. Primo Levi, *The Drowned and the Saved* (New York: Vintage, 1989), p. 42.

7. "Twilight zone" has already been preempted by science fiction. In any case, if the only reason it might work is because of the color of the twilight, it isn't really an alternative.

8. See Isaiah Trunk, *Judenrat: The Jewish Councils in Eastern Europe Under Nazi Occupation* (Lincoln: University of Nebraska Press, 1996), and Raul Hilberg, *The Destruction of the European Jews,* revised and definitive ed. (New York: Holmes and Meier, 1985).

9. Calel Perechodnik, who became a ghetto police officer in a small town near Warsaw, left a memoir recording his inner conflict over that decision and his ultimate remorse, *Am I a Murderer?* (Boulder, Colo.: Westview, 1996).

10. See also Miklos Nyiszli, *Auschwitz: A Doctor's Eyewitness Account,* trans. Tibere Kreme and Richard Seaver (New York: Arcade, 1993).

11. On lost innocence, see Herbert Morris, "Lost Innocence," in *On Guilt and Innocence: Essays in Legal Philosophy and Moral Psychology* (Berkeley: University of California Press, 1976), pp. 139–61.

12. On "dirty hands," see Michael Stocker, *Plural and Conflicting Values* (New York: Oxford University Press, 1990).

13. See, for example, Kathleen M. Blee, *Women of the Klan: Racism and Gender in the 1920s* (Berkeley: University of California Press, 1991); Claudia Koonz, *Mothers in the Fatherland: Women, the Family, and Nazi Politics* (New York: St. Martin's, 1987); Patricia Pearson, *When She Was Bad: Violent Women and the Myth of Innocence* (New York: Viking, 1997); and Renate Sieberg, *Secrets of Life and Death: Women and the Mafia,* trans. Liz Heron (London: Verso, 1996).

14. On rape as a male protection racket, see Susan Rae Peterson, "Coercion and Rape: The State As a Male Protection Racket," and Susan Griffin, "Rape: The All-American Crime," in *Feminism and Philosophy,* ed. Mary Vetterling Braggin, Jane English, and Frederick A. Elliston (Totowa, N.J.: Littlefield, Adams, 1977), pp. 360–71 and 313–32. For further development, see Claudia Card, *The Unnatural Lottery: Character and Moral Luck* (Philadelphia: Temple University Press, 1996), pp. 97–117.

15. Joyce Trebilcot, "Dyke Methods," in *Lesbian Philosophies and Cultures,* ed. Jeffner Allen (Albany: State University of New York Press, 1990), p. 17.

16. See Elizabeth V. Spelman, *Fruits of Sorrow: Framing Our Attention to Suffering* (Boston: Beacon, 1997), for thoughtful reflection on the misappropriation of others' pain.

17. For more on resistance within the camps, see Eugen Kogon, *The Theory and Practice of Hell* (New York: Berkley Medallion, 1960); *The Buchen-*

wald Report, trans. David A. Hackett (Boulder, Colo.: Westview, 1995); and Hermann Langbein, *Against All Hope: Resistance in the Nazi Concentration Camps 1938–1945* (New York: Paragon, 1994).

18. Norma Alarcon, "Chicana's Feminist Literature: A Re-Vision Through Malintzin/or Malinztin: Putting Flesh Back on the Object," in *This Bridge Called My Back: Writings by Radical Women of Color,* ed. Cherríe Moraga and Gloria Anzaldúa (Watertown, Mass.: Persephone, 1981), pp. 182–90.

19. See Francisco López De Gómara, *Cortés: The Life of the Conqueror by His Secretary,* trans. Lesley Byrd Simpson (Berkeley: University of California Press, 1964), pp. 56–57, and Bernal Díaz del Castillo, *The Discovery and Conquest of Mexico,* trans. A. P. Maudslay (New York: Da Capo, 1996).

20. Stephen E. Ambrose, *Undaunted Courage: Meriwether Lewis, Thomas Jefferson, and the Opening of the American West* (New York: Simon and Schuster, 1996), p. 187.

21. See, for example, Ella E. Clark and Margot Edmonds, *Sacagawea of the Lewis and Clark Expedition* (Berkeley: University of California Press, 1979).

22. On southern white women's collaboration with black women in resistance to slavery, see Adrienne Rich, "Disloyal to Civilization: Feminism, Racism, Gynephobia," in *On Lies, Secrets, and Silence: Selected Prose, 1966–1978* (New York: W. W. Norton, 1979), pp. 275–310. See also Larry Koger, *Black Slaveowners: Free Black Slave Masters in South Carolina, 1790–1860* (Columbia: University of South Carolina Press, 1995), on prosperous mulattoes and African Americans of lighter skin who not only bought family members and other slaves for humanitarian reasons but also acquired slaves for labor primarily because they had little access to other sources of labor and also to elevate themselves above the masses. Milton Meltzer also writes of slaves in ancient Rome who were themselves owners of yet other slaves. See his *Slavery: A World History* (New York: Da Capo, 1993).

23. I owe this observation to Paula Gottlieb, who read and commented on a draft of this chapter.

24. See John Sack, *An Eye for an Eye,* with a new preface (New York: Basic Books, 1995), on former prisoners of Nazi camps who were hired in 1945 by Russians to staff camps for German inmates who were accused or suspected of having been Nazis or of having served Nazis.

25. Cf. Fyodor Dostoevsky, *The Brothers Karamazov,* trans. Constance Garnett (New York: New American Library, 1957), bk 5, chap. 4, pp. 218–27.

26. Mary Daly, *Gyn / Ecology: The Metaethics of Radical Feminism* (Boston: Beacon, 1978).

27. Audre Lorde, "Open Letter to Mary Daly," in *Sister Outsider: Essays and Speeches* (Trumansburg, N.Y.: Crossing Press, 1984), p. 67.

Part One
Character and Moral Luck

2 / *In Defense of Guilt*

SANDRA LEE BARTKY

THE PARADOX OF BLEEDING HEARTS
AND GUILTY LIBERALS

"Bleeding heart liberal!" "Guilty liberal!" Two terms of opprobrium, one thrown out by the American Right, the other by the Left. I shall try to show that both charges, although from opposing political perspectives, are embedded in a series of masculinist polarities. Revisiting guilt points up the difficulties, whatever our politics, of escaping from the pervasiveness of sexist conceptual frameworks.

The term "bleeding heart liberal" is typically uttered with scorn, not so much by rightwing politicians as by the *enragees* who elect them. One hears this phrase often, especially on right-wing talk radio, virtually the only talk radio on the U.S. airwaves. "Liberal" is the ultimate term of opprobrium in these right-wing times, since a domestic "radical" is virtually unimaginable. Thus, "bleeding heart liberal" has become consummate abuse.

Now this has always perplexed me: Why isn't it a good thing, a praiseworthy thing, to have a bleeding heart? Normally, no one, not even a liberal, would have a heart that bled for Bill Gates.[1] Those for whom the bleeding hearts bleed are the less fortunate. Why, then, is such scorn heaped upon those who feel compassion for them? Isn't compassion a virtue? What would a world without compassion be like? Isn't it better to have a compassionate heart than a cold, cold heart? I am further perplexed by the fact that many of those who excoriate "bleeding heart liberals" belong to the Christian Right, a congeries of organizations that regard the United States as a Christian, or (in their less anti-Semitic and more "multicultural" moods) a "Judeo-Christian," country. Now Jesus Christ and the Virgin Mary are often pictured with hearts emanating divine rays or with hearts that bleed; oftentimes their hearts emanate divine rays *and* they bleed. So "bleeding heart" is consummate abuse in the mouths of the very people who worship members of a holy family with hearts that bleed. How can this be? How can the politics of the Christian Right stand in such sharp contradiction to the religious iconography of traditional Christianity? "A foolish consistency is the hobgoblin of little minds," as Emerson once said, but this is taking inconsistency too far. Jesus is all right as a deity, but you wouldn't want him making policy; you hope the Virgin will plead your case before God, but you wouldn't elect her to Congress.

The compassion of bleeding hearts, they tell us, is corrosive, for bleeding hearts refuse to cut off the poor from welfare, and welfare creates dependency. We rob the poor of their initiative when we provide them with a "safety net." The bleeding hearts are too "permissive": what we need is "tough love." Here, clearly, is a gendered subtext of tender and tough, permissive and disciplinary, dove and hawk: the first term suggests the feminine, the second the masculine. The bald eagle that represents our country is a predator; the Paraclete is a dove. Jesus and the Virgin Mary, the effeminate and the feminine, indeed all the bleeding hearts are soft; neocons (neoconservatives) are hard.

Most of us always thought that poverty came first, then welfare; but George Gilder et al. want us to believe that welfare creates poverty![2] Welfare rewards the lazy and shiftless; take it away and they will develop the work ethic—or starve. Never mind that the majority of persons on welfare are children, or that the average recipient spends two years on welfare, not a lifetime.[3] Never mind that single mothers are disproportionately represented on the welfare rolls: their dependency, so it is said, stems from "liberal do-gooders," not from women's historic low wages or from the scarcity and, when available, the expense of decent day care. Never mind that life on the minimum wage will not lift a family above the poverty line, and if it should, goodbye perhaps to Medicaid and food stamps—holdovers from the "War on Poverty" that has been supplanted, so it seems, by a war on the poor. Never mind that "downsizing" has impoverished whole communities or that hundreds of thousands of jobs, both skilled and unskilled, have been automated out of existence or else exported to low-wage Third World countries whose governments are only too glad to guarantee, often by repression and torture, "stability."

I turn now to another liberal persona, this time an object of contempt not for the Right, but for the Left—the "guilty liberal."[4] In the political culture I sought out in the late sixties as the limitations of liberalism became more and more apparent to me, no one, not even hard-bitten reactionaries, was regarded with more contempt than "guilty liberals." (This made me very uncomfortable, because prior to my embrace of radicalism, I had been a liberal for many years and I knew in my secret heart that I was, well, guilty.) So who were these pariahs? They were well-meaning folk who were pricked by conscience—"liberal guilt"—in the face of clear injustice, but who made merely token gestures (like paying the black cleaning lady a few dollars more) and who were unwilling to forgo privilege (all liberals were assumed to be privileged) in order to make the kinds of sacrifices that social revolution was supposed to require. Since they were not prepared to make sacrifices, when "push came to shove" liberals would just disappear or even go over to the other side. Hence, they were untrustworthy, fickle. These guilty liberals were, in other words, hypocrites and cowards.

But have we not seen some strange departures from principle on the part of notable radicals? Rennie Davis (of the Chicago Seven) dropped out and became a disciple of the thirteen-year-old Perfect Master (a leading guru of the day); Jerry Rubin (also one of the Chicago Seven), a Wall Street broker; Eldridge Cleaver, a born-again Christian and shill for American megacorporations. Nor is it the case that liberals never stand on principle when the going gets rough or even sacrifice for it. Thousands of white northerners, many liberals among them, went south as volunteers during the civil rights movement. They went with no guarantee that they would return; indeed, some did not return.

Another ground of condemnation of liberal guilt is associated with the belief that guilt is not a proper motivator of political action, because an emotion can never take the place of a correct analysis. The construction of such an analysis typically is not believed to spring from any particular emotion. This idea is thoroughly Cartesian: emotion is at best superfluous; at worst, a snare that can lead us to incorrect conclusions. Cognition trumps emotion once again.

Radicals, we believed, have a tough and complex analysis—a class analysis accompanied perhaps by considerations of gender or race. Radicals permit themselves certain emotions, to be sure—outrage at the action of right-wing dictators, joy at the prospect of the triumph of socialism. We did not permit ourselves guilt. Guilt was for liberals. Liberals had only a few woolly-minded ideas about the efficacy of electoral politics, "bourgeois right," and—guilt (an unclean emotion in which, like self-pity, some are thought to wallow). Also, liberals were typically regarded as fickle: just when you think they are on your side, they disappear or temporize.

The gendered subtext is a bit harder to see here than it was in the case of the "bleeding heart liberal," but it is visible nonetheless. On the one hand, tough-minded, hard-edged, even "scientific" analysis, courage, and the readiness to sacrifice; on the other, woolly-minded political theory that shrinks from the implications of its political values—namely, that the achievement of genuine liberty and true equality will require an overthrow of the existing order—hence intellectual cowardice, but also personal cowardice, fickleness, and unclean emotions like guilt. It cannot escape attention that the qualities ascribed to liberals by both their right-wing and left-wing critics are those traditionally associated in our culture with women and "the feminine."

LET'S HEAR IT FOR GUILT

In the balance of this chapter, I take a thread from the preceding discussion and follow it out. I shall argue, against the conviction of the American Left, that guilt can be one among many acceptable motivations for political action. I shall argue too that although the standard characterizations of guilt in the literature of moral psychology are not inaccurate, they are simplistic and somewhat shallow when examined in a political context. (More about this in the next section). It should be clear in what follows that the political action in question is taken on behalf of others less fortunate than oneself.

I want to specify at the outset two among the many uses and forms of guilt that I shall *not* be discussing. First, guilt used as a weapon, usually by one person against another, a practice known colloquially as "guilt-tripping." This tendency can be extremely damaging not just in personal relationships, but in political organizations as well, especially women's organizations. This is a big topic, and I shall save it for another time. A second form of guilt I shall not be discussing (and possibly the cause of the phobic reaction of my comrades to any discussion of guilt) is the unconscious guilt, left over from childhood, that can manifest itself in neurotic symptoms. The same people who oversaw my radicalization were or had been heavy consumers of psychotherapeutic services (myself included); among the more favored members of the middle class, "going into therapy" was (and probably still is) the most common way of dealing with emotional crises and/or pervasive unhappiness. The kinds of guilt we were encouraged to recognize and to try to purge in therapy were thought to stem from tabooed infantile erotic and aggressive desires. Setting these aside, there remain forms of guilt worth taking seriously from a political point of view.

Guilt by Complicity

In the analytic tradition of moral psychology, guilt is a subjective experience of self-assessment called forth by the violation of principles that a person values and by which she feels herself bound.[5] It is not necessary to have violated such principles herself; a person can be guilty of complicity with those who have, such as her government. There is required for complicity (1) the knowledge that certain deeds have been done; (2) the recognition that these deeds violate principles that a person values and by which she feels herself bound; and (3) the knowledge that so far she has done nothing to make the doer cease violating moral and/or legal norms. Now, the U.S. government has violated many principles that I value—principles of international law and of common human decency. What this government does, it does in my name, by my elected representatives, with my tax money, so to speak, over my signature. All of this makes me, as long as I acquiesce, an accomplice in the crimes of my government: I am guilty of complicity.[6]

Now everyone knows that the U.S. government is largely an instrument of the concentrations of capital that have bought the White House and the Congress. I say "largely," not "entirely," because some resistance to the government and its actions is still possible. Government is a site of contestation, even though the corrosive effects of capitalism have brought it about that the contest is always between

David and Goliath. What happens at the grass roots does sometimes matter. Even though some people have been sacrificed, martyred (the Black Panthers), it is often possible in the United States today for a person to be politically effective (of course in concert with others) without running much risk of imprisonment, loss of employment, or death. This realization makes continued complicity in the crimes of the government especially reprehensible.

The landmark Civil Rights Act of 1964 was passed after seven years of intense political agitation. The war in Vietnam might have dragged on forever if not for mass dissent and mass mobilization. Agitation led to the cutoff of funding for the Contra War; avenues for funding had to be found illegally. Similarly, the women's movement has made the mistreatment of women in every area of life visible to millions of people; in response (a response that has been feeble, but detectable), government has granted rights and enacted remedial measures in areas to which it was heretofore oblivious.

The recognition that one is guilty of complicity is not incompatible with righteous indignation or with feelings of solidarity with the victims of injustice, the latter two "respectable" motivations for the "correct" radical.

Guilt by Virtue of Privilege

An awareness of the guilt of complicity can be called forth by specific acts or policies of my government. But government is only one institution in the social totality in which we discover our enjoyment of privilege or our exclusion from it. The guilt of the privileged is not attached to any particular act or policy; guilt of this sort is occasioned by something far more global, namely, the very structure of the social totality itself, that positions some as privileged, others as "underprivileged." These positions are determined largely, but not always irrevocably, by accidents of birth. The guilt people sometimes experience in the recognition of complicity with government is generally occasioned by specific events, such as the CIA's involvement in the overthrow of a legally elected president or an imperialist military intervention. But the social totality that produces privilege (and hence the guilt of the privileged) need do nothing out of the ordinary. It needs only to continue to function *normally.* Joseph K. in Kafka's *The Trial* is arrested "in a country with a legal constitution, there was universal peace, all the laws were in force."[7] Seeing the social world we inhabit as normal, generally lawful, resting on the consent of the governed, and so forth makes it more difficult (especially if we are its beneficiaries) to see the ways in which, even though "all the laws were in force," it is also a complex network of systemic injustices.

"Privilege" in this context is a special advantage or favor that is granted to some individuals or groups of individuals and not to others; the term also carries the connotation of an exemption from some duty or burden. The guilt that emerges from my recognition that I occupy a privileged position in the social totality has to do not only with the benefits I enjoy that I have not earned but also and equally with the fact that others have been excluded from their enjoyment unjustly by a mere accident of birth. Here is a double consciousness: the recognition of my unearned privilege and the concomitant recognition that the unjust denial of privilege to others is the result of the "normal" workings of the social order. In my own case, the unearned privileges I enjoy are white-skin privilege, class privilege, and heterosexual privilege. Now, it is often the case that one is privileged in some ways and disadvantaged in others. As a woman, for example, I am denied phallic privilege, although this denial is usually (but not always) tempered by the fact that I am heterosexual, that I have a decent income and a steady job, and that I do not suffer the additional disadvantages that accrue to women of color and lesbians.

Let us consider first the question of earned and unearned privilege. If our society were a perfect meritocracy, what appears to be a gross maldistribution of social goods would have a rationale that some would argue is just. People would get what they earned—no more and no less. Conservatives like to pretend that our society is sufficiently meritocratic to justify the uneven distribution of money and power. They are fond of pointing to the disadvantaged backgrounds of specific individuals (for example, President Clinton) who pulled themselves up by their bootstraps and thus earned the privileges they enjoy. True, for many individuals there is a connection between hard work, commitment, sacrifice, and success. Conservatives have played compellingly on this connection. But no matter how hard a poor black boy from Arkansas might have struggled to improve his lot (as Clinton struggled to improve his), it is highly unlikely that this black boy could have been elected president. At any rate, the true test of the justice of social arrangements is not whether from time to time they allow extraordinary individuals with extraordinary abilities to rise to the top, but how well the system as a whole works for ordinary people.

The idea of meritocracy is tied logically to the image of society as a contest. Now a fair contest requires a "level playing field," i.e., an original situation in which the competitors begin at roughly the same place with the same or with comparable qualities. But the majority of advantaged individuals never shared a level playing field with their disadvantaged competitors. I take myself again as an example. I worked very hard and very long to climb the academic ladder, faced what was for me the sheer terror of Ph.D. examinations, agonized over a writer's block that delayed the writing of my dissertation, suffered terribly during the dreadful probationary period, published barely enough to get tenure, and generally had a psychology that combined substantial ambition with pervasive feelings of inadequacy and with fears both of failure and of success. Yet there were also factors quite beyond my control that helped me all along the way: my skin color, culturally associated more with intelligence than are the skin colors of others; a failure of female socialization that had made me into a marriage resister, shrinking in something like horror at the destiny to which most young women of my class and background aspired in those days—suburban housewifery; an intellectual father who made me into his intellectual companion; philosophical discussions with my father, who would sometimes change sides just to give me practice; a house full of books and a community that valued education, even for women; no pressure from my parents to marry and have children; complete financial support from home through an undergraduate degree, which, while it was "only" at the state university (all my parents could afford), freed me from the necessity of getting even a campus job to study and to spar over endless cups of coffee with other young wanna-be intellectuals about music, art, and the "big ideas." When I developed psychosomatic illnesses due to the stresses of graduate school and the later probationary period prior to the granting of tenure, my parents paid for me to see specialists not available through the student health plan.[8]

The very idea of society generally or the job market particularly as a level playing field is an ideological mystification that flies in the face of everything we know about the complex relationships of individuals to their communities and families, their schools, their parents' income level, their educational histories, temperaments, and psychologies. Alison Jaggar argues in *Feminist Politics and Human Nature* that the liberal values of freedom and equality (as long as "equality" carries with it the idea of competition on that level playing field) are in conflict, thus making liberal political theory itself incoherent. The only way to secure a level playing field would be to take children from their parents at birth and educate them identically in identical environments. This plan is unworkable in the current political climate, as it would incur astronomical expense. (The same politicos who maunder on about our no longer needing affirmative action because that level playing field is now a reality will not even appropriate sufficient funds to keep the worst of our scandalously unequal schools from collapsing, sometimes on the very heads of their students.) To level the playing field, anything more than token contact with parents would have to be denied, as would many preferences, say for toys or books, of children themselves. These intrusions into the family, flawed as the institution is, deny very basic rights.

It surprises me that so few people who call for a level playing field have thought through the implications of creating one. The nightmare scenario of massive state intervention cannot help but be implicated in any political perspective that imagines even modest success in life to be the earned consequence of a fair contest: the conditions required to make such a contest fair are repugnant.[9] I am not suggesting that competitors in all contests be physically and mentally identical, which is, of course, impossible. Some contests select for certain traits in their winners (like height in basketball). But the great contest of life in this capitalist system also selects for certain advantages in *its* winners: these advantages are simultaneously the goods that it takes to come out on top and the prizes waiting at the finish line, such goods as money and connections. This is indeed a vicious circularity.

The conservative view of society as a meritocracy not only denies the real effects of race, class, gender, sexual orientation, as these are played out in the lives of ordinary people, but it also very conveniently saddles the victims of these systemic biases with responsibility for their effects. Thus, poor people are poor because of a deficiency of personal responsibility or the lack of a work ethic, because they are promiscuous or are socialized into a defective culture of poverty. There is merit in none of these charges. The same politicians who appear to agonize over the alleged lack of personal responsibility on the part of the poor seem sublimely unconcerned with their own personal responsibility for ridding this rich nation of its persistent poverty. It is not accidental that there is a large overlap between poverty and race. Widespread bigotry, one among many causes of poverty, can easily incorporate poverty into its racist view of the world, a marriage made in hell. In point of fact, most of the poor in this country are children; most welfare recipients are white.

If guilt by virtue of privilege fits the standard view of guilt in moral psychology, then the enjoyment of privilege must involve the violation of a moral principle. Here is a candidate for such a principle: *it is wrong to enjoy privileges from which other people have been unjustly excluded, especially if one's privileges have been predicated upon the unjust exclusion of others.* We examined above one kind of thinking that would make the excluded responsible for their own exclusion, thus canceling the "unjust" before "excluded." But there is another strategy also at work to exonerate the system and those it advantages. What if the disadvantaged are not just morally but biologically unfit? Biological explanations for inequality abound. The newspapers seize on any study that purports to prove that there are biological differences between men and women that account for their social disparities, even while the popular press ignores the mountain of studies that point to differential treatment of the sexes in virtually every domain. A few academics with respectable credentials seem unable to abandon the idea that Blacks are genetically inferior to whites in regard to intelligence.[10] The "findings" are announced periodically to the reading public with some fanfare on the Right; in centrist publications such as the *New York Times,* the seriousness with which these claims are taken, even when they are (often hesitantly) rejected, grants these "scientific" studies a respectability they do not merit. I cannot review this debate here, which is, by now, centuries old.[11]

For the sake of argument, let us assume that findings of racial and gender inferiority are at least superficially plausible. Still, the racial and sexual differences these studies purport to uncover are generally quite slight; hence, if there are genetic differences between races or sexes, it is plausible that changes in childhood socialization could wipe them out altogether. In a speech lambasting *The Bell Curve,* the latest best-seller that purports to demonstrate the inferiority of African Americans in regard to intelligence, Stephen Jay Gould of Harvard demonstrated this point quite dramatically. Taking off his glasses, he said, "I am myopic. My myopia is genetically determined." Letting this statement sink in for a bit, he put his glasses back on with a flourish. "Now," he said, "what has happened to my myopia?" But this gesture is hardly Gould's last word on the subject: he unconditionally rejects both the methodology and the conclusions of *The Bell Curve*.[12] Unfortunately, however, it is likely that most privileged people believe one or the other (or both) of the twin pillars of institutional privilege: the alleged biological and the alleged moral inadequacy of the un- and underprivileged.[13]

So far, my analysis suggests that privileged people in general are not innocent of injustice; nevertheless, only a fraction recognize this to be the case. There is a striking encounter in Sartre's *Dirty Hands* that can perhaps teach us something about the recognition—or the nonrecognition—of responsibility. The play is set in a Balkan country in the closing days of World War II. Hugo, the son of a wealthy industrialist, has joined the Proletarian Party. George and Slick, two working-class members of the party, resent Hugo's class privilege—his fine clothes, his trophy wife—and have been taunting him. He joined the party, they think, "because it was the thing to do"; they joined out of brute necessity, out of hunger. Finally Hugo bursts out angrily:

> For once you're right, my friend. I don't know what appetite is. If you could have seen the tonics they gave me as a kid; I always left half—what waste! Then they opened my mouth and told me: "One spoonful for Papa, one spoonful for Mamma . . . and they pushed the spoon down my throat. . . . Then they had me drink blood fresh from the slaughterhouse, because I was pale; after that I never touched meat. My father would say every night: "This child has no appetite." Every evening he would say: "Eat, Hugo, eat. You'll be sick." They had me take cod-liver oil; that's the height of luxury, medicine to make you hungry while others in the street would sell their souls for a beefsteak. I saw them pass under my window with their placards: "Give us bread." And then I would sit down at the table. "Eat, Hugo, eat." A spoonful for the night watchman who is on strike, a spoonful for the old woman who picks the parings out of the garbage can, a spoonful for the

family of the carpenter who broke his leg. I left home. I joined the party, only to hear the same old song: "You've never been hungry, Hugo, what are you messing around here for? What can you know? You've never been hungry." Very well, then! I have never been hungry. Never! Never! Never! Now perhaps you can tell me what I can do to make you stop throwing it up to me.[14]

The taunting doesn't stop. Finally, Hoederer, the party leader, intervenes on Hugo's behalf: "You heard him? Come on now, tell him. Tell him what he has to do, Slick, what do you want of him? Do you want him to cut off a hand? Or tear out one of his eyes? . . . The hunger of others is not so easy to bear, either." One of the men says, "There's plenty who manage to put up with it very nicely." And Hoederer replies, "That's because they have no imagination."[15]

In Illyria, Sartre's mythical country, the social order is so skewed that some children are stuffed to the point of nausea, while others are starving. The contrast between the more privileged classes and the underclass in our own country is not quite so grim. Nevertheless, the abject poverty of the homeless and the hopelessness and destitution of the urban black underclass in the United States mirror the hunger of Illyria. Even though Hugo is a child, he is able to imagine the misery of the population, this in a very literal sense: he carries in his mind images of the poor—the old woman who picks parings out of the garbage, the destitute family of the injured carpenter who cannot work. How do these images get into Hugo's head? Perhaps he has seen old women picking parings out of the garbage, perhaps not; but certainly he has seen the strikers in front of his father's house, carrying signs that say "Give Us Bread."

Hoederer is right: we need to imagine, in the most vivid sense, what it would be like to be one of the insulted and injured of this world, for the insults and injuries of others, when we open ourselves up to them as best we can, are indeed not easy to bear. But for Hugo adequately to grasp the wrongness of his privilege, he needs more than imagination: he needs to unmask the moralizing or the Social Darwinist mystifications that regularly justify unredeemed human misery. Like most emotions, guilt, when it is acknowledged as a judgment of self, has an affective dimension that is inextricable from a cognitive dimension (in this case, rejections of the kinds of rationalizations for poverty that are pervasive in bourgeois society).

What I have called "guilt by reason of privilege" is now revealed as a variant of "guilt by reason of complicity." Hugo recognizes his complicity in an unjust social order, indeed the complicity of his *class.* The two kinds of guilt differ in regard to their objects: acts and policies of government in the one, the structure of an entire social totality in the other.

Of course a social totality does not spring into being from nowhere; its character has been slowly and steadily formed precisely by human actions and government policies sedimented over time. But there are historical and psychological factors that have played an important role as well. Moreover, the social totality is riven by contradictions, and it is always in the process of change. Guilt by reason of privilege is more interesting theoretically than simple guilt by complicity, just because its object is difficult, perhaps impossible, to grasp fully. Terms like "social totality" or "the established order" fall easily enough onto the page, but their referents contain regions of confusion and opacity.

Most human beings do not want to feel that they are in any way guilty of perpetuating human misery, which is undoubtedly the reason why my white middle-class students respond regularly with anger, defensiveness, or denial when I suggest to them that we whites enjoy privileges that are systematically denied to nonwhites. "I've never abused or insulted a black person!" or "My parents came here thirty years ago from Croatia: my forebears were peasants, not slaveholders." My students are onto something, namely, the normal distinction between having done something wrong and having done nothing wrong. I am making the counterintuitive claims that one can be guilty *without having done anything wrong* and that one can be guilty without feeling guilty. I am guilty by virtue of my relationship to wrongdoing, a relationship that I did not create but have not severed either.

Thus, the standard characterization of guilt in moral psychology is too "psychologistic." On my view, I am guilty by virtue of simply being who and what I am: a white woman, born into an aspiring middle-class family in a racist and class-ridden society. The existentialists were fond of saying that guilt was endemic to the human condition: I confess to never having fully understood this idea until now. The recognition of unearned privilege does not necessarily or inevitably engender guilt feelings in the heart of the one privileged. The response might well be anger or dismay. But if a person feels guilty because her or his location in the social totality has been a source of unearned privilege, then, in my view, that person is, so to speak, "entitled" to her guilt. There is complicity involved in this second kind of guilt, just as there is in the first, that is, in the recognition that I am implicated in (for example) my government's violation of international law. My role in the maintenance of an unjust social order is a fact, *whether I recognize it or not*. Guilt, then, need not be felt as emotions are typically felt: it is an existential-moral condition that can be, but need not be, accompanied by "feeling guilty."

A Note on White-Skin Privilege

When Hoederer in Sartre's *Dirty Hands* tells George and Slick that the hunger of others is hard to bear, they reply, quite rightly, that "there's plenty who manage to put up with it very nicely." How is it that so many respectable, even pious persons do manage to "put up with it very nicely"? In my view, this is one of the most important and still unanswered questions in political theory. In addition to the role played by the ideological mystifications of "personal responsibility" and Social Darwinism, there is the standard reply: Most people will struggle, even to the point of taking up arms, to maintain their privilege.[16] Their resolution is grounded not only in self-interest and self-serving ideologies but, for some persons, in a number of complex psychological factors that I have analyzed elsewhere.[17] There is also self-deception and morally culpable ignorance on a large scale. The more fortunate perceive few links between their own privilege and the misery of the underprivileged. The two are perceived as entirely unconnected. The radical friends of my youth were right when they emphasized the necessity for an analysis, one that links these phenomena. Moreover, much privilege—be it white-skin, phallic, class, or hetero-normative—although substantial and pervasive, is also *imperceptible*.

Peggy McIntosh, associate director of the Center for Research on Women at Wellesley College and architect of the S.E.E.D. (Seeing Educational Equity and Diversity) Project on Inclusive Curriculum, has made an extraordinary contribution to our understanding of white-skin privilege; her work goes a long way toward answering the question why so many of the privileged "put up with it" so easily. "I think whites are carefully taught not to recognize white privilege, as males are taught not to recognize male privilege. So I have begun in an untutored way to ask what it is like to have white privilege as an invisible package of unearned assets which I can count on cashing in each day, but about which I was 'meant' to remain oblivious."[18] McIntosh's final list has forty-nine items; she invites us to add to it. I will reproduce below about a third of the list so that white-skinned persons of conscience will be motivated to hunt down the rest of her work:

1. I can if I wish arrange to be in the company of people of my race most of the time.
2. If I should need to move, I can be pretty sure of renting or purchasing housing in an area which I can afford and in which I would want to live.
3. I can be pretty sure that my neighbors in such a location will be neutral or pleasant to me.
4. I can go shopping alone most of the time, pretty well assured that I will not be followed or harassed.
5. I can turn on the television or open to the front page of the paper and see people of my race widely represented.
6. When I am told about our national heritage or about "civilization," I am shown that people of my color made it what it is. . . .
9. I can go into . . . a supermarket and find the staple foods which fit with my cultural traditions, into a hairdresser's shop and find someone who can cut my hair.
10. Whether I use checks, credit cards, or cash, I can count on my skin color not to work against the appearance of financial reliability.
11. I can arrange to protect my children most of the time from people who might not like them.
12. I can swear, or dress in second hand clothes, or not answer letters, without having people attribute these choices to the bad morals, the poverty, or the illiteracy of my race.
13. I can speak in public to a powerful male group without putting my race on trial. . . .

15. I am never asked to speak for all the people of my racial group.
16. I can remain oblivious of the language and customs of persons of color who constitute the world's majority without feeling in my culture any penalty for such oblivion. . . .
18. I can be pretty sure that if I ask to talk to "the person in charge," I will be facing a person of my race.
19. If a traffic cop pulls me over . . . I can be sure I haven't been singled out because of my race. . . .
22. I can take a job with an affirmative action employer without having co-workers on the job suspect that I got it because of race.
23. I can choose public accommodation without fearing that people of my race cannot get in or will be mistreated in the places I have chosen. . . .
25. If my day, week, or year is going badly, I need not ask of each negative episode or situation whether it has racial overtones.[19]

When I read this for the first time, not so long ago, I was astonished: how could I have failed to notice so much about being white, I, who had at least on one occasion risked my life in the civil rights movement? I was disturbed, too, at my ignorance of what it must be like for people of color to bear the daily burden of racism. McIntosh says that whites are "carefully taught" not to notice all this. Paradoxically, we whites have thoroughly learned something we were not in fact "carefully taught." "Carefully taught" implies that there were other whites, not so oblivious, who taught us to be oblivious. But I think that the people who taught me were themselves as oblivious as I have been myself. Segregation was carefully maintained as I was growing up (in the North) in virtually every domain of life. Without black friends or neighbors, with nary a black teacher from kindergarten through graduate school, who was there to teach me the difference? I have read all the "important" black writers, but their topic is largely their experience of racism, not the phenomenology of white-skin privilege. McIntosh makes another quite crucial observation about privilege: some of the items on her list characterized as "privileges," such as fair housing, shouldn't be characterized as privileges at all but as entitlements available to all; nor is number 16, obliviousness to much of the world's culture, properly a privilege; it is described more accurately as a form of domination as well as an intellectual and moral impoverishment of the one dominating.

Guilt in the Form of a Debt

Nietzsche makes much of the nonmoral origins of moral notions. In *The Genealogy of Morals* he finds the genesis of guilt in a sense of indebtedness; to be guilty is to owe someone something. Indeed, the German word *Schuld* has both meanings, guilt and debt.[20] Here is another gloss on the gulf between feeling and fact: one can in fact owe someone a debt without knowing it or, as in the case of the chronic deadbeat, without feeling any urgency, ever, to repay it.

To owe a debt to someone and to overlook it is blameworthy. What I am about to say now is very personal; it may be more a personal confession than a social fact. For many years, Jews and Blacks had a special relationship. In comparison with other white Americans, Jews supported black causes financially and politically, far in excess of their representation in the white population. Reasons for this support are not hard to find. Both groups had then and still have common enemies (the KKK, the Aryan Nation). Jews, who had been oppressed for centuries, were able more easily than many white Americans to identify with oppressed Blacks. Recently, however, these ties have been weakened considerably, chiefly by the rise of black anti-Semitism (how sad that one of the few things Blacks are allowed to share with "real Americans" is Jew-hating and Jew-baiting), the identification of many persons of color in this country with the Palestinians, and the emergence of a small but influential group of Jewish neoconservatives who have polemicized against what most Blacks see as in their interest, such as affirmative action. But in spite of all, these ties have not been entirely broken. Jewish financial support is still strong, nor did Jesse Jackson's "Hymietown" remark keep a majority of Jews from voting for him some years ago when he ran in the New York presidential primary.

Whatever the vicissitudes of relations between Blacks and Jews, I have always seen Blacks in this country as stand-ins for Jews in the following sense: they are standing in a place where we would be if they were not already in it. They have been the first ordered out of the trenches; we Jews are behind the lines, protected in the victim-reserves. There is a place in the mass American psyche (and, so it appears, in the collective psyches of many other peoples as well) for a kind of murderous bigotry. Blacks have mainly occupied this place in this country. In the West, the Chinese were in it for a short time; there are parts of this country in which prejudice against Hispanics is very vicious and very widespread. But in the East, the South, and the Midwest, anti-Black racism is clearly the principal form of bigotry and the one that has had the most baneful consequences—from the lynching, rape, and mutilation of Blacks to de jure and de facto segregation.

But anti-Semitism has been a persistent theme as well. Though he was only one (even one is one too many), Leo Frank, the Jewish manager of a textile plant in the South, was accused falsely of rape, dragged from his cell, and lynched—largely because he was a Jew. I do not mean by referring to this one incident to put in shadow the regular lynching, the castration, and often the burning of black bodies that was common practice in the South but also in the North for decades, ignored by federal law enforcement and often aided and abetted by local police.[21] Children were often brought to these lynchings, which sometimes took on the character of a festival. The Ku Klux Klan reached its peak membership not in the South but in the Midwest in the early twenties. In 1922, for example, 30 percent of white native-born males in Indiana were members of the Klan. In this incarnation, the Klan was at least as anti-Catholic and anti-Semitic as it was anti-Black.[22]

My sense of it is this: they, the Blacks, took the heat and the hate and the persecution that might otherwise have been visited upon us, the Jews. Perform a thought-experiment: close your eyes and imagine that overnight all the Blacks and Hispanics disappear: who would be on the front lines then? Of course, no one can know for certain, but even a superficial acquaintance with American history and contemporary politics suggests an answer: gays, lesbians, Hispanics, and, most likely, Jews. We would move up a notch on the register of national scapegoats. Hence, as a Jew I have often felt indebted to Blacks; they suffer the persecution some form of which might well have been visited upon us if the course of U.S. history had been different. Jews in this country have, at least since World War II, not only been little affected by anti-Semitism (one can always think of exceptional cases) but have been allowed to prosper. It is now and has always been payback time: one way to deal with this incalculable debt is to strike a blow, indeed, many blows, against anti-Black racism.

IN LIEU OF A CONCLUSION

I have been arguing, in line with traditional moral psychology, that guilt is a response to the recognition that the more privileged Americans have been complicit in the violation of moral principles. Moreover, guilt is not simply an "emotion" of self-assessment, involving, as it does, acts of cognition and certain ideological commitments. In contradistinction to traditional moral psychology, I have argued that guilt is also a moral-existential predicament, that is, that the reactionary goals pursued by our foreign policy as well as the very structure of everyday life place the relatively privileged in a morally compromised position, whether we know we are in it or not. One can be guilty without feeling guilty and without having authored the social arrangements that involve one in complicity. So conservatives are quite right to pillory "bleeding hearts"—if bleeding is all they do. The liberal social policies that have been adopted in one or another "war on poverty" may be flawed, but if they are, it is unlikely that their flaws are due to an excess of compassion on the part of policy makers. It is sometimes difficult to believe that conservatives have hearts at all. It is unlikely that the "welfare reform" they supported (with the collusion of Democrats) will reduce either poverty or racism to any appreciable degree, and it has the potential to impose new forms of suffering and denial on the poor.

There are, of course, extenuating circumstances. Whites grew up in a land that managed to make us oblivious to white-skin privilege. I was in my thirties before I began to grasp the enormity as well as the imperceptibility of male privilege under patriarchy; only later was I led to a recognition of the imperceptibility of my own white skin. It is true in law, but is it not true in ethics as well that "ignorance of the law is no excuse"?

I would distinguish between ordinary ignorance and culpable ignorance. I have some extremely sheltered white students from distant suburbs who have grown up, as I did myself, in entirely white communities, educated by school and media to be unaware of the inequality and injustice that deforms our society. Most have never been in downtown Chicago, which has been represented to them as mortally dangerous, have never had a friend of color, and have never come up against a view of U.S. society that is in conflict with what they were taught. When they finally see a ghetto (our university is in the middle of the inner city) or talk to a welfare recipient or meet with an "out" gay person, their confusion and astonishment are palpable. I think that these young people suffer—to use one of their favorite expressions—"cluelessness."

I am less sure of what to say about their parents. Many parents commute; they have some familiarity with the city; they read the papers. How can anyone read the Chicago papers day after day without coming to see that conditions in the ghetto are so terrible that a collective escape from them—without help—would be nothing short of miraculous? Unlike their children who know very little, they know something about "capital flight," rising inequalities in income, our irrational and unfair system of school funding; perhaps they know that 300,000 manufacturing jobs have left the Chicago area in the last fifteen years. I am also certain, from my own experience, that Peggy McIntosh's claims about the imperceptibility of white-skin privilege are perfectly on target and apply to these parents just as they did to me. Their behavior does not manifest simple ignorance: they exhibit culpable ignorance, the willful not-knowing of what is staring them in the face, the bad faith of pretending not to know what they do indeed know, and the retreat under the two-pillared shelter— the disadvantaged are personally responsible; the disadvantaged are biologically unfit—for whites endangered by the possibility of guilt.[23]

How much effort on the part of a person will cancel her complicity, hence remove her guilt? Can this cancellation ever be complete? In regard to the first form of complicity I discussed, complicity in the crimes of my government, I think that the answer to the second question is "yes." The people of Operation Plowshares (symbolically) attacked missile silos containing nuclear bombs and then, in some cases, were given long jail sentences when they refused to show contrition or promise that there would be no further such actions. These protesters, to my mind, successfully detached themselves from the insanity of Mutually Assured Destruction. But what about antinuclear protestors—protestors of many mad and oppressive policies—who do not devote the better part of their lives to what offends them most, who have not risked their lives or even their jobs, who have not gone to jail? What about the many who "only" wrote letters and sent checks and perhaps attended a few demonstrations?

Again, how much effort on the part of a person will cancel her complicity, hence remove her guilt? I am inclined to the view that in many respects it cannot be canceled; hence my designation of a certain kind of guilt as "existential," my sympathy with Sartre's view (and Plato's) that one cannot have clean hands where the polity is unclean. It is important to remember that there are some inequalities from which we cannot entirely divorce ourselves, no matter how hard we try. White-skin privilege is a case in point, as a good part of this privilege consists in experiences that, as a white person, *I will never have.* I cannot be stopped by the police because I am driving "too good a car" for a person of my color. On the other hand, I can try in my day-to-day living and working to be cognizant of my situation and especially to be cognizant of the situations of my colleagues, students, and friends of color. Julia LeSage, film critic, filmmaker, and activist, once told me that any class that does not mention racism perpetuates it. This point seems especially salient to those of us who teach feminist studies, ethics, and political philosophy.

In my view, we accomplish little as individuals; in the spirit of Mother Jones, we need to organize, not to mourn and not merely to "bleed." We certainly need not worry over degrees of complicity—which can become a new and insidious form of white evasion, a backhanded way of keeping ourselves still in the center. We need to find those organizations that appear to be making a difference, join them, and support them. I do not believe that personal change must precede political action, a common New Age belief. Meaningful political action will change us. The relationship between personal change and political empowerment is complex: each needs the other; neither can be fully successful in the absence of the other. How much time, effort, money, and sacrifice are required for the verdict "no longer complicit?" Or even "no longer *as* complicit?" This is a question for which there is, I think, no possibility of a blanket answer, for much depends on the kind of injustice that moves us to action, on the state of our health and strength, on our circumstances and responsibilities to those close to us, and, to some extent, on the political climate of the country. My conclusion, then, is that this discussion has raised questions about the shedding of guilt and the termination of complicity for which there are no conclusive answers.

NOTES

I would like to thank Claudia Card for her inestimable help in the preparation of this chapter. But I alone am responsible for the ideas expressed herein; she bears no responsibility for my limitations. I would also like to thank Ted Precht for his invaluable assistance as well.

1. Bill Gates, CEO of Microsoft, is at the time of this writing (1998) said to be the richest man in the United States.

2. George Gilder, *Wealth and Poverty* (New York: Bantam Books, 1982).

3. See David Zucchino, *Myth of the Welfare Queen: A Pulitzer Prize–Winning Journalist's Portrait of Women on the Line* (New York: Scribner, 1997).

4. None of what I say here should be construed as a defense of liberalism as a political theory.

5. See Gabriele Taylor, *Pride, Shame and Guilt: Emotions of Self-Assessment* (Oxford: Oxford University Press, 1985).

6. The sort of complicity I have in mind is "moral" complicity, but perhaps "legal" complicity is not far off the mark if we think primarily not of U.S. law but of international law. Black's Law Dictionary defines "complicity" as "participation in guilt."

7. Franz Kafka, *The Trial* (New York: Alfred A. Knopf, 1959), p. 7.

8. The suburban specialists told me unequivocally that I should quit graduate school and get married. It was not until I found a doctor on my own, Bertram Carnow, that I was taken seriously. Carnow told me that the graduate students (from the University of Chicago) he saw in his Hyde Park practice suffered more from stress-related illnesses than soldiers he had seen as a frontline surgeon in World War II.

9. Alison Jaggar, *Feminist Politics and Human Nature* (Totowa, N.J: Rowman and Allanheld, 1983), esp. chap. 3.

10. Richard J. Herrnstein and Charles Murray, *The Bell Curve* (New York: Free Press, 1994).

11. But see Ruth Bleier, *Science and Gender: A Critique of Biology and Its Theories About Women* (New York: Pergamon Press, 1989).

12. Herrnstein and Murray, *The Bell Curve*. Gould's extremely persuasive critique of research of this sort is based in part on a very telling attack on the scientificity of I.Q. tests, Herrnstein and Murray's principal research instrument. See Steven Jay Gould, *The Mismeasure of Man* (New York: Norton, 1981).

13. There is some debate currently about the biological bases of homosexuality. Many lesbians, however, claim to have made a choice—for many feminists, a principled political choice. The "reasons" offered by homophobes for denying gays and lesbians not just privileges but basic rights are either empirically false (homosexuals are always recruiting the naive into the homosexual lifestyle) or are based on readings of the Bible that (a) have been challenged by many scholars of religion and (b) have no place in a secular society anyhow. See John Boswell, *Christianity and Social Tolerance* (Chicago: University of Chicago Press, 1978).

14. Jean-Paul Sartre, *Dirty Hands*, in *No Exit and Three Other Plays* (New York: Vintage, 1955), pp. 170–71.

15. Ibid., p. 171.

16. However, many people tithe; there is sharing in times of emergency, even extraordinary acts of courage. We are egotists, but also, under certain conditions, altruists.

17. See Sandra Bartky, "Sympathy and Solidarity: On a Tightrope with Scheler," in *Feminists Rethink the Self*, ed. Diana Meyers (New York: Routledge, 1997).

18. Peggy McIntosh, "White Privilege and Male Privilege: A Personal Account of Coming to See Correspondences Through Work in Women's Studies," Working Paper No. 189 (Wellesley, Mass.: Wellesley College Center for Research on Women, 1988).

19. McIntosh, "White Privilege and Male Privilege," p. 44.

20. Friedrich Nietzsche, *On the Genealogy of Morals*, trans. Walter Kaufmann and R. S. Hollingdale (New York: Vintage, 1969), pp. 62–65. Nietzsche's discussion of this connection is rich in both psychoanalytic and theological insights.

21. Seventy Blacks were lynched in 1919 alone; fourteen were burned. M. William Lutholtz, *Grand Dragon: D. C. Stephenson and the Ku Klux Klan in Indiana* (W. Lafayette, Ind.: Purdue University Press, 1991), p. 154.

22. Ibid., p. 55.

23. On this form of bad faith, see in particular Lewis Gordon, *Bad Faith and Antiblack Racism* (Atlantic Highlands, N.J.: Humanities, 1995).

3 / On the Malleability of Character

MARCIA L. HOMIAK

John Stuart Mill was one of the first philosophers to chart the ways in which temperament and inclination are molded by antecedent circumstances. He was one of the first to argue that both women's *and* men's abilities to live virtuously and morally are seriously impeded by societies that have systematically subordinated women.[1] In Mill's view, oppressive circumstances mold all of us and make relationships of healthy intimacy and genuine understanding almost impossible. How, then, can we become better? Mill's answer is that becoming better (let's say becoming an egalitarian or a feminist) requires more than a rational revision of belief—more, for example, than a recognition of how societies wrongfully subordinate women or how radical social change is needed to liberate women. Becoming a feminist, for Mill, requires more than being persuaded of something. It requires a deeper and different transformation—a transformation in character.

Mill's interest in character, and his realization that becoming better involves a change in something fundamental about oneself, has not gone unnoticed in contemporary feminist literature. Recognizing that becoming a feminist takes a "profound personal transformation,"[2] not only in behavior but also in consciousness (of oneself, others, and one's relation to others and the world), feminist writers have begun to think more systematically than Mill did about the constitution of character and the nature of identity and integrity.[3] Moreover, feminist writers aren't alone among moral philosophers in finding character and integrity worthy of serious discussion: within the last two decades, there has been a resurgence of philosophical interest in "virtue ethics" (sometimes inspired by feminist concerns, sometimes not), where character is said to play a central role.[4] But these discussions have introduced disturbing questions about the nature and extent of moral agency and moral responsibility: We might agree that becoming better involves a fundamental change in character; but if our characters are, as Mill recognized, the products of oppressive circumstances and oppressive social conditions, perhaps we are not in control of our characters at all and becoming better isn't a real possibility.[5] Claudia Card introduced the first volume of *Feminist Ethics* with these and related worries. She asked: "If oppressive institutions stifle and stunt the moral development of the oppressed, how is it possible, what does it mean, for the oppressed to be liberated? What is there to liberate? What does it mean to resist, to make morally responsible choices, to become moral agents, to develop character?" (1991, 25). This chapter is a contribution to this long-standing feminist discussion. I try to show how we can overcome the effects of antecedent circumstances, how we can take responsibility for our character and become better. I'll argue that it is possible for nearly everyone to become better. But my account will also explain why women often face different obstacles in this process than do men.

I approach these questions—of the nature of character, the possibility of character change, and the extent of our responsibility for character and the actions produced thereby—not from the perspective of contemporary feminist writing or even from a modern direction, but from an Aristotelian direction. Because Aristotle's discussions of character are among the most detailed and insightful in the western philosophical tradition, it makes good sense to turn to him. But learning from Aristotle isn't easy or straightforward, because he does not seem to have a consistent position on the extent to which character change is possible. Consider the following:

1. "To the unjust and self-indulgent person it was open at the beginning not to become men of this kind, and so they are such voluntarily; but now that they have become so it is not possible for them not to be so" (*Nicomachean Ethics* 1114a20–21).[6]
2. "The man who pursues the excesses of things pleasant, or pursues to excess necessary objects, and does so by choice, for their own sake and not at all for the sake of any result distinct from them, is self-indulgent; for such a man is of necessity without regrets, and therefore incurable, since a man without regrets cannot be cured" (1150a19–22).

3. "Man has reason, in addition, and man only. For this reason nature, habit, reason must be in harmony with one another; for they do not always agree; men do many things against habit and nature, if reason persuades them that they ought" (*Politics* 1332b5–9).[7]

4. "And it is possible to become bad instead of good or good instead of bad. (For the bad man, if led into better ways of living and talking, would progress, if only a little, toward being better. And if he once made even a little progress it is clear that he might either change completely or make really great progress. For however slight the progress he made to begin with, he becomes ever more easily changed toward virtue, so that he is likely to make still more progress; and when this keeps happening it brings him over completely into the contrary state, provided time permits)"(*Categories* 13a23–31).[8]

Sometimes—in passages (1) and (2)—Aristotle writes as though settled states of character are fixed and unalterable. Once formed, we can do nothing about them. If that is correct, we might wonder how we can be held morally responsible for actions produced by our states of character.[9] If my consuming the entire cake results from my intemperance and I cannot now change that intemperance, how are my actions up to me and under my control? Maybe my actions are no different from those of a paranoid afflicted with mania or from those of a compulsive kleptomaniac. Yet my consuming the entire cake, as an action produced by my intemperance, seems paradigmatic of action for which I am morally accountable.

I shall challenge the idea (which Aristotle seems to endorse in his more skeptical moods) that we are not responsible for actions produced by our states of character. My strategy is to take seriously Aristotle's more hopeful remarks about the possibility of character change—as suggested in (3) and (4) above. I argue that Aristotle has resources in his moral philosophy to show us how we can alter our fundamental beliefs and desires, how we can, in effect, become different—though not all at once. I argue that, just as the *Categories* passage—(4) above—claims, agents can become better little by little, "if led into better ways of living and talking." On my interpretation, agents with settled states of character can change who they are. But I approach these questions in the opposite direction from much contemporary discussion on responsibility and agency. Contemporary discussion begins from the intuitively plausible position that responsible agents are distinguished by their capacity to "listen to reason." It must then be in virtue of some *rational* feature or capacity that people are vulnerable to rational persuasion and thereby responsible agents of change.[10] In contrast, I argue that specific *nonrational* psychological capacities must be realized for rational argument to be effective, for us to be creatures who can listen to reason.

My Aristotelian account thus supports the view (held by Mill) that arguments alone will not effect fundamental change and that change must call upon other, nonrational aspects of the person. Although I indicate why women in the contemporary United States often face different obstacles in developing the requisite nonrational desires and attachments than do men, I argue that it is nevertheless possible for most people to develop them, even people who have grown up in oppressive or stultifying circumstances. Thus I do not conclude, as Susan Wolf seems to do in *Freedom Within Reason* (1990), that citizens of racist or misogynist states are not psychologically free to change who they are and hence cannot be held fully responsible for their adult racist and sexist actions. On the view I propose, most people have the nonrational psychological capacities that are realized in becoming better. Hence most can listen to reason and be responsible agents.

The rest of this chapter is organized as follows. Section I summarizes difficulties one confronts by holding (as Aristotle does) both that only adults with settled states of character are responsible agents and also that formed states of character are unalterable. Aristotle thinks most adults have the capacity to reflect about what goals to pursue and what values to embrace and that they can develop and implement strategies to realize their aims. Developing and implementing such strategies show they have formed states of character. His discussion suggests that it is because they have formed states of character that they are responsible for the actions produced by those states. But, as I have indicated, Aristotle also seems to think that, once acquired, states of character are unalterable. This claim calls into question our status as responsible agents, since it suggests we are no longer agents of change. Section II considers the extent to which agents of settled character are vulnerable to rational argument aimed at change. At first sight, their vulnerability to argument seems insufficient to sustain a connection between rational capacity and character change. Section III considers evidence from Aristotle's *Nicomachean Ethics* and *Rhetoric* that there is considerable agreement in ordinary people's beliefs about the nature of the good life. If there is such agreement, one might think all people (whether morally virtuous or vicious) are susceptible to argument directed toward the good. But it is unclear how such argument might work. Agents' sensitivity to reason still appears limited.

Section IV examines examples of fundamental change, from (relatively) bad to (relatively) good character. Section V argues that such change depends on actualizing at least one of two nonrational psychological capacities: (i) the capacity to take pleasure from the exercise of our characteristic rational powers and (ii) the capacity to form, and to enjoy, ties of friendship and association. My argument is that a person's beliefs about the nature of the good are altered, then, not directly (through rational revision of beliefs), but indirectly (through actualization of one or both of the above nonrational capacities). Finally, section VI considers briefly Susan Wolf's discussion of responsible agency and takes up implications of her view for feminist concerns about the possibilities of resistance to oppressive social structures. Although my discussion should prove congenial to many feminist writers who find women particularly well-placed to enjoy ties of friendship and community, my view also suggests that both men and women face obstacles in developing the exercise of their characteristic rational powers—obstacles whose elimination requires radical social change.

I

Let me begin by summarizing what seems to be Aristotle's view on moral responsibility. Aristotle believes that only human adults, with the rational capacities distinctive of human adults, are morally responsible. (He excludes women, slaves, and children.) What are the requisite rational capacities, and why are they the critical factor for determining moral agency?

Aristotle insists that virtue and vice are objects of praise and blame (1109b30–34); he explicitly associates "decision" (*prohairesis*) with virtue and vice (1111b7; cf. 1105a31, 1106b36, 1134a17, 1135b25); he denies that children and animals share in decision (1111b9); and he asserts that decision distinguishes character better than actions (1111b5–6) or beliefs (1112a1–3). The ability to act from decision thus seems to be what distinguishes morally responsible agents, whose actions are appropriate candidates for moral praise and blame, from those who are not morally responsible. What then is a "decision"? Decisions are rational desires, which issue from an agent's deliberation about the good (1113a10–12; 1113a25–33). Decisions thus reflect an agent's choice of values and goals, her choice, one might say, of how to live. Human adults have life-plans and settled states of character. The (voluntary) actions produced by their states of character (for example, a generous person's helping action, a brave person's defense of a besieged town, an irascible person's insulting behavior, and an intemperate person's consumption of the whole cake) are thus reasonable candidates for moral praise and blame.

Now we can see why Aristotle thinks only adult human agents who can form and act on decisions are morally responsible agents. For the deliberation necessary for decision, because it is about how to live, will likely include development of stategies designed either to promote the growth of desires one does not have now or to eliminate desires one does have. Thus only beings who have some control over who they are and over what they can do can fruitfully undertake the deliberation involved in forming decisions. Were a being simply the passive subject of her desires, such deliberation would have no useful practical role in her life. The capacity to deliberate in this fashion carries the suggestion that we can implement our deliberative desires in action and thereby bring about change in our present set of desires. Thus the central idea behind associating responsibility with the formation of rational desires is that these desires, which we construct, can effect change in us; in this way we are agents of change and are thereby responsible for who we are and what we do. Thus Aristotle seems to hold a view like that of many contemporary philosophers—that a morally responsible agent "listens to reason" in the right way and can, when necessary, respond to rational argument (her own or others') aimed at altering her behavior.

I mentioned earlier that Aristotle seems not to have a consistent position on how adults with settled states of character are vulnerable to rational persuasion and hence are able to change. On one hand, he claims that since doing virtuous and vicious actions is up to us (is voluntary), and since this is what it is to be virtuous or vicious, then being good or bad is up to us (1113b11–14).[11] On the other hand, a page later he asserts that whereas "it was originally open to the person who is [now] unjust or intemperate not to acquire this character, hence he has it willingly, though once he has acquired it he can no longer get rid of it" (1114a20–23). Aristotle seems to be saying that although steps we took to become virtuous or vicious were voluntary and up to us, we can't now be rid of our virtue or vice—we can't now be different. But why not?

Presumably, because being virtuous or vicious involves more than simply believing that one way of life is better for us than another. States of character are complex combinations of thought and feeling: they are the result of educating both rational and nonrational desires (including emotions, feelings, and appetites), so that we form attachments to persons, objects, and ways of acting, which, once formed, are hard (perhaps even impossible) to alter. But if states of character are unalterable, how can ordinary virtuous and vicious actions be paradigmatic of voluntary action? Such actions, we thought, were reasonable candidates for actions for which we can be held accountable, because these actions are "ours": they reveal our deliberated commitments and goals; they show us as agents of self-creation. Now it looks as though the acquisition of a state of character, which we thought necessary for forming decisions (1111b5–6 and 1112a1–3) and hence for morally responsible action, has undermined our status as agents of change and hence as morally responsible agents: intemperate people cannot be temperate; unjust people cannot be just. No wonder Aristotle hopes for properly brought up students in his classes (1095b4–9; 1179b23–29). If states of character are resistant to deliberative arguments whose aim is to move agents toward a different choice of values and goals, then Aristotle's efforts would prove futile with badly brought up students who have inappropriate nonrational habits.

If Aristotle wants to say that it is in virtue of our deliberative capacities that we are agents of change and morally responsible, then he needs some way to explain how having a settled character does not render an agent invulnerable to rational persuasion. I argue that Aristotle has the resources to show how agents with settled states of character are vulnerable to reason and hence to change—to show how, for example, agents raised under oppressive institutions can come to question the character they developed. The resources are the above-mentioned nonrational psychological capacities: (i) the capacity to take pleasure from exercising our characteristic rational powers and (ii) the capacity to form, and to enjoy, ties of friendship and association. Actualizing these capacities, I argue, is necessary for rational argument to be effective.

II

To begin, I explore ways in which agents with settled states of character might evidence a sensitivity to reason and hence a capacity to change. As a test case, I use an example suitable to Aristotle's texts and evaluative concerns and also to his deeply sexist culture: Paris's sexual attraction to Helen and his abduction of her to Troy. Mythological tradition is unclear about Helen's response: was she also attracted to Paris? Did she succumb to her own sexual desires when she left Sparta for Troy? (In *Iliad* III.171ff., Homer implies she believes she could have refused his advances.) Whether Helen did or didn't "consent," her wishes in this case are not what is important in her culture, just as they weren't when her father married her off to Menelaus. That women's desires generally did not count in their relations with men is a central aspect of her culture's sexism. However, I want to approach this example as it would have been viewed by Aristotle and his peers. What interests them are Paris's moral defects, for it is Paris who counts. Looking at the example this way may prove more instructive for feminists than to concentrate on Helen's condition and fate. For we are trying to understand how someone deeply influenced by the basic institutions of his culture can come to reevaluate and alter his desires and aims.

If we look at the example from this direction, then, it seems clear that Paris risks the disfavor of his fellow aristocrats, not to mention the destruction of his family and city, for sexual pleasure. I'll assume his action is voluntary (produced by his intemperate character) and blameworthy (because intemperate).[12] As a result, it is reasonable for his peers and for us to hold him morally responsible for what he has done. If he is responsible for (i) abducting Helen and (ii) acting intemperately, then, on the Aristotelian view I've been considering, he should be sensitive to reason and capable of altering his desires. Presumably, then, someone should be able to convince Paris (i) not to seduce Helen and (ii) not to act intemperately. If there are no such arguments, then Paris's (i) desire for Helen and (ii) his intemperate desire will seem compulsive. He can't help acting on them. What might such arguments look like?

(1a) We might begin by looking at arguments that do not call into question Paris's deep evaluative commitments. Suppose someone persuaded him that abducting Helen is time-consuming and the outcome of the long journey uncertain. There are easier, more predictable ways to satisfy his sexual appetites. There's an attractive slave-girl nearby. Suppose he opts for the easier methods and decides against abducting Helen.

If Paris is persuaded by this reasoning, then should we conclude that his intemperate desire is not compulsive? Not if we think that alleged compulsives will also choose the easier means of satisfying their compulsive desires. (The manic might find the desire to express his creative powers irresistible. But it is not silly to think we can convince him to do so on a personal computer, rather than on the walls of his hospital room.) Because the argument doesn't challenge Paris's evaluative commitments, we can't conclude that Paris's intemperate desire for sexual gratification is not compulsive. Although his decision to take easier, less problematic means to satisfy his lust shows he is sensitive to reason in a weak, evaluatively neutral, sense (he accepts an elementary principle of rational choice), it does not show he can control whether he is intemperate or not. We can hold him accountable for his ineptitude, but not (yet) for his intemperance.

(1b) Again, let's assume Paris is persuaded not to abduct Helen. This time the argument is different: he is told that either he satisfies his lust and faces certain death at the hands of Menelaus, or he leaves Sparta in sexual frustration. He opts to preserve his life. Responding positively to this argument, Paris shows us he is not self-destructive. Faced with a threat of death, he chooses life rather than indulge his desires. He need not, if the stakes are sufficiently high, act on his sexual desires. Does this show us these desires are not compulsive, that his desire for Helen is not compulsive? Again, not if we think alleged compulsives (addicts, those who are phobic) faced with similar options would also choose life.[13]

(1c) We might look at a different argument, one that does challenge Paris's evaluative commitments. Someone might try to convince Paris that it is impermissible for aristocrats to violate laws of hospitality; or that, by stealing Helen, he will bring on Greek armies and risk destruction of his family and city. Let us assume Paris is persuaded: he agrees that aristocrats are bound by conventions of hospitality or that the welfare of one's community is more important than sleeping with the most beautiful woman in the world. He decides not to satisfy his lust for Helen.

What does this show? We might think it shows that Paris has been argued into continence: that is, he now knows and does what he ought to do, although tempted otherwise. (Incontinent people know what they ought to do but follow temptation to act otherwise, whereas a continent person successfully resists the temptation; virtuous people know what they ought to do and are not tempted to do otherwise.) Paris still feels great sexual desire for Helen but doesn't act on it. Surely this result depends on how strongly Paris holds the values of community, family, or aristocratic convention. If he finds these values of slight importance, it is hard to see how he can be persuaded to pursue them rather than indulge his lust. But if he finds them extremely important, he does not seem intemperate at all. Perhaps he is at most continent. But then we haven't persuaded him of anything, for he was continent to begin with. Or, he is no different from the Paris in (1b): with stakes sufficiently high, that Paris, like this one, refuses to indulge his lust. But then how is he different from other alleged compulsives?

Let us now take the opposite course and assume Paris is resistant to our arguments. First (2a), assume Paris is unpersuaded by the arguments in (1a) above. He prefers to satisfy his lust in circumstances requiring a maximum of practical inconvenience, risk, and uncertainty. It is hard to make sense of this preference. What we know about Paris from mythological tradition doesn't suggest that he enjoys the risk and uncertainty of a challenge, so it's not that he has a reason to prefer risk. Rather, Paris seems to be rejecting an elementary principle of rational choice (the principle of choosing the most effective means). If so, it is hard to avoid concluding that he is deeply irrational.

(2b) Assume Paris is unpersuaded by the threat of death in (1b). This alternative, too, is odd, since it is hard to see what reason Paris has for scorning death in these circumstances. He is not, after all, scorning death to secure some noble end (which would be understandable). Does he then have no love of life? That doesn't seem to fit with what we know about him—that he is wealthy, of good family, an admired man. Here, too, it is hard to avoid concluding that he is deeply irrational.

(2c) Finally, assume that Paris is unpersuaded by our arguments in (1c). As we probably expected, he thinks these are the arguments of fools. He continues to want to satisfy his sexual appetites and is not dissuaded from seducing Helen. If we conclude that he is not responsible for seducing Helen, then, by extension, no one of settled character is responsible for acts produced by that character, and no one whose character is firmly established by the demands of sexist institutions could be expected to change.

What do these examples show? Most plausibly, that Paris is vulnerable to reason in a weak, evaluatively neutral, sense. If made aware of an easier, more effective means of satisfying his intemperate desire, he will choose it. Or, if stakes are high enough, he will decide not to indulge his intemperate desire. But in these ways he does not seem different from persons conventionally labeled compulsive. If Paris does not respond to reason in even this weak sense, we cannot make sense of his actions; he appears deeply irrational. On the other hand, if Paris responds to arguments aimed at altering his evaluative commitments, then he is responsive to reason in a stronger sense.[14] But we did not find it plausible to think an intemperate (as opposed to a continent) Paris would find such arguments persuasive. The examples, then, seem to confirm Aristotle's skeptical position that states of character are resistant to rational alteration. We are left wondering why agents with settled states of character can reasonably be thought responsible for the voluntary actions produced by their states of character. Although agents may deliberate about how to satisfy their (character-expressing) desires, they are not persuaded by arguments that call those desires into question. Such agents do not seem appreciably different from people who are conventionally thought to be compulsive.

III

Someone who hopes to explain how agents of settled character are vulnerable to arguments directed at character change may say that we have drawn the alternatives too narrowly, expected too much too quickly. Our examples in section II showed little because they were simplistic. When we thought it plausible for Paris to be persuaded, the argument succeeded by offering Paris better means to satisfy desires he already had. He listened to reason in that he accepted some elementary principles of rational choice and exhibited a preference for self-preservation. Will an Aristotelian framework allow for a different approach? Can we develop arguments to appeal to desires that various agents have, whether they are virtuous or vicious, continent or incontinent, but which aren't merely formal preferences for inclusion, greater effectiveness, or for self-preservation? Perhaps these are the desires that, over the course of time (as the *Categories* passage suggests), can be deliberatively reshaped into values that Aristotle associates with virtuous people. If so, then persons of deficient character can still effect character change in themselves and hence can be held responsible for their morally deficient behavior.

An Aristotelian framework does seem to permit a deliberative alternative that is directed to beliefs and desires held by agents of various moral characters. For the starting point of Aristotle's ethics is the beliefs of the many (the common beliefs or *endoxa*). If his considered views fail to accommodate enough of the common beliefs, Aristotle takes himself to have failed in providing an adequate account of fundamental ethical notions or an adequate resolution of an ethical problem. In the famous introduction to the discussion of *akrasia* (incontinence, weakness of will), for example, he writes that "we must set out the appearances, and first of all go through the puzzles. In this way we must prove the common beliefs (*ta endoxa*) about these ways of being affected—ideally, all the common beliefs, but if not all, then most of them, and the most important. For if the objections are solved, and the common beliefs (*ta endoxa*) are left, it will be an adequate proof" (1145b3–7).[15] Although the many will find strange and uncompelling Plato's belief in the Form of the Good and Socrates' belief in the ability of knowledge to master passion (1095a17–28), they will accept the idea that happiness is the chief good (*EN* I.4). As such, happiness is a combination of such important goods as virtue, pleasure, material well-being, family, and community (*EN* I.7); it is characteristically human and something that is properly one's own doing (*EN* I.5). Of course, these common beliefs are highly abstract. Yet Aristotle thinks that because people agree on them, they can recognize some ways of life as better than others. Anyone can see, for example, that the best life isn't focused on honor (1095b22ff.). Since honor is bestowed by others, it can easily be taken away. But the good life is something that is our own (*oikeion ti*, 1095b26) and thus hard to take from us. (Aristotle's common beliefs are psychologically accurate enough to apply to contemporary life. That we accept some version of the idea that a happy life is one's own doing explains why we are reluctant to think women live well when they live through the accomplishments of their spouses or children.)

Like his *Nicomachean Ethics*, Aristotle's *Rhetoric* seems to assume that persons of vastly different moral character share important common beliefs and that because of this fact they are vulnerable to deliberative argument about how best to live. For the *Rhetoric* explores the effect of argument on ordinary people of varying moral character, that is, on people who accept the common beliefs we have already described. Because a good orator's task is to persuade ordinary people, rather than simply to manipulate them for his own purposes (*Rhetoric* 1355b10–11, b18–21), he must know enough about what they believe and about how they feel to find bases for effective argument. To persuade, he avoids specialized knowledge (which would fail to instruct many) and instead uses "notions possessed by everybody" (*Rhetoric* 1355a28). So rhetoric works with common beliefs and common emotional reactions.[16]

Thus a good orator will recognize, as Martha Nussbaum has pointed out, that some elements of a person's emotional character are malleable by argument and in predictable ways.[17] For example, people will pity someone they come to believe has suffered some undeserved misfortune (*Rhetoric* 1385b13–15); they will fear someone they come to believe is about to harm them, if they cannot prevent it (*Rhetoric* 1382b30–83a1); they will feel warmly toward someone they come to believe has acted to benefit them (*Rhetoric* 1381a13–14). Nussbaum's point is that alteration in belief will often alter emotion and feeling, for "at least much or most of the time the belief does sufficiently cause the complex passion" (1996, 310–11).

How then do we alter another's beliefs so as to produce the appropriate emotion? The answer, on this view, is that we address arguments directly to the beliefs characteristic of specific emotions. We explain, for example, that the situation was an accident, not a deliberate assault, so that anger isn't appropriate here. As Nancy Sherman has put it, we must try to persuade the offended person to "compose the scene in the right way" (1989, 171). The offended person's judgment was mistaken; once it is corrected, she will respond appropriately.

The problem with this approach to character change is that it does not go very far. How can we tell the right way to compose the scene? What one person sees as constitutive of the scene, another may not. Perhaps, then, everything rests on our tutor: Paris just needs the right sort of person to help him refine his beliefs and aims in the right way. Again it isn't clear what the right way is. Presumably, the deliberative arguments in section II above weren't the right way. Then does Paris need Aristotle's course on moral philosophy? This seems an unreasonably stiff requirement. But if it is not unreasonable, why does Aristotle suggest that it is precisely people like Paris who *cannot* benefit from such a course? Consider: "For someone whose life follows his feelings would not even listen to an argument turning him away, or comprehend it [if he did listen]; and in that state how could he be persuaded to change? And in general feelings seem to yield to force, not to argument" (1179b26–29; cf. 1095b4–9). If Paris's problem is that his beliefs and his intemperate desires are simply too entrenched to be altered by even the most astute deliberation, then we seem forced back on our earlier view: that Paris is not accountable for his intemperate actions. Nussbaum ends her own account of emotional change at just this pessimistic point. Since she believes that early family life paves the way for adult emotional responses, she acknowledges that one can rightly wonder "how far philosophical examination can reach in altering those [emotional] structures, should they be judged to be defective" (1996, 318).

I believe we can escape these difficulties and show that persons of deficient moral character are responsible both for their morally deficient actions and for their morally deficient character. We can, I think, ultimately transform Paris's intemperate desires and his belief that the pleasures of sexual gratification take precedence over other goods. But the right way to do this isn't to address our arguments directly to Paris's intemperate desires or his endorsement of principles of rational choice (as did the examples above in section II). Nor is the right way to address directly the specific beliefs constitutive of Paris's emotional responses (as suggested in this section). Rather, we must allow for revised beliefs to emerge indirectly by first enabling other, nondeliberative, nonrational capacities to be realized.

These nondeliberative capacities can be realized, and our beliefs can be revised, in the course of full-scale deliberation about how to live—but only if deliberation takes place under special circumstances. So let us turn to what these circumstances might be.

IV

Under what circumstances might a morally vicious person undertake the full-scale deliberation that brings into question his long-standing values? I can imagine variations on two possibilities, which are distinguished by the agent's attitude toward complex deliberation.

(i) In the first type of situation, a personal emergency or crisis in the morally vicious person's life prompts full-scale, wide-ranging, moral deliberation. The individual has no positive attitude toward complex deliberation and undertakes it because circumstances seem to require it.

(ii) In the second type of case, the morally vicious person undertakes an activity that he knows is broadly deliberative in nature and does so because he enjoys this kind of activity. For example, he might be hired by a company or civic body to solve a difficult practical problem (say, an escalating budget crisis) that is broad in scope and wide-ranging in its implications.

I consider (i) first and in detail, since it may be the more common sort of circumstance under which full-scale deliberation is begun. I comment briefly on (ii) later in this section.

Here are examples of (i): (a) Consider a prisoner on death row, accused of a vicious double murder and rape. He is poor, completely without resources, abandoned by his contacts on the outside. To ease his intense loneliness, he turns to charitable organizations, asking for someone to visit. A nun volunteers. At first, their conversations are tense. He reveals despicable traits of character, shows no remorse for his deed, belittles and insults the nun. The nun does not flinch and responds forcefully but kindly. She insists that he treat her with respect, as she does him. Her insistence that he treat her properly gradually merges into a conversation about the value of human beings, the value of human life, and the importance of taking responsibility for one's actions. When she agrees to help him secure a lawyer who can fight for the commutation of his sentence, her commitment to helping him is broadened. Now she provides both emotional care and practical help. Although the lawyer's efforts fail, the nun continues to offer moral guidance and love until the convict's death. When he dies, he is finally able to admit what he did and to recognize its wrongness. At his death, he is no longer arrogant. He asks the parents of his victims to forgive him.[18]

In this example, the prison inmate reflects on his past actions and on the person he has been. Eventually, he acknowledges the wrongness of what he did and of how he has lived, and he decides to be different. He is a better person at his death than he was for most of his life.

How does this character change come about? It seems clear that it is not produced simply by reflection on past actions. What is important in helping us understand this change is the circumstances under which the deliberation takes place. The nun offers the inmate practical assistance, human warmth and kindness, even love, not for any self-interested reason but for the inmate's good for his own sake. It is not unreasonable to think that the inmate recognizes that she is offering to help for his sake, and that he responds to her actions with his own friendly attachment to her (cf. *Rhetoric* 1381a11–13). At the same time, because of the vigor and strength of her moral prodding, and because her prodding is clearly for his sake, he begins to think more deeply about his life and about how persons ought to be treated. He comes to enjoy being with her and talking to her (cf. *EN* 1168a5–9; *Rhetoric* 1381a28–29), even though some of these conversations are at first difficult for him because they require more introspective honesty than he is willing to undertake.

(b) Next consider a student in an introductory philosophy course. He has no interest in philosophy, but his parents, who fund his education, demand that he take it. Suppose he is an unpleasant sort: self-serving, disdainful of others, unjustifiably self-confident, whose main goal in life is material success. His instructor proceeds to argue for an ethical view (imagine it close to Aristotle's) that challenges his own. But the instructor is not autocratic, impatient, unfair, or inappropriately demanding. She is clearly committed to her students' intellectual development. She constructs assignments that require them to think carefully and analytically and to engage with each other in thoughtful and constructive conversation. The students respond to her obvious enthusiasm and commitment. By the end of the

course, our self-serving student has become a better person: he recognizes the value of having his peers' respect, of friendship, of intellectual exchange, and he sees the disadvantages of devoting one's life
to material success.

How are we to explain this change? As in the case of the prison inmate, the nature of the circumstances under which deliberation takes
place is crucial. If his professor is contemptuous and impatient, if she
does not take his views seriously and rewards sloppy and superficial
thinking, he will likely remain hostile to the views she discusses. If
his peers are sullen and unresponsive, even if the instructor does her
best, he might also remain indifferent. But if his peers do their part
in carrying on intellectual exchange in the classroom and the instructor offers the sort of stimulation and challenge that we have described, then it is not unreasonable to think that our self-serving
student will experience an important change in his character. Like
the prison inmate, he responds with friendly feelings toward both his
instructor and his peers, because they treat him fairly (cf. *Rhetoric*
1381a11-13). The instructor has, as we have said, his intellectual
growth at heart. He senses that she wants him to thrive, and he
develops friendly feelings toward her.

So far, this situation is the same sort as in case (a). The morally deficient person responds with friendly feelings toward those who clearly mean to assist and support. But there is a feature of (a) that is more
prominent here in (b). Because the class operates as the instructor
hopes, classroom discussions and paper assignments are interesting,
engaging, even exciting. Our morally deficient student comes to enjoy the work of the class and the stimulation his peers provide. He
enjoys, in effect, the realization of his own abilities brought about by
the instructor's successful pedagogical techniques (cf. *EN* 1168a5-9).
Hence, he comes to like himself more and his classmates also (cf.
Rhetoric 1381a28-29). He is less arrogant and self-satisfied and treats
others better.

I imagine variations on these two cases. Victor Hugo's Jean Valjean
may be a variation on (a). Hugo portrays Valjean as thoroughly warped
by his unjust imprisonment. When he emerges, he is considered dangerous and vicious, a man whose sole concern is for his own preser-
vation. But his character is altered by his encounter with the compassionate Bishop of Dignes, from whom Valjean steals two silver
candlesticks. When pressed by authorities to identify Valjean as the

thief, the bishop insists the candlesticks have been a gift. The bishop's kindness prompts Valjean to begin a long process of introspection and self-assessment. For some years thereafter, Valjean lives a life devoted to improving the lives of others, especially the poor.

As a variation on (b), imagine the self-serving, egotistical, materialist son of a wealthy aristocrat, who wastes his father's fortune through gambling. In exasperation, the father threatens to cut him off completely unless he begins to earn an honest living. The son finds work in a factory that turns out to be worker-controlled and worker-owned. Each worker shares equally in skilled and unskilled labor, and in managerial decisions about the nature of the process, conditions, and outcome of production. Here there may be no individual source of disinterested benevolence (like the nun or philosophy professor) whose honest concern undermines resistance to warmer or more egalitarian attitudes. But the structure of the work process serves to create feelings of equality and solidarity among workers; the workers take pride in what they do and enjoy it. One can imagine the son's being affected by his surroundings to emerge a better person.[19]

In these examples character changes are explained by two psychological phenomena. First, more obvious in (a) than in (b), is the capacity to respond with affection to another's sincere efforts to assist and benefit us. We come to like for their own sake those who seek to help us, when we see that their help is not given to achieve some self-interested purpose (*Rhetoric* 1381a11–13). The nun who visits the prison inmate, the Bishop of Dignes, and the philosophy professor all want to assist and benefit others for their own sakes. The second phenomenon, more obvious in (b) than in (a), is that we come to enjoy the realization of our own abilities, and the more complex and subtle these abilities are, the more we enjoy their realization (1168a5–9). Not only do we enjoy the realization of our own complex abilities, we also enjoy such realization in others (1169b35–1170a1; 1170b14–17). A result is that we come to like those others and ourselves (more than we did), and for no ulterior reason. So the philosophy student comes to like the other students in his class, and the factory worker comes to like his fellow workers.

These examples suggest that for deliberation to issue in revision of values and character change, the activity of deliberation must be motivated in one of two ways: the first is some element of exigency, crisis, or requirement (impending death, threatened disinheritance, a parental demand); the second is sheer pleasure taken in the activity of complex deliberation. It is harder to illustrate the second motivation plausibly. It is possible that a person who enjoys complex deliberation might set himself the task of addressing metaphysical, and ultimately ethical, issues, for the sheer challenge of it. Yet such earnest reconsideration of one's values is not usually undertaken for the fun of it. More likely, it is undertaken in response to a crisis or demand.

It shouldn't surprise us, then, that we weren't able to convince Paris not to be intemperate. This does not mean his values are not alterable by deliberation. Rather, his resistance to our arguments suggests that in his culture he won't easily find himself in circumstances that would enable him to revise his values in the right way. Since his Homeric culture is not set up to restrain self-seeking, even when self-seeking endangers others, Paris may not easily encounter a crisis that could effect serious reconsideration of his commitment to the pursuit of sensual pleasures.[20] But it is not impossible. Consider this scenario: Aeneas and his father are not the only men to survive the burning of Troy. Paris escapes deep into the countryside, is taken in by a poor farmer, is taught the rudiments of self-sufficient farming, comes to depend on his wits and skill, takes pleasure in the cultivation of the earth, and no longer chooses sensual enjoyment at the cost of other pleasures. Unlikely. But if my argument is correct, only unusual circumstances could provoke Paris to serious deliberative reconsideration of his aristocratic values.

V

Significantly, the circumstances under which deliberation takes place highlight the psychological phenomena we have described. For these two capacities—(i) to enjoy the realization of our complex abilities and (ii) to form friendly feelings toward those who intend to benefit us or whose abilities we admire—are precisely the abilities, which, fully realized, form the psychological basis of Aristotle's virtues. Aristotle's virtuous person enjoys most the unimpeded exercise of his characteristic human abilities of judging, choosing, deciding, and deliberating (1095b26; 1098a12–18; 1099a7–21; 1153a14–15; 1168a5–9; 1176a26–29). Because he enjoys this activity more than any other, he has the best and most appropriate kind of "self-love" (1169a3). Moreover, a virtuous person realizes these abilities fully in a democratic community of fellow citizens who enjoy the exercise of their abilities (and those of their fellow citizens) in the same way (1168b34–1169a3). Citizens know each other well enough to know that they share the major aims and values that guide the decisions and practices of their community; what they value and enjoy about each other is what they value and enjoy about themselves. Hence they regard each other as "other selves" (1166a32) and become friends in varying degrees (1097b6–11, 1160a8–14; 1170a4–7, 1170b17–19; *Politics* 1280a31–34, 1295b14–27, 1332b26–27; *Rhetoric* 1381a30). As friends, they care for each other for each other's own sake (1155b31). In contrast to friendships among the nonvirtuous, friendships between the virtuous are especially strong and long lasting because they are grounded in the pleasure individuals take in who their friends are as realized human beings.

I have argued elsewhere that virtuous people are distinguished from various nonvirtuous people by having realized these psychological abilities fully (Homiak 1981, 1985, 1990). But because "it is natural" (*touto de phusikon*, 1168a8) for human beings to love the exercise of their powers and to form friendships on the basis of sharing that enjoyment (1168a4–9; *Rhetoric* 1381a28–29), almost every person realizes her human abilities, if only partially or incompletely. Vicious people, then, do not fail to enjoy the exercise of their deliberative capacities; the problem is that they may enjoy them for the wrong reason or in service of the wrong end, such as some other activity or state that they enjoy more. Many vicious people use their deliberative powers to secure "external goods" (reputation, influence, material wealth), which they prefer to self-realization (1168b15–19). Their self-love, then, is precarious.[21] Just as almost everyone has some self-love, so, too, does almost everyone have relations of affection or comradeship. Even vicious people have friendships, although these friendships are short-lived because the friendly feelings are not based on essentially human characteristics. The nonvirtuous come to like others not for who they are as realized beings, but for their useful or pleasant qualities (1156a10–21). This, in turn, is attributable to their precarious self-love. Nevertheless, the instability of their friendships does not mean they are incapable of limited care and concern for others' own sake (1157b1–5).

Since virtuous and nonvirtuous people do not have wholly disparate psychologies, it makes sense to think of these character types as falling along a single spectrum, with the morally vicious at one end, followed by the incontinent, then continent people, and finally, the morally virtuous. To see character types in this way fits with the characterization of Aristotle's moral philosophy as a perfectionist view in which the virtuous person, living in a community of virtuous people, represents the full and unimpeded exercise of human abilities in full and unimpeded friendships with fellow citizens. No individual can fully realize her human powers in isolation from other self-realizers. This is the sense in which human beings are "political" (1097b11)—they require a specific kind of democratic community in order to live well.

VI

I close by considering contemporary views of responsible agency that seem similar to the Aristotelian view I've developed here. I am especially interested in their implications for the possibility of resistance to oppressive practices and beliefs. The Aristotelian view, I argue, offers a decidedly more optimistic picture of the human potential for moral improvement.

I have indicated that contemporary philosophers who delineate the rational capacities that make agents responsible, on one hand, or the circumstances under which these capacities are called into play, on the other, are developing lines of thought that have roots in Aristotle's views. Several philosophers have argued that responsibility rests on the extent to which we can govern our actions by our "will" (desires, purposes, and goals) and on the extent to which we can determine our wills by reflection about our "values" (what we "really want," the kind of life we want to lead).[22] Responsibility is being able to form and act upon these second-order reflective desires. These desires constitute our "real self" (Wolf 1990); responsible action expresses (or could express) our real self. Aristotle agrees with this view to the extent that he thinks responsible agents form *prohaireseis* ("decisions"), which are reflective desires about how to achieve the kind of life to which we have committed ourselves. As we become adults, we develop a sense of what we most want from our lives and strategies for achieving our basic ends: we develop desires about which desires we ought to have (1111a29–31). These desires, our values, are expressed in our character; responsible action expresses (or could express) our character.

Susan Wolf offers an interesting departure from Aristotle's view. She accepts only some "real selves" as responsible, namely, those whose values are based on a recognition and appreciation of what is "true and good." If we have what she calls the ability to "recognize the true and the good" (to recognize what we should do) and to "appreciate the true and the good" (to act in accordance with our recognition), then we have the ability to do the right thing for the right reasons. Selves with this ability are responsible for the actions that express (or could express) that recognition and appreciation. But Wolf allows that there may be many selves who "can't help doing the wrong thing" or who are "psychologically determined to do the wrong thing" (1990, 80), in that they cannot alter their selves to adopt different values. They cannot change toward the good and become better (Wolf 1990, 86). Hence they are not responsible.

Exactly which selves cannot change? Wolf suggests that almost any morally problematic upbringing could be coercive and render the agent unable to see what he should do or unable to act upon that recognition. As an example, she cites Tony, son of a Mafia don, who may be unable to lead a life as an honest schoolteacher because fear of his father's wrath, should he decide to abandon a life of organized crime, makes him unable to abandon that life (1990, 112–13). Other examples, for Wolf, are ordinary citizens of Nazi Germany, white children of slaveowners in the 1850s, and people brought up to embrace conventional sex roles (1990, 121), who may all be unable to recognize what is of value. If they cannot see the injustice of their lives, they are, according to Wolf, less blameworthy, and therefore less responsible, for actions expressing the values of their upbringings. These agents are able to make some moral judgments, according to Wolf, but gaps in their moral understanding render them less blameworthy for certain actions. She closes with the claim that there is no method for determining which upbringings and influences are consistent with an ability to see and appreciate the good, and hence that there is always the risk that we are less responsible than we may hope (1990, 146).

Like Wolf, I've also argued that responsibility depends on our abil-

ity to alter ourselves toward the good, on our ability to become better. But on the Aristotelian view I've proposed, the ability to correct
ourselves and become better depends on our ability to experience the
pleasures of self-expression and the pleasures of friendship and community. These abilities are natural, nonrational psychological responses, which most people experience without difficulty. Hence
most people have the psychological resources to recognize and appreciate the true and the good, that is, to listen to reason and to become
better, no matter how warping their upbringing may seem, no matter what their present state of character. We have no good reason to
think Tony lacks these resources or that ordinary citizens of unjust
social environments lack them.

This is not to suggest that change is straightforward, easy, or quickly achieved. Change may require exposure to the proper transforming
forces, which may not be readily available. As we've seen, Paris's culture gives him no easy access to transforming forces. Nor does contemporary United States culture, if by culture we mean the way major
economic and political institutions inform the nature of work and its
relation to family life. Many if not most adults in the United States
still work at alienating jobs that do not afford opportunity to realize
the human powers and to experience the pleasures of self-expression.
Women in particular, because of nearly total responsibility for child
care and many employers' resistance to accommodating young children at work, often endure low-paying, dead-end jobs that encourage
feelings of self-hatred. Women who live with men are usually economically dependent on men. Economic dependence undermines the
realization of women's decision-making abilities and their development of Aristotelian "self-love," since important family decisions are
often made for others by the individual with economic power. Moreover, economic inequality between women and men distorts and limits the affection and love women and men may develop for each other.
In the context of unequal power relations, affection may serve to sustain inequality. Mill was among the first to recognize that in such circumstances affection may harm both parties (1970, 25–26). Thus,
women in the contemporary United States are not well positioned to
develop fully either of the capacities central to becoming better.

Moreover, when transforming forces are available, change will most
likely be slow and uneven, especially if the agent's self-hatred has a
long history. The realization of one's talents takes time, and the effort

often involves setbacks and frustrations.²³ Radical change is slow. But, as the *Categories* passage reminds us, it is psychologically possible: "For the bad man, if led into better ways of living and talking, [will make progress toward being better]. . . . For however slight the progress he made to begin with, he becomes ever more easily changed toward virtue, so that he is likely to make still more progress; and when this keeps happening it brings him over completely into the contrary state, provided time permits" (13a23–24, 25–31).

Nevertheless, there are people for whom change is presumably not psychologically possible. Perhaps Aristotle's "bestial" people (1148b19–24) or the insane are such. If bestial people are called such because they cannot experience the pleasures of self-expression and can take pleasure only in physical sensations, then they cannot be shifted toward the good. If people suffering from chemical imbalances in the brain or from the effects of potent drugs or psychological manipulation do not respond to efforts to help with feelings of friendship, that is a sign that, at least while they are suffering from these conditions, they cannot alter who they are.

Because fully experiencing pleasures of self-expression and of association depends on having access to transforming forces, exposure to proper moral education and membership in the right kind of adult democratic community are crucial. These structures provide the environment in which the psychological capacities for self-love and love of others can be fully actualized. If we are correct that realizing these psychological capacities forms the basis of the virtues (and that failure to do so explains the various vices), then moral education, in particular, is not a matter of practicing specific activities relevant to specific virtues: of standing one's ground in dangerous circumstances as education in courage, of avoiding sweets as education in temperance. Nor is moral education most importantly focused, as Sherman and Nussbaum have argued, on providing appropriate constituent beliefs for emotions: so that we grieve when we believe we have suffered a serious loss, feel pity when we believe that someone else has suffered undeservedly, or feel angry when we believe serious wrongs have been done to us or our loved ones. Moral education is not the acquisition of desires specific to one virtue rather than another or the acquisition of beliefs specific to one passion rather than another. Rather, to say, as Aristotle does in II.3 of the *Nicomachean Ethics*, that moral education is fundamentally a matter of taking pleasure in the right activities in the right ways is to say that it consists fundamentally in practicing the most generalizable human activity which, because it is so easy to extend and apply to specific activities, is relevant to every virtue.

On the view I have defended, moral education, and hence responsible agency, is located further down, so to speak, in the agent's psychology. Responsible agents are capable of listening to reason, of acknowledging and accepting arguments for acting differently. But listening to reason, as a rational ability, requires for its realization the realization of ordinary nonrational psychological capacities. Fortunately, most people have the nonrational capacities to take pleasure from self-expression and from social relationships. Hence most can both listen to reason and act responsibly—even those whose moral development has been stifled and stunted by oppressive institutions. Aristotle's views, I think, offer a decidedly optimistic picture of the human potential for moral improvement. Practically everyone can become *better*.

But if we accept Aristotle as a good guide to what moral virtue is, we cannot be as sanguine about our chances of becoming *good*. If being good requires being members of a community in which we are all able to fully realize our human powers and ties of friendship, then being good requires radical social change. To fully realize their characteristic decision-making powers, individuals need fulfilling, challenging, creative work to do. They need to participate meaningfully in decisions that importantly affect how they live. To fully realize their ties of friendship and association, individuals need adult relationships that encourage a healthy sense of individuals' own value and importance, rather than immature dependence or despotism. Such wholesale restructuring of work and family life presupposes drastic changes in our current political, socioeconomic, and educational institutions. It seems to me that there are many legitimate ways to contribute to these changes and that each contribution is part of the process of becoming better.[24]

NOTES

1. See, for example, Mill (1970).
2. So Sandra Bartky puts the point (1979, 252).

3. See, for example, Herman (1983, 1996), Sherman (1989), Kahan and Nussbaum (1996), Moody-Adams (1990), Homiak (1990), and Nussbaum (1996). For discussions of character and integrity overtly inspired by feminist concerns, see Card (1990) and Davion (1991).

4. See, for example, Annas (1993), Baier (1985, 1991), Homiak (1990, 1993), Hursthouse (1991), Nussbaum (1986, 1990), and Sherman (1989).

5. So Susan Wolf seems to suggest (1990). Cheshire Calhoun (1989) defends an earlier rendering of Wolf's view. I take up Wolf's position (and by implication Calhoun's) in section VI of this chapter.

6. As translated by Irwin (1985). I use this translation throughout. All subsequent references to Aristotle's writings are to the *Nicomachean Ethics* (hereafter *EN*) unless otherwise indicated.

7. As translated by Jowett in Barnes (1984).

8. As translated by Ackrill in Barnes (1984); hereafter "the *Categories* passage."

9. For an argument against the prevailing view in contemporary philosophy that responsibility for character is necessary for responsibility for action, see Meyer (1993). For a sketch of worries about Meyer's approach, see Homiak (1995).

10. See, for example, Frankfurt (1971), Taylor (1976), Watson (1975), and Wolf (1990).

11. Here I assume that if "doing virtuous and vicious actions" is what it is to be virtuous or vicious, Aristotle must be referring to actions done from the relevant rational desires, that is, actions done as virtuous or vicious persons would do them. For a different interpretation, see Meyer (1993, 131).

12. Paris can plausibly be viewed as incontinent rather than intemperate. For a consideration of Paris as paradigmatically weak-willed, see Homiak (1997).

13. We are reminded of Kant's famous example, in the *Critique of Practical Reason*, of a man before a gallows, who is confronted with the object of his, presumably irresistible, sexual desire. If he chooses to indulge his desire, he faces immediate death by hanging. Kant says we know that he will conquer his desire.

14. Here I am influenced by Fischer (1987). Paris seems to fit Fischer's description of someone who is "weakly" reasons-sensitive, since he responds to (1a) and (1b) kinds of arguments. Fischer finds sensitivity to such reasons sufficient for holding an agent morally accountable. Presumably, if Paris responded to a (1c) type argument, he would be "strongly" reasons-sensitive. Fischer suggests that agents of morally suspect character are not strongly reasons-sensitive.

15. For the classic discussion of Aristotle's dialectical method, see Owen (1961). For a discussion of the method as applied to ethical questions in particular, see Irwin (1978). For the use of this (essentially Socratic) method by contemporary philosophers, see Rawls (1971) and Brink (1989).

16. For a more detailed discussion of the relationship between the task of the rhetorician and that of the moral philosopher, see Irwin (1996).

17. See Kahan and Nussbaum (1996) and Nussbaum (1996) for detailed discussions of Aristotle's treatment in the *Rhetoric* of the cognitive structure of various emotions. Nussbaum's remarks are guided by Sherman (1989), especially chaps. 2 and 6.

18. This example is influenced by and roughly patterned after the exchanges between Sister Helen Prejean and Matthew Poncelet in the film *Dead Man Walking*.

19. I discuss this kind of example in more detail in Homiak (1990).

20. For a useful discussion of this aspect of Homeric ethics, see Irwin (1989), chap. 2.

21. See, for example, Aristotle's descriptions of various vicious types at *EN* 1095b19 (intemperate people), 1128a21 (vulgar buffoons), 1126a7–8 (inirascible people), and 1127a7–9 (flatterers).

22. For references, see note 10.

23. For discussion of difficulties involved in realizing one's talents, see Elster (1987).

24. I am grateful to Burton Dreben, Janet Levin, Charles Young, and especially Claudia Card for helpful comments on earlier versions of this chapter.

REFERENCES

Annas, Julia. 1993. *The Morality of Happiness*. Oxford: Oxford University Press.
Aristotle. 1985. *Nicomachean Ethics*. Trans. Terence Irwin. Indianapolis: Hackett.
Baier, Annette. 1985. *Postures of the Mind*. Minneapolis: University of Minnesota Press.
_____. 1991. *A Progress of Sentiments: Reflections on Hume's Treatise*. Cambridge: Harvard University Press.
Barnes, Jonathan, ed. 1984. *The Complete Works of Aristotle*. 2 vols. Princeton, N.J.: Princeton University Press.
Bartky, Sandra Lee. 1979. "Toward a Phenomenology of Feminist Consciousness." In *Philosophy and Women*, ed. S. Bishop and M. Weinzweig, pp. 252–58. Belmont, Calif.: Wadsworth.
Brink, David O. 1989. *Moral Realism and the Foundations of Ethics*. Cambridge, Eng.: Cambridge University Press.
Calhoun, Cheshire. 1989. "Responsibility and Reproach." *Ethics* 99:389–406.
Card, Claudia. 1990. "Gender and Moral Luck." In *Identity, Character, and Morality: Essays in Moral Psychology*, ed. O. Flanagan and A. O. Rorty, pp. 199–218. Cambridge, Mass.: MIT Press.
_____. 1991. "The Feistiness of Feminism." In *Feminist Ethics*, ed. Claudia Card, pp. 3–31. Lawrence: University Press of Kansas.
Davion, Victoria M. 1991. "Integrity and Radical Change." In *Feminist Ethics*, ed. Claudia Card, pp. 180–92. Lawrence: University Press of Kansas.
Elster, Jon. 1987. "Self-Realization in Work and Politics: The Marxist Conception of the Good Life." In *The Main Debate: Communism vs. Capitalism*, ed. T. R. Machan. New York: Random House.
Fischer, John M. 1987. "Responsiveness and Moral Responsibility." In *Responsibility, Character, and the Emotions*, ed. F. Schoeman. Cambridge, Eng.: Cambridge University Press.

Frankfurt, Harry. 1971. "Freedom of the Will and the Concept of a Person." *Journal of Philosophy* 68:5–20.

Herman, Barbara. 1983. "Integrity and Impartiality." *Monist* 66:233–50.

_____. 1996. "Making Room for Character." In *Aristotle, Kant, and the Stoics: Rethinking Happiness and Duty*, ed. S. Engstrom and J. Whiting, pp. 36–60. Cambridge, Eng.: Cambridge University Press.

Homiak, Marcia L. 1981. "Virtue and Self-Love in Aristotle's Ethics." *Canadian Journal of Philosophy* 11:633–51.

_____. 1985. "The Pleasure of Virtue in Aristotle's Moral Theory." *Pacific Philosophical Quarterly* 66:93–110.

_____. 1990. "Politics As Soul-Making: Aristotle on Becoming Good." *Philosophia* 20:167–93.

_____. 1993. "Feminism and Aristotle's Rational Ideal." In *A Mind of One's Own: Feminist Essays on Reason and Objectivity*, ed. L. Antony and C. Witt, pp. 1–17. Boulder, Colo.: Westview Press.

_____. 1995. Review of Susan Sauve Meyer's *Aristotle on Moral Responsibility*. *Philosophical Books* 36:256–58.

_____. 1997. "Aristotle on the Soul's Conflicts: Toward an Understanding of Virtue Ethics." In *Reclaiming the History of Ethics: Essays for John Rawls*, ed. A. Reath, B. Herman, and C. Korsgaard, pp. 7–35. Cambridge, Eng.: Cambridge University Press.

Hursthouse, Rosalind. 1991. "Virtue Theory and Abortion." *Philosophy and Public Affairs* 20:223–46.

Irwin, T. H. 1978. "First Principles in Aristotle's Ethics." *Midwest Studies in Philosophy* 3:252–72.

_____. 1989. *Classical Thought*. Oxford: Oxford University Press.

_____. 1996. "Ethics in the *Rhetoric* and in the *Ethics*." In *Essays on Aristotle's Rhetoric*, ed. A. O. Rorty, pp. 142–74. Berkeley: University of California Press.

Kahan, Dan M., and Martha C. Nussbaum. 1996. "Two Conceptions of Emotion in Criminal Law." *Columbia Law Review* 96:269–374.

Meyer, Susan Sauve. 1993. *Aristotle on Moral Responsibility*. Oxford: Blackwell.

Mill, John Stuart. 1970. *The Subjection of Women*. Cambridge, Mass.: MIT Press.

Moody-Adams, Michelle. 1990. "On the Old Saw That Character Is Destiny." In *Identity, Character, and Morality: Essays in Moral Psychology*, ed. O. Flanagan and A. O. Rorty, pp. 111–31. Cambridge, Mass.: MIT Press.

Nussbaum, Martha C. 1986. *The Fragility of Goodness: Luck and Ethics in Greek Tragedy and Philosophy*. Cambridge, Eng.: Cambridge University Press.

_____. 1990. *Love's Knowledge: Essays on Philosophy and Literature*. Oxford: Oxford University Press.

_____. 1996. "Aristotle on Emotions and Rational Persuasion." In *Essays on Aristotle's Rhetoric*, ed. A. O. Rorty, pp. 303–23. Berkeley: University of California Press.

Owen, G. E. L. 1961. "tithenai ta phainomena." In *Aristote et les problèmes de la méthode*, ed. S. Mansion, pp. 83–103. Louvain: Symposium Aristotelicum.

Rawls, John. 1971. *A Theory of Justice.* Cambridge: Harvard University Press.

Sherman, Nancy. 1989. *The Fabric of Character.* Oxford: Clarendon Press.

Taylor, Charles. 1976. "Responsibility for Self." In *The Identities of Persons,* ed. A. O. Rorty, pp. 281–99. Berkeley: University of California Press.

Watson, Gary. 1975. "Free Agency." *Journal of Philosophy* 72:202–20.

Wolf, Susan. 1990. *Freedom Within Reason.* Oxford: Oxford University Press.

4 / *Moral Failure*

CHESHIRE CALHOUN

Moral revolutionaries are people who succeed in thinking from a moral point of view that both exceeds and improves upon the conventional moral understandings that are broadly shared in their social worlds. They get it right under social circumstances that make it difficult to do so. And we admire them for it. In this chapter I pursue the paradoxical thought that their getting it right actually produces a particular kind of moral failure of their lives. Thus, such revolutionaries are likely to have reason for regret about how their lives turn out morally.

FAILURES, MORAL FAILURE, AND MORAL LUCK

Failure is not the same as culpable error. For culpable errors one is held responsible, downgraded, chastised, penalized, punished, disapproved, resented, held in contempt. One may feel guilty about, repent, make amends, for culpable errors. Failures, by contrast, are not culpable—at least, the failures that interest me are not. For want of talent, one might fail to be a good philosopher; or, for want of the inner resources to be cheerful, one might fail to have friends; or, for want of natural grace or rhythm, one might fail to be able to dance. Nor are failures simply excused errors. A good excuse gets one off the evaluative hook. To be excused is to have no reason to think badly of oneself or for others to think badly of oneself. To have failed, by contrast, is to have a reason to think badly of oneself and to expect others to do the same. However unavoidable it may have been to turn out to be a bad philosopher or a friendless person or incapable of dance, these failures leave their evaluative mark. They are sources of regret, shame, loss of self-esteem, and of the thought that one's character or life is blemished by falling short of some standard for what lives should look like.

One might, of course, deny that there are any such failures as I have described. Either one is culpable or one isn't; evaluation tracks those two conditions. Much moral philosophy, in its focus on the will, obligation, and responsibility, gives the impression that no one simply fails. But without a space for the notion of failure, it is hard to make sense of many of the things that shame us or inspire the thought that our lives have not turned out as human lives are supposed to—our uncomeliness, lack of talent, gracelessness, competitive poor showings, and crumbled marriages.

In addition, without space for the notion of failure, there will be no way to acknowledge that what we expect from other people and ourselves is not, in fact, confined to what is under voluntary control. Some of our expectations are tied to thoughts about what is statistically normal for persons or for persons of a certain sort.[1] Normal people have some modicum of talent or cheerfulness or grace. Those who don't are failures. Other expectations are tied to an ideology of the normal that is disconnected from what real people are typically like. Normal people are supposed to be self-supporting and capable of sustaining long-term marriages. Those who aren't are failures. Other expectations are tied to ideals rather than to normalcy. To embark on a career is to hold up for oneself an ideal of excellence, or be held to it by others. To fall short is to fail, sometimes in a minor way, sometimes thoroughly.

In moral philosophy, the notion of moral luck captures one sense of specifically moral failures. As Thomas Nagel developed the notion, our actions and characters are vulnerable to moral assessment so long as we have made some contribution to what our actions are and what our character is, even if most of what we actually do or actually turn out to be is a matter of luck, pure and simple.[2] So, for example, we morally assess the accidentally successful rescue attempt and the accidentally botched rescue attempt differently, even though succeeding or botching was a matter of luck. We morally assess the character of those who participated in Nazi Germany differently from those who didn't, even though it was luck that some people but not others faced the particular moral tests posed by life in Nazi Germany. Victims of bad moral luck fail to perform well, and we blame them for it, even though much of what contributed to their deeds being what they were was not under their control.

In Nagel's view, the moral part of moral luck hinges on our having made *some* contribution to our deeds or our character. It is the fact that we can be held partly responsible for what we do or what we are that gives moral assessment a foothold. Underlying this view is a remnant of the Kantian notion that the domain of morality extends only to what we can control. Thus, moral failures must partially connect to that domain.

A quite different account of the moral part of moral luck seems to be at work in Martha Nussbaum's use of that notion.[3] For her, the ideal of a morally excellent life is what makes moral failure possible. Oedipus, for example, fails to live a morally excellent life. Through no fault of his own, his life becomes blemished by acts of incest and patricide. Although he made contributions to these deeds, that is not what, on this account, makes him vulnerable to *moral* bad luck (as opposed to just plain bad luck). Rather, his bad luck and failure are moral because the ideal in the light of which he is assessed is a moral ideal of what human lives should be.

Claudia Card also develops an account of moral luck that differs from Nagel's.[4] Whereas Nagel emphasized the luck that enters into our being *held* responsible, blamed, or praised, Card emphasizes the luck that enhances or undermines our capacity to *take* responsibility for ourselves. Taking responsibility for ourselves includes taking responsibility for the social meaning of our lives and actions. For example, when being lesbian is socially defined as unnatural and perverse, taking responsibility for being lesbian will involve creating and imposing new meanings so that one can stand behind one's life. Success, however, depends on how others receive these new meanings. Thus, taking responsibility will be a matter of luck. The luck is moral because taking responsibility is a basic form of moral activity.

The notion of moral failure that I have in mind is closer to Nussbaum's and Card's than to Nagel's. I suggest that among the ideals of what a human moral life should be is the ideal of living a moral life within a shared scheme of social cooperation where one's moral understandings are shared by others. Under these conditions one's moral activity and one's moral reasons will be intelligible to others. Given sufficient bad luck, our moral lives can fail because they are characterized by abnormally frequent unintelligibility to others or abnormally frequent inability to defend one's actions in terms that others find meaningful. Our attempts to be self-respecting, to avoid misplaced gratitude, to offer generously what is not owed, may be received by others as arrogance, ingratitude, and mere dutifulness. Under such conditions, our moral practice is idiosyncratic, not part of a common scheme of social cooperation. If this is, in fact, a kind of moral failure, it is a failure from which impeccable exercises of responsibility cannot protect us.

Obviously, it will take some work to make the case that there is such an ideal, that falling abnormally short of it is a *moral* failure, and that trying to do the right thing can produce this failure. Let me begin, then, with doing the right thing.

FEMINIST RESISTANCE AND DOING THE RIGHT THING

Trying to do the right thing, to live morally well, is not just one thing but many. Realizing that moral philosophers disagree among themselves about what these moral tasks are, let me propose the following four commitments as relatively uncontroversial and basic to (if not exhaustive of) any attempt to do the right thing:

1. *The principle of self-respect.* I am a being with self-respect; and as a being with self-respect, I will affirm my place in the moral world.
2. *The principle of mutually agreeable rules.* I am a reasonable being; and as a reasonable being, I will act according to principles that could be mutually agreed to by free, equal, reasonable, and rational beings.
3. *The principle of pursuing the good.* I am a rational being with the powers to frame a conception of the good; and as a rational being, I will act on my conception of the good.
4. *The principle of character.* I am a being with moral character; and as a being with moral character, I will cultivate and express the virtues.

These principles, if correct, express the moral commitments any agent, in any social context, must have and act on if she is to do the right thing. In this sense, doing the right thing is always the same thing. However, these moral commitments must be enacted in the agent's own social world where a moral practice is already under way and where there are established and broadly shared social understandings of what counts as doing the right thing. In morally well-formed social worlds, doing the right thing will be a matter of compliance with shared moral understandings. But in morally ill-formed social worlds, doing the right thing will require resistance to the existing practice of morality. In this sense, doing the right thing is *not* the same thing across all possible social contexts.

Feminist moral philosophers, unlike more conventional moral philosophers, have been interested in describing the shared moral understandings that operate in sexist, heterosexist, classist, and racist social worlds. They have also been interested in what it means, particularly for members of subordinate groups, to try to do the right thing in these social contexts. In particular, feminists have drawn attention to the facts that in our social world (1) some groups are socially constructed as moral inferiors to be treated as second-class citizens in the moral world; (2) unjust practices to which members of subordinate groups could not possibly agree absent coercion are socially institutionalized; (3) some healthy conceptions of the good are deemed inappropriate for certain social groups (for example, fulfilling same-sex erotic relationships, marriage, and family for gays and lesbians), whereas damaging conceptions of the good are deemed appropriate (for example, for women, the pursuit of excessive slimness and the use of plastic surgery); and (4) the images of virtue, or of what it takes to avoid vice, that are offered to women, blacks, gays and lesbians, and the poor are deformed and demeaning images (for example, avoiding arrogance means deferring to male and white authority, being civilly respectful of others' feelings means concealing one's lesbian identity, and having a work ethic means accepting poverty as one's own fault).

The four principles for doing the right thing, when put into play in ill-formed social worlds—particularly when put into play by members of subordinate groups—will be principles of resistance. From the standpoint of those who are subordinated, for example, the principle of self-respect is primarily a principle of intolerance: "I am a being with self-respect, and as a being with self-respect, I will not tolerate _____." To be self-respecting is to refuse to put up with humiliation, abuse, unfair denial of opportunities, objectification, demeaning or defaming stereotypes,[5] silencing, and domination. It is to refuse to offer misplaced gratitude for treatment that is simply one's due.[6] And it is to resist the idea that members of subordinate groups are not entitled to judge morally members of dominant groups and, thus, are not entitled to express anger at moral mistreatment.[7] Because one's own mistreatment is connected to that of fellow subordinates, the resistance required by a principle of self-respect is likely to be not just resistance to one's own mistreatment but general resistance to a system of domination.

Similarly, from the standpoint of those who are subordinated, the principle of accepting only mutually agreeable rules is primarily a principle of resistance. Since we are not now in Rawls's "original position" (a position of ideal freedom and equality, from which the principles to govern our choices would be chosen) but find ourselves immersed in a practice of morality already under way, and since much of that practice supports systems of domination, to accept only mutually agreeable rules will inevitably mean to refuse to abide by existing social norms to which women, blacks, gays and lesbians, and the poor would not have consented had they occupied positions as free and equal participants in the social scheme.[8] This principle may also require resisting decision-making arrangements that exclude participation by those whose lives will be significantly affected by those decisions (for example, the policy of having experts within welfare bureaucracies make unilateral decisions for their clients).[9] At a theoretical level, it may require resisting philosophical constructions of impartial decision making that exclude the very dialogue with real others that might secure the genuine impartiality necessary for locating rules that in fact could be mutually agreed to by all.[10]

Acting on the principle of pursuing one's own conception of the good will also largely be a matter of resisting those conceptions socially prescribed as appropriate for one's social group—as women have historically tried to resist patriarchal marriage by refusing to marry, by constructing "Boston marriages" with other women, by cross-dressing and marrying women, and by divorcing out of inegalitarian marriages. As these examples suggest, it may also require pursuing conceptions of the good that are socially deemed unwise, unnatural, or irrationally risky—conceptions that are inconceivable within the dominant view as possible conceptions of the good. In addition, it will require resistance to culturally normalized but unfair distributions of resources to those who are subordinated (distributions that constrain their pursuit of the good) and resistance to their lack of credibility as judges of the good (a lack that undermines social negotiation for conditions more conducive to their flourishing).[11]

Finally, the principle of moral character will be a principle of refusing to comply with social definitions of the virtues appropriate to one's station that in fact crush or cramp genuine expressions of virtue. Central to the application of this principle of moral character will be resistance to ideologies and social practices that naturalize and normalize the idea that there are different, and differently valued, virtues for different social groups. In particular, it will be necessary to resist the maddening idea that there is a set of virtues appropriate to generic, mature humans, but a different, incompatible set of virtues appropriate to women or other social groups.[12] Sometimes it will be necessary to resist ideologies and practices that construct the absence of virtue as a natural, unalterable feature of some social groups.

THE MORAL IDEAL OF DOING THE RIGHT THING

Although resistance is often personally costly, it is also morally attractive. These four principles, which under unjust conditions become principles of resistance, are connected to a particular moral ideal. That ideal is the ideal of a life beyond reproach. One aim of moral life is to become sufficiently critically reflective, sufficiently motivated, and sufficiently alive to one's own moral status, to the importance of a cooperative scheme, to one's options for constructing a good life, and to one's possibilities for virtue that one need not reproach oneself later for having been servile or unfair or thoughtless about the good or vicious. It is an ideal fit for self-determining beings who are custodians of their own lives and who are capable of deciding for themselves what shape those lives should take. It is, I think, a correct ideal. This is, in part, what we are trying to do when we participate in the enterprise of morality.[13]

To say that it is an ideal is to say that real human lives are not, in fact, going to be beyond reproach. Negligence, narrow-mindedness, a desire to retain privileges, cowardice, and the like will make for culpable fallings short of the ideal. In addition, when dominance and subordination are conventionalized and rendered natural, normal, and unproblematic, when necessary knowledges are suppressed (for example, knowledge of the history of oppression), or when critical moral concepts are not socially available (for example, the concept of date rape or marital rape), then there is a live possibility that a person just will not be able to see how morally badly her or his life is going. Loving devotion turns out to have been servility. Living up to one's station and its duties turns out to have been complicity with injustice. Being a good X turns out to have meant the cultivation of vice rather than virtue. These are moral failures. They are failures of one's life to embody the ideal of doing the right thing, in spite of one's best efforts. One kind of moral failure, then, that is an especially live possibility when injustice is conventionalized so that agents themselves are not well positioned to determine what the right thing is, is the possibility that trying to do the right thing might *end* in failure.[14] The more paradoxical possibility, which I pursue here, is that resistantly trying to do the right thing might *produce* moral failure. How could that be? I begin by describing the kind of failure that I think resistantly trying to do the right thing produces. I then turn to reasons for thinking this a specifically moral form of failure.

ILLEGIBILITY AND UNREASONABLENESS

One of the most important effects of liberation movements is that they produce critiques of conventional moral norms. Such critiques show why compliance with conventional moral norms is not, in fact, a way of doing the right thing but is instead a way of participating in and sustaining systems of domination. The feminist movement, for example, challenged a conventional assumption that wives who take on the principal burden of unpaid domestic labor are simply doing their fair share—fair, because this is what wives owe their families. It also challenged the idea that a good life for women must include child rearing and personal attachment to a man. The lesbian and gay movement challenges a conventional assumption that making one's lesbianism or homosexuality known is, among other things, rude and shameless. Some of the moral critiques produced by liberation movements have now been conventionalized. They have become part of our common stock of moral understandings. This is not to say that everyone endorses those critiques. It is to say that everyone finds them familiar and comprehensible. A black man's angry response at being called "boy" or a woman's filing sexual harassment charges are now legible as affirmations of self-respect. What both are morally up to doesn't need explaining.

However, when large portions of dominance systems continue to be conventionalized, formulating moral critiques will produce what I have elsewhere called "abnormal moral contexts."[15] Abnormal moral contexts occur when some segment of a society produces advances in moral knowledge that outrun the social mechanisms for disseminating and normalizing that knowledge in the society as a whole. In that case, a gap opens between what "everyone knows" is the right thing to do and what from a (presumably) advantaged epistemic position is viewed as the right thing to do. The gap, of course, will be obvious only to those who take themselves to be reasoning from a more advanced, socially critical point of view—as feminists, for example, generally take themselves to be doing. It is that gap that makes doing the right thing, as determined from this socially critical point of view, necessarily a form of resistance.

To do the right thing under circumstances where dominance systems are conventionalized requires rejecting broadly shared social assumptions about the moral place persons are entitled to claim for themselves, about which practices are morally legitimate, about what counts as courage, generosity, proper pride, and so forth, and about which forms of life count as good ones. Of course, from the point of view of those who don't have access to these critiques and the evidence that supports them, these acts of resistance will not be legible either as acts of resistance or as attempts to do the right thing. They will look simply like doing the wrong thing. Refusing to be grateful for help with the housework will appear to be ingratitude. Refusing custody of one's children upon divorce will appear coldly unloving rather than a resistance to compulsory motherhood. Kissing one's domestic partner in public will appear confrontationally obscene rather than affectionate.

I have chosen the terms "legible" and "illegible" to underscore the fact that the social practice of morality depends heavily on our being able to "read" the meaning of others' actions. To take a simple example, were expressions of gratitude, such as saying "thank you," not interpretable by recipients as an expression of gratitude, this particular moral exchange would break down. Under these conditions, a person might privately intend to express gratitude, and yet, if the expression is illegible, there is a real sense in which no gratitude is actually *expressed.*

When moral resisters have the opportunity to explain what they are doing and, thus, make their actions legible, they may still be unable to make themselves seem reasonably justified. Their justifications may be received as wildly implausible, irrational, based on patently false assumptions, and, thus, not really justifications at all. The difficulty of justifying oneself is often further complicated by the fact that subordinate groups typically are also socially constructed as defective reasoners.

Moral resisters' commitment to doing the right thing thus risks producing two forms of failure: a failure to make what one is morally up to legible to others and a failure to provide justifications that are recognizable to others as justifications.

MORAL FAILURE AND THE IDEAL
OF A SHARED SCHEME OF SOCIAL COOPERATION

But why think that these failures are moral? Why think that a life characterized by abnormally frequent illegibility or by abnormally frequent inability to defend one's actions in terms others find meaningful is morally defective, lacks the moral excellence one expects of a moral life, and is an occasion for moral regret and possibly also moral shame? Quite the contrary, living a genuinely self-respecting life, refusing to comply with unjust practices, correctly conceiving and enacting the virtues, and living out a genuinely estimable lifeplan all seem reasons for moral self-congratulation. If failure is to attach anywhere, it seems more reasonable to attach it to those whose lack of critical distance from social moral norms prevents them from seeing and finding meaningful what moral resisters are up to. If another cannot see that being out of the closet is an affirmation of self-respect, isn't the failure theirs rather than the uncloseted person's?

In addition, moral philosophers standardly distinguish between morality as a system of social norms—a culture's moral code—and morality as a set of prescriptions that are justifiable from a critical, reflective, theoretical point of view. Because social moralities may not survive critical review, they are better thought of simply as social norms rather than as constitutive of morality. It is from the point of view of social norms that moral resisters' actions are illegible or without minimal justification. From a genuinely moral point of view, what they are up to morally is perfectly legible. To view failures of social legibility and justifiability as moral failures thus seems to confuse social norms with genuine morality. If there is any failure here, it is merely social, not moral. Indeed, moral resisters may well be social failures, regarded as deviant, outlaw, perverse, crazy, extremist. Being so regarded does not reflect on their moral excellence.

These are compelling objections. However, I think they rest on three interconnected, mistaken assumptions: (1) that the moral ideal of doing the right thing is the only relevant ideal for assessing the moral excellence of lives; (2) that the successful social enactment of morality is not itself a moral ideal; and (3) that if there are multiple moral ideals, they cannot be in such fundamental tension with each other that it is impossible to orient one's life toward all of them simultaneously.

I take the second assumption first, since it is the heart of the matter. Morality is fundamentally social, and one common way of stating this idea is to say that morality is a scheme of social cooperation. The fact that morality is a scheme of social cooperation suggests that to contrast social norms with genuine morality is misleading. Indeed, any attempt to cleanly distinguish social norms from genuine morality is like the attempt to imagine an unperceived world. As empiricist philosopher Bishop Berkeley pointed out, in the very process of imagining an unperceived world, we covertly insert a perceiver— ourselves. So, too, in conceiving a distinction between genuine morality and social norms. We do not purify morality of the social. Instead, we covertly insert a different social world into the picture, one in which what we take to be genuine moral norms are also socially normative. Kant's "kingdom of ends" is a hypothetical social world. In that world, universal moral laws are social norms. The "ends" in this kingdom are social participants in a practice of morality. They share common moral understandings of what things mean morally (for example, of when gratitude is misplaced or of what treatments are humiliating). The correct contrast, then, is not between genuine and merely social morality but between two different social moralities, one hypothetical and the other actual, where we take the hypothetical one to be preferable to the actual one.

The original objection to counting as a moral failure resisters' failure to make legible what they are morally up to might, then, be more accurately put this way: moral resisters, whose actions are illegible according to actual social norms, have not failed morally, because their actions are legible according to a more nearly correct, although hypothetical, set of social norms. In other words, the only thing that really matters so far as moral success or failure is concerned is the ideal of getting it right.

But is it? Is getting it right the only thing we aim to do when we participate in the practice of morality? Or do we aim at other things as well, things that might depend upon our being able to make what we are morally up to comprehensible and justifiable to others?

Let us return to the idea that morality is a scheme of social cooperation, which means that even though individuals are to guide their behavior by moral rules, moral rules are not designed for individuals. They are designed instead for the social worlds that individuals inhabit. Similarly, even though individuals are to cultivate virtues, the point of virtues is not just to make individual lives good but to make our common lives good. The shared cultivation of virtue enables us to count on others to do the things that need doing. Because morality is a scheme of social cooperation, both the attempts of philosophers to frame justifiable schemes of social cooperation and the efforts of individuals to do the right thing have the same practical aim: to put into play in our social world a shared set of understandings about how we are to do things morally together. It makes no sense to engage in critical moral reflection or to attempt to do the right thing without this practical aim. To do so would require treating morality as a kind of private language whose rules or conceptions of virtue need not be accessible or meaningful to anyone else.

It is no surprise, then, that moral theories so often articulate justification as a matter of justifying ourselves *to others,* with the aim of securing shared moral understandings that can guide our common life together. Role reversal tests embody this social conception of justification in a modest way by focusing our attention on what individual others might think of our proposals. Social contract theories like those of Hobbes and Rawls, dialogic models like Habermas's, and legislative models like Kant's in the third formulation of the categorical imperative (that of the kingdom of ends) employ more fundamentally social conceptions of justification (even if the society is a hypothetical one). More obviously social conceptions of justification (because they are less hypothetical) are communitarian models, where justification appeals to traditions and understandings that are actually shared, and some feminist reconstructions of dialogic models that employ real, rather than ideal, discourse situations.

Common to all of these approaches is the assumption that we aim, in the process of justification, at mutual agreement to a common scheme of social cooperation. The moral ideal operating in theories of justification is the ideal of making ourselves intelligible to others—so that, for example, any contractor behind a Rawlsian "veil of ignorance" can take up our position—and of actually reaching shared moral understandings.[16]

Now, whether we are in truth justified in what we do as real moral actors may depend only on what would happen in a hypothetical social world, like that of the Rawlsian original position, in which we attempt to justify our choices to hypothetical others. Thus, orienting our lives toward the ideal of doing the right thing may not require that we be able to justify ourselves to real others in our actual social world. This is especially true in social worlds where the real participants suffer from epistemic defects, such as socialization to accept dominance systems as natural, normal, and legitimate. But even if being justified is detachable from how others receive us in our actual social, moral world, the ideal of being able to make ourselves intelligible and to reach shared moral understandings continues to operate in our actual social world. Hypothetical social worlds, like those of the Rawlsian original position and the ideal discourse situation, help us to specify what the ideal is, what we ultimately want out of our moral lives—namely, shared moral understandings.

But that ideal does not operate only in hypothetical worlds. As participants in an actual moral practice, we operate under the ideal of participating in a shared scheme of social cooperation. Maximally, a shared scheme is one in which there is full consensus on who has which moral status, on which principles and practices are legitimate, on what constitutes particular virtues, and on what falls within the range of possible conceptions of the good. Minimally, a shared moral scheme means that we share enough moral understandings that we can successfully interpret what others are morally up to and see their reasons as providing some justification, even if we ultimately disagree. To abandon the ideal of a shared scheme of cooperation would be to give up hope for the possibility of a moral practice in our actual social world.

TWO IDEALS

I suggest, then, that there are two ideals for moral lives. One is the familiar ideal of getting it right. The search for correct principles and adequate justifications is part of realizing this ideal. The other is the ideal of participating in a shared scheme of social cooperation. Communicating our moral views to others, offering explanations and justifications, and seeking consensus are part of realizing this ideal.

What distinguishes the two moral ideals is that orienting our lives toward the first is up to us in a way that orienting our lives toward the second is not. It is substantially up to me whether I govern my life by principles, conceptions of virtue, and a conception of the range of possible good lives that would be shared in a hypothetical social world.[17] It is substantially not up to me whether my life is at the same time also oriented toward reaching common moral understandings. Whether it is also so oriented largely depends on who my fellow moral practitioners are and on the possibilities for reception. Bad moral luck may undermine the aim of participating in a shared scheme of social cooperation in which we can make what we are morally up to legible to others. Self-respect may be persistently received as arrogance, integrity as irrational extremism, generosity as merely fulfilling an obligation, love as perversity, demanding fairness as demanding "special rights," sustaining a family as leaching off the system, and so on.

What the two ideals share in common is that both provide yardsticks, independently of considerations of praiseworthiness or blameworthiness, for measuring the excellence and success of our moral lives. I may not be to blame for the fact that my life has been one of servility or arrogance or unfairness. But to discover after the fact that it has been so because of my moral misconceptions is to discover moral failure. It is a failure that merits moral regret and also shame, since I am now revealed, particularly in the eyes of others about whose opinion I care most, not to have measured up to a standard that applies to me. Similarly, although less obviously, to find that one's moral life is marked by abnormally frequent occasions of being morally illegible to others and of having one's reasons rejected as not even minimally justifying is to find that one's moral life has failed. It has failed in much the way that Van Gogh might have thought his life as a participant in the social practice of art had failed. No matter how good his work was, his life as an artist was in part a failure because art also aims at being shared. So, too, no matter how much one gets it morally right, one's life as a moral practitioner may end in failure because the practice of morality also aims at a common moral life together.

This failure merits moral regret. It is less obvious that it merits shame. What would seem to bar this sort of failure's being a fit subject for shame is that if one really is getting it right, then one has nothing to be ashamed *of*. If others mistake objecting to unfair treatment as arrogance, nagging, shrillness, demanding special treatment or special rights, that is their mistake. The moral resister is not really any of these things; she has no reason for shame. But the line between reality and appearance may not be so sharp. Our actions have meanings in the social world, and individuals cannot change those meanings at will.[18] A woman who persistently complains that her husband is not doing enough domestic labor really is a nag. That is what her actions mean in this social world, even if, from the point of view of the hypothetical social world that guides her decision making, her actions also mean standing up for fair treatment. Because our actions have social meanings, who we are and, thus, our sources of shame are partly determined by who others take us to be.

This result may seem unfair. Morality sets before us the task of living well. Now it seems that one might fail simply because of the collective backwardness of those with whom we must interact. But this objection rests on a mistake. Morality sets before us the task of *doing the right thing*. Success on this dimension is not a function of how others receive us. Living a moral life that is successful on all relevant dimensions, however, includes more than successfully executing this task. Consider an analogy with teaching. Successful teaching only partly depends on successfully executing such tasks as preparing and giving comprehensible lectures and grading fairly. It also depends on class chemistry, students' willingness to work, their interest in the subject, and the like. These are not tasks. Teaching may fail, owing

to these nontask factors. In this case, the only way to avoid the conclusion that one has failed as a teacher is to reduce teaching to a set
of tasks performable by the teacher alone. But this approach wrongly
treats teaching as an individualistic enterprise. Teaching is a fundamentally social activity. Successful participation in this social activity depends both on the parts that are up to oneself and the parts that
are up to others. So, too, in the case of morality.

If success depends both on what is up to us (correct task execution
in getting it right) and on what is up to others (reception of what one
does as a meaningful part of a shared scheme of social cooperation),
then there is no guarantee that both moral ideals will be realized simultaneously. Indeed, as I have been suggesting, when getting it right
requires repudiating shared moral understandings, success on this
dimension may *produce* failure on the other.

Central features of moral philosophizing often work to obscure
both the ideal of participating in a shared scheme of social cooperation and the possible conflict between this ideal and that of getting
it right. The (perfectly appropriate) focus on determining correct
moral principles and adequate justifications can easily lead to the
impression that getting it right is all that matters. Moral philosophizing may also make the reception of one's moral activity seem far
less problematic than it actually is. Using hypothetical worlds peo-
pled by reasonable beings who would, of course, agree to correct
moral principles is one way of doing so. Relying heavily on shared
intuitions is another way.[19] Eschewing radical social critique in favor
of moral fine-tuning or more theoretical topics is yet another.

In a different way, the highly discursive nature of philosophical
practice works to obscure how problematic real-life moral communication may be. Making one's choices legible and one's reasons acceptable as justifying reasons is much more likely of success when choices
and reasons can be carefully formulated in essays and books. As a
philosopher, for example, Claudia Card can devote an entire chapter
to articulating what she means by "lesbian" and, thus, what she is
morally up to when she stands up for her lesbian life. As a participant
in the daily practice of morality, she does not have this luxury. As a
result, exercises of integrity, like hers, that involve rejecting conventional meanings are bound to be and to remain illegible to others as
an exercise of integrity or even as minimally justified.

In making moral communication with others seem unproblematic, moral philosophy obscures the possibility that our moral lives will not in fact be conducted within a minimally shared scheme of social cooperation and that our moral practice will be an idiosyncratic performance. The point here is not that there is something wrong with moral philosophy. The point is that central features of moral philosophizing make it difficult to entertain thoughts about what is happening to moral resisters' lives in abnormal moral contexts as they try to get it right. Thus, we aren't invited to think about what we would say about such a life, especially if it were our own. Would we think it tragic that a life devoted to doing the right thing was incomprehensible to others or vilified as perverse, irrational, or immoral?[20] Would we think our lives had turned out as moral lives are not supposed to? Would our pride in doing the right thing be spoiled with shame for the other, social meanings of our actions? And would we find it forgivable, because understandable, if someone chose participation in a common moral life over doing the right thing?

The answer to all of these questions seems to me to be yes. Indeed, there would be something perverse about a person who cares only about how things would go between herself and others in a hypothetical, morally more perfect social world and who is morally untroubled by the fact that in her actual exchanges with others, she is received as arrogant, unfair, ungrateful, selfish, uncivil, and intolerant.[21]

In sum, moral revolutionaries are to be admired for their commitment to doing the right thing. Even so, their lives will be, in part, moral failures. It is part of the tragedy of morally ill-formed social worlds that those who are morally best will have reason to regret how their lives turn out morally.

NOTES

In 1990, Colleen Stameshkin mentioned that she thought failure was an interesting and neglected philosophical topic. I owe to her the topic of failure. Two works have particularly influenced the content of this chapter: Claudia Card, *The Unnatural Lottery: Character and Moral Luck* (Philadelphia: Temple University Press, 1996), and Margaret Walker, *Moral Understandings: A Feminist Study in Ethics* (New York: Routledge, 1998). My particular approach to moral failure grows out of themes I developed in "Responsibility and Reproach," *Ethics* 99 (1989): 389–406; "Kant and Compliance with Conventionalized Injustice," *Southern Journal of Philosophy* 32 (1994): 135–59; and "Standing for Something," *Journal of Philosophy* 92 (1995): 235–60.

1. On the idea that our attributions of responsibility are connected to expectations about what is statistically normal, see Ferdinand Schoeman, "Statistical Norms and Moral Attributions," in *Responsibility, Character, and the Emotions: New Essays in Moral Psychology,* ed. Ferdinand Schoeman (Cambridge, Eng.: Cambridge University Press, 1987), and Jeffrie G. Murphy, "Moral Death: A Kantian Essay on Psychopathy," in *Ethics and Personality,* ed. John Deigh (Chicago: University of Chicago Press, 1992).

2. Thomas Nagel, "Moral Luck," in *Mortal Questions* (Cambridge, Eng.: Cambridge University Press, 1979).

3. Martha C. Nussbaum, *The Fragility of Goodness: Luck and Ethics in Greek Tragedy and Philosophy* (Cambridge, Eng.: Cambridge University Press, 1986), especially chap. 11.

4. Card, *The Unnatural Lottery.*

5. See Claudia Card, *Lesbian Choices* (New York: Columbia University Press, 1995), pp. 151–68, on the construction of gay and lesbian identities as demeaning and defaming ones.

6. Thomas E. Hill Jr., "Servility and Self-Respect," in *Autonomy and Self-Respect* (Cambridge, Eng.: Cambridge University Press, 1991). The principle of self-respect that I proposed in my list of four basic principles is derived from this essay.

7. Elizabeth V. Spelman, "Anger and Insubordination," in *Women, Knowledge, and Reality: Explorations in Feminist Philosophy,* ed. Ann Garry and Marilyn Pearsall (Boston: Unwin Hyman, 1989).

8. On the "original position," see John Rawls, *A Theory of Justice* (Cambridge: Harvard University Press, 1971), pp. 17–22.

9. See Iris Marion Young, *Justice and the Politics of Difference* (Princeton, N.J.: Princeton University Press, 1990), and Kathryn Pyne Addelson, *Moral Passages: Toward a Collectivist Moral Theory* (New York: Routledge, 1994).

10. See Seyla Benhabib, *Situating the Self: Gender, Community, and Postmodernism in Contemporary Ethics* (New York: Routledge, 1992); Young, *Justice and the Politics of Difference;* and Marilyn Friedman, *What Are Friends For? Feminist Perspectives on Personal Relationships and Moral Theory* (Ithaca, N.Y.: Cornell University Press, 1993).

11. On epistemic credibility, see Walker, *Moral Understandings.* I argued in "Family Outlaws: Rethinking the Connections Between Feminism, Lesbianism, and the Family," in *Feminism and Families,* ed. Hilde Lindemann Nelson (New York: Routledge, 1996), that gays and lesbians lack definitional authority with respect to the family and, thus, do not have the same standing that heterosexuals have to recommend changes in family law.

12. Kathryn Pauly Morgan, "Women and Moral Madness," in *Science, Morality, and Feminist Theory,* ed. Marsha Hanen and Kai Nielsen (Calgary: University of Calgary Press, 1979).

13. Feminists have been highly critical of conventional accounts of the autonomous person. But those criticisms are, I think, less of the ideal of living beyond reproach than of the lack of realism, often characteristic of moral philosophies that ignore our actual social context, about how possible it is to live such a life.

14. For discussion of difficulties involved in "getting it right," as well as critical evaluation of some now standard attempts to "get it right" in aca-

demia (by, for example, promoting affirmative action), see Marilyn Frye, "Getting It Right," in *Willful Virgin: Essays in Feminism 1976–1992* (Freedom, Calif.: Crossing Press, 1992).

15. Calhoun, "Responsibility and Reproach."

16. On the "veil of ignorance," which screens out the particulars that enable us to distinguish one individual (such as ourselves) from another, see Rawls, *A Theory of Justice*, pp. 136–42.

17. I say "substantially" because the control we have over getting it right is a matter of degree and also vulnerable to luck. As actual moral reasoners, we are embedded in social worlds that may provide better or worse resources for successfully conducting the sort of inquiry required by hypothetical contract or discourse scenarios. It has for that reason been a central feminist critique of Rawls that the method of going behind a veil of ignorance and of imagining oneself in multiple social positions or as bearers of multiple conceptions of the good is not a method that real moral reasoners can employ in its pure form.

18. Claudia Card develops this point more elegantly and forcefully than I do here (*The Unnatural Lottery*, pp. 140–62).

19. "Shared" here amounts to one of two things. Either moral arguments draw on the most conventionalized and socially legitimated moral beliefs (such as that it is wrong to inflict gratuitous suffering), or they draw on moral beliefs that are shared by those who also share the philosopher's gender, race, and class location (for example, the belief that contractors in the Rawlsian original position should, of course, be heads of households).

20. I owe to my colleague, Jill Gordon, the idea that such a life is tragic.

21. One might try to capture the idea that it matters how our actual exchanges with others go by placing moral value on the activity of sustaining relationships. Unfortunately, this strategy factors considerations about how others will receive us into decisions about what the right thing to do is. Others' misguided responses, however, should not be decisive in decisions about what, morally, ought to be done.

Part Two
The Ethics
of Feminist Politics

5 / *Public Address As a Sign of Political Inclusion*

IRIS MARION YOUNG

Democracy means nothing as a normative ideal if not political equality. A democratic system of political decision making, as opposed to an aristocracy or monarchy, provides all citizens with the equal opportunity to influence outcomes.[1] An important implication of the ideal of political equality is a norm of inclusion. A principle of inclusion says that democratic processes, discussion, and decision making ought to include everyone affected by the decisions. Recent civil rights and liberation movements have made it clear that political inclusion requires a great deal more than having a formally equal right to vote. Feminists, in particular, have insisted that the full inclusion of women in political democracy entails that individual women, and the gendered perspectives they often express, have a recognized and effective voice in political deliberations that lead to decisions.

The welfare reform debate of 1993–1996 illustrates how far American politics remains from meeting this basic requirement of democratic ethics, although this failing is hardly unique to American politics. Discussion and debates were loud and long during this period; participants from varying political and ideological perspectives cajoled, exhorted, accused, and ridiculed one another. At least one social segment crucially affected by the outcome of this debate, however, was blatantly and persistently excluded from discussion, namely, lower income single mothers. An important sign of this exclusion, I suggest, is the fact that the participants in the debate, whatever their substantive positions, rarely spoke as though they were *addressing* members of this social segment. They instead positioned these women primarily as part of the problem to be solved.

In this chapter I theorize this intuition. I elaborate a particular aspect of an ethics of democratic inclusion, which I call greeting or public address. For persons, groups, or social segments to be included in public discussions, others in those discussions must publicly acknowledge their inclusion by publicly addressing them among others. To elaborate this category of greeting or public address, I assume a model of democracy that relies on a communicative ethics rather than a model that describes democracy merely as a voting process that aggregates preexisting preferences. I derive a norm of democratic ethics from an aspect of everyday communicative interaction whose significance for ethics is undervalued, namely, activities of greeting.

I rely on the philosophy of Emmanuel Levinas for an understanding of the function of greeting in an ethical theory of everyday communication. I then explain how this function appears or ought to appear in the context of political communication. Since the primary purpose of the elaboration of normative ideals is critical, I then apply this account of public address as a sign of inclusion to the American welfare reform debate of 1993–1996.

DEMOCRATIC THEORY AND COMMUNICATION

Several recent books and groundbreaking articles define a model of deliberative or discursive democracy, give an account of its normative principles, and justify deliberative democracy as the best understanding and practice of democracy.[2] Briefly stated, the theory of deliberative democracy conceptualizes democratic politics primarily as a process in which citizens work out problems and resolve conflict by discussion that leads to decision. Voting and other means of registering preference, on this account, are only a moment in a larger democratic process, which consists of public discussion about the issues, among both citizens and political officials, where participants aim to persuade one another about the best politics and actions. Although partly descriptive, deliberative democracy is primarily a normative theory. It identifies deliberative activities that actually appear in working democratic processes and systematizes these into a normative theory of the conditions of fair public procedures that involve political discussion and debate. Such normative principles and criteria then provide means for evaluating actual democracies. A policy, political institution, public media process, constitution, or political history can all be evaluated as more or less democratically *legitimate* according to the extent and quality of their deliberations.

Most deliberative theorists agree that political equality or inclusion is a major criterion for determining democratic legitimacy. Laws, policies, and decisions are normatively legitimate, on the deliberatively democratic view, only if all affected by them have been included in the discussion that leads to them. The full inclusion of all members of the polity in the deliberatively democratic process promotes democratic legitimacy in at least two ways. First, inclusion increases the chances that deliberation and its decisions will take account of all the interests bearing on a question. Second, inclusion increases the chances that deliberators will transform their positions from an initial self-regarding stance to a more objective appeal to justice, because they listen to others with different positions to whom they are also answerable. The inclusion of all social positions and perspectives, finally, I believe, promotes more wise and just decisions, because such inclusion maximizes social knowledge available to decision makers.

Despite agreement that inclusion is important, most theories of deliberative democracy say little about the conditions of inclusion.[3] When they do consider such conditions, theorists of deliberative democracy tend to focus on the important set of conditions for inclusion that are *external* to the process of discussion itself.[4] Inequalities of wealth and income, power, prestige, expertism, and other forms of social structural disadvantage prevent some persons or social segments from equal presence on processes of discussion and decision making. I use presence in the sense that Anne Phillips gives to the term. Phillips distinguishes between a politics of ideas, where what matters is the opinions and positions citizens have in the political process, and a politics of presence, where what matters is who the people are, what social positions and life experiences they have come from, and who is present in forums of discussion and decision making. One of the reasons that a politics of presence has become important, according to Phillips, is that attention to presence in this sense reveals forms of political inequality and exclusion that are less apparent when one attends only to ideas.[5] Although it is important to the theory and practice of democratic communication to respond to these external conditions of exclusion, in this chapter I am concerned with a condition of exclusion and inclusion that is more *internal* to the process of discussion itself.

Although I endorse the general discursive turn in democratic theory, I have some specific criticisms of certain expressions of a theory of deliberative democracy in particular. As it has been developed, the idea of deliberative democracy tends to privilege specific forms of communication that are coded as articulate, dispassionate, orderly, and formal. Even when people are formally included in a forum guided by certain ideas of what counts as proper deliberation, they may find that those norms of deliberation are culturally biased, that they are regulated in ways that some people find intimidating, that they hold standards of "articulateness" that ignore political substance, or that they dismiss forms of communication judged too emotional or disorderly. Even when people are present, they may not be encouraged to express their views, their attempts to express themselves may be silenced, or they may not be taken seriously. In these ways individuals and groups may be *internally* excluded.

I suggest that a discussion-based democratic theory should be called a theory of communicative rather than deliberative democracy to indicate that it makes a broader account of political communication, which includes, but is not limited to, argument. Elsewhere I have proposed three additional forms of political communication that can aid the theory and practice of communicative democracy: greeting, rhetoric, and storytelling.[6] Here I elaborate the moral and political function of the first of these forms of communication, greeting, which in the context of politics I will also call public address. The claim of this chapter is not that this form of communication occupies a more important place than other communicative actions in political life, but only that it serves uniquely important functions that so far have not been noticed by theories of discursive democracy.

GREETING

I assume, with writers like Jurgen Habermas, Seyla Benhabib, and others, that a good way to theorize the norms and practices of an inclusive discussion-based democracy is to reflect on the ethics implicit in everyday communication. The idea here is that democratic norms can be discovered through a reflective interpretation of the basic norms of moral respect that everyday communicative interactions express and to which they often appeal. For reasons that I leave aside, I find some limitations in Habermas's own theory of communicative ethics, however, and I look to Levinas's communicative ethics to supplement it.

"Greeting" refers to those moments in everyday communication where people acknowledge one another in their particularity. Thus, it includes literal greetings, such as "hello," "how are you?" and addressing people by name. In the category of greeting I also include moments of leave-taking: "good-bye," "see you later," as well as the forms of speech that often lubricate discussion with mild forms of flattery, stroking of egos, deference, and politeness. Greeting includes handshakes, hugs, the offering of food and drink, and making small talk before getting down to real business.

In *Otherwise Than Being, or Beyond Essence,* Emmanuel Levinas distinguishes an aspect of communication as a process of subject-to-subject recognition, on the one hand, from an aspect of expressing content or referring to something between the subjects, on the other. The former he calls "Saying" and the latter, the "Said." Prior to and a condition for making assertions and giving reasons for them is a moment of opening up to and directly acknowledging the others without the mediation of content that refers to the world. The gesture of opening up to the other person, where the speaker announces "here I am" for the other and "I see you," is prior to the thought to be conveyed, a world to refer to, act in, and share.

For Levinas, this act of signification is one of exposure, vulnerability, risk. In such announcement the speaker responds to the other person's sensible presence by taking responsibility for the other's vulnerability but without promise of reciprocation. Communication would never happen if someone did not make the "first move" out of responsibility for the other to expose herself without promise of an answer or acceptance. Greeting (my term, not Levinas's) is this communicative moment of taking the risk of rebuff in order to establish and maintain the bond of trust necessary to sustain a discussion about issues that face us together.

Levinas describes the most primordial moment of an ethical relation between one person and another as a condition of being *hostage.* To recognize another person is to find oneself already claimed by the other person's potential neediness. The sensual, material proximity of the other person in his or her bodily need and possibility for suffering makes an unavoidable claim on me, to which I am hostage. Often a person turns her back on or is indifferent to this claim that the other makes upon her. Sometimes she may react with selfish greed or cruelty to the claim. But when she acknowledges the other, she responds to the other and acknowledges an ethical relation of responsibility for the other person: "It is through the condition of being hostage that there can be in the world compassion, parody, and proximity—even the little that there is, even the simple, 'After you, sir.' The unconditionality of being hostage is not the limit case of solidarity, but the condition for all solidarity."[7]

In the moment of communication that I call greeting, a speaker announces her presence as ready to listen and to take responsibility for her relationships to her interlocutors at the same time that it announces her distance from the others, their irreducible particularity. Greetings in this broad sense are a constant aspect of everyday communicative interaction. Without these gestures of respect and politeness that are only Saying without anything said, communicative interaction would feel like the science fiction speech of an alien, some sort of heartless being for whom speech is only for getting things said, interrogating their truth or rightness, and getting things done. Greeting has a very important place, moreover, in situations of communication among parties who have a problem or conflict and try to reach some solution through discussion.

THE ROLE OF GREETING IN
POLITICAL COMMUNICATION

I have described the functions of greeting in everyday communication. But how does this account transfer to the context of political communication in which citizens and public officials engage in discussions and debates about public issues? Before answering that question, let me review some examples of greeting gestures in politics.

Rituals of greeting are a formal part of the political practices of many non-Western and traditional societies. Meetings of different villages or klans among the Maori people, for example, begin with several stages and forms of greeting; Maori engage in these rituals today in their political life, which has also influenced the political practices of New Zealand society more generally.[8] The gestures of greeting function to acknowledge relations of discursive equality and mutual respect among the parties to discussion as well as to establish trust and forge connection based on the previous relationships among the parties. In modern Western political processes the role of greeting is not so self-conscious, but I suggest that it is often quite ritualized. Most forums of political discussion, dispute, and negotiation are peppered with gestures of greeting, as are most nonpolitical interactive situations. The political functions of such moments of greeting are to assert discursive equality and establish or reestablish the trust necessary for discussion to proceed in good faith.

Before the guest speaker begins her speech on an issue of the day to a public forum, she must be introduced by an official of the hosting organization. The official recites the speaker's background and achievements, often incorporating a narrative about the hosting organization and its connection with the speaker and her activities. When the speaker finally takes the podium, she does not usually get right to the point but instead thanks her introducers, says some words of praise about her hosts, and tells a narrative of her own about their connection.

Delegates come to the annual convention of a large, citizens' organization, or to a legislative session, in each case knowing that the agenda is fraught with some hotly contested issues. Especially when groups or factions confront one another over issues about which they will disagree, rituals of greeting and politeness are important for starting and maintaining discussion through difficult times. Contentious meetings often begin or end with receptions during which individuals greet each other personally. People disagreeing with each other often acknowledge the importance of the group on the other side, its integrity and goodwill, before they give their reasons for disagreement. Such gestures do not offer information, nor do they further arguments directly by giving reasons or criticisms. But without such spoken moments of politeness, deference, acknowledgment of the particular perspective of others, their goodwill and their contribution to the collective, discussion itself would often break down. To be sure, such gestures of flattery and deference are often absent from political contests, frequently making discussion impossible because some or all contestants do not believe that the others respect them as political equals. Then there is only power politics.

Gestures of greeting are most elaborate and ritualized in international relations. Indeed, much of diplomacy consists in state leaders, ambassadors, and other high officials visiting high officials of other states to do little else than greet one another. They give speeches that affirm that country's friendship and mutual respect but say nothing of substance about policy. They attend balls and dinners. A cynic can say that such activity is simply playing to the media and crowds, while the real international politics goes on as a power struggle behind closed doors. If gestures of greeting are divorced from ongoing processes of political discussion, debate, and decision making, they do indeed become diverting political window dressing. Too often they are so divorced, or no serious public political discussion takes place.

The term "greeting" or "public address" names communicative political gestures through which those who have conflicts and aim to solve problems *recognize* others, especially others with whom they differ in opinion, interest, or social location, as included in the discussion. By such Sayings, as discussion participants we acknowledge that the others they address are part of the process. We implicitly promise to make our contributions to discussion accountable to them, as theirs are to us. Following the intuition underlying Levinas's account of Saying, this acknowledgment cannot come in the form of a general appeal to "all reasonable persons." It must be more particular. That is, I or we must try to persuade you, who are in this social situation. We must be responsive to you, who have this claim on us, listen seriously to you, even though we may perceive that our interests conflict fundamentally, or else we may come from different ways of life with little mutual understanding.

In mass politics, individuals do not usually enter political contestation and discussion by themselves. They usually join with others with whom they share affinities of interest, ideology, or social position. Although the group character of modern politics ought to be fluid, democratic debate in mass societies is inevitably debate among and between social groups and social segments. Thus, in practice, what it means in mass politics to address publicly the others with whom one shares political problems and seeks a solution is to address groups of others in their socially differentiated specificity.

Charles Taylor has proposed that a politics of recognition is a basic element of justice. He expresses it as a political end, an ultimate goal that cultural groups seek in their interaction with others. Attention to the importance of greeting gestures in politics raises questions for me about whether Taylor has correctly articulated the significance of recognition. In a diverse society with complex problems and conflicts, I suggest, at least one level of recognition is best thought of as a condition of rather than as a goal of political communication that aims to solve problems justly. A deliberative or communicative model of democracy says that democratic legitimacy requires that all those affected by decisions should be included in discussions that reach them. Greeting names those communicative political gestures through which participants in democratic discussion recognize other specific groups as included in the discussion that will issue in decisions. By such gestures of greeting, discussion participants acknowledge that they are together with those they name, and that they are obliged to listen to their opinions and take them seriously. As a political issue of inclusion, recognition is primarily a starting point for political interaction and contest rather than a goal.[9] This meaning of recognition is considerably thinner than the meaning that Taylor gives to the term. Political greetings name the others with whom one is discussing issues in their situated specificity. It acknowledges the legitimacy of their situated and differentiated points of view. This is far from the affirmation of cultural understanding and independence that Taylor gives to the term. For the purposes of this argument, I reserve judgment on the question of whether political cooperation requires such a deep recognition. The important point for now is that at least one level of recognition should be understood as a condition and as a means for beginning to cooperate politically rather than as the end that groups seek.

To be sure, public gestures of acknowledgment more often than not are pro forma and superficial. Political discussants too often fail to respect those whom they have acknowledged. Thus, less powerful groups often must struggle for recognition time and again, calling on the political public to make good on the promise of inclusion contained in its gestures of public address. Without the moment of greeting, however, no discussion can take place at all, because the parties refuse to face one another as dialogue partners. When Yasir Arafat and Yitzhak Rabin shook hands in 1993, some wrongly celebrated this moment as the arrival of peace. The moment was and remains a historical turning point, however, as the moment when Israel for the first time gave greeting to the Palestinians as a group with whom they are obliged to discuss their mutual problems and conflicts. When, as in this case, discussion has broken down, greetings must often be renewed for further discussion to take place.

APPLICATION: THE AMERICAN
WELFARE REFORM DEBATE

The uses of a theory of communicative democracy are primarily critical. With the norms and ideals expressed in the theory, one can evaluate how most political processes fall short of what is necessary to do justice. Understanding the political function of greeting gives an important criterion for assessing actual political processes. Actual political discussion should be examined not only for what it says, whether the issues are well formulated, the arguments coherent, and so on. We should also ask whether the major contributions to a political debate show discursive signs that they are addressing all those who should be included in the debate.

One sign of the absence of such greeting is that a public debate refers to persons or social segments only in the third person, never addressing them in the second person. If a social segment rarely if ever appears as a group to whom deliberators appeal, and if there are few signs that public participants in deliberation believe themselves accountable to that social segment among others, then that social segment has almost certainly been excluded from discussion.

I suggest that the American welfare reform debate of 1993–1996 fails this test of inclusion, and that public discussions of welfare reform largely remain exclusionary in this sense. Lower income people, and in particular lower income single mothers—the social segment arguably the most directly affected by the reforms—on the whole have not been included as participants in the deliberations. In this debate lower income single mothers have not been treated as equal citizens with opinions and perspectives that deserve to be taken into account to make just and wise decisions about public assistance. Instead, they have been treated almost entirely as the *objects* of the debate. There has been a great deal of talk about lower income single mothers, especially those on welfare, as a *problem*. Many experts have analyzed the sources of this problem and have made predictions about how policy will produce behavioral change in this problem group. The actual voices, evaluations, and reasons of lower income people have rarely been heard in the public debate. When lower income people have been invited to speak, it is usually not to say what they think but to provide an "object lesson" about the difficulty of living, or the possibilities of change, to support one side or another in the debate. Nor have lower income single mothers had very much in the way of representatives or advocates for their points of view on welfare. As the 1996 debate came to a head, the Children's Defense Fund came out as a strong advocate for considering the effects of welfare reform on children. But it did not speak for mothers.

If lower income single mothers had been considered participants in the welfare reform debate, then a congressman would not have been able to show a sign saying "Don't Feed the Alligators" on the floor of the House at one point in that debate. Is there any reason to think that the congressman felt obliged to justify his views to *everyone*? Could he have used the House floor for the act if he had sensed that a significant number of others there considered the congressional debate accountable to lower income single mothers (among others)? Inclusion is, thus, an important principle of deliberative democracy, because it expands the meaning of reciprocity and accountability in public. It is not simply that deliberators should have reasons that others can accept. Deliberators must both explicitly *address* the others whom they aim to persuade, and they must listen to their claims.

I am not suggesting that if lower income single mothers had been properly included in the welfare reform debate, they would have argued for keeping welfare as we knew it. Far from it. I am saying, however, that it would have been more difficult for some of the things claimed in the debate about the laziness and irresponsibility of poor people to carry weight. The punitive and disciplinary aspects of the current reforms that are premised on such disrespect for fellow citizens would have been less likely to hold the center of the legislation if the people most affected had been publicly acknowledged as party to the discussion and decision and not simply as their object.

Since June 1996 public discussion of welfare policy has given some minimal forum to the voices of those mothers whose futures are at stake in these changes. Rarely, however, are these women asked to say what they think the policies should be, what is really needed to make them just. Instead, they are usually treated once again as objects of observation: here's what I used to be doing, and here's what I am doing now. In my experience, most lower income single mothers need little prodding to express savvy analysis of the system and to make claims about what would improve both it and their lives. To the extent that their subjectivity as citizens is not publicly addressed in deliberations about welfare policy, the outcome of those deliberations cannot be morally legitimate, no matter what that outcome is.

CONCLUSION

Democratic norms mandate inclusive communication as a criterion of political legitimacy. Laws, policies, and decisions are normatively legitimate only if they are the outcome of a transparent process of public debate in which all members of the polity have had an effective chance to participate and influence the outcome. Inclusive public debate increases the chances that the process of arriving at policies has taken account of all interests. Inclusion increases the chances that those who make proposals will transform their position from an initial self-regarding stance to a more objective appeal to justice because they listen to others with different positions to whom they are also answerable. Even when a process of public discussion ends in a majority decision whose justice or wisdom some question, they can regard it as legitimate if they have reason to believe that they had an effective voice in making their case.[10] Even if they disagree with an outcome, political actors must accept the legitimacy of a decision, if it was arrived at through an inclusive process of public discussion.

In this chapter I have offered an idea of greeting or public address as one important norm of political inclusion and as a test of exclusion. Before a deliberation about substantive policy can proceed, those deciding must acknowledge one another in their particularity and recognize that they are accountable to one another. Speaking and acting without such acknowledgment of some parts of the society is an effective and often unnoticed mode of exclusion, even when there are no formal bars to their participation. Although the conditions of internal inclusion involve other communicative actions, I have suggested that greeting functions as an important condition of recognition. I have illustrated this claim with an example from recent politics in the United States. I have no reason to think, however, that the context of American political discussion and decision making is very much worse in this regard than many other contexts.

NOTES

1. See Charles Beitz, *Political Equality* (Princeton, N.J.: Princeton University Press, 1990), p. 4.

2. For statements of the theory of deliberative democracy, see Joshua Cohen, "Deliberation and Democratic Legitimacy," in *The Good Polity*, ed. Alan Hamlin and Philip Pettit (London: Basic Blackwell, 1989), pp. 17–34; Benjamin Barber, *Strong Democracy* (Berkeley: University of California Press, 1984); John Dryzek, *Discursive Democracy* (Cambridge, Eng.: Cambridge University Press, 1990); James Fishkin, *Deliberative Democracy* (New Haven: Yale University Press, 1991); Amy Gutmann and Dennis Thompson, *Democracy and Disagreement* (Cambridge: Harvard University Press, 1996); and James Bohman, *Public Deliberation* (Cambridge, Mass.: MIT Press, 1996).

3. See Iris Marion Young, "Justice, Inclusion and Deliberative Democracy," in *Democratic Disagreement*, ed. Stephen Macedo (Oxford: Oxford University Press, 1999). In this chapter I discuss the theory of deliberative democracy offered by Amy Gutmann and Dennis Thompson and suggest that it would be strengthened by a more explicit discussion of norms of inclusion.

4. See Beitz, *Political Equality*, pp. 97–122. See also Joshua Cohen, "The Economic Basis of Deliberative Democracy," *Social Philosophy and Policy* 6, 2 (1992): 25–50.

5. Anne Phillips, *The Politics of Presence* (Oxford: Oxford University Press, 1996).

6. I have developed this argument in an extended way in an essay where I also elaborate on the political functions of these three modes of communication in addition to argument ("Communication and the Other: Beyond Deliberative Democracy," in *Democracy and Difference*, ed. Seyla Benhabib [Princeton, N.J.: Princeton University Press, 1996], pp. 120–36; reprinted in Iris Young, *Intersecting Voices: Dilemmas of Gender, Political Philosophy, and Policy* [Princeton, N.J.: Princeton University Press, 1997]). For some stronger criticisms of the idea of deliberative democracy, see Lynn Sanders, "Against Deliberation," *Political Theory* 25, 3 (1997): 347–76.

7. Emmanuel Levinas, *Otherwise than Being, or Beyond Essence*, trans. Alphonso Lingis (The Hague: Martinus Nijhoff, 1981), p. 117.

8. For one account of Maori greeting protocol, see Joan Metge, *The Maoris of New Zealand: Tautahi* (London: Routledge and Kegan Paul, 1976), pp. 249–53.

9. I have argued that Nancy Fraser wrongly construes a politics of recognition as an end in itself rather than as a means toward political engagement and material justice. See Nancy Fraser, "From Redistribution to Recognition? Dilemmas of Justice in a 'Post-Socialist' Age," *New Left Review* 212 (1995): 68–93, and Young, "Unruly Categories: A Critique of Nancy Fraser's Dual Systems Theory," *New Left Review* 222 (1997): 147–60.

10. See Bernard Manin, "On Legitimacy and Political Deliberation," *Political Theory* 15, 3 (1987): 338–68.

6 / (Re)reading Mary Daly
As a Sister Insider

AMBER L. KATHERINE

In response to Mary Daly's *Gyn / Ecology: A Metaethics of Radical Feminism* (1978), Audre Lorde wrote her a letter in 1979, eventually published as an open letter, in which she said: "This letter has been delayed because of my grave reluctance to reach out to you, for what I want us to chew upon here is neither easy nor simple. The history of white women who are unable to hear Black women's words, or to maintain dialogue with us, is long and discouraging. But to assume that you will not hear me represents not only history, perhaps, but an old pattern of relating, sometimes protective and sometimes dys-functional, which we, as women shaping our future, are in the process of shattering and passing beyond, I hope" (1984, 66–67). Be-cause Audre Lorde's critique of *Gyn / Ecology* was (and is) so com-pelling, and because Mary Daly did not respond in kind to Lorde, there has been very little discussion of *Gyn / Ecology* by white fem-inists in the United States.[1] This is unfortunate, because there is much to be learned from reading and thinking about this book, espe-cially about unfruitful patterns of relating among women of differ-ent racial and ethnic identities. I offer a way for "third wave" feminists to read (and for "second wave" feminists to reread) Mary Daly's radical feminism, which takes up Audre Lorde's open invita-tion to dialogue.[2]

OUTSIDERS AND INSIDERS

The rereading that I propose is a project in coming to see how radi-cal feminists in the European-American tradition are, at once, out-siders and insiders. A genealogy of European-American radical feminism can be a reflective starting point. In her aspirations to live as an "Outsider" to patriarchal reality, Mary Daly drew from Virginia Woolf, and before her, Matilda Joslyn Gage, and before her, those burned in Europe as "witches." The title of Audre Lorde's 1984 collection of essays, *Sister Outsider,* suggests that Lorde understood herself as an "Outsider" in relation to her "sisters" inside this European-American feminist tradition. As Lorde's title implicitly points out, even though Daly, Woolf, and Gage chose to live as gender outsiders, they were raised as racially and geopolitically privileged insiders.

I focus on two insider / outsider relations: (1) that between patriarchal loyalists and radical feminists of the European-American tradition and (2) that between radical feminists of the European-American tradition and women of other traditions. In the former relation radical feminists, such as Daly and I, are outsiders; in the latter, we are insiders. I use "insider" and "outsider" to refer to our situatedness in relation to historically constituted material axes of power. In a race supremacist society, insiders live with racial power or privilege, whereas outsiders live with racism. In a patriarchal society, men are insiders, women are outsiders. The rich are insiders, the poor outsiders in class society. Insiders move through the world more comfortably and empowered than the outsiders they ignore, exploit, and oppress. An Insider may have access to privileged knowledge or language, an authorized vantage point or resources, or the right to speak or act on behalf of others. Insiders are often judges, teachers, scholars, psychotherapists, gynecologists, bosses, fathers. They have relations of power with outsiders who are often prisoners, students, patients, domestic workers, daughters. Insiders are "in" dominant / privileged social / political groups; outsiders are "out" of these groups.

Insiders may share the benefits of power, and outsiders, the burdens of oppression, but one's placement within a complex of power relations does not necessarily determine how one views one's situation or that of others. Still, there are patterns in the perspectives of both insiders and outsiders that seem directly related to one's sociopolitical placement. I have been most influenced in my thinking about the patterns in perspective among insiders and outsiders by María Lugones (1987, 1991, 1992, 1994), but also by W. E. B. DuBois (1969 [1903]) and by feminist standpoint epistemology (Alcoff and Potter 1993). In general, insiders do not recognize themselves as insiders, nor do they see outsiders as such. Rather, they claim to view everyone as individuals. Outsiders, on the other hand, are more likely to have a perspective from which they view people as excluded or included on the basis of their group membership. This outsider perspective is often characterized as a "double consciousness," a pluralist self-consciousness, or, sometimes, as fragmented. Outsiders are more likely to know themselves both from the insider perspective and from their own outsider perspective. In contrast, insiders usually lack this double consciousness and see themselves as unified. A likely explanation for this difference is that insiders have a greater stake in maintaining (or justifying) their identity, practices, and projects. It is not that insiders never have pluralist-consciousness or that only they have a unified sense of themselves. Everyone is, in principle, capable of understanding themselves and others from more than one perspective. The point is that within a regime of oppressive power relations, insiders are less likely to be conscious of themselves and others as double or multiple. For such consciousness would risk their having to acknowledge their privilege and power over others. In contrast, outsiders motivated to resist have a stake in revealing the ways in which insider / outsider relations shape perspectives.

For example, I see myself as an Outsider who rejects the patriarchal insider perspective on me as a normal "Woman" in favor of a radical feminist consciousness of myself as "Other" than normal. But when I look in the mirror and see the Outsider, the radical feminist who says no to the patriarchal scholar, I see only one of my selves. Maintaining this sense of self, I can also see myself through the eyes of Audre Lorde's "Sister Outsiders" as an insider. In cultivating this pluralist self-understanding, I choose to interrupt the dysfunctional patterns of relating that Lorde names in her letter, to hear women of color and dialogue with them.

Although I did not know Audre Lorde and have not met Mary Daly in person, both are my teachers. What I found inspiring in their works when I first read them in college classrooms in the early eighties was the vision of feminist interaction and connection that they named "sisterhood." One can hear the title *Sister Outsider* as finding *Gyn / Ecology*'s omissions and assumptions a betrayal, because they construct Lorde as an outsider to the sister relation that she and Daly sought to affirm. Perhaps sharing Lorde's reaction, María Lugones argues, "Sisterhood is neither an appropriate metaphor for the existing relations among women nor an appropriate ideal for those relations when put forth by white feminists" (Kramarae and Spender 1992, 406). She offers as a reason the absence of analysis or defense of the sister relation by white / Anglo feminists, who have critiqued the American family. I agree with Lugones's proposal of aspiring to a feminist ideal of pluralist friendship that begins with "compañerismo" rather than sisterhood. Yet I also find critical reflection on the sister relation, as constructed in feminist discourse, necessary and a fruitful place to begin.

I am hopeful that Daly's work can be used to reflect on things we do with little, if any, awareness—especially as radical feminist insiders—which, had we awareness, we might do differently or not at all. Daly and Lorde have taught me that history is present in our patterns of relating, that by studying history we can dis / cover those oppressive foreground patterns side by side with and intertwined with the inspiring and empowering patterns that Mary Daly calls the "Background." I find the mirror idea in María Lugones's work helpful for discovering this intertwining of patterns and the historical, geopolitical constitution of our many selves, our cultural identities. Lugones suggests in "On the Logic of Pluralist Feminism" that one way white feminists can begin to notice women of color is to "realize that we are mirrors in which you can see yourselves as no other mirror shows you." She says: "It is not that we are the only faithful mirrors, but I think we *are* faithful mirrors. Not that we show you as you *really* are; we just show you as one of the people you are. What we reveal to you is that you are many—something that may in itself be frightening to you. But the self we reveal to you is also one that you are not eager to know for reasons that one may conjecture" (Card 1991, 41–42).

We can look at Mary Daly's *Gyn / Ecology* in the mirror of Audre Lorde's criticisms. But my ultimate interest is not in what we might learn about *Gyn / Ecology* from analysis at this level. I am interested ultimately in what critiques by radical women of color in the United States (particularly Audre Lorde's) reveal about European-American radical feminists in general. I want to learn about white feminists, including myself, by looking at the historical tradition of European-American radical feminism in the mirror of sister outsiders, like Audre Lorde. The trick, I think, is to develop the skills to (re)read Daly's *Gyn / Ecology* in a way that reveals both the feminist Outsider and the Eurocentric insider. The challenge for those of us who

trace, or re-member, genealogies similar to Mary Daly's is to maintain self-awareness as sister insiders and to let that awareness inform
our feminist practices, discussions, and projects.

A BACKGROUND HISTORY OF OUTSIDERS

The history of radical feminism, as Daly presents it, is a "Crone-
ology of Outsiders."[3] She "re-members" radical feminism by exploring its roots in a buried gynocentric tradition.[4] On her reconstruction,
yesterday's witches and the late twentieth century's radical feminists
are related in lines that run through Matilda Joslyn Gage and Virginia
Woolf. Uniting the tradition is the standpoint of the Outsider in
patriarchy.

Daly re-members Matilda Joslyn Gage as "a major radical feminist
theoretician and historian whose written work is indispensable for
an understanding of the women's movement today" (1980, vii). Her
foreword to Gage's *Woman, Church and State* identifies Gage as a
"foresister of contemporary feminists" who dared to reveal and name
the enemy (1980, vii). Gage's book brings together studies of matri-
archal societies, female sexual slavery, witchcraft, and marriage, with
critiques of civil and ecclesiastical law, in order to reveal the systematic nature and consequences of patriarchal oppression: "The
most stupendous system of organized robbery known has been that
of the church towards women, a robbery that has not only taken her
self-respect but all rights of person; the fruits of her own industry;
her opportunities of education; the exercise of her own judgment, her
own conscience, her own will" (Daly 1980, 238). Hence Gage dedicated her book to "all Christian women and men, of whatever creed
or name who, bound by Church or State, have not dared to Think for
Themselves" (1980, 2). Their standpoint is, in Daly's terms, that of
the Outsider in patriarchy.

Gage's *Woman, Church and State* is the major source for Daly's
chapter on the European witch burnings. Among the scholars of the
witch craze whom Daly surveys in this chapter, only Gage exemplifies a "Hag-identified vision" (1978, 216).[5] In this chapter, Daly develops Gage's claim that many women were persecuted as witches
because their independent thinking and healing practices presented a
threat to the patriarchal church. Daly's expanded thesis is that the

witch craze was a "primal battle" between "an aspiring 'intellectual' elite of professional men" and "a spiritual / moral / know-ing elite cross-section of the female population of Europe," which "was at heart concerned with the process of know-ing" (1978, 194). Following Gage, Daly argues that the witch craze "masked a secret gynocidal fraternity, whose prime targets were women living outside the control of the patriarchal family, women [Outsiders] who presented an option—an option of 'eccentricity' and of 'indigestibility'" (1978, 186). This is not to say that either Gage or Daly held that only eccentric or scientifically minded women were persecuted. Both were aware that the threat of being accused of witchcraft functioned to keep all women *inside* the control of the patriarchal church and family.

Undoubtedly Gage was the primary influence on Daly's "Remembering" the witches as early modern Outsiders. Yet the term "Outsider" comes not from Gage but from Virginia Woolf. Important as Gage was to Daly's thinking about witches, Virginia Woolf was equally important to the overall project of *Gyn / Ecology.* By coincidence, Virginia Woolf (1882–1941) who was, on Daly's reconstruction, a symbolic daughter of Matilda Joslyn Gage, was eleven years old (1893) when Gage's *Women, Church and State* was published in the United States, and Daly, symbolic daughter to Woolf, was ten years old (1938) when *Three Guineas* was published in England. I find Woolf the single most important influence on Daly's radical feminist thought. The index of *Gyn / Ecology* contains fifteen references to Virginia Woolf (three times as many as to Simone de Beauvoir), and Daly repeatedly identifies Woolf as her feminist foresister. Like Gage, Woolf sets a precedent for Daly's emphasis on daring and independent thought. But Woolf's influence runs even deeper than Gage's. It is there in the conceptual framework of *Gyn / Ecology,* in the Outsider's journey from the patriarchal "foreground" to the feminist "Background." Two sources of influence on *Gyn / Ecology* are Woolf's essay "A Sketch of the Past" (in *Moments of Being* 1976) and her book *Three Guineas* (1977 [1938]).[6]

In "A Sketch of the Past" Woolf writes, "behind the cotton wool is hidden a pattern" of human connectedness (1976, 72). "Cotton wool" is her term for "non-being," that level of existence constituted by the moments "one does not remember," moments "not lived consciously." For example, she says: "One walks, eats, sees things, deals with what has to be done; the broken vacuum cleaner;

ordering dinner; writing orders to Mabel; washing; cooking dinner; bookbinding" (1976, 70). In contrast, Woolf describes "moments of being" as engaged, satisfying, highly conscious experiences which are "embedded" in the "nondescript cotton wool." As examples of "moments of being" she offers the activities of her previous day, including enjoying her writing, walking along the river, noticing the country very closely, reading Chaucer with pleasure, starting a book of memoirs that interested her. Behind the "cotton wool" appearances of people who live "very much like the characters in Dickens," she finds "the scaffolding in the background," patterns of satisfying and highly conscious moments (1976, 73). Awareness of these patterns comes as a shock, as "a revelation of some order; it is a token of some real thing behind appearances" (1976, 72).

Consider, for a moment, Daly's ontological vision of radical feminism as "the journey of women becoming." Like Woolf, Daly appears interested in how women, enmeshed in the cotton wool, come to be fully conscious, engaged, inner-directed individuals able to see through the cotton wool existence. Daly announces this process of radical becoming, which she calls "Be-ing," as a journey from the phallocentric "foreground" to the gynocentric "Background." Daly's "foreground" seems to me to be developed from Virginia Woolf's "cotton wool," and Daly's "Background" (the "realm of the wild reality of women's Selves") from Woolf's "scaffolding in the background." Level of awareness is a defining feature of each arena. In the foreground we move through the world mechanically, according to patriarchal norms; in the Background, we move in a highly reflective, Self-centering way, which acknowledges the organic connections among all things. In *Gyn / Ecology,* the African mother who silently, without reflective awareness, subjects her daughters to excision and infibulation exemplifies foreground movement, whereas the American feminist who speaks out of her self-conscious interconnection with all women to challenge the conspiracy of silence upheld by "objective" Western scholars on the subject exemplifies Background movement.

Woolf provides further insight into this ontological distinction in her autobiographical reflections. On Virginia's telling, her mother, Julia Jackson, and sister, Stella Duckworth, were caught in the "cotton wool" of pouring tea for distinguished men. Virginia remembers them as sad and silent. She notes that neither left anything to remember them by (1976, 83–88). Her brothers and her father, on the other hand, were engaged in a lively existence, which included the finest education money could buy and abundant opportunities for making a mark on the world as "a Headmaster, an Admiral, a Cabinet Minister, a Judge" (1976, 132). Virginia remembers her father, Leslie Stephen, as a Victorian patriarch who engaged in weekly breast-beating tirades over the accounting books, tirades vented in "brutal" rages against Virginia's sister Vanessa (1976, 125).

Virginia's brother George, who took social responsibility for the family, was critical and domineering. She remembers George criticizing her dress: "He was thirty-six when I was twenty. He had a thousand pounds a year and I had fifty. Those were reasons that made it difficult to defy George that night. But there was another element in our relationship which affected me as I stood there that winter's night exposed to his criticism in my green dress. I was not wholly conscious of it then. But besides feeling his age and his power, I felt too another feeling which I later called the outsider's feeling" (1976, 131–32). Note that in this encounter Virginia not only identifies the financial inequality as a cause of her beholden situation, but she also identifies the origin of her resistance in the standpoint of the "outsider." This riveting sketch, published in the midst of Daly's writing *Gyn / Ecology*, must have appeared to Daly as a time capsule from a radical feminist foresister. Although Daly's life was very different from Woolf's, Daly's identification with Woolf is deep. Both understood themselves as outsiders emerging from the cotton wool or patriarchal foreground in search of engaged, satisfying, highly conscious life experiences: Woolf's "moments of being" became Daly's "Background Be-ing."

In *Three Guineas* (1977 [1938]) Woolf seeks a path for "the daughters of educated men" who, for the first time in history, have the means to make a mark in the world. Woolf sums up the revolutionary potential of this new influence:

The educated man's daughter has now at her disposal an influence which is different from any influence that she has possessed before. It is not the influence which the great lady, the Siren, possesses; nor is it the influence which the educated man's daughter possessed when she had no vote; nor is it the influence which she possessed when she had a vote but was debarred from the right to earn a living. It differs, because it is an influence from which the money element had been removed. She need no longer use her charm to procure money from her father or brother. Since it is beyond the power of her family to punish her financially she can express her own opinions. (1977 [1938], 32)

Woolf saw economic independence from men as the condition for women's independent thought and action. On this model, freedom is won with "the weapon of independent opinion based upon independent income" (1977 [1938], 73).

The question of *Three Guineas* is how women will use this new influence. Will they follow in the processions of ruling class men? Woolf argues that there is a difference between the social situations of women and men that could enable women to maintain their freedom without joining the patriarchal processions. The difference is not of social or economic class, she notes, because women and men of the "the educated class" "speak with the same accent, use knives and forks in the same way; expect maids to cook dinner and wash up after dinner; and talk during dinner without much difficulty about politics and people; war and peace; barbarism and civilization" (1977 [1938], 9). Rather, the difference is a gendered one: "Take the fact of education. Your class has been educated at public schools and universities for five or six hundred years, ours for sixty. Take the fact of property. Your class possesses in its own right and not through marriage practically all the capital, all the land, all the valuables, and all the patronage in England. Our class possesses in its own right and not through marriage practically none of the capital, none of the land, none of the valuables, and none of the patronage in England. That such differences make for very considerable differences in mind and body, no psychologist or biologist would deny" (1977 [1938], 33). This difference is the effect of having been excluded from all professions of the public sphere in the name of God, Nature, Law and Property, which gives one very little stake in "civilization" (1977 [1938], 119). Thus, Woolf famously declared: "As a woman, I have no country. As a woman I want no country. As a woman my country is the whole world" (1977 [1938], 197). In a similar vein Angela Davis (1995 [1971]) and Adrienne Rich (1979) argued in the seventies that being disenfranchised—made an outsider—endows one with a particularly unique and useful political perspective, ground for agency, and set of possibilities.

Rather than join the processions of educated men, Woolf argues, the daughters should work for liberty, equality, and peace as outsiders (1977 [1938], 192). She calls for an "Outsider's Society," which would have no office, no committee, no secretary, no meetings, and would hold no conferences. It would have no oaths or ceremonies or pageantry. Outsiders would live by the lessons of their own "unpaid-for" tradition of education.[7] According to Woolf, this tradition offers four great teachers: "poverty, chastity, derision, and freedom from unreal loyalties" (1977 [1938], 145). Poverty teaches that one must earn enough money to maintain one's independence, but not a penny more (1977 [1938], 145). Chastity teaches that one must refuse to sell one's brain for money (1977 [1938], 146). Derision teaches to "refuse all methods of advertising merit, and that ridicule, obscurity and censure are preferable, for psychological reasons, to fame and praise" (1977 [1938], 146). Finally, freedom from unreal loyalties teaches one *not* to identify with people on the basis of nation, religion, college, family, and sex (1977 [1938], 146). If we live by these lessons, Woolf promises, we "can join the professions and yet remain uncontaminated by them" (1977 [1938], 151).

In her introduction to *Gyn / Ecology* Daly singles out Woolf's *Three Guineas* as a particularly important source of inspiration (1978, 33). Daly charts the journey from the foreground to the Background on the basis of Woolf's strategic attempts to think about how daughters of educated men can at once maintain economic independence and break with the processions of their fathers. For Daly, radical feminism is about not only economic independence from the fathers, but independence in all dimensions, mind / body / spirit, in the midst of the ever-present invitations of assimilation and tokenism. She insists that in the process of creating our Selves, we must embrace our Otherness, re-membering our Selves as members of the Outsider's Society who pledge allegiance to no flag, acting only in the interest of our conscious freedom to move in the Background.

Through re-membering Gage and Woolf, Daly re-constructs a radical feminist tradition of strong, knowledgeable, resistant women, linked "Crone-ologically" with the European women burned as witches. Uniting the tradition is the independent standpoint of the Outsider in patriarchy.

In the mirror of Lorde's "Open Letter to Mary Daly" the history of radical feminism re-constructed by Daly can be read as a Crone-ology of Sister *Insiders.* After reading *Gyn / Ecology,* and finding everywhere Witches and Outsiders from a European Background, Lorde asked, "Where was Afrekete, Yemanje, Oyo, and Mawulisa? Where were the warrior goddesses of the Vodun, the Dahomeian Amazons and the warrior-women of Dan?" (1984, 67). If yesterday's European witches and radical feminists of the late twentieth century are related in lines that run through Gage and Woolf, where does that leave the radical feminist who traces her Background traditions through India, China, or Africa? Lorde insists, "Assimilation within a solely western european herstory is not acceptable" (1984, 69). Since the only Background tradition re-membered in *Gyn / Ecology* is European, a feminist from another tradition is constructed in the text as a racial or ethnic outsider, a *Sister Outsider.* What unites the European-American feminist tradition, from this perspective, is implicit allegiance to the standpoint of a gender outsider who is also, without awareness, a racial or ethnic insider.

The most widespread response by European-American feminists who have become aware of the construction of the Sister Outsider has been to advocate inclusion. On the inclusion view, Daly should have included strong, resistant female symbolic figures and Background histories from the traditions of women in all of the patriarchal cultures she interrogates. However, although the inclusion solution might enable us to recognize important differences in Background traditions, it ignores the patterns of *relation* between women from different feminist traditions, as if all women were similarly situated geopolitically as Outsiders to patriarchy. Without interrogation of the relation between the African and European women, it might appear that African women could aspire to become Outsiders just like European women. Because the problem is not a failure to hear and dialogue about differences but a failure to hear and dialogue about the *relations* that construct differences, I recommend, as an alternative to the inclusion solution, a (re)reading of Daly's *Gyn / Ecology* that highlights ways in which radical feminist Outsiders from the European-American tradition are also Insiders in relation to Outsiders from non–European-American traditions. *Gyn / Ecology* offers a case study in the construction of an Insider perspective that lacks self-awareness as such. My proposed (re)reading is a consciousness-raising project, designed to enable European-American radical feminists to choose pluralist self-conceptions that can facilitate dialogue and connection across differences.

A FOREGROUND HISTORY OF SISTER INSIDERS

In response to Lorde's criticisms, I take to heart María Lugones's suggestion that white women in the United States block identification with their self that constructs the woman of color as a sister outsider. She says white women block identification because "knowing us in the way necessary to know that self would reveal to you that we are also more than one and that not all the selves we are make you important. Some of them are quite independent of you. Being central, being a being in the foreground, is important to your being integrated as one responsible decision maker. Your sense of responsibility and decision-making are tied to being able to say exactly who it is that did what, and that person must be one and have a will in good working order" (1991, 42). I propose a self-critical reflective investigation to reveal how we who were raised as racial or ethnic insiders have separated ourselves from women raised as racial or ethnic outsiders. Hence, I suggest a return to Daly's text as an exercise in unblocking identification with the historically and geopolitically constituted insider self. The goal is to move beyond old patterns of relating that cause pain and thwart feminist connection.

Mary Daly wrote in 1990: "I hope that in its richness, as well as in its incompleteness, *Gyn / Ecology* will continue to be a Labrys enabling women to learn from our mistakes and our successes, and cast our Lives as far as we can go, Now, in the Be-Dazzling Nineties" (1990, xxxiii). The task of the radical feminist who wishes to unblock identification with, or dis / cover, the patterns of relating that constitute her as an insider is to re-read the history of radical feminism in the United States as a Crone-ology of Sister Insiders in relation to those it constructs as Sister Outsiders. Begin with what Daly says about the relationship between foreground and Background. She suggests that much of what appears as foreground reality is a reversal of

Background reality. For example, the Christian myth of the trinity, Father, Son, and Holy Ghost, reverses the Triple Goddess (Mother, Maiden, Moon) in early mythology (Daly 1978, 75–79). Radical feminists need to "reverse the reversals": "In order to reverse the reversals completely we must deal with the fact that patriarchal myths contain stolen *mythic* power. They are something like distorting lenses through which we *can* see into the Background. But it is necessary to break their codes in order to use them as viewers; that is, we must see their lie to see their truth" (Daly 1978, 47).

I propose a self-reflective shift in European-American radical feminist thinking. If we can see into the Background only through the distorting lenses of foreground phenomena, we must acknowledge that the Background we are re-membering is a reversed reversal and, therefore, inevitably bears traces of the foreground. Traces I note here are the racist and ethnocentric assumptions and practices of the patriarchal foreground. If Lugones is right that each of us is multiply constituted (not univocal), then part of a European-American radical feminist politic must necessarily include raising awareness about historical patterns of relations between women from traditions differently situated with regard to racial, ethnic, and geopolitical axes of power. Lugones challenges individualist notions of responsibility regardless of whether the responsible person is a patriarchal loyalist or a radical feminist. We might frame Daly's Outsider with Lugones's words (1991, 42) by saying: "Being central, being a being in the [Background], is important to your being integrated as one [who governs Hag-ocracy]. Your sense of responsibility and decision-making are tied to being able to say exactly [what men have done to women], and that [Outsider] must be one and have a will in good working order." With this shift in mind, let us re-view Daly's history of radical feminism to dis / cover the Sister Insider.

What Matilda Joslyn Gage passed down to Mary Daly was a radical feminist vision of resistance and transformation based on the power of independent thought and judgment. Recall that Daly develops Gage's claim that many women were persecuted as witches because of the threat their independence presented to the church. Daly's thesis is that the witch craze was an epistemological battle between the rising class of professional men and "a spiritual / moral / know-ing elite cross-section of the female population of Europe" (1978, 194). Now, consider how the central value of independence looks from the perspective of women whose survival and resistance were based on the power of *inter*dependence. According to Lorde, this was true of women of African traditions whose struggle was, by necessity, based on the power of female bonding (1984, 69). Notice how this difference in values points to a different focus on relations. For women of European descent the focus has, historically, been on independence from men. This was clearly the case for Woolf, who understood the challenge faced by the daughters of educated men as a struggle to maintain economic independence from men. In contrast, for women from non-Western traditions, the focus has been on dependence on women in the extended family and community. The Sister Insider, in this case, is one whose focus has been on independence from men to the exclusion of interdependence with at least some women. She is an insider insofar as she is loyal to the order of values of the fathers who have traditionally understood freedom as an independent rather than collective interest.

Daly is a case in point. Although she seeks to identify the global nature of patriarchal oppression, the focus of each chapter in the Second Passage of *Gyn / Ecology* is on the relation between the Western patriarchal scholar, whose "objectivity" distorts and erases gynocidal intent, and the feminist Searcher, whose "gynaesthetic" perception reveals and names this same intent. The project of this Passage is not to detect positive patterns of relation among women from the diverse patriarchal locations she investigates, with the exception of establishing the relation between the European witches and contemporary feminists which I mentioned earlier. The project is to dis / cover and create a feminist Self by engaging the epistemological battle of early Modern Europe, present today between academic feminists and patriarchal scholars. Daly does not ask, as Lorde suggests she might have, about "real connections" among women from diverse traditions.

However inadvertently, Daly replicates historical patterns of relating to women of non-Western cultures characteristic of Western women and men. Her chapter on Indian sati champions Katherine Mayo as an independent feminist Searcher, discredited and erased for her "daring" efforts to name the atrocities against Indian women.[8] However, by adopting Mayo's perspective, Daly situates herself in the tradition of white women saving brown women from brown men, a classic moral "justification" for British imperialism. Because

Daly focuses on independence from patriarchal scholars, she fails to interrogate the patterns of relation between Mayo and Indian women. By siding with Mayo, Daly situates herself more in relation to imperialist men than in relation to Indian women.[9]

I have argued that Virginia Woolf influenced Mary Daly's thinking about the Outsider's journey of consciousness and practice from the patriarchal foreground to the feminist Background. This influence is present in Woolf's distinction between "cotton wool" moments of nonbeing and conscious moments of being, which Daly echoes in her distinction between patriarchal foreground and feminist Background. In order to reveal the Sister Insider perspective embedded in this distinction, consider it from the perspective of Mabel, the domestic servant Woolf mentions in her examples of activities that constitute the level of existence she calls "non-being." Recall her comment that among the things one does that are not remembered, "not lived consciously," is "writing orders to Mabel." From Mabel's perspective, the *relation* between Woolf's engaged, satisfying, highly conscious "moments of being" (enjoying her writing and reading Chaucer with pleasure) and Woolf's unremembered "moments of nonbeing" (writing her orders to cook and clean) is obvious. Yet the power relation between them is obscured by Woolf's construction of Mabel's work as "non-being." More importantly, Woolf's freedom *depends* on Mabel's servitude. The foreground / Background distinction is forged and constituted on Mabel's back. Woolf is independent of the men of her own class, but not independent of the women of Mabel's class. Unconscious of her relations with women outside her class, Woolf is a privileged insider. It is not the collective interests of all women but only the individual interests of a privileged class of women that concern Virginia Woolf.

Similarly, Daly's insider self is revealed through an interrogation of the distinction she inherits from Woolf. Like Woolf, who constructs the distinction between moments of non-being and be-ing on Mabel's back, Daly constructs the distinction between foreground and Background in part on the backs of women from India, China, and Africa. Note that Daly's feminist Searcher (descendant of the witch) makes her Background self by uncovering the victimization of women who, in the text, have no Background existence at all. Of course, there really are women (in America and beyond) so victimized that they experience no significant moments of be-ing. The problem in *Gyn / Ecology* is that Daly only sees women from non-Western cultures in these situations. Hence, the feminist Searcher discovers the following basic difference between women of European descent and those of non-Western cultures:

> The situation of those accused of witchcraft was somewhat different from that of the footbound Chinese girls and of the genitally maimed girls and young women of Africa, for these were mutilated in preparation for their destiny—marriage. It was also somewhat different from the situation of the widows of India, who were killed solely for the crime of outliving their husbands. For the targets of attack in the witchcraze were not women defined by assimilation into the patriarchal family. Rather, the witchcraze focused predominantly upon women who had rejected marriage (Spinsters) and women who had survived it (widows). The witch-hunters sought to purify their society (The Mystical Body) of these "indigestible" elements—women whose physical, intellectual, economic, moral, and spiritual independence and activity profoundly threatened the male monopoly in every sphere. (Daly 1978, 184)

The witch craze was not a slaughter of helpless victims but a "battle" over knowledge fought by men against daring independent "Outsiders." In contrast, sati, foot binding, and genital mutilation are represented as crimes against helpless victims with no gynocentric traditions that might explain the patriarchal forces pitted against them or from which they might draw the strength to resist. *Gyn / Ecology*'s feminist Searcher is constructed through and dependent on representations of non-Western women as victims rather than both as victims and as descendants of gynocentric Background traditions. The radical feminist Journeyer's Background existence depends on deconstructing (in Daly's lexicon "A-mazing") the foreground, which is constituted by perpetrators and victims of patriarchal violence.

Of course, Daly believed these non-Western women really were only victims and, therefore, that naming their situation was the responsible and daring thing to do. Consider her position on the African woman silenced by pain, subject to a conspiracy of silence of academics, Catholics, liberal reformers, population planners, "politicos of all persuasions":

> I have chosen to name these practices for what they are: barbaric rituals / atrocities. Critics from Western countries are constantly being intimidated by accusations of "racism," to the point of misnaming, non-naming, and not seeing these sado-rituals. The accusations of "racism" may come from ignorance, but they serve only the interests of males, not of women. This kind of accusation and intimidation constitutes an astounding and damaging reversal, for it is clearly in the interests of Black women that feminists of all races should speak out. Moreover, it is in the interest of women of all races to see African genital mutilation in the context of planetary patriarchy, of which it is but one manifestation. (1978,154)

On Daly's view, accusations of racism are intended to keep white Western women, like herself, from speaking out. Because she does not attend to the history of relations between Western women and African women, the possibility does not occur to her that the feminist act of speaking out against patriarchal violence might, at the same time, be a racist or ethnocentric act. Although aware that others will be critical of her exposé, she is not aware of how racism and ethnocentrism are embedded in her radical feminist perspective. She cannot see how speaking *for* the African woman implicates her in a relation that contributes to their oppression and constitutes her as an insider. Part of what keeps Daly from seeing the racism and ethnocentrism of her perspective is the responsibility to speak out that she feels as a Feminist Searcher who knows. She understands this responsibility as transcending the foreground ethics of race and racism. In Lugones's terms, her commitment to being a responsible decision maker, to being able to name patriarchal oppression, blocks her ability to see the duplicitous meaning and effects of her actions.

In Daly's defense one might argue that her case is different from that of Virginia Woolf. Whereas Woolf explicitly limits her project to discovering a liberatory path for the daughters of educated men, with little concern for the liberation of working class and poor women, Daly argues explicitly that radical feminism must concern itself with the plight of all women. Woolf's stake in not seeing her relation to Mabel is obvious; Daly's stake in not seeing her geopolitical relation to the non-Western women she represents in *Gyn / Ecology* is less so, at least to white women. In fact, forging the foreground / Background distinction on the backs of Indian, African, and Chinese women in the book jeopardizes her intention to further the liberation of all women. It would be unfair not to acknowledge this difference. Yet acknowledging it further illustrates my point. Daly's Outsider who strives to break silence and speak out against genital mutilation is also the Insider who silences the other by speaking on her behalf. In naming genital mutilation "barbaric," Daly inadvertently situates herself with "civilized" men of the educated class who "use knives and forks in the same way; expect maids to cook dinner and wash up after dinner; and talk during dinner without much difficulty about politics and people; war and peace; barbarism and civilization." Simultaneously, and ironically, she is right to refuse to be silenced by white Western critics charging her with "racism!" This is the very multiplicity that Lugones suggests we must acknowledge in the interest of feminist friendship.

GLOBAL FEMINISM

Finally, let us re-view Woolf's Outsider declaration, "As a woman, I have no country. As a woman I want no country. As a woman my country is the whole world" (1977 [1938], 197). Recall that she makes this proclamation from the standpoint of one who has been excluded from participation in the public sphere. By systematically embracing this outsider status she attempts to maintain independence from patriarchal values without losing the freedom secured by the economic privileges of the patriarchal professions. Daly follows Woolf, arguing that by re-membering our Selves as members of the Outsider's Society who refuse to pledge allegiance to any flag, we affirm our freedom. How is the Sister Insider revealed in this seemingly noble declaration?

In a recent essay, Susan Friedman reminds us that Adrienne Rich answered this question in a critique of Woolf's ethnocentrism. Rich offers this critique in the context of a self-criticism advanced along the lines that I have been arguing are called for by the politics of feminist bridge-building. Whereas previously Rich had understood her feminism unproblematically in the tradition of Woolf's declaration, in 1984 she reflected: "As a woman I have a country; as a woman I

cannot divest myself of that country merely by condemning its government or by saying three times 'As a woman my country is the
whole world.' Tribal loyalties aside, and even if nation-states are now
just pretexts used by multinational conglomerates to serve their
interests, I need to understand how a place on the map is also a place
in history within which as a woman, a Jew, a lesbian, a feminist I am
created and trying to create" (1984, 22). The Sister Insider is revealed
in the Outsider's declaration of having no country insofar as it constitutes a denial, or lack of awareness, about how she bears the history of imperialism in her present patterns of relation. According to
Friedman, however, Rich's critique misreads Woolf, a result of Rich's
felt need "in the 1980s to define a locational politics that did not
erase the differences among women in the service of a false global
sisterhood that potentially obscures the structure of power relations
between different groups of women at home and abroad" (1998, 197).
But, Friedman argues, since Woolf advocated "a transnational oppositional identity that replaces patriotism," rather than "a global sisterhood where gender oppression links women everywhere in a
common sisterhood," her work "exhibits an early feminist formulation of a locational politics, not a repudiation of it, as Rich implies"
(1998, 198–99).

Friedman offers her critique of Rich in the context of a larger effort
to sever a genealogical link between Daly and Woolf. Friedman reads
Daly the same way she reads Rich, as author of a misguided attempt
to "globalize feminism" (1998, 181). Pointing to the problem with
the global feminist theory in this radical feminist tradition in the
United States, Friedman says:

> The difficulties and dangers of such an internationalization are sig-
> nificant. Unless one's field is itself comparative, learning about
> women and gender systems in other parts of the world from one's
> base of specialization requires a considerable time investment to
> acquire sufficient contextual knowledge about other societies and
> histories. Feminist bricolage or patchwork so beautiful and
> provocative in the arts is not so beautiful in theory and scholar-
> ship. Plucking bits and pieces of women's lives and gender systems
> from here and there is seriously ahistorical, oblivious to the local
> overdeterminations of cultural formations. (1998, 182)

In a footnote Friedman comments, "Mary Daly's *Gyn / Ecology* is the most notorious example of such decontextualized internationalization of feminism" (1998, 217). I think it is important to reflect critically on this dismissal of *Gyn / Ecology*. On Friedman's view, attempting to make global connections among gender systems is "dangerous" for anyone without a "base of specialization" or a "considerable time investment," that is, for those in the most privileged knowledge / power positions. Her language here shares a family resemblance with language used by scholars in the United States in the seventies who tried to discredit the efforts of feminists who were attempting to make connections that revealed patriarchy as a planetary phenomenon. A large part of *Gyn / Ecology* is devoted to deconstructing scholarship that tried to persuade women that making such connections was itself racist or ethnocentric. For example, Daly argues, many female scholars use the deceptive language of "objective scholarship" because "the temptation to identify with the male viewpoint—which is legitimated by every field—is strong, and the penalties for not doing so often intimidate women into self-deception" (1978, 126).

My point in highlighting this resemblance is to caution against trusting that scholars with "specializations" are better situated than others (such as domestic workers, artists, people who listen to public radio, even self-reflective Sister Insiders) to globalize feminism. If the goal is to raise awareness of global patterns of oppression in order to change them, we should all try, in every way we can, using whatever resources and skill we have, to make the connections. Of course, we will not always get the picture right (if there is such a beast as "the right picture"), but we will surely get it wrong if we fail to study past mistakes for what they can teach us about historical patterns of relation that thwart our best efforts to make connections across difference. Hence, the problem with severing the genealogical link between Daly and Woolf—as Friedman does by arguing that Daly's global feminism is decontextualized, whereas Woolf's is not—is that it obscures the lessons that I have been arguing we can learn from (re)reading Daly in the radical feminist Outsider tradition of Gage and Woolf. It does a serious disservice to the project of understanding the historical relations that have constituted radical feminism to deny, as Friedman implicitly does, that Woolf and Daly can be and should be read together in the tradition of the Sister Insider.

CONCLUSION

I believe we can learn much, from (re)reading *Gyn / Ecology*, about moving dialogues forward among feminists across racial and ethnic differences. I have suggested that María Lugones's work provides useful insights for developing a way to (re)read Daly's radical feminism that is responsive to Audre Lorde's criticisms. Such a (re)reading can help us develop a sense of our selves in relation to others, which makes possible a deeper kind of hearing. I hope that realizing this possibility will contribute to the practical development of a model for feminist relating across differences.

I have recently experimented with this (re)reading in coming to be friends with Debra Barrera Pontillo, a Chicana artist and teacher with whom I've had the good fortune to work (in a predominantly white academic context). At times, the process has been harrowing and painful. However, coming to know myself as a radical feminist in relation to Debra, unblocking identification with my historically constituted ethnic and racial insider self, has enabled me to hear her more fully. It has enabled us to engage fruitfully in dialogue across our differences by helping me shift my thinking from the value of independence to that of interdependence. It has enabled me to choose awareness of myself and others as victims of oppression, yes, but also as resistors who disrupt the insider / outsider logic in various ways through our attention to each other. My awareness of myself as both an Outsider and an Insider has made me a better ally, enabling dialogues that have led Debra and me, with others, to become effective forces for change within our academic community. My experience, informed by my rereading of radical feminism as an insider perspective, affirms Gloria Anzaldúa's proclamation: "Caminante, no hay puentes, se hace puentes al andar (Voyager, there are no bridges, one builds them as one walks)" (Moraga and Anzaldúa 1981, v).

NOTES

This chapter began as a part of my dissertation. It grew from my studies with Marilyn Frye, who has been my ally, respectful critic, and model of how to do philosophy since 1988. I am grateful to Claudia Card for her patience and thoughtful suggestions throughout the revision process. And thanks to Debra Barrera Pontillo for the walks and the talks.

1. Audre Lorde attached a note to the version of the open letter published in *Sister Outsider*, which said, "The following letter was written to Mary Daly, author of *Gyn / Ecology*, on May 6, 1979. Four months later, having received no reply, I open it to the community of women." Daly reports in her "New Intergalactic Introduction" to *Gyn / Ecology* (1990) that she had a meeting with Lorde to discuss the letter on 29 September 1979 at the Simone de Beauvoir Conference in New York City. She reports: "I explained my positions clearly, or so I thought. . . . Apparently Lorde was not satisfied, although she did not indicate this at the time." Daly concludes her brief comments on Lorde's letter: "It continues to be my judgment that public response in kind would not be a fruitful direction. In my view, *Gyn / Ecology* is itself an 'Open Book' " (1990, xxix–xxxi). Audre Lorde died of breast cancer in 1992.

2. The "first wave" of feminism in the United States is the period from the famous Seneca Falls Convention of 1848 through, according to some, the 1920 ratification of the Nineteenth Amendment to the Constitution or, according to others, through the Second World War. The "second wave" refers to a period beginning in 1963 with the publication of Betty Friedan's *The Feminine Mystique.* There is no definitive moment that can be said to mark the beginning of the "third wave." However, several anthologies published in the nineties have declared the arrival of third-wave feminism.

3. This is not the only historical reconstruction of this sort. Another original effort is offered by feminist philosopher Claudia Card in "What Is Lesbian Culture?" *(Lesbian Choices* [New York: Columbia University Press, 1995]).

4. Mary Daly uses several gynocentric (woman-centered) strategies to signify her standpoint outside patriarchal language and thought. She makes up new words ("Crone-ology") and divides words to unmask hidden meanings or invite readers to listen to words differently ("re-member"). She engages in "irregular" capitalization, as in "Crone" and "Hag" to signify feminist reclamation. A Hag is "a Witch, fury, Harpy who haunts the Hedges / Boundaries of patriarchy" (1987, 137). A Crone is a "Survivor of the perpetual witchcraze of patriarchy, whose status is determined not by chronological age, but by Crone-logical considerations" (1987, 114). In general Daly capitalizes words naming the feminist "Background" and its inhabitants and does not capitalize words naming the patriarchal "foreground" and its inhabitants (e.g., "christians"), except to indicate a meaning from a Background perspective (as in "The Godfather") (1978, 22–27). In this chapter I sometimes choose to follow her nonstandard usage to reveal her influence and engage her work on her own terms.

5. According to Josephine Donovan, Gage is "the first to see the witches as bearers of alternative feminine traditions, which established them as community powers feared by the church" (1992, 41).

6. The influence of Woolf's *A Room of One's Own* (1929) on Daly's *Gyn / Ecology* is also evident, although I do not explore it here. See, for example, "Separation: Room of One's Own" (Daly 1978, 380–84).

7. In reconstructing this outsider tradition Woolf consults the biographies of Florence Nightingale, Ann Clough, Emily Brontë, Christina Rossetti, and Mary Kingsley.

8. For insightful critical studies on this pattern of relation, which implicates Daly, see Mrinalini Sinha,"Reading Mother India: Empire, Nation,

and the Female Voice," *Journal of Women's History* 6, 2 (Summer 1994), and Gayatri Spivak, "Can the Subaltern Speak? Speculations on Widow-Sacrifice," *Wedge* 7/8 (Winter-Spring 1995).

9. This pattern raises questions for many feminists working for social change with women who are situated differently with regard to dominant axes of power. For example, my college emphasizes service learning, which many feminist colleagues support. A pedagogical rationale often cited is to empower students; through serving those in need, students realize their potential to make positive change. The focus is on establishing an independent student capable of exercising her own judgment, conscience, will. Why not service learning projects designed around the value of interdependence, with the goal of restructuring power relations between those who "serve" and those who "need"? Who designs these projects? Whom do they serve?

REFERENCES

Alcoff, Linda, and Elizabeth Potter. 1993. *Feminist Epistemologies.* New York: Routledge.

Card, Claudia. 1995. "What Is Lesbian Culture?" In *Lesbian Choices.* New York: Columbia University Press.

Daly, Mary. 1978. *Gyn / Ecology: The Metaethics of Radical Feminism.* Boston: Beacon.

———. 1980. Foreword to *Woman, Church, and State: The Original Exposé of Male Collaboration Against the Female Sex,* by Matilda Joslyn Gage. Watertown, Mass.: Persephone.

———. 1987. *Webster's First New Intergalactic Wickedary of the English Language.* Boston: Beacon.

———. 1990. "New Intergalactic Introduction." In *Gyn / Ecology: The Metaethics of Radical Feminism.* Boston: Beacon.

Davis, Angela. 1995 (1971). "Reflections on the Black Woman's Role in the Community of Slaves." In *Words of Fire: An Anthology of African-American Feminist Thought,* ed. Beverly Guy-Sheftall. New York: New Press.

Donovan, Josephine. 1992. *Feminist Theory: The Intellectual Traditions of American Feminism.* New expanded edition. New York: Continuum.

DuBois, W. E. B. 1969 (1903). *The Souls of Black Folk.* New York: New American Library.

Friedman, Susan. 1998. "Geopolitical Literacy: Internationalizing Feminism at 'Home'—The Case of Virginia Woolf." In *Mappings: The Locations of Feminism in the Borderlands.* Princeton, N.J.: Princeton University Press.

Gage, Matilda Joslyn. 1980 (1893). *Women, Church, and State: The Original Exposé of Male Collaboration Against the Female Sex.* Watertown, Mass.: Persephone.

Kramarae, Cheris, and Dale Spender, eds. 1992. *The Knowledge Explosion: Generations of Feminist Scholarship.* New York: Teachers College Press.

Lorde, Audre. 1984. *Sister Outsider: Essays and Speeches.* Freedom, Calif.: Crossing Press.

Lugones, María. 1987. "Playfulness, 'World'-Traveling, and Loving Perception." *Hypatia* 2, 2: 3–19.

_____. 1991. "On the Logic of Pluralist Feminism." In *Feminist Ethics,* ed. Claudia Card. Lawrence: University Press of Kansas.

_____. 1994. "Purity, Impurity, and Separation." *Signs* 19, 2: 458–79.

Lugones, María, with Alake Rosezelle. 1992. "Sisterhood and Friendship As Feminist Models." In *The Knowledge Explosion: Generations of Feminist Scholarship,* ed. C. Kramarae and D. Spender. New York: Teachers College Press.

Moraga, Cherríe, and Gloria Anzaldúa, eds. 1981. *This Bridge Called My Back: Writings by Radical Women of Color.* New York: Kitchen Table Press.

Rich, Adrienne. 1979. "Disloyal to Civilization: Feminism, Racism, Gynephobia." In *On Lies, Secrets, and Silence: Selected Prose, 1966–1978.* New York: Norton.

Woolf, Virginia. 1929. *A Room of One's Own.* New York: Harcourt, Brace.

_____. 1976. *Moments of Being: Unpublished Autobiographical Writings.* Sussex: University Press.

_____. 1977 (1938). *Three Guineas.* London: Hogarth.

7 / *Revolutionary Community*

JACQUELINE ANDERSON

Will feminism devote itself to the elimination, not the containment, of rape, battery, incest, prostitution, and pornography, the most egregious violations of women's human rights; or will feminists settle for nearly everyone saying how much we deplore the violence as the violence continues unabated? Will feminism continue the difficult and costly politics of confrontation—rebellion against the power of men in public and in private, resistance to a status quo that takes the civil inferiority of women to be natural, sexy, and a piece of political trivia; or will an elite of women, anointed to influence (not power) by the media, keep demonstrating (so the rest of us will learn) how to talk nice and pretty to men, how to ask them politely and in a feminine tone to stop exploiting us? (Dworkin 1988, 325)

Recently, a few events have occurred that have made these questions resurface in my political imagination. It is possible, I think, to dismiss as so much sophistry and rhetoric Andrea Dworkin's dismissal of reform. As women, after all, we can count some victories, and they are not insignificant. Her question, however, is similar to that posed by the Black Muslims and Black Nationalists to those with faith in reform during the civil rights struggle. But of course we are able to count some victories, and they were not insignificant. Malcolm X questioned the possibility of African Americans and white Americans marching together for social justice. Lesbian separatists have posed a parallel question with respect to women and men. Andrea Dworkin's not so polite nudging of women to not be so polite might seem extreme, but only to the extent that it is possible to believe that social justice will result from a national guilty conscience or from important conceptual analysis.

Mitsubishi, the car maker, is currently defending itself against a class action sexual harassment suit brought by its women employees.

The behavior of the men at this factory can only be described as primitive. Earlier this year, a thirteen-year-old African American boy was viciously beaten by three white teens because he had crossed a racial boundary on his way to play basketball with friends. I spoke with a friend a short time ago who listed with great dismay the astonishing number of feminist bookstores no longer in business. These events returned me to the Dworkin question because they reminded me of just how far we have not come. Whatever we might list as victories—as lesbians, women, people of color, or members of another vulnerable group—I think that we can safely assume that the net effect has been neither significant nor meaningful.

Sarah Hoagland, in *Lesbian Ethics: Toward New Value,* says: "I want a moral revolution. I don't want greater or better conformity to existing values. I want change in value. Our attempts to reform existing institutions merely result in reinforcing the existing social order" (1988, 25). There are certainly some measures by which my claim is simply wrong that the success of virtually all social justice efforts in this country, with the exception of one, has resulted in fragile and easily crippled reforms. (The exception is of course the social justice victory for white men signaled by the practical death of affirmative action. This country was quite determined to remove all taint of reverse discrimination.) Lesbians and gay men have joined together in an effort to gain the right to marry legally. A lesbian is now star of a popular television comedy. Her "coming out" captured national attention. We are nothing, if not visible, and visibility is certainly critical to any struggle. Lesbians are comothering and attempting to protect their families legally. We can be in the military as long as we are willing to be quiet and refrain from sex. A number of corporations now recognize our relationships as real and extend to us some ordinary benefits. There are states with legislation enacted to protect our civil rights. These reforms do count as gains. But they are more icing than cake; they give the impression of greater substantive change than is the case.

These lukewarm concessions are also threats. They threaten our sense of ourselves as members of an "out group." They promise the possibility of "normalcy," that is, that we can be or that we already are like everyone else except for the small details that we are not heterosexual, white, and male. This apparent willingness to begin assimilating us tempts us to devalue the institutions that we created where we celebrated our difference. The loud and proud voices and rabble-rousing actions of radical lesbians are not pushing us to construct alternative contexts to empower ourselves or to construct political models different from those offered by the present sociopolitical order.

The post–civil rights period for Americans of African descent may have some lessons for us as women and lesbians that point to the sincerity and promise of our current victories. The most egregious and visible systems of bigotry practiced against African Americans—the separations imposed by separate drinking fountains, back seats and back doors, the terrorism of the Klan, the barriers to voting—were finally made illegal. Affirmative action legislation was passed and its protection extended to a variety of "out groups." Officially sanctioned bigotry ended. The cynicism and distrust of some seemed gratuitously negative and demoralizing in the face of our optimism that things would continue to get better. And for those who were prepared, there was a limited expansion of opportunity.

Within the African American community, there was a flourishing of creative and entrepreneurial activity. Bookstores, theater, music, dance, literature, and small businesses were all present, and they were sources of pride and promise. In Chicago, for example, there was a somewhat renovated old theater on the southside that was renamed the Afro Arts Theater. Dance, drama, music, performance poetry, and speakers, such as Imamu Baraka, were most often weekly events. As we moved more into the mainstream of America, these cultural institutions began to fade so that now they are practically nonexistent.

However, it is clear that the promise was far greater than the net result. The public face of crime and economic dependency remains black, although now that face includes some other "others." Most schools in this country remain segregated. The economic disparity between whites and African Americans is increasing. The final successful assault on affirmative action has already culminated in a reduction in the college enrollments of American students of color. It is also within the realm of possibility that the success of welfare reform had something to do with the (false) impression by many that those who benefited most were degraded black men and African American women with many children. So, our movement into the mainstream of America has not been meaningful, and we no longer have much community culture with the exception of "rap" music. (Interestingly, the largest consumers of this genre are young and white.)

Bigotry has become a more complex phenomenon as it has ceased to be reducible to black/white relations. But the process has not changed. As African Americans have become marginalized, other "out-groups" can be found occupying some place in the hierarchy of deception. Because women and lesbians, in my view, are a microcosm of the complexity, I believe that it is possible to make some relevant comparisons.

Women and lesbians are so visible that many may have the impression that we have made considerable process. Our media image is much more improved. Some of our concerns have even become part of the public discourse, for example, domestic violence, breast cancer, sexual intimidation, and even gay rights. Chicago has a city-sponsored Gay and Lesbian Hall of Fame (although sponsorship does not here mean financial support) and a community liaison position that pays a living wage. These concessions to our complaints would seem to portend our imminent acceptance into the mainstream, and that is the nature of our peril: that we will allow what has been built to suffer a premature death, because we (mistakenly) believe that it is no longer necessary.

It is my contention that we must measure our approximation to social justice by the quality of life and hope of *most* women and lesbians. By that standard very little, if anything, has changed. The most privileged among us have been halted by the reality that today 95 percent of corporate executives and 85 percent of elected officeholders are male. Domestic violence continues to be the leading cause of injury to adult women. Although it is true that women now earn 74 percent of what men do, that is largely the result of men earning less; 44 percent of women still earn wages below the level of poverty. In these statistics lesbians are included as women, generally not married to men, and often with children. The lesbians most at risk by any economic discrimination are going to be those who are poor and white, along with those who are members of another "out group." So, poverty is still feminine, and when women are in jeopardy, lesbians are likely to be in greater jeopardy than most.

We are now living in a nation in which it seems that the distance between rich and poor is increasing at a rate faster than anywhere else in the world. The real wealth that is being created in this country is enriching the already rich. Over 90 percent goes to the top 20 percent of all wage earners, while 62 percent enriches the top 1 percent of the population. The middle class is shrinking, even though in some particular groups, such as African Americans, it is now larger that at any other time in our history. This is not good news for women, who may find themselves forced to be in relations with men for bare survival. For many lesbians, this form of coercion could be a tragedy.

This country has the highest reported frequency of rape among Western industrialized nations. We still do not have the secure right to a legal and safe abortion, and for some women access is virtually impossible. Even with our visibility, it remains an act of great courage to "come out," and for most of our sisters, coming out is still not possible. The reforms that have occurred are important. I am not interested in constructing a utopian description of our more radical past efforts at community building. But we have not made a "moral revolution"—the existing social order is in no current jeopardy from us.

A most effective strategy is that of divide and conquer. Given the complexity of our various cultural, racial, class, and sexual identities, we can easily be set against each other. Recently in Chicago, Mountain Moving Coffee House (MMCH) was threatened with a discrimination complaint because of its "womyn born womyn only" policy. This lesbian space has been in continuous existence for twenty-three years. It is the only space of its kind in the city and virtually the only space of its kind in the country. The complainant, a self-defined woman born with a physical defect (a penis that is still present), identifies as a lesbian, performs with an African American performance ensemble, and writes the transsexual column for one of the gay newspapers.

The most articulate expression of the complaint was forwarded by a lesbian-identified postoperative transsexual and supported by the Chicago Lesbian Avengers (CLA) and the Women's Action Coalition (WAC). Their objection was to the "born womyn" component of the policy. The issue for them was simple: The coffeehouse policy was transphobic—phobic about transgendered people and transsexuals. A petition was composed and signatures requested at the annual International Women's Day dance. (The petitioners did not attend the dance. They gathered in the lobby of the hotel.)

The coffeehouse is space rented in a church once a month for, at most, eleven months. The total amount of time per year is approximately forty-four hours. The original complaint concerned being excluded from performing at the coffeehouse. Admission was not an issue, because the coffeehouse collective does not challenge women at the door. Transphobia was also not an issue, and it certainly was not *the* issue. The policy under which transsexuals are excluded from performing was obviously established to exclude men.

However, we no longer have the luxury of conceptual simplicity. Identity is a more fluid and complex matter now for many. So a policy designed to exclude men collides with the notion that some biological males are self-identified women who may not have been surgically altered. Without the "born womyn" component of the policy, the coffeehouse is positioned to accept everyone who claims to be a woman. This position would set a standard of open admission not required of any other organization. For example, the original complaint was made by someone who is a member of an ensemble closed to all who are not of African descent. In this country, that requirement can be met with one drop of "black blood." Yet their standard is more rigid, and it has not been challenged.

Vulnerable communities have a very long history of struggle for the right to assemble, which has been possible only because others have chosen to respect it. Lesbians are vulnerable, and the coffeehouse is lesbian space. So, the issue was one of respect. The CLA supported the complaint by co-signing the petition without communicating with the coffeehouse collective at any time prior to or subsequent to the complaint. The MMCH collective, along with some of its friends, has extended to them the opportunity to meet and discuss their concerns.

The poignancy of this conflict rests in the absence of relationship between the Chicago Lesbian Avengers, the Women's Action Coalition, and the Mountain Moving Coffee House collective. The CLA is the organizer of the Dyke March here in Chicago, and MMCH collective members have participated as volunteers for assorted pre-march tasks. The WAC has performed at the coffeehouse. We are not strangers to each other. And yet it is only subsequent to the complaint that the CLA and WAC lesbians conveyed to the MMCH collective through a petition that the policy was problematic.

Lesbians in conflict with lesbians, when the issue is the presence of a penis in lesbian space, borders on the absurd. However, the most cogent concern, in my view, was the absence of an identifiable ethic. The possibility that there might be some method of resolution other than a contentious and public conflict was not explored by the coffeehouse critics. The stage was set and the issue defined by the nonlesbian.

The effort to isolate the coffeehouse from the larger community of lesbians as an institution in violation of someone's human rights suggests that we need to talk to each other as lesbians. Even though the coffeehouse policy remains, there was no victory in this entire scenario, even though there was a victor. The person who lodged the original complaint and threatened legal action has now decided to move on and go only to those places that are welcoming. But now there are lesbians in the community who are hurt and angry with each other.

We cannot afford to play divide and conquer with each other, because we will most certainly be the conquered. We need only attend to what probably has been the most successful use of this strategy, that is, the political reification of race. Our efforts to come together as women and lesbians have consistently been undermined by our inability to transcend the racial divide. Our obsession with race and color ironically facilitates ignorance of the relevant social and political determinants that have situated all of us in this society.

The race construct enmeshes us in essential group identities that can be manipulated easily to set us against each other. The post–civil rights period should make us very suspicious of change that does not foster a moral revolution. Affirmative action provisions have been completely impoverished precisely because they were doing their work. The view has currency that the playing field is now level and that, therefore, the time is right for us to get on with the business of creating a truly "colorless" society. Yet racism continues to plague people of color, but with a difference. People of color are to a larger degree fighting with each other for the same small piece of the pie. We more often see each other through the lenses of stereotypes provided by a bigoted culture. The effort to make a moral revolution failed in the face of insincere reforms.

Thus, we may want to question more seriously the importance of the right to marry and the right to serve in the military as uncloseted lesbians. Women in the military are raped, and they are victims of sexual harassment and of domestic violence. Rape has been used as a military strategy against women of other nations. The presence of an army creates populations of vulnerable and exploited women and children who are never counted as casualties of war. So, although social justice demands that our sisters who choose military service have an undeniable right to serve as uncloseted lesbians, I would argue that this reform should not be viewed as unproblematic. If we struggle for the right to be in the military without questioning the existence of military institutions and values, we are not fostering a moral revolution.

Similar questions can be raised concerning the institution of marriage. The practical benefits of gaining legal recognition of our relationships are clear. But what do we gain by having them sanctioned by a bigoted, heteropatriarchal society? The institution will not change just because we might be admitted as members, and we are not demanding basic social change but only admission into existing practices. The norms of a woman-hating culture should not be left unquestioned in our struggle against exclusion as lesbians.

Reform fundamentally means finding a place for us—women, lesbians—within the existing system. The most critical lesson that the post–civil rights era has for lesbians is that there really is no place within the existing system for us as uncloseted lesbians. There are also very sound reasons for us not to accept uncritically the concessions offered by the present system. So, we must talk. We must organize. We must insist that we be acknowledged on our own terms as women and lesbians. To get this result we will need to promote a moral revolution.

Because we need to talk, we need community. Our community will be complicated because we are complicated. Andrea Dworkin pointed to one expression of this complexity with the idea of an identity of primary emergency, that is, the identity that places us in greatest peril. For all of us, it might be that we are women; for some of us, our racial/ethnic/religious identity. Our identity of primary emergency is both temporal and situational. Bigotry has no parameters. It is not rational. But it is always dangerous. So, we have not outgrown the need for community, but we are smarter. We will not always have the same priorities at the same time. We have made mistakes. But we are more savvy than we were twenty-five years ago.

If we are to circumvent the inevitable attempts to set us against each other as we foster a moral revolution, the values of our community must embrace principles that respect our essential complexity.

Joyce Trebilcot, in her book *Dyke Ideas,* offers the following three values/principles for her ideal of a "wimmins" community:

> First Principle: I speak only for myself.
> Second Principle: I do not try to get other wimmin to accept my beliefs in place of their own.
> Third Principle: There is no given. (Trebilcot 1994, 43)

These values/principles facilitate lesbian communication because they provide for a community whose members also have a radical sense of personal autonomy. They set the conditions for relations of respect, not only among lesbians but also between lesbians and other women.

Communication among us has often been problematic. Yet there are some very important and fundamental areas of agreement. If we suppose that an important reason for our gathering together is to empower each other and construct the basis for a moral revolution, then our environments must be free of hierarchy and oppressive values and behaviors. The ethic contained in the three principles allows for the possibility of coming together and also for the possibility of separating, because there are times when each is required.

Joyce Trebilcot does not intend the ethic contained in the three principles as a set of rules to be followed but, rather, as providing a framework within which a community or gathering of women might be intentionally created and within which more specific values might be derived. The appropriate context for these principles, according to Joyce Trebilcot, is a community of women, because that means implicitly the rejection of hierarchical and oppressive values and behaviors. If those values and behaviors are present, then the community cannot be considered a woman's community, regardless of who lives there.

The personal autonomy of each woman in the community is assured, because the three principles are not intended as *rules* to be adhered to by anyone in the community and may be violated at any time without guilt. One kind of allowable violation would be any context in which patriarchal values are present, which is, in any case, outside their intended application (Trebilcot 1994, 43). This community would be one of autonomous lesbians choosing to come together and also choosing to separate whenever they cease to be compatible. This flexibility would serve as a check on any woman who was inclined to impose her will on others.

It does not benefit us to fight each other. But if we construct rules of belief and conduct, fighting will be the result. In imagining a community that would embody her three principles, Joyce Trebilcot offers the analogy of a potluck supper: "We each contribute something and thereby create a whole meal. It is understood that our contributions may be diverse and may seem, on some standards, not to go well together, but we are not bothered by that; we each choose according to our own and/or other dishes. The food I bring is usually something I like myself, but also I like to share it—I hope that some others will like it too" (1994, 49).

My point is not to say whether transgendered or transsexual self-identified lesbians should or should not be welcomed into the community. My point is that a community that is committed to radical change needs an ethic for making decisions about such issues. Joyce Trebilcot's three principles offer an ethic that could give us a revolutionary community.

The community that I imagine being created and guided by the three principles would not be characterized by stability, because each member would be her own authority. The personal and political must intersect in ways that are true to the intricacies of our lives. Although this information is not new, we have not always been very successful in our response to it. The women and lesbians at greatest personal risk, most of us, have still been virtually untouched by the changes that we tend to count as successes. So, it remains essential that we confront and rebel against the power of men. For that we will need to build new institutions. We need to create new values and new ways of being in community.

REFERENCES

Dworkin, Andrea. 1988. *Letters from a War Zone: Writings, 1976–1982*. New York: Dutton.
Hoagland, Sarah Lucia. 1988. *Lesbian Ethics: Toward New Value*. Palo Alto, Calif.: Institute of Lesbian Studies.
Trebilcot, Joyce. 1994. *Dyke Ideas: Process, Politics, Daily Life*. Albany: State University of New York Press.

8 / Beyond Pluralism and Assimilationism in the Politics of Gender

ANNA STUBBLEFIELD

As feminist citizens, we must consider the ethical implications of supporting or advocating gender-neutral, as opposed to gender-sensitive, social politics. Assimilationists and cultural pluralists have tended to disagree over this issue.

Assimilationists and cultural pluralists disagree over the value and meaning of social group identity and social group differences. Assimilationists argue that certain social group identities, such as gender and racial identities, are arbitrary and essentially meaningless. They argue that the way to eliminate oppression is to transcend these identities so that people do not identify as members of these supposedly different groups. We are all inherently the same and should be treated without reference to unnecessarily limiting, arbitrary group classifications.

In contrast, cultural pluralists argue that social group identities and differences are empowering and an important source of value and meaning in people's lives. Social group identities and differences should not be used to limit people. But the solution to oppression is not to eliminate these identities. Rather, people should celebrate and affirm their social group identities and particularities so that everyone will perceive these identities positively rather than negatively. Public policy should recognize different needs of different social groups and respond to them in such a way that the result is not the exclusion of members from full participation in social and political institutions.

Iris Young criticizes Richard Wasserstrom's assimilationist understanding of sexist oppression. She offers a version of cultural pluralism that she applies to the case of women as well as to other social groups that she finds to be oppressed. I use the work of these two philosophers as examples to discuss the relevance of the assimilationism/cultural pluralism distinction to the case of sexist oppression. Many of Iris Young's criticisms of assimilationism, I argue, do not apply to Richard Wasserstrom's version of assimilationism, which I call "radical assimilationism." Neither philosopher works with an adequately developed view of what it means to be a woman in a sexist society. Catharine MacKinnon offers a theory of women's gender socialization more developed than (but in accord with) Iris Young's. Yet, Catharine MacKinnon's theory is undermined by aspects of women's experience that have been identified by German feminist theorist Frigga Haug and her colleagues. I propose an alternative theory of women's gender socialization that accommodates Frigga Haug's insights. On my proposal, Iris Young's cultural pluralist recommendations, if practiced, would yield the genderless society envisioned by Richard Wasserstrom. The assimilationism/cultural pluralism distinction would collapse in the case of sexist oppression. Richard Wasserstrom's vision, however, is not a useful model for addressing present problems of sexist oppression. Rather, we should abandon the assimilationism/cultural pluralism distinction as a basis for policy and focus instead on how women are socialized in a sexist society and on what can be done to mitigate sexist gender socialization.

RADICAL ASSIMILATIONISM

In 1980 Richard Wasserstrom published an essay articulating and defending an assimilationist ideal, which since then has often been used as an example by others. In his ideal society, gender and race would matter as little as eye color does in ours.[1] No basic political rights and obligations are (officially) determined on the basis of eye color, and no important institutional benefits and burdens are connected with it (Wasserstrom 1980, 24). In the case of gender, the assimilationist ideal would be incompatible with psychological and sex-role differentiation: "in the assimilationist society in respect to sex, persons would not be socialized so as to see or understand themselves or others as essentially or significantly who they were or what their lives would be like because they were either male or female" (Wasserstrom 1980, 26).

Iris Young, in contrast, believes that eliminating group identification is derogatory to those group members, and that eliminating oppression requires that group identification be constructed in positive ways rather than eliminated:

> While I agree that individuals should be free to pursue life plans in their own way, it is foolish to deny the reality of groups. Despite the modern myth of a decline of parochial attachments and ascribed identities, in modern society group differentiation remains endemic. . . . Even when they belong to oppressed groups, people's group identifications are often important to them, and they often feel a special affinity for others in their group. I believe that group differentiation is both an inevitable and a desirable aspect of modern social processes. Social justice, I shall argue in later chapters, requires not the melting away of differences, but institutions that promote reproduction of and respect for group differences without oppression. (1990, 47)

We need to distinguish Richard Wasserstrom's assimilationist vision from what it would mean to implement assimilationist policies in current American society. His vision is radical. He describes a society with no sex roles, no notions of masculinity or femininity, no gendered notions of sexuality. Bisexuality (neither heterosexuality nor homosexuality) would be the norm. Families need not consist of two adults of different sexes or even two adults. There might be no nuclear family structure as the norm. Procreation might be accomplished differently (for example, with artificial insemination). Parenting roles after birth would be genderless (Wasserstrom 1980, 26 and 31).

Certain of Iris Young's criticisms of generic "assimilationism" (not aimed specifically at Richard Wasserstrom, although she uses him as an example) are not applicable to a society with no sex roles or gendered identity. They apply, rather, to policies that do not differentiate between men and women in a society in which sex roles and expectations are forceful.

First, according to Iris Young, the assimilationist ideal assumes that equal social status for all requires that everyone be treated according to the same principles, rules, and standards. She argues that equality, defined as the participation and inclusion of all groups in a society's institutions, sometimes requires different treatment for oppressed or disadvantaged groups (1990, 158). Richard Wasserstrom, however, does not argue that men and women should be treated identically, to the derogation of women, in a society differentiated by sex. He suggests that if and only if there were no social meaning attached to sexual differentiation (if and only if, in effect, there were no men and women), there would be no reason to treat men and women differently. Nor does he suggest that everyone be treated identically. In response to the argument that women and men may have different physical capacities that render most women less capable of performing some of the work that most men are more capable of performing, he argues that in a technological society such differences in physical capacity, if substantial enough to undermine the transcendence of gender roles, should be removed by accommodations for the less capable party.[2] Furthermore, he strongly advocates preferential treatment to address the present oppression of women (1980, 51–82). Thus, his vision is not of identical treatment but of identical access to opportunities (1980, 31–33, including notes).

Iris Young argues that in contemporary American society, where group differences and group privileges continue to exist, the assimilationist insistence that equality and liberation entail that social policy should ignore difference has three oppressive implications: (1) "[ignoring] difference disadvantages groups whose experience, culture, and socialized capacities differ from those of privileged groups. The strategy of assimilation aims to bring formerly excluded groups into the mainstream. So, assimilation always implies coming into the game after it is already begun, after the rules and standards have already been set, and having to prove oneself according to those rules and standards"; (2) "the ideal of a universal humanity without social group differences allows privileged groups to ignore their own group specificity," thus perpetuating cultural imperialism; and (3) the goal of assimilation holds up to people a demand that they "fit" into the mainstream in behavior, values, and goals. This demand leads to inferior status for groups that deviate from the allegedly neutral, mainstream standard, and it produces an internalized devaluation of themselves by members of those groups (Young 1990, 164–65).

Again, these points are cogent for attempts to implement policies that do not recognize the different situations and needs of men and women in our society and that rest on the presupposition that treating men and women the same means treating women as if they were men. They do not apply, however, to Richard Wasserstrom's ideal, which does not involve bringing women into the mainstream. His ideal throws out the mainstream. It does not privilege a male perspective but produces an entire shift in perspective. It does not demand that women "fit in" to male standards but demands, rather, that the standards be changed.

Thus, it is important not to identify Richard Wasserstrom's radical assimilationist vision with misguided attempts to "assimilate" women into a societal mainstream that favors men. That confusion cleared up, we can focus on questions that bring out the real difference between Richard Wasserstrom's assimilationism and Iris Young's cultural pluralism. Should group identification be so identified with group oppression that eliminating oppression requires eliminating group identification? Or does eliminating oppression require affirming group identification? Does either position adequately address sexist oppression?

THEORIES OF WOMEN'S GENDER SOCIALIZATION

I find neither of these views a strong foundation for attacking sexist oppression. Neither adequately addresses the role played in sexist oppression by gender-specific social norms—social norms that specify appropriate behaviors on the basis of gender. A case has been made within feminist theory for abandoning essentialism (Adams and Cowie 1990). Historically, gender essentialists have held that to be a woman (man) is to possess a stable core of nonrelational physical or psychological properties that one shares with all other women (men). Gender nonessentialists hold that gender is not determined by the possession of particular reproductive organs or psychological qualities. They hold, rather, that to be a woman (man) is to be identified as a woman (man) in particular social contexts, and that what makes one count as a woman (man), as well as the value placed on gender distinctions in that context, are matters of social construction.

Both Richard Wasserstrom and Iris Young are nonessentialists about gender, and both discuss the role of gender-specific social norms in their arguments about sexist oppression. They suggest that such norms pressure women to be subservient to men and to provide men services (sexual, domestic, ego stroking, physical caring for both

them and their children, nurturing, and the like). Iris Young develops this analysis further than Richard Wasserstrom does. She argues
that women are devalued relative to men because they are perceived
as more earthy, defined more in terms of bodily functions and hence
as more primitive, less pure. Work identified as women's is similarly
devalued, and it is considered appropriate for women to perform im-
pure, bodily oriented functions. Furthermore, she argues that people
devalued in this way easily come to devalue themselves, which
undermines their resistance to being devalued (1990, 136–48).

These analyses of the role of gender-specific social norms in sexist
oppression are limited in the following ways. Richard Wasserstrom
sees gender-specific social norms as unfair constraints on individual
development, and he sees the roles women are supposed to play and
the functions they are to perform as tantamount to slavery (1980,
399–40). He assumes women would prefer to be free from these constraints, pressures, and expectations, that they comply to the extent
that they are coerced or perceive no better options for themselves. Iris
Young stresses the devaluation aspect of gender-specific social norms.
She argues that women comply with norms either for the reasons
Richard Wasserstrom gives or because they feel bad about themselves.

Although Iris Young's view is more sophisticated than Richard
Wasserstrom's, neither involves a complete enough understanding of
what it means to be a woman in a sexist society. Iris Young's views,
however, resonate with Catharine MacKinnon's view of the gender
socialization of women, which attempts a more complete account.
Catharine MacKinnon claims that what it means to be a woman is to
be an object for men's sexual use. To be socialized as a woman is to
become what men desire sexually (and she argues, in discussing pornography, that men's desires are also socially constructed, not naturally given). Human social structures worldwide have been produced
by and for men. What it is to be feminine is to fit into a social structure that caters to male desires, such that each "type" of woman—
maiden, whore, mother, wife—has a place and meets a need. One
becomes a woman through experiencing sexuality as the subordinate
participant, the one who attracts and who caters to the other's needs.

Feminist theorist Jacqueline Rose suggests that in addressing the
question of how to characterize women's gender socialization, we
must grapple with a problem arising from the failure of what she
calls the "sociological" account of gender socialization. On this

account, one is socialized to become a woman (man) by internalizing norms of femininity (masculinity). She finds this characterization inadequate, as it fails to account for incompleteness in gender identification. If the sociological picture were correct, she argues, we would all be perfect women and men, living out our gendered roles contentedly. But in fact, people constantly fail to live up to feminine and masculine ideals. She observes further that the sociological account does not support the political case for challenging women's oppression. If people slip comfortably into gender roles, why challenge those roles?

Jacqueline Rose suggests that psychoanalysis offers a more nearly accurate and politically useful account of the gender socialization of women. She argues:

> What distinguishes psychoanalysis from sociological accounts of gender . . . is that whereas for the latter, the internalisation of norms is assumed roughly to work, the basic premise and indeed starting-point of psychoanalysis is that it does not. The unconscious constantly reveals the "failure" of identity. Because there is no continuity of psychic life, so there is no stability of sexual identity, no position for women (or for men) which is ever simply achieved. Nor does psychoanalysis see such "failure" as a special-case inability or an individual deviancy from the norm. . . . Feminism's affinity with psychoanalysis rests above all, I would argue, with this recognition that there is a resistance to identity at the very heart of psychic life. Viewed in this way, psychoanalysis is no longer best understood as an account of how women are fitted into place. . . . Instead psychoanalysis becomes one of the few places in our culture where it is recognised as more than a fact of individual pathology that most women do not painlessly slip into their roles as women, if indeed they do at all. (1986, 90–91)

I agree with her about this, although her account does not exhaust the possibilities of sociological approaches to the gender socialization of women. One of her principal concerns is that characterizations of the gender socialization of women often portray women as passive recipients of femininity. Whether these characterizations assume that femininity is sociologically or biologically determined, they "have in common the image of utter passivity they produce: the woman receives her natural destiny or else is marked over by an equally ineluctable social world" (Rose 1986, 7). This picture does not allow, she argues, for the active role that women play in becoming women. The challenge for theorists is "how to reconcile the problem of subjectivity which assigns activity (but not guilt), fantasy (but not error), conflict (but not stupidity) to individual subjects—in this case women—with a form of analysis which can also recognise the force of structures in urgent need of social change" (1986, 14).

Thus, the challenges for a sociological account of women's gender socialization are to accommodate its incompleteness and to accommodate women's own participation in it. Although Catharine MacKinnon shares Jacqueline Rose's concerns, her characterization of the gender socialization of women does not meet these challenges. It can be contrasted with the account presented by Frigga Haug and her colleagues, who argue that women participate in their own gender socialization by actively acquiring skills they need to approximate ideals of femininity. Their gender socialization is incomplete because they are unable to meet these ideals fully; at most, they become masters of deception, using dress and behavior to conceal their innate lack of womanliness. This account does meet Jacqueline Rose's challenges.

I propose a revision of present notions of gender socialization that is supported by the work of Frigga Haug and her colleagues (hereafter, Frigga Haug), although she does not specifically articulate it. In my revision, women's gender socialization is not a process resulting in one's becoming a certain kind of person (a woman). Rather, to be socialized as a woman is to live in an ongoing state of affairs in which one is recognized as a woman and to whom, therefore, norms of femininity apply. To be a woman is constantly to have to cope with norms of femininity, to have to take them into account, to be judged in terms of them. If this picture is accurate, neither Richard Wasserstrom's nor Iris Young's views of sexist oppression and how to remedy it are adequate.

CATHARINE MACKINNON'S THEORY OF WOMEN'S GENDER SOCIALIZATION

Catharine MacKinnon acknowledges the ambivalent sense of self, apparent in women's experiences in our society, for which Jacqueline

Rose argues that an adequate theory of women's gender socialization must account. Catharine MacKinnon describes women as thoroughly feminine, meaning subordinate to men and lacking a sense of self. Yet, she also notes women's discontent and anger. She claims that women are forcibly limited to places in the social structure that men created for them and that they are coerced into submission to men by witnessing what happens to other women: "fathers who raped them; boyfriends who shot at them; doctors who aborted them when they weren't pregnant or sterilized them 'accidentally'; psychoanalysts who so-called seduced them, committing them to mental hospitals when they exposed them; mothers who committed suicide or lived to loathe themselves more when they failed; employers who fired them for withholding sexual favors or unemployment offices that refused benefits when they quit" (1989, 89). She argues, "Patterns of treatment that would create feelings of incapacity in anybody are seen to connect seamlessly with acts of overt discrimination to deprive women of tools and skills" (1989, 90).

Furthermore, she claims, women so internalize their subordination to men that they cannot perceive what has been done to them. Citing Rowbotham (1973, 43),Catharine MacKinnon argues that: "one form of the social existence of male power is inside women. In this form, male power becomes self-enforcing. Women become 'thingified in the head.' Once incarnated, male superiority tends to be reaffirmed and reinforced in what can be seen as well as in what can be done. . . . Given the imperatives of women's lives, the necessity to avoid punishment—from self-rejection to involuntary incarceration to suicide—it is not irrational for women to see themselves in a way that makes their necessary compliance tolerable, even satisfying" (1989, 99–100). Thus, through violence perpetrated against them and in order to avoid punishment and tolerate living within the system, women, it seems, become thoroughly feminine. They embrace subordination, their place, what it means to be a woman. "Women are systematically deprived of a self and . . . that process constitutes socialization to femininity" (1989, 100).

Catharine MacKinnon also notes "women's feelings of discontent," however (1989, 100). Arguing that the submissive qualities attributed to women's "natures" are actually the result of socialization geared to produce those qualities, she argues that that socialization is incomplete: "When one gets to know women close up and without men present, it is remarkable the extent to which their so-called biology, not to mention their socialization, has failed. . . . Women become angry as they see women's lives as one avenue after another foreclosed by gender" (1989, 91).

Catharine MacKinnon is making a dual claim. On one hand, she argues that the feminization of women is so complete that they embrace the social structure and their subordinate position within it to the extent that they are unable to perceive what is being done to them. On the other hand, she points to women's discontent, lack of conformity to standards of femininity, and their anger at what has been done to them. This apparent inconsistency raises again the question that leads Jacqueline Rose to embrace psychoanalytic theory over sociological accounts of gender socialization: how can women be so thoroughly feminized and yet perceive and resist their continued subordination?

Catharine MacKinnon's answer is that this is the wrong question. To wonder how women can be both fully feminized and also able to perceive and resist their subordination presupposes two assumptions, which she identifies as patriarchal. The first is that genuine knowledge must be objective. The second is that socialization from which one can at least partially escape is not oppressive. She claims that to ask how women can be both fully feminized and perceive their subordination is to suggest that if women can perceive their subordination, they must be able to adopt an objective standpoint, outside their subjective experience of feminization, and thus not be fully feminized. She worries that finding women's perception of their own subordination as indicative that they are not fully feminized will lead to the conclusion that women are not really oppressed (1989, 96–105, 114–17).

I do not disagree with Catharine MacKinnon's response to the question as she understands it. Her description of women's feminization and resistance to it reflects a real duality in the world and does not impugn feminism. I object, however, to her understanding of the substance of the question. There is a different interpretation, pertinent and appropriate to feminism.

I take the question to be about the nature of women's gender socialization and how it relates to feminization. Catharine MacKinnon has identified a duality crucial to understanding what it means to be a woman. On one hand, as she observes, the social structure is such that there is a "slot" for women. Anything a woman does is interpreted by reference to the slot into which she fits (that is, by reference to her being a woman): "Socially, femaleness means femininity, which means attractiveness to men, which means sexual attractiveness, which means sexual availability on male terms. What defines woman as such is what turns men on, and everything any kind of woman is, does. Virtuous girls, virginal, are 'attractive,' up on those pedestals from which they must be brought down; unvirtuous girls, whores, are 'provocative,' so deserve whatever they get" (1989, 110). On the other hand, as she also observes, most women do not conform to the standards of femininity that circulate as social norms. It would seem, therefore, that although all women fit into the slot reserved for women, this "fitting" does not require conformity to norms of femininity.

Catharine MacKinnon's own theory of femininity cannot accommodate this important observation. She argues that one comes to be a woman "not so much through physical maturation or inculcation into appropriate role behavior as through the experience of sexuality: a complex unity of physicality, emotionality, identity, and status affirmation, in which sexual intercourse is central" (1989, 111). Neither being physically a woman nor "being ladylike" is definitive of "being a woman." Rather, to be a woman is to experience sexuality as constructed for women: to be the subordinate participant in sexual encounters, the one who attracts, who caters to the other's needs: "So many distinctive features of women's status as second class—the restriction and constraint and contortion, the servility and the display, the self-mutilation and requisite presentation of self as a beautiful thing, the enforced passivity, the humiliation—are made into the content of sex for women. Being a thing for sexual use is fundamental to it" (1989, 130).

She seems to suggest that to the extent that women achieve being a thing for sexual use—to the extent that they mutilate themselves, display themselves—they are women, that self-mutilation and display are what make a woman a woman in the definitive sense: "I think that sexual desire in women, at least in this culture, is socially constructed as that by which we come to want our own self-annihilation. That is, our subordination is eroticized in and as female; in fact, we get off on it to a degree, if nowhere as much as men do. This is our stake in this system that is not in our interest, our stake in this system that is killing us. I'm saying femininity as we know it is how we come to want male dominance, which most emphatically is not in our interest" (1987, 54). In this picture, the more women mutilate themselves, the more they constrain and display themselves, the more they succeed at being women.

Let us return to the duality that Catharine MacKinnon notes. On one hand, women fit into their slot in the social structure. On the other hand, they conform imperfectly to standards of femininity. On her view of women's gender socialization, however, mutilation and display are what it means to be a woman, and norms of femininity also dictate mutilation and display. Thus, the slot set aside for women is the slot for people who mutilate and display themselves, and conforming to standards of femininity means conforming to standards of mutilation and display. Thus, to fit into the slot is also to conform to standards of femininity. To be socialized as a woman is identical to being feminized. But this socialization does not allow for the duality, for women resisting feminization. On this account, the more women fail or refuse to conform to standards of femininity, the less they count as women. A lesbian who refuses to conform in any way to standards of femininity would not count as a woman at all.[3] This position is controversial, however. Lesbians in our society are commonly perceived as alarming and revolting (both senses) women. Nonetheless, most people do count lesbians as women, which is why lesbians experience censure for not being feminine enough and not being readily available for men's sexual use. If lesbians were not taken to be women, they would not be punished for being unwomanly.

The problem is easily resolved if we adopt an essentialist understanding that defines gender in terms of genitalia. Then lesbians are women, regardless of whether they are feminized, just because they have female reproductive organs. If we maintain a commitment to gender nonessentialism, however, we need a social constructivist understanding that allows even unfeminine or incompletely feminine females to count as women. We need an account that maintains a distinction between being a woman and being feminized.

FRIGGA HAUG'S *FEMALE SEXUALIZATION*

Frigga Haug offers an explanation of feminization that shows how females can count as women even though they fail to conform fully to norms of femininity. Her proposal also meets Jacqueline Rose's challenge of accounting for women's active participation in their own gender socialization. According to Frigga Haug, women do not become feminized by succeeding in meeting standards of femininity. Rather, they become socialized as women through expending effort to meet these standards, most often through mastery of skills of artifice that allow them to hide their innate lack of femininity.

Frigga Haug uses the analogy of the slave girl (as in the "Tales of the 1,001 Nights") to illustrate this notion of feminization. A passive slave girl with no accomplishments and no initiative would not beguile her master. The one who delights her master has developed arts to charm him, knows how to make the most of her beauty and disguise flaws, understands and skillfully caters to his desires. Despite the odious context, these accomplishments are nonetheless accomplishments and result in a sense of self-confidence and satisfaction as does the acquisition of any skill: "An ability to handle given rules with proficiency and the security that the sense of their general acceptability affords—for example in the games we play with our men, or for the attentions of men in general—give power and strength to individual women. The subjective feelings of happiness and satisfaction accompanying our manipulation of systems of rules are thus more than an illusion, a product of the 'imagination' of individual women; they are a practice through which both sexual ordering, and the oppression within it, are reproduced" (1992, 144–45).

According to Frigga Haug, one's obsession with the norms grows in relation to one's failure to meet standards of femininity effortlessly. She describes a process wherein women are surrounded by standards that insinuate themselves into their judgments, but in which a woman becomes fully aware of a particular standard only at the moment when she perceives herself as not meeting it (1992, 117–19). Women's feminization, on this account, is the obsession with meeting feminine standards through artifice, since they rarely can be met without it. This account rests on the claim that most standards of femininity require artifice. Feminine gait and posture are learned rather than representing how anyone naturally moves. Eating in certain ways, dressing in certain ways (corsets, push-up bras, and so on), and sometimes exercise are required to present a feminine figure, whether more or less corpulent, as standards change. Hair requires attention even when styles are "natural" (one must "fix" one's hair to appear "natural"). Meeting standards of femininity requires effort. A woman might conceivably meet those standards without effort, but that is unlikely. For most, being feminine is the experience of expending attention, time, energy, and money in attempting to meet standards of femininity.

If this is what feminization is and how it occurs, then the implications of feminization are quite different from those of Catharine MacKinnon's picture. Femininity becomes women's responsibility, a reflection on women's character. In Catharine MacKinnon's account, to be feminized is to have had something done to you. In Frigga Haug's account, because women are supposed to come by femininity naturally (although none do), the necessary behaviors become a responsibility. Something has been done to women in that this responsibility has been foisted upon them, with negative consequences if they do not live up to it. The point that Frigga Haug emphasizes, however, is that women are active participants in, not just passive recipients of, their feminization. On her view, women buy into the program of feminization, because to do otherwise would be to shirk their responsibility, to present to the world their weak characters (1992, 127–28). Femininity becomes an issue of self-respect in an odd way: women do things that are not self-respecting in the sense of taking care of themselves and liking themselves for who they really are in order to maintain their self-respect in the sense of rising to a challenge, not making excuses, and overcoming perceived failings through willpower. On this account, women do not participate in their feminization only to avoid censure; rather, they experience positive feelings about themselves for doing so.

BEING A WOMAN VERSUS BEING FEMININE

Frigga Haug's account of feminization opens the way for an even more radical redefinition of women's gender socialization than the one that it explicitly offers, a more radical redefinition that distinguishes between being a woman and being feminized. I propose that what it means to be a woman is to be someone to whom norms of femininity are applied just because she is identified as female. Feminization is not a process as the result of which a person becomes a woman. Rather, to be a woman is to be entangled by and to constantly have

to deal with and think in terms of norms of femininity. To be socialized as a woman is to know that these norms are applied to you, that
you are judged in terms of them, that every action you make is given
meaning by them.

This view, if correct, complicates the possibility of resistance to
sexist oppression. Women cannot escape from the pressures exerted
by norms of femininity simply by choosing to be unfeminine. Resisting norms involves acknowledging them as much as does attempting to conform to them. For example, Frigga Haug argues, women
choose to purchase and wear particular clothes to appropriate for
themselves attributes associated by norms with particular "types"
of women: mother, sex symbol, chaste maiden, and so on (1992, 15).
Women who are trying to resist femininity, however, also choose
their clothing in response to norms, purposely choosing the opposite
of what is advertised as feminine. Understanding clothing *as* unfeminine—androgynous, sloppy, "functional"—depends on the same
norms that give "sexy" clothing its meaning and message. Frigga
Haug alludes to this phenomenon, arguing: "Once trapped in a network of prevailing standards, we see no way out. A simple reversal—
'it's fun to be fat,' or whatever—merely reinforces the validity of the
negative evaluation of fatness in the very act of affirming it. Change
cannot be a matter of simple opposition to certain limited standards,
nor of living against and in spite of them" (1992, 130).

Of course, there are other reasons to make unfeminine choices.
Unfeminine clothing may be chosen because it is more comfortable
or practical. But there are costs associated with such a choice, because others perceive it as resistance to femininity, even if that was
not the intent. Women experience censure (frequently severe—being
fired, beaten, raped) for appearing to resist femininity, and they experience censure as much from other women as from men. Furthermore, women who resist or appear to resist norms of femininity are
held up as examples of why it is so important to conform to these
norms: "You don't want to look like that—*she*'ll never get a date."
Their acts of nonconformity are used by others to reinforce feminine
norms. Finally, if, as Frigga Haug argues, being feminized is the experience of expending attention, time, energy, and money in the project of attempting to live up to standards of femininity, being an un-
feminized woman may require similar expenditures in the service of
resisting norms of femininity or dealing with the consequences of

being unfeminine. What it means to be a woman, feminized or not, is always to be coping with norms of femininity.

ASSIMILATIONISM, CULTURAL PLURALISM, AND GENDER

Let us now consider the implications of this conclusion for assimilationism and cultural pluralism. Iris Young, advocating cultural pluralism, argues that for groups that have found themselves objectified and marked with a devalued essence "the assertion of a positive sense of group difference . . . is emancipatory because it reclaims the definition of the group by the group, as a creation and construction, rather than a given essence" (1990, 172). She describes her vision of the good society as an idealized "city life," a "vision of social relations affirming group difference. . . . Different groups dwell in the city alongside one another, of necessity interacting in city spaces. If city politics is to be democratic and not dominated by the point of view of one group, it must be a politics that takes account of and provides voice for the different groups that dwell together in the city without forming a community" (1990, 227). Her vision is based on a politics of "democratic cultural pluralism" (which she sometimes calls "radical democratic pluralism"). She states that "in this vision the good society does not eliminate or transcend group difference. Rather, there is equality among socially and culturally differentiated groups, who mutually respect one another and affirm one another in their differences" (1990, 163).

How do these proposals and visions play out for women? If women's gender socialization (therefore, sexist oppression) is entanglement with norms of femininty, then Iris Young's notion of affirming a women's culture must work in either of two ways to adequately address the problem of sexist oppression. I refer to these as the "strong sense" and the "weak sense."

In the strong sense, affirming a women's culture would require development of women's norms that completely reject sexual and nurturing subservience to men (although Iris Young, in fact, appears not to advocate feminist separatism). If being a woman means experiencing constant pressure from norms that demand sexual and nurturing subservience to men, and if trying consciously to resist those norms consumes as much energy and acknowledges the existence of those norms as much as conforming to them does, then affirming a women's culture in a way that would actually help remedy the problem would require separation. Women would have to separate themselves from men in fundamental ways and demand respect for their lifestyle from men, but not cultivate men's attraction or even expect their approval.

Such a society would be unstable, however. If no women were sexually available to men, men would, presumably, look to each other for sexual satisfaction. So we would have "female families" and "male families." Suppose the mechanical logistics of reproduction were worked out. There might be negotiations between the male group and the female group regarding sperm, gestational services, and so forth. Sex selection would assure the gender of each child, so that men could contract with women to produce male children who, presumably, would be raised by men, whereas women would acquire X-chromosome sperm from men in order to have female children for themselves. Sex selection and segregation would be necessary, because if children of both sexes were raised by women, women's culture would be transmitted to both. We would then have a generation of "genderless" children. But this "genderlessness" would bring about the transcendence of gender that Richard Wasserstrom describes and to which Iris Young's position is supposedly in opposition. In fact, if being a woman means being someone to whom norms of femininity apply, this culture could not even be properly called a "women's" culture, because there would be no more women (or men), only adult females (and males) of the human species.

However, even if male children were raised by men, and female children were raised by women, the society would still be unstable. One of two things would happen. One possibility is that men would nurture their (male) children. This scenario would require men to perform work currently identified as women's, which would undermine many of the masculine norms that now complement oppressive feminine norms (norms encouraging certain sorts of aggressiveness, depicting caring for others as weakness, and so forth). So men would end up appreciating what are now taken to be women's perspectives and needs. Again, we would be on our way to transcending gender norms, to the genderless society Richard Wasserstrom describes.

Another possibility is that some men would become the nurturers and come to have the subservient role to other men that women now have. Given that people of color and poor people of both genders have shouldered the responsibilities of caretaking and maintenance in our society, it would not be surprising if in the end the "newly subservient" in this case were men already subordinated on the basis of race or class or both. In any case, we would have a new group of oppressed people (or of the already-oppressed being oppressed in a new way), who eventually would either break off on their own (affirm their own difference) or join the women whose perspective they would have come to share. Again, over time, we would move toward a genderless society, as more and more men, in effect, become "women" (feminized). Thus, affirming a women's culture in the strong sense simply would not lead to a stable society with continuing differences between genders. It would evolve instead into a society that had transcended gender.

But Iris Young's proposal also can be understood in a weaker sense. Rather than proposing a fundamental separation of women and men, it could be seen as proposing that the needs and perspectives of women that relate to such aspects of our lives as motherhood, our roles as nurturers, our tendency to be less aggressive and more cooperative, and so forth, should be respected by men. The idea is that the world should accommodate rather than punish people having these needs and these perspectives, that men should respect values that women often have.

One complication of affirming a women's culture in this sense is that the intersection of gender with racial, ethnic, class, and other social identities creates many different understandings of "women's" values, which are unlikely to be reconcilable. Furthermore, this view also leads to the transcendence of gender. Whichever attributes or behaviors come to be perceived as valuable and respected—truly valued and respected, not in the "woman on a pedestal" sense but in the way that men in our society value and respect certain attributes and behaviors in each other—would then come to be valued in men, too. If workplace policy should support parents, it should support parents of any gender. If raising a child is seen as the most important job in the world, men will be expected to do it too and will want to. If women are not pressured to be sexual objects for men, to dress and behave in certain ways in order to attract them, then sexual relations will lose much of their emphasis on gender. Indeed, in her suggestions for workplace policy regarding pregnancy and parenting, Iris Young suggests that policies that would accommodate women as parents should also be extended to fathers. This recommendation moves toward transcending gender rather than asserting continuing gender differences.

Iris Young's proposal, examined carefully and in light of a more complete understanding of the role of gender-specific social norms in sexist oppression, evolves into Richard Wasserstrom's proposal. His proposal, however, also comes up short. The problem with his vision of the genderless society is that it is not a useful model for us. If we base present policy on what policy would be like in such a world, we will in some cases actually contribute to rather than reduce gender oppression. For example, in his society gender would never be considered a factor in a hiring decision, because people would not think in terms of gender. But there also would not be significantly differential representation of women and men in any area of work, because women and men would not be socialized to think of work as feminine or masculine; girls would not be sent the message that they are less capable in mathematics, nor would boys be teased if they wanted to be nurses. If in a society like ours, however, we ignore gender as a factor in hiring, in a misguided effort to emulate Richard Wasserstrom's society, we perpetuate the differential representation of women and men in certain fields and reinforce the social norms that cause that differentiation. As Richard Wasserstrom acknowledges, we need to treat women and men differently by, for example, granting preferential treatment in hiring to women in male-dominated fields, in order to mitigate the effects of present social norms.

Furthermore, in cases where we need to devise policies to address present discrimination against women, Richard Wasserstrom's vision supplies us with no information. For example, Iris Young discusses funding for collegiate sports and suggests that rather than funding on a per athlete basis, which results in lesser funding for women's sports (because there are fewer participants), men's and women's program be equally funded regardless of numbers of participants (except where disparities in numbers are particularly large), facilities be equally good, coaches equally well paid, and so on. Richard Wasserstrom's vision adds nothing to consider in regard to this question because sports would be very different in his world. There would, presumably, be no separate men's and women's teams because the gender distinction would not be made. There would be no masculine or feminine sports in the way that football is considered masculine and field hockey feminine. His vision is useless as a model. We have to deal more directly and specifically with the effects in our world of particular gender-specific social norms.

If we examine policy disputes between advocates of gender-sensitive policies and advocates of gender-neutral policies, we see that the policy situations in question involve gender-specific social norms. In the workplace, issues about policy responses to pregnancy and breast-feeding involve social norms about how women should (not) combine motherhood and other work. The question about whether women-only learning environments constitute inappropriate or necessary segregation involves social norms about girls' or young women's behavior in front of male peers (is classroom assertiveness appropriate? is it attractive to men to demonstrate your intelligence?). It involves the question of whether girls are "supposed to be" so disinterested in math and science that they forgo opportunities to learn because they feel the need to feign disinterest, or, alternatively, whether teachers simply perceive them as less interested or less capable at these subjects in ways that influence how those teachers address, encourage or discourage, and evaluate girls in these subjects. The idea that certain uses of free speech such as pornography may silence women brings up norms about women and sexuality and what it means for women to be sex objects.

In each of these cases, gender-specific social norms for women may result in physical, psychological, or developmental harm to women. Unless women are protected and supported in certain ways, these norms may pressure them to make choices that reinforce and perpetuate the norms. The Frigga Haug material suggests that women who resist norms, even if they belong to resisting groups, often expend as much energy and acknowledge the strength of the norms as much as women who work to conform to them. Resisting oppressive gender-specific norms cannot be done effectively on a personal level. It has to be done on a public, policy, and institutional level. We need policies that protect women from immediate repercussions of existing gender-specific social norms. On this point Iris Young and Richard Wasserstrom would agree. But neither his model of a genderless society nor her notion of affirming a distinctive women's culture helps to further this project. I conclude that the assimilationism/cultural pluralism distinction is not helpful for ending sexist oppression.[4]

NOTES

1. Eye color, in fact, matters more than Wasserstrom thought it did. See Morrison (1972).

2. He extends this argument from the claim that such accommodations are appropriate for people with physical disabilities, such as those who use wheelchairs.

3. Some lesbian theorists (Wittig 1992; Hoagland 1988) insist that they are not women.

4. I am writing a book in which I argue that the assimilationism/cultural pluralism distinction is not helpful in addressing how to fight the racial oppression experienced by black people in the United States. My arguments in that case are substantially different from the ones presented here. I do not believe that the indefinite maintenance of separate but genuinely equal group identities and cultures is impossible in the case of race. Although it is helpful in some ways to examine what oppressions based on different social group identities have in common, as Iris Young does, it is also important not always to lump them together. Each case has unique features, unique histories, and unique problems that must be taken into account if our conclusions are to be relevant.

REFERENCES

Adams, Parveen, and Elizabeth Cowie, eds. 1990. *The Woman in Question: A Collective Work of Memory.* Cambridge, Mass.: MIT Press.

Haug, Frigga, ed. 1992. *Female Sexualization.* Trans. Erica Carter. London: Verso.

Hoagland, Sarah Lucia. 1988. *Lesbian Ethics: Toward New Value.* Palo Alto, Calif.: Institute of Lesbian Studies.

MacKinnon, Catharine. 1987. *Feminism Unmodified: Discourses on Life and Law.* Cambridge: Harvard University Press.

_____. 1989. *Toward a Feminist Theory of the State.* Cambridge: Harvard University Press.

Morrison, Toni. 1972. *The Bluest Eye.* New York: Washington Square.

Rose, Jacqueline. 1986. *Sexuality in the Field of Vision.* London: Verso.

Rowbotham, Sheila. 1973. *Woman's Consciousness, Man's World.* Harmondsworth: Penguin.

Wasserstrom, Richard. 1980. *Philosophy and Social Issues: Five Studies.* Notre Dame, Ind.: University of Notre Dame Press.

Wittig, Monique. 1992. *The Straight Mind and Other Essays.* Boston: Beacon.

Young, Iris Marion. 1990. *Justice and the Politics of Difference.* Princeton, N.J.: Princeton University Press.

Part Three
Violence and Harm

9 / *Philosophical Reflections on War Rape*

ROBIN MAY SCHOTT

The attempted genocide in Bosnia-Herzegovina has intensified the effort by politically and morally engaged thinkers to understand the existence of evil—the destruction of human beings by other human beings[1]—which has haunted European and American intellectual life since World War II. How is it possible for human beings to have the capacity not only of killing other people, but of experiencing this killing as nothing extraordinary? (Staub 1989, 6).

It has been documented that among the atrocities committed during the civil war in the former Yugoslavia was war rape—rape committed against civilian women in their homes or in rape/death camps. These rapes have been committed with a political purpose, to ensure that women and their families will flee and never return,[2] and thus war rape has been an instrument of "ethnic cleansing." Men have also been raped and are thus arguably "feminized" by the enemy. Both parties to the conflict have used rape as a weapon of war, although according to Beverly Allen in her book *Rape Warfare: The Hidden Genocide in Bosnia-Herzegovina and Croatia,* the largest number of reported victims have been Bosnian Muslims.[3] She has described this form of rape as "genocidal rape," because it is a crime aimed at the systematic annihilation of another people and their culture by rape, death, and pregnancy (1996, 21). The violence of war rape is experienced through the degradation of a girl or woman and of those affected by her suffering. A fifty-four-year-old woman who was raped in her home in the municipality of Kljuc said afterward, "They denigrated me, which will bear hard upon my body and soul as long as I live" (Allen 1996, 178). Survivors of war rape suffer from multiple trauma: genital trauma, psychological trauma, physical trauma from severe burns, amputations, infected incisions, and the damage done to their throats because of repeatedly having been forced to swallow vast amounts of urine and sperm (Allen 1996, 74).

The violence of war rape is also enacted through the possibility of pregnancy, a key point in Allen's claim that these war rapes should be viewed as genocidal. A thirty-nine-year-old Croatian woman from the town of Prijedor, who was raped by a reserve captain of the "Serbian Army," was told that "I needed to give birth to a Serb—that I would then be different" (Helsinki Watch 1993, 164). Women are often convinced that the offspring they bear as a result of war rape are also the enemy, leading many survivers to attempt third-trimester abortions, commit suicide, or remove themselves from any contact with the infant after birth (Allen 1996, 99). A team of experts who visited six major medical centers in the former Yugoslavia in January 1993 on behalf of the U.N. Human Rights Commission concluded that "it is not possible to know precisely the actual number of rapes or the number of pregnancies due to rape that have occurred." Nevertheless, the team believed that "the incidence of rape in the conflict . . . has been widespread" (Allen 1996, 22). In the view of Helsinki Watch, the forcible impregnation of women constitutes an abuse separate from the rape and should be denounced as such (1993, 22). It is also noted that the failure to punish rapists is as widespread as the act of rape itself.

Documenting the sexual abuse, including rape, is difficult because of women's reluctance to report rape as a result of fear of retribution both to themselves and their families and of shame, lack of trust, and fear of awakening bad memories (Helsinki Watch 1993, 23; Allen 1996, 94). "What happened to me, happened to many, but the women keep it secret. It is shameful. Thus, the mother conceals it if it happened to her daughter so she can marry and if it happened to an older woman, she wants to protect her marriage. It is a huge embarrassment, you know" (Helsinki Watch 1993, 178). It is an additional emotional hardship to subject women to interviews about rapes, and there have been reports of attempted suicide by women after they have been interviewed by the media and delegations (Allen 1996, 95).

Rape and sexual abuse constitute not only violations of international human rights standards and humanitarian law but also can be a constituent crime against humanity (as that term was defined in the Nuremberg trial and in Article 6[c] of the Nuremberg Charter) if it is part of a mass pattern of such crimes (Helsinki Watch 1993, 20).

THE ROLE OF PHILOSOPHICAL REFLECTION

Although there is a long tradition in philosophy that reflects on the nature of good and evil, there is a much smaller range of philosophers who reflect on particular phenomena of good and evil. Hannah Arendt is a notable exception in her studies *The Origins of Totalitarianism* and *Eichmann in Jerusalem: A Report on the Banality of Evil.*[4] An even narrower range of philosophers have taken up the question of evil in the form of sexual violence. Feminist philosophers are beginning to demarcate a path here, notably Claudia Card in her essays "Rape Terrorism" and "Rape As a Weapon of War."[5]

For a feminist philosopher and "bystander" to war rapes, one of the most compelling questions in the present age is how to understand the evil enacted by war rape and in what ways understanding such violence might contribute to its reduction. Is the task of the engaged bystander to give words to pain, as Elaine Scarry proposes, "to communicate the reality of physical pain to those who are not themselves in pain"?[6] Can the "verbal representation of pain" contribute to its political representation and hence social recognition as a problem? (Scarry 1985, 12).

Or is the task, as Julia Kristeva proposes, one of self-knowledge, of recognition that the existence of abjection—of that which is beyond the thinkable and the tolerable—is at the same time that which constitutes the I? The horror of Nazi crime that one feels, for example, in seeing the heap of children's shoes and dolls in the museum of Auschwitz is a horror based on a recognition of a threat to one's living universe. But this threat does not come from outside identity, system, or order; it comes from the frailty of such systems, from the "want on which any being, meaning, language, or desire is founded."[7] Kristeva describes abjection as an ambiguity that does not radically cut off the subject from what threatens it—on the contrary, abjection acknowledges it (the subject) to be in perpetual danger (1982, 9). On this view, only through individual and cultural self-awareness is it possible to soften the boundaries between the subject, placed within the symbolic order, and that which is viewed as threatening to this order.

Or, alternatively, the task of the engaged bystander might be to reflect on the conditions of judgment, the possibility of distinguishing between good and evil when one is surrounded by moral and political breakdown, as Hannah Arendt proposes in her *Lectures on Kant's*

Political Philosophy.[8] On this view, the role of imagination is crucial in enabling the possibility of (an imagined) dialogue between self and others that can contribute to an enlarged mentality.

In what follows I consider three different strategies, not all proposed by philosophers, for interpreting the phenomena of evil. Although none of these strategies addresses the violence of war rape in particular, it is fruitful to consider that application.

First, the structuralist anthropologist Mary Douglas, in *Purity and Danger,* offers a groundbreaking analysis of purity and pollution that can be applied to interpreting cultural perceptions of evil.[9] Although Douglas does not use the term evil, Kristeva adopts her analysis of pollution to explain the cultural identification of women with radical evil. Both Douglas's and Kristeva's accounts are particularly useful for their focus on the symbolics of the body.

Second, the psychological analysis offered by Ervin Staub in *The Roots of Evil* probes the practice of evil in terms of a continuum of destruction (1989, 6). The radical evil of destroying other human beings through torture or systematic annihilation becomes possible because individuals have acclimated themselves first to committing lesser forms of evil. Bystanders have a crucial role to play in either acquiescing to or protesting against acts of destruction.

Finally, Hannah Arendt's analysis of evil focuses on the failure of judgment. The closing sentence of *Eichmann in Jerusalem* introduces the infamous phrase the "banality of evil," which is meant to focus on the thoughtlessness out of which evil can occur (Arendt 1958, 252). In the face of the collapse of moral standards in civil society, such as occurred in Germany during Hitler's regime, the only defense against evil can be found in individual imagination and judgment. In her later work Arendt offers an interpretation of Kant's political philosophy via a reading of his *Critique of Judgment,* which focuses attention on the judging spectator rather than the deeds of the actor.[10]

None of the above three analyses focuses on the problem of evil as it is manifested in war rape. Nonetheless, they can be useful interpretive tools in answering the following questions: Why does political violence take the form of sexual violence? How does a situation move from "normality" to massive war rape, where young women are raped by their former high school teachers, and female medical workers are raped by doctors who were formerly their colleagues (Helsinki Watch 1993, 217)? What role do bystanders play in accelerating or diminishing violence? Does sexual violence pose a special challenge to philosophical thinking, requiring a theory that explicitly thematizes the body? Does the existence of war rape place the demand of changing the cultural symbolics of the body?

POLLUTION AND MORAL EVIL

Many of the examples of war rape cited in the Helsinki Watch report refer to violations of taboos—neighbors rape the women next door, and young men rape women old enough to be their mothers. One fifty-four-year-old women reported that she pleaded with the Serbian soldiers who were raping her on the cold concrete floor: "Children, don't. I could be your mother" (Helsinki Watch 1993, 174).

In the face of this trespassing of prohibitions that constituted the order of daily life in the former Yugoslavia, one is tempted to seek an explanation of war rape in terms of prohibitions and their violations. From this perspective, the analysis offered by the structuralist anthropologist Mary Douglas in *Purity and Danger* seems compelling. Douglas's work takes as her central focus questions not of moral evil but of systems of purity and pollution. Pollution, including our ordinary sense of revulsion at dirt where it doesn't belong— at the dirt in somebody else's bathroom that is visible certainly to the visitor's eyes, at the menstrual blood that stains the guest sheet one is using in a friend's house, at the vomit on the bedroom floor where one's son has just gotten sick, at the pus instead of dewy tears streaming from someone's eyes—points to disorder, to matter out of place (Douglas 1966, 2). Beliefs about punishing transgressions and purifying serve to impose a unified system on an inherently untidy experience (Douglas 1966, 4). Dirt, or pollution, is never an isolated event but is an effect of a systematic classification of matter (Douglas 1966, 35). Avoiding anomalous forms serves to reinforce approved patterns (Douglas 1966, 39).

Douglas not only takes up the analysis of the relation between outside / inside—that which is outside the border of a system is itself necessary for the maintenance of a given symbolic order—but she explicitly addresses the question of bodily pollution and of the symbolics of the body. She notes that "the body is a model which can stand for any bounded system. Its boundaries can represent any boundaries which are threatened or precarious. The body is a complex structure. The functions of its different parts and their relation afford a source of symbols for other complex structures. We cannot possibly interpret rituals concerning excreta, breast milk, saliva and the rest unless we are prepared to see in the body a symbol of society, and to see the powers and dangers credited to social structure reproduced in small on the human body" (1966, 115).

On her view, sexual pollution, by which each sex endangers the other through contact with sexual fluids, does not express actual relations between the sexes but mirrors designs of hierarchy or symmetry in the larger social system (1966, 3–4). She notes that pollution fears cluster only around contradictory norms of sexual behavior (as with the case of the Enga, who fight enemy clansmen yet marry the enemy clanswomen) (1966, 157), because social pressures that constrain sexual relations are so potentially explosive.

Douglas's analysis is principally concerned with patterns of pollution and rituals of purity that protect or cleanse one from contact with pollution (for example, in adultery). Is an analysis of pollution and purity relevant to instances of war rape? One could speculate about the culturally induced psychological beliefs about sexual pollution that may be entwined with war rape. A raped woman most surely feels herself polluted by the enemy seed and perhaps seeks purification through abortion or severance of contact with an infant at birth and through the effort to forget. Perhaps men who rape are motivated by beliefs in women's sexual pollution, beliefs that originate with prohibitions and the incitement to transgress such prohibitions (for example, through pornography). The breakdown of social order that takes place during civil war, on this view, could result in a determination to transgress prior prohibitions. (Here we may find an echo of Freud's notion of the returned of the repressed: the stronger the repression, the stronger the rebellion against the taboos.)

But an analysis of war rape in terms of pollution and danger would not address the moral dimension: the knowing violation and destruction of human persons. Douglas views the relation between patterns of purity (or pollution) and moral codes as complex. Beliefs about pollution can be used to uphold moral codes, to marshall public opinion on the side of right when the moral code itself is not strong enough to accomplish this task. Alternatively, purification rituals can provide the ground for breaking with the moral code, to make possible surviving that which is not morally permissible (for example, the effectiveness of purification rituals could increase the incidence of adultery) (Douglas 1966, 133–38).

How could Douglas's analysis of the relation between moral codes and pollution beliefs contribute to understanding war rape? Implicit here is the suggestion that questions of moral good and evil can never be understood in isolation from the complex social structure of society. This complexity leads Douglas to describe society as "a complex set of Chinese boxes, each sub-system having little sub-systems of its own, and so on indefinitely" (1966, 138). Thus, to take up the question of the moral evil evidenced in war rape would require an analysis of how moral codes interact with pollution beliefs. How, for example, under "ordinary" social conditions do beliefs about pollution (for example, the danger of adultery) reinforce moral codes that teach that right inheres in monogamy and heterosexuality? Under what circumstances do beliefs about pollution and purity shift from being a buttress to existing moral codes to justifying a break with such moral codes? For example, if general social breakdown and chaos weaken moral codes, some men might believe that they can be exposed to certain sexual "dangers" with impunity (such as raping a woman old enough to be one's mother), especially if one is acting on the orders of a commanding officer.

Furthermore, if Douglas is right in suggesting that the powers and dangers attributed to the social structure at large are reproduced in small on the body, and that sexual danger expresses relations of symmetry or hierarchy between parts of a society, one may also have a clue to why the violent breakdown of a social order is mirrored in the violent transgression of sexual relations. If, on this structuralist hypothesis, the body is represented as mirroring the social system, then the danger attributed to one member of the social system (for example, one ethnic group) that appears to threaten this system may be reflected by threatening human bodies through torture, mutilation, and killing. If sexual danger represents relations of asymmetry between different members of the body politic (such as hierarchies between ethnic groups, between urban and rural populations), then a violent upheaval against these relations in the social system may explode into a violation of prohibitions concerning sexual danger. Hence, the sexual violence of war rape may spiral into genocidal rape, the attempt to annihilate one member of the body politic. If sexual relations are a symbol for social conflicts, then these conflicts will never be resolved by the physical violence done to women in war rape but will relentlessly continue on the path of destruction until other factors intervene (such as moral protest or punitive measures by other members of the society).

Why are sexual relations so vulnerable to being used to represent the maintenance or breakdown of social systems? In part to answer this question, Julia Kristeva, in *Powers of Horror*, modifies Douglas's analysis of pollution. Kristeva takes issue with Douglas's assumption that the symbolic system is transparent to itself through its representation of the human body. Such an analysis cannot account for the subjective dynamics or variations or the significance of linguistic structures for the "symbolic order." Therefore, Kristeva's focus on language and subjectivity highlights the "different subjective structures (that) are possible within the symbolic order" (1982, 67). She focuses on how a particular symbolic organization affects and benefits the subject and on the desiring motives that are required to maintain a given social symbolics (1982, 67).

Not only does Kristeva shift the conception of the symbolic system to a linguistic understanding of system, but she also identifies the concept of pollution or defilement with evil: "Let us posit that defilement is an objective evil undergone by the subject" (1982, 69). Here Kristeva collapses the distinction between morality and pollution beliefs that Douglas distinguishes with such care. Possibly the discussion of the interdynamics between morality and pollution draws one into sociohistorical variables that are not relevant for Kristeva, since her own analysis of symbolic systems is based on structural features of language. Additionally, this shift to the notion of evil is no doubt motivated by Kristeva's emphasis on the subjective dimension. Pollution undergone by the subject is evil, since that which is excluded from the system/subject at the same time founds this subject. "If it be true that the abject simultaneously beseeches and pulverizes the subject, one can understand that it is experienced at the peak of its strength when that subject . . . finds the impossible within; when it finds that the impossible constitutes its very *being*, that it *is* none other than abject" (Kristeva 1982, 5).

Kristeva also significantly modifies Douglas's treatment of the body as representative of the symbolic system. Her starting point is the social and symbolic importance of women, particularly the mother. The ritualization of defilement is accompanied by a view of the feminine as synonomous with a radical evil to be suppressed (Kristeva 1982, 70). Therefore, Kristeva's treatment of the body is informed by the primary status she sees accorded women and mothers as symbols of evil. Instead of focusing, as Douglas does, on boundaries of the body in any of its aspects ("excreta, breast milk, saliva and the rest" [Kristeva 1982, 115]), she proposes only two fundamental types of polluting objects: excremental and menstrual (1982, 71). Excrements stand for danger to identity from without; menstrual blood stands for danger from within. Both pollutions, she argues, stem from the maternal. Ultimately both language and culture maintain an order among their discrete elements "by repressing maternal authority and the corporeal mapping that abuts against them" (Kristeva 1982, 72).

But how could Kristeva's analysis of abjection, which reworks Douglas's analysis of pollution, contribute to understanding war rape? Kristeva's project of redefining the concept of symbolic system would mean that in order to analyze social conflicts, it is necessary to recognize how social symbolics reverberate with the symbolic dimension of language. That is, to interpret the sexual violence of war rape in Bosnia-Herzegovina would demand an inquiry into the discourses of ethnicity and nationality in the former Yugoslavia. (And if symbolic systems are based on defining certain identities as ambiguous, marginal, and dangerous, one could speculate that in multicultural societies there are competing, conflicting symbolics.)

Moreover, Kristeva's analysis points to the possibility of subjective variations; thus her theory can take into account the fact that individuals respond differently amidst the proliferation of violence (for example, some officers protected women against rape, and others urged soldiers onto further gruesome acts). Her focus on the primacy of the mother (based on a psychoanalytical account) in the symbolics of the body may be used to explain why the breakdown of a system of social relations takes the form of sexual violence. Genocidal rape aims at the destruction of maternal authority both practically and symbolically (through the killing of women after they are raped or the impregnation of women by the enemy, thereby endangering the possibility of reproduction of particular ethnic groups).

In other words, both Douglas's and Kristeva's analyses make at least one crucial contribution to the understanding of war rape: they focus on the symbolizing of the body, and the symbolizing of sexual relations, as primary for understanding a cultural order. The particular challenge posed to ethics by sexual violence is to understand the corporality of evil in its specific sexual manifestations. Kristeva's intervention in the analysis of abjection, moreover, shifts the emphasis from structural relations (Douglas's "Chinese boxes") to subjective effects. Through her psychoanalytic approach she raises the question of desire (what desires are necessary to maintain particular social symbolics) and of subjective variation. In other words, she might argue that an analysis of war rape must focus both on the symbolic systems and the variable subjective effects through the tools of psychoanalysis. Finally, her placing the mother as the primary figure of abjection and evil is one possible answer to the question of why social violence is expressed in the particularly cruel forms of war rape. But neither Douglas nor Kristeva offers tools to answer this question: Why does the eruption of violent acts take place? Whether war rape is understood as an expression of a breakdown of a moral code or as a revelation of the truth of this code, it nonetheless signifies a radical change in social acts. What is the nature of threats that come from inside or outside the system? At what point do such threats bring about violent eruptions? How can subjective responses (from those within or outside the system, e.g., bystanders) resist such eruptions?

LEARNING EVIL BY DOING

In order to understand the process whereby relatively ordinary people can become directly or indirectly responsible for awful human destruction (as in the case of Eichmann), some psychologists have focused on processes whereby individuals, as members of a group, progress along a continuum of destruction (Staub 1989, 17). Ervin Staub writes: "Evil that arises out of ordinary thinking and is committed by ordinary people is the norm, not the exception. . . . Great evil arises out of ordinary psychological processes that evolve, usually with a progression along the continuum of destruction" (1989, 126). By the concept of continuum, Staub underlines his theory about the practical element of morality—people learn by doing—either by acts of good or acts of evil. Small acts of helping a child on the street, a friend, or their relatives can lead a bystander to become a rescuer. (And this continuum characterizes not only individual "rescuers" but groups, as in the famous example of the efforts of the people of Le Chambon to save thousands of Jews.)[11] By a similar process, people become capable of committing great acts of evil by first committing smaller acts of evil. When one begins to harm others, it becomes difficult to shift course in part because one's images of oneself and of others change through these acts. One minimizes suffering for those harmed and justifies their suffering by their evil nature or, as Eichmann claimed for himself, by higher ideals (Staub 1989, 82).

Staub proposes that there are psychological developments that occur along this continuum of destruction: compartmentalization, which enables individuals to act on goals that conflict with other important values, and the exclusion of moral values in order to maintain personal integration while allowing for destructive behavior. These processes are linked with two other psychological developments: a reversal of morality and a relinquishing of feelings of responsibility for the welfare of victims (Staub 1989, 83). As the destruction process continues, harming victims becomes accepted as "normal" behavior. Once the process of destruction begins, it is more diffficult to stop it (the "completion" tendency: the closer one is to achieving a goal, as in the carrying out of genocide, the harder it is to give it up). In addition to social and political factors (such as difficult life conditions), there are other cultural factors that contribute to the possibility of evil as evidenced in genocide: cultural values of obedience to authority, values of aggression, monolithic instead of pluralistic cultures, outward pressure to conform (for example, to totalitarian systems) that can diminish internal resistance.

Staub also underlines the crucial role of bystanders, either in passively participating with the commission of evil acts (as was typical of so many Germans, who saw such benefits of Hitler's rule as increased production, reduced unemployment, and moral and political unification of Germany [1989, 116]) or in active resistance. Where active resistance to Hitler's orders took place (for example, in Bulgaria and Denmark), the attempt to eradicate the Jewish population was much less successful.

Staub's inquiry into the roots of evil takes as its focal point the

Holocaust but also considers other examples of genocides and mass killings: for example, the Turkish genocide of the Armenians, the genocide in Cambodia, the mass killing in Argentina. By a curious omission, he does not consider war rape (even though he notes that when inhibitions against harming diminish, extraneous motives can enter: "greed, the enjoyment of power, the desire for sex or excitement" [1989, 84]). This is a regrettable omission, since there is documentation of systematic and widespread rape of Belgian, Jewish, Polish, and Soviet women by the Nazi army (as well as of German women by the Soviet army, Italian women by Moroccan mercenaries in the French Army, and Korean and Chinese women by Japanese soldiers during World War II).[12] Nonetheless, one can speculate about the usefulness of Staub's concept of a continuum of destruction in an analysis of war rape.

His theory that larger acts of evil grow from smaller acts of evil may be corroborated by reports that some soldiers raped women in Bosnia-Herzegovina because they were ordered to by officers and were promised houses as rewards, or because their own families were threatened. One act, such as taking (or desiring to take) the house that belongs to another family, could lead to more brutal acts. Moreover, the widespread incidence of gang rape in war rape in Bosnia-Herzegovina could be one means by which soldiers overcome their individual resistance through pressure to conform to group behavior that supports a perverted sexuality and a perverted nationalism (Arcel 1998, 199). Such external conformity may lead to internal transformations, which seek to integrate one's actions by excluding moral considerations from the justification of one's behavior. Moreover, since war rape was clearly a part of ethnic cleansing (contributing to the displacement of the civilian population in areas that were crucial for military aims [Arcel 1998, 195]), the ability of male soldiers, police officers, camp guards, teachers, and doctors to commit rape could be linked to the desire to complete the project of annihilating the "enemy." If there are no signs of resistance (for example, from other officers or soldiers), there is little to stop the process of destruction from accelerating.

What Staub's analysis of practical morality contributes is an attention to the process of evil acts—how people become capable of committing great evil. Whereas Douglas and Kristeva focused on symbolic systems (and with Kristeva, a focus on "subjective effects"), Staub focuses on processes, such as processes by which moral values become gradually degraded or excluded from an individual's self-concept. He does not, however, raise questions of sexual violence, even though it would be appropriate in the context of his analysis of the Holocaust and torture in Argentina. And he alludes to the "desire for sex" as an extraneous motive in the commission of harm. Such an analysis implies that rape, if it occurs, is an act of sexual desire instead of an act of violence, as it has been defined by feminists over the last two decades. In other words, Staub's discussion of evil does not face questions that are explicit in war rape: Why does destructive behavior take the form of sexual violence in which women's bodies and psyches are violated? As is clear in his own study, the omission of thematizing sexual violence, the violation of female bodies, may contribute to covering up the incidences of war rape. One of the pioneer researchers on psychological trauma connected to the Holocaust, the psychoanalyst Henry Krystal, admitted that he was an examiner of Holocaust survivors for three years without inquiring about rape, and no case was reported. When he began to inquire about rape, five women reported it in one year (Arcel 1998, 196).

Moreover, Staub remains committed to a fundamentally psychological analysis of evil. He writes of the Holocaust: "Especially in the last decade historians have offered increasingly complex analyses of economic and political forces that preceded the Holocaust and presumably contributed to it. . . . I believe, however, that the basic sources of genocide are cultural characteristics, difficult life conditions, and the needs and motives that arise from them. . . . Leaders who consciously manipulate the people to serve their political purposes are likely to share these needs" (1989, 32). Although he does not deny political purposes, he speaks of them as a means of channeling psychological needs. Such an approach would imply that the mass use of war rape for ethnic cleansing is rooted in psychological needs, such as the need to express anger and revenge for acts committed against Serbs in World War II, the need to express feelings of ethnic superiority and of rage against women (Arcel 1998, 196). In other words, the focus of Staub's analysis is on the motives of individuals and groups and their consequences. Such an analysis fails to address how these motives themselves are effects of political or military institutions or other symbolics systems.

THE BANALITY OF EVIL

Hannah Arendt is one of the few philosophers of this century who has seriously considered the problem of evil in the context of the political affairs of the world—for example, in her major study, *The Origins of Totalitarianism*, and in *Eichmann in Jerusalem*. Her book on Eichmann, as well as her *Lectures on Kant's Political Philosophy* (the final work before she died), focused on the problem of judgment. Faced with the need to arrive at a moral judgment of Eichmann, a historical judgment of the events contributing to the Final Solution, and with Eichmann's own evident failure of judgment, judgment seemed to her the crucial issue in the trial of the man who facilitated the mass destruction of the Jews.[13]

In her book on the Eichmann trial, Arendt sought the lesson of "this long course in human wickedness" and found it in the "fearsome, word-and-thought-defying *banality of evil*" (1958, 252). By this phrase she did not mean to minimize or trivialize evil, to treat it as an everyday affair of no import. Rather, her point was to show that the greatest wickedness in human history—beyond the scope of comprehension—could occur because of the failure of judgment among individuals responsible for these acts. When the legal order is no longer that of a civilized country, where law becomes the enactment of Hitler's command "Thou shalt kill" (Arendt 1958, 150), when there is no guidance but one's own judgment, then it is judgment to which we must turn to tell right from wrong: "Those few who were still able to tell right from wrong went really only by their own judgments, and they did so freely; there were no rules to be abided by, under which the particular cases with which they were confronted could be subsumed. They had to decide each instance as it arose, because no rules existed for the unprecedented" (1958, 295). But the ability to retain judgment was obviously the exception, and Eichmann did not share in this exception.

Arendt repeats the question of Judge Landau at the trial of Eichmann, whether the accused had a conscience. Her answer is yes: he did on one occasion ship 20,000 Jews and 5,000 Gypsies from the Rhineland not to Riga or Minsk, where they would have been immediately shot, but to Lodz where no preparations for extermination were yet being made. But three weeks later, he agreed to ship 50,000 Jews to Riga and Minsk. Thus, "yes, he had a conscience, and his conscience functioned in the expected way for about four weeks, whereupon it began to function the other way around" (Arendt 1958, 95). The "other way around" meant that he claimed to live by Kant's moral precept—that is, to live by duty, to obey the law. But by obedience to duty, he did not mean obedience to a universal moral law; rather it was obedience to the words and laws of the Führer. And this obedience led Eichmann to diligently seek personal advancement while carrying out the Final Solution, because he "never realized what he was doing" (Arendt 1958, 287). He lacked imagination; he was thoughtless. "That such remoteness from reality and such thoughtlessness can wreak more havoc than all the evil instincts taken together which, perhaps, are inherent in man—that was, in fact, the lesson one could learn in Jerusalem" (Arendt 1958, 288).

The diagnosis of "failure of judgment" seems a compelling one in the case of Eichmann, since his responsibility in carrying out the Final Solution was primarily in terms of decisions. In deciding to follow all orders from his superiors, he abdicated responsibility for making any further decisions himself. The context of decision making, as Arendt also stresses in *The Origins of Totalitarianism*, was one of depersonalization and objectification. Arendt gives the following example of the "objective" attitude typical of the SS: Eichmann's defense lawyer claimed during the trial that the accused was innocent of charges bearing on his responsibility for "the collection of skeletons, sterilizations, killings by gas, and *similar medical matters.*" When challenged by the judge, the lawyer proceeded to defend his description: "It was indeed a medical matter, since it was prepared by physicians; *it was a matter of killing, and killing, too, is a medical matter*" (Arendt 1958, 69).

Eichmann, among others, might really have believed that the gassing chambers were "Charitable Foundations for Institutional Care"— a more attractive alternative to the shooting or the horrible deaths of the war (Arendt 1958, 109). But Eichmann's insulation from contact with "normal" knowledge of murder, helped by what Arendt calls rigid "language rules," was not a foolproof shield against reality. Thus Eichmann reported that when he saw the preparation for the gas chambers at Treblinka, he thought it was monstrous: "I am not so tough as to be able to endure something of this sort without any reaction. . . . If today I am shown a gaping wound, I can't possibly look at it" (Arendt 1958, 87). And when he saw the Jews entering mobile gas vans in Kulm and heard the shrieking, he was very upset. He saw the corpses being thrown into an open ditch "as though they were still alive, so smooth were their limbs. They were hurled into the ditch, and I can still see a civilian extracting the teeth with tooth pliers. And then I was off—jumped into my car and did not open my mouth any more" (Arendt 1958, 88). So on the few occasions where Eichmann was forced to face the horror of the Final Solution, he felt sick and horrified. But generally, Arendt notes, he was not forced to see much because it was easy to avoid the killing installations.

Can Arendt's analysis of the failure of judgment apply to the cruelty committed during war rape? Can one also say, as she does in reference to Eichmann and his contemporaries, that war rape was committed by people whose judgment failed them when there were no other guideposts to follow? Do those who commit war rape reveal their inability to achieve impartiality, their failure to take the viewpoints of others into account in order to achieve what Kant called "enlarged thought"? (Arendt 1982, 42–43).

There is, of course, some sense in which this conclusion seems warranted. Had a Serbian soldier who was raping a Bosnian Muslim woman old enough to be his mother sought to take her viewpoint into account, it is hard to imagine that he could have raped her. Aggression in war requires an ability to dehumanize those defined as enemies. This dehumanization is explicitly trained—from drill songs in the American army that dehumanized the Vietcong during the Vietnam war to training sessions in killing where Serbian soldiers trained other young men to wrestle pigs, pin them to the ground with their heads held back, and then cut their throats.[14]

Yet there is one crucial difference between the form of evil in war rape and that of the Final Solution. In the latter, genocide was carried out in response to orders and by means of the gas chambers (in addition, of course, to the massive numbers of deaths that occurred in the camps because of cold, starvation, overwork, and cruelty).[15] But what specifically characterizes war rape is that a man uses his own body as a weapon of war: his hands, his mouth, his genitals are used to inflict pain, injury, degradation, and often death. The distancing from seeing the actual results of evil that characterized Eichmann's crime is not present in the example of rape. (Arendt notes that it was not the accusation of having sent millions of people to their death that caused real agitation in Eichmann, but only the accusation by one witness that he had beaten a Jewish boy to death [1958, 109].) Of course, one might argue that the leaders who instigated the program of war rape as part of "ethnic cleansing" did feel such distance.

In this context, to speak of the evil of war rape as a failure of judgment would be grossly inadequate to describe this crime. It is not enough to ask, why did soldiers follow orders (and there were orders to rape), but, rather, how is it possible (whether because of orders or as a release of the anxiety and physiological tension that builds up from long waitings in barracks and fields, as one European military officer explained [Arcel 1998, 201]) to radically alter one's physcial comportment so that relations of ordinary cordiality in peacetime can be turned into sexual violence? Arendt's focus on judgment cannot address the specific corporeal aggression involved in the act of war rape.

The limitation of her notion of judgment to consider war rape could be linked to what feminists somewhat infamously refer to as the "missing body" in Arendt's political theory—the omission of any reference to gender or the sexed body in her writing. Linda Zerilli seeks to rescue Arendt from crude accusations about the missing body and notes that there is indeed a prohibition, in *On Revolution* and *The Human Condition*, on speaking the body in public, a taboo that never directly names sexuality.[16] Contrary to Kristeva, Arendt never names the body as sexed and does not focus on the female / maternal body's relation to the life cycle (Zerilli 1995, 173). But Zerilli argues that in treating the body as genderless, Arendt brings men's bodies into question by focusing on the sheer terror of having a body, the anxiety about mortality and the loss of symbolic mastery that haunts every speaking subject (1995, 174). But even if this blind spot in Arendt's thinking may be productive, as Zerilli proposes, in loosening the grip of gender on our cultural imaginary, it nonetheless constitutes a limit for considering the kind of evil manifest in war rape. For it is, nonetheless, the sexed body that remains a pivotal marker of this crime—the sexed bodies of the men who rape and of the women who are raped.[17] Moreover, it is remarkable that Zerilli's stress on the terror of embodiment and mortality overlooks what is one of Arendt's unique contributions: the significance of natality, "the new beginning inherent in birth."

In *The Human Condition* Arendt writes, "Since action is the political activity par excellence, natality, and not morality, may be the central category of political, as distinguished from metaphysical, thought" (1958, 9). Had she thematized more explicitly the concrete dimensions of the human body, she might have been able to think about evil acts that involved bodily engagement and not only those, like Eichmann's, that were characterized by bodily disengagement. Had Arendt turned her attention to concrete embodiment, it would have been possible to develop the concept of natality, which she only schematically introduces in the *The Human Condition*. If natality is the mark of a new beginning, the capacity for the newcomer to begin something anew, then what are the ethical and political features of a world where natality is a product of violence and can forseeably lead to future violence? But in focusing on judgment, Arendt treats evil as an affair of the intellect (a product of thoughtlessness or a failure to judge). Hence Benhabib finds Arendt a "cognitivist" in her moral reflection, with the consequence that Arendt "leaves unexplored the motivational question of how perspicacious thinking and good judgment could be translated into action" (1996, 192). Had Arendt considered the corporeal engagement in evil, it would have been possible to consider not only "motivational" questions but also how bodily sensibilities themselves are transgressed and transformed by evil acts.

Arendt develops her views on judgment through an interpretation of Kant's *Critique of Judgment.* She argues that although Kant never really wrote a political philosophy, one can surmise the political philosophy he would have written through his focus on human plurality and sociability in this, his third, *Critique*. In her *Lectures on Kant's Political Philosophy,* she turns to Kant's notion of impartiality, of taking the viewpoints of others into account, as an exercise of the imagination. Critical thinking, she writes, still goes on in isolation, "but by force of the imagination it makes the others present and thus moves in a space that is potentially public, open to all sides; in other words, it adopts the position of Kant's world citizen. To think with an enlarged mentality means that one trains one's imagination to go visiting" (1982, 43).

Enlarged thinking does not consist in an enlarged empathy through which one can know what actually goes on in other's minds. "To accept what goes on in the minds of those whose 'standpoint' . . . is not my own would mean no more than passively to accept their thought, that is, to exchange their prejudices for the prejudices proper to my station" (Arendt 1982, 43). Enlarged thought, on the other hand, is the result of disregarding self-interest (and the self-interest of others). The greater its reach, the more "general" thinking will be. And here Arendt uses the term "general" not to apply to an abstract concept. Rather, it is a generality she claims that is closely connected to particulars, that is, to "the particular conditions of the standpoints one has to go through in order to arrive at one's own 'general standpoint'" (Arendt 1982, 44).

What kind of role could this notion of enlarged thinking or impartiality play in the context of war rape? This question is in part ill-suited to Arendt's purposes, since in her writings on judgment in the 1970s she is no longer interested in judgment in the sense of actors deliberating on future courses of actions. Instead, she looks to judging as reflection on the past: "Such reflections will inevitably arise in political emergencies."[18] Although neither Arendt nor Kant ever clarify the relation between judging and acting, they do not deny that acting occurs in both its grandiosity and its horror. Arendt cites Kant's own equivocal reaction to the French Revolution, his estimation of its grandeur and his condemnation of those who prepared it. Kant wrote: "The revolution of a gifted people which we have seen unfolding in our day may succeed or miscarry; it may be filled with misery and atrocities to the point that a sensible man, were he boldly to hope to execute it successfully the second time, would never resolve to make the experiment at such cost—this revolution, I say, nonetheless finds in the hearts of all spectators (who are not engaged in this game themselves) a wishful participation that borders closely on enthusiasm."[19]

Perhaps this privileging of the spectator in Kant's philosophy, which Arendt reiterates in her later work on judgment, arises from the awareness that enlarged thinking is only possible from the point of view of the spectator. To return to the issue of war rape, it is obvious that a rapist has failed to take into perspective the point of view of the woman he is raping. But it would be both tasteless and morally absurd to demand of the woman that she take into account the viewpoint of the rapist (to remember, for example, that he may be motivated by the desire for transgenerational revenge for acts committed during World War II or during the Ottoman occupation of the Balkans)[20]—at least, until she has the luxury of being a spectator of her own past. It may be that "enlarged thinking" should be a moral proposal; but when faced with its brutal transgression, we can no longer expect enlarged thinking from the person violated.

A difficulty with Arendt's appropriation of Kant's concept is that she never specifies what this "general standpoint" entails—only that it is connected with the particular conditions of the standpoints one has to go through in order to arrive at impartiality. It involves making present to myself what the perspectives of others involved could be and whether I could "woo their consent" (Benhabib 1996, 190), how through imagination I could simulate a moral dialogue with all concerned. This enlarged mentality is distinguished from empathy; it is not a feeling with others but a thinking with others that takes as its starting point the view that human beings have an interest in the world and in those who constitute it.

But there remain a number of puzzles in Arendt's notion of enlarged thinking. Is it a form of reconciling conflicting points of view? Is there an interpretation that is large enough, adequate enough, to explain differences in point of view? Or are some interpretations superior to others, and if so on what grounds? Or shall we instead settle for the reality of differing interpretations, some of which may be acceptable because they point to different fields of experience (such as science or common sense) and some of which must simply be acknowledged to conflict (such as the different points of view of partners in marital conflict)?[21] And how in the face of conflict are right and wrong to be apportioned? (It would surely be a distortion of the situation to argue that a man who is physically abusing his children and threatening violent reprisal against his ex-wife has a point of view as "legitimate" as those who are most vulnerable in this situation. When she struggles for her own and her children's physical safety and personal dignity, for their moral survival, one cannot demand of her a disengagement from her own perspective.) Not only does Arendt's view have difficulty in settling the question of conflict (and the necessity of commitment in the face of conflict), but she also assumes that a desire for unity and consistency is the basis for a principled moral standpoint. As Benhabib notes, however, consistent viewpoints can be quite compatible with the deeds of the likes of Eichmann, while "enlarged thinking" may in fact lead to moral conflict and alienation (1996, 190–91).

Arendt's notion of enlarged thinking also seems to come up short by emphasizing the construction of a dialogue with imagined persons and thus underestimating the importance of dialogue with real persons. Ronald Beiner notes that "in judging, as understood by Arendt, one weighs the *possible* judgments of an imagined Other, not the actual judgments of real interlocutors."[22] But this view attributes to imagination: (1) an interest in and respect for another's point of view and (2) an ability to seek a viable "truce" between differing standpoints. This view assumes a normative account of imagination that may be far from its manifest motivations. ("To think with an enlarged mentality means that one *trains* one's imagination to go visiting" [my emphasis; Arendt 1982, 43].)

As Kristeva notes in *Powers of Horror,* imagination may express instead a fascination with horror through voyeurism rather than a respectful donning of another's position (1982, 46). In the context of war rape, the normative activity of the imagination described by Arendt is lacking; one has not trained oneself properly to go visiting. But Arendt's account cannot deal with the facets of the imagination that resist this socializing norm and allow sexual violence: the eroticizing of violence that takes place through pornography (as Catharine MacKinnon has argued[23]); the abjection and fascination of death and of the birth-giving scene—the ultimate abjection—that in Kristeva's view forms "the other facet of religious, moral, and ideological codes on which rest the sleep of individuals and the breathing spells of societies" (1982, 150, 155, 209). The literature of abjection suggests that when sociability entails destruction, Arendt's account of imagination in terms of sociability is too thin.

Benhabib argues that although Arendt's conception of politics is unintelligible without "a strongly grounded normative position in universalistic human rights, equality, and respect" (1996, 194), there is a lacuna in her thinking, since one finds no attempt at normative justification. Arendt's analysis in *The Human Condition,* continues Benhabib, is a form of anthropological universalism that presupposes but does not justify an attitude of respect for the other. Although I agree with Benhabib's diagnosis of the normative presuppositions at work in Arendt's writings, I differ with her about the urgency of normative justification. It is true, as Benhabib notes, that the moral attitude of enlarged thought seems to be missing when we most need it—in the face of National Socialism and totalitarianism, as analyzed by Arendt; in the face of massive war rape, as noted here. But the philosophical task of sustaining viable conceptions of morality cannot be fulfilled through procedures of justifying universalist norms.

The task, it seems to me, is to understand the breakdown of *practical* morality, how people commit acts that are contrary to what they themselves initially believe is right. When faced with corpses dumped in a pit, Eichmann felt sick. And I find it plausible that the doctors who raped women they had worked with cordially for ten years also might have felt an initial nausea at their acts. It may be that procedures of normative justification can provide individuals with moral and psychological supports in the face of social breakdown. In this case, however, the value of justification is not in the theorizing alone but in the role of theory in strengthening an individual's resistance to moral dissolution—that is, in its practical benefits. There may be other tools as well that can similarly strengthen individual resistance to wrongdoing (as in Staub's proposal of the habit of helping others). And it may well be that for some individuals, universalist justification of norms may coexist with wrongdoing (for example, as evidenced by the massive support for Hitler among academics and religious leaders in Germany). Faced with acts of mass-scale evil in the contemporary world, the task for philosophers is less one of justification of norms (is it really necessary to justify the judgment that murder and rape is wrong?) than of diagnosing the conditions for moral breakdown and of the possibility of altering these conditions.

Arendt's theory of enlarged thinking, based as it is on Kant's theory of judgment, ultimately prioritizes the spectator over the actor. And there are some good reasons for such a choice: for example, the old argument in philosophy that only the spectator can see the whole, whereas the actor's view is partial by definition. On this view, it is only the spectator who can escape the cave of opinions and go hunting for truth. Or the view that there is something else involved in action than what is consciously willed by the actor, and therefore the actor's perspective should not be privileged. Or, as Arendt also emphasizes, the view that spectators are always involved with other spectators, and thus that the spectator's viewpoint is an achievement of plurality (1982, 55–65). All of these features point to what Arendt considered most crucial in human affairs: sociality, communicability, and publicity. And indeed the role of the spectator is crucial in adjudicating the course of history, as Kant argued. Certainly the presence of Western journalists and investigative groups during the civil war in the former Yugoslavia has contributed to an increased public outrage against war rape, in contrast to the history of silent indifference toward it. The publicity brought about through spectators, or bystanders, has contributed to legal changes in which for the first time a United Nations tribunal has given indictments for rape as a war crime.[24]

As Ervin Staub has noted, the role of bystanders in protesting or acquiescing to violence is a crucial factor in the future development of events. But in defining the witness to events as the spectator, as Kant and Arendt do, as opposed to the bystander, as Staub does, we miss one crucial factor: the bystander can also "stand in," that is, provide a moral conscience in a context where that is lacking (consider, for example, the success of Amnesty International in gaining release of political prisoners) or "stand back," that is, remain passive (as in the case of the passivity of German bystanders in the face of increasing persecution of the Jews). According to Kant, "in the hearts of all spectators" to the French Revolution there was a "wishful participation," a sympathy that would be dangerous to express but could lead to a philosophical prediction about the progress of the human race (Arendt 1982, 45–46). The spectator in Kant's and Arendt's notion of enlarged thinking does not have a practical function but a predictive one. In other words, enlarged thinking is premised on a disengagement from participation in crises that is inimicial to moral intervention.

TOWARD A PHILOSOPHICAL ANALYSIS OF WAR RAPE

In evaluating the interpretations of evil in these theories and their relevance to an analysis of war rape, I have found certain contributions and lacuna:

First, as indicated in Douglas's and Kristeva's analysis, it is crucial to understand the way bodies are symbolized by given cultural, linguistic, and social systems. Sexual symbolization may be linked to the representation of hierarchies in the social symbolic, as Douglas argued, or it may be linked more explicitly to views of women's bodies, and of the mother's body as abject, as Kristeva argues. But if moral reflection is to be able to deal adequately with crises of sexual violence, it must include an understanding of the symbolics of the body as a central moral concern. Otherwise, moral thinking shows itself to be incapable of addressing the corporality of evil—of how bodily comportment and sensibilities are radically transformed through the infliction/suffering of violence. Both Staub and Arendt fail to take account of sexed bodies in their reflections on moral crises, with disturbing consequences. Moreover, it is crucial to examine the symbolic meaning of the mother's body in a particular cultural context, since this is the site of vulnerability in war rape. Arendt's concept of natality could be developed to reflect on the specific conditions of natality instead of treating natality as simply an abstract moment in philosophical anthropology. Contextualizing natality could raise new questions: What is inherent in birth when birth itself is a product of violence? What new beginnings, new actions, might birth from sexual violence spawn?

Second, reflections on sexual violence need to account for the processes of breakdown, as Staub makes evident. Although crisis might be imminent in a given symbolic order by virtue of the exclusions and repressions that constitute that order, one must still ask how and why particular instances of breakdown occur. An investigation into the processes of moral breakdown entails a differentiated analysis of the context and circumstances of war rape, as Libby Tata Arcel argues; one must focus on different historical cases of war rape, differences of motives between leaders and the civilian population, differences among individual men, and so forth (Arcel 1998, 200). Such an analysis is necessarily cross-disciplinary, drawing resources from psychology, history, philosophy, linguistic analysis. Moreover, it involves giving an account of the process of evildoing, by which prevailing moral norms break down during the emergence of crisis. This view of moral reflection does not constitute an abandonment of philosophy as a project for the present. Rather, it underlines the philosophical task of self-reflection, which calls for an investigation into the conditions for the possibility of moral thinking and behavior.

Finally, reflections on sexual violence need to diagnose the conditions of moral breakdown, as Arendt sought to do in reference to the genocide of the Jews during Hitler's rule. Such a diagnosis may include, as Arendt argued, an account of imagination and communication amid human plurality. But one must go beyond the implicitly normative account of imagination found in Arendt's writing to inquire into the role of imagination in voyeurism and the fascination with horror, as in rapists' fascination with the humiliation and degradation of their victims. Moreover, a diagnosis of moral breakdown must deal with how to sustain moral reflection in the face of conflicting points of view. Arendt's notion of enlarged thinking deals neither with radical conflicts among perspectives nor with the necessity of commitment in the face of conflict.

In terms of the change that is demanded, three related questions emerge: How is it possible to change the symbolization of the sexed body, the mother's body, and birth so as to reduce the threat of violence?[25] How can moral reflection focus on the practice of morality, the doing of good and evil, so as to encourage the former rather than the latter?[26] And how can one develop a perspectivist theory of morals, which acknowledges conflicts of point of view, without resorting to "impartiality" or universalist norms?

Of course, the problematic status of universals remains on the agenda for theoretical and political debate. I would argue that universalist claims can have vital strategic value. The United Nations Universal Declaration of Human Rights from 1948 is a vital document for the protection of individuals, although subsequent declarations about children's and women's rights point to lacuna in the formulation of universal human rights. Nonetheless, my claim is that it is not the strength or weakness of universal norms that is at stake in moral crises. I disagree with the claim that rape in wartime can be avoided by a soldier's understanding the universal right to be secure in one's person and free from torture (Articles 3 and 5 of the United Nations Universal Declaration of Human Rights). Rather, what is required is the soldier's acknowledgment of wrongdoing in the particularity of his physical transgression. In other words, it is necessary to move away from a cognitive account of morality if cognition implies a rational recognition of norms. Instead, it is crucial to incorporate the bodily element of judgment, which places a demand to revise and expand the concept of cognition.[27]

The kind of moral theory that emerges from reflections on war rape will be multifaceted. As Michele le Doeuff writes, it would be a nonhegemonic theory, based on the recognition of the "necessarily incomplete character of all theorization."[28] It would be based on multidisciplinary work that can take account of the differential contexts in which war rape occurs. And it would emphasize the inevitable partiality of vision without the illusion of omniscience.[29] Feminist philosophical inquiries into war rape seek to contribute to an analysis of this horror. By implication they embroil philosophy in an enquiry into war and violence that has hitherto occupied only a point of peripheral vision in that discipline.

NOTES

1. Ervin Staub, *The Roots of Evil* (Cambridge, Eng.: Cambridge University Press, 1989), p. 25.

2. Helsinki Watch, *War Crimes in Bosnia-Hercegovina*, vol. 2 (New York: Human Rights Watch, 1993), p. 21.

3. Beverly Allen, *Rape Warfare: The Hidden Genocide in Bosnia-Herzegovina and Croatia* (Minneapolis: University of Minnesota Press, 1996), p. 78.

4. Hannah Arendt, *Eichmann in Jerusalem: A Report on the Banality of Evil* (Chicago: University of Chicago Press, 1958), and *The Origins of Totalitarianism* (New York: Harcourt, Brace, 1951).

5. Claudia Card, "Rape Terrorism," in *The Unnatural Lottery: Character and Moral Luck* (Philadelphia: Temple University Press, 1996), pp. 97–117, and "Rape As a Weapon of War," *Hypatia* (Special Issue on Women and Violence, ed. Bat-Ami Bar-On) 11, 4 (Fall 1996): 5–18.

6. Elaine Scarry, *The Body in Pain* (New York: Oxford University Press, 1985), p. 9.

7. Julia Kristeva, *Powers of Horror: An Essay on Abjection*, trans. Leon S. Roudiez (New York: Columbia University Press, 1982), p. 5.

8. Hannah Arendt, *Lectures on Kant's Political Philosophy*, ed. Ronald Beiner (Chicago: University of Chicago Press, 1982).

9. Mary Douglas, *Purity and Danger* (London: Routledge and Kegan Paul, 1966). This book was influential for the analysis of sexual pollution I developed in *Cognition and Eros: A Critique of the Kantian Paradigm* (Boston: Beacon, 1988; University Park: Pennsylvania State University Press, 1993).

10. Ronald Beiner, "Hannah Arendt on Judging," in Arendt, *Lectures*, p. 104.

11. See Philip Hallie, *Lest Innocent Blood Be Shed: The Story of the Village of Le Chambon, and How Goodness Happened There* (New York: Harper and Row, 1979), for an account of how a group can organize to save victims of persecution.

12. Libby Tata Arcel, "Sexual Torture of Women As a Weapon of War—The Case of Bosnia Herzegovina," in *War Violence, Trauma, and the Coping Process*, ed. Libby Tata Arcel, with Goana Tocilj Simunkovic (Copenhagen: International Rehabilitation Council for Torture Victims, 1998), p. 184.

13. Seyla Benhabib, *The Reluctant Modernism of Hannah Arendt* (London: Sage, 1996), p. 185.

14. Ed Vulliamy, *Seasons in Hell: Understanding Bosnia's War* (London: Simon and Schuster, 1994), p. 193.

15. See Primo Levi's accounts of life and death in the concentration camps in his *Survival in Auschwitz,* trans. Stuart Woolf (New York: Collier Macmillan, 1993), and *If This Is a Man: The Truce,* trans. Stuart Woolf (London: Penguin, 1979).

16. Linda M. G. Zerilli, "The Arendtian Body," in *Feminist Interpretations of Hannah Arendt,* ed. Bonnie Honig (University Park: Pennsylvania State University Press, 1995), p. 171; Hannah Arendt, *On Revolution* (New York: Viking, 1963); Hannah Arendt, *The Human Condition* (Chicago: University of Chicago Press, 1958).

17. In "Gender and 'Postmodern War,'" *Hypatia* 11, 4 (1996): 19–29, I argue that faced with sex-specific violence and dislocation, gender remains a crucial interpretive category, which is not to deny that women can participate in the raping of other women (by the use of verbal assaults and physical objects such as bottles), or that men can also be raped. Nonetheless, the massive rape that has been an instrument of war is the rape of women by men.

18. Quoted in Beiner, "Hannah Arendt on Judging," in Arendt, *Lectures,* p. 109.

19. Immanuel Kant, "An Old Question Raised Again," in *On History,* trans. and ed. Lewis White Beck (Indianapolis: Bobbs-Merrill, 1963), quoted in Arendt, *Lectures,* p. 45.

20. Arcel discusses this transgenerational revenge as one of the common elements in the war rapes ("Sexual Torture of Women," p. 196).

21. These questions parallel the questions raised about Nietzsche's theory of truth and perspectivism. See Maudemarie Clark, *Nietzsche on Truth and Philosophy* (Cambridge, Eng.: Cambridge University Press, 1990).

22. Beiner, "Hannah Arendt on Judging," in Arendt, *Lectures,* p. 92.

23. Catharine MacKinnon, "Turning Rape into Pornography: Postmodern Genocide," *Ms.* 4, 1 (July/August 1993): 24–30.

24. Claudia Card, "Addendum to 'Rape As a Weapon of War,'" *Hypatia* 12, 2 (Spring 1997): 217.

25. Claudia Card makes one proposal in "Rape As a Weapon of War."

26. Note that Benhabib calls for, among other factors, the "motivational habits of civic courage and civic virtue" (*The Reluctant Modernism of Hannah Arendt,* p. 193).

27. These comments are in part a response to the challenging questions posed to me when I presented a shorter version of this chapter at the Department of Philosophy, Århus University, Århus, Denmark, in March 1998.

28. Michele le Doeuff, "Women and Philosophy," in *French Feminist Thought,* ed. Tori Moi (Oxford: Blackwell, 1987), p. 208.

29. See Donna Haraway's "Situated Knowledges," in *Simians, Cyborgs, and Women* (New York: Routledge, 1991).

10 / *The Uses of Narrative in the Aftermath of Violence*

SUSAN J. BRISON

Dori Laub quotes a Holocaust survivor who said, " 'We wanted to survive so as to live one day after Hitler, in order to be able to tell our story.' "[1] As Laub came to believe, after listening to many Holocaust testimonies and working as an analyst with survivors and their children, such victims of trauma "did not only need to survive in order to tell their story; they also needed to tell their story in order to survive" (Felman and Laub 1992, 78). Telling their story, narrating their experiences of traumatic events, has long been considered—at least since Freud and Janet[2]—to play a significant role in survivors' recovery from trauma. Despite many decades of clinical and theoretical work on the subject of trauma and narrative, just why narratives play such an important role in surviving the aftermath of trauma remains somewhat of a mystery. In this chapter I examine some of the ways in which telling, writing, reading, listening to, and, sometimes, embodying first-person narratives can play a significant role both in recovering from trauma and in researchers' and clinicians' arriving at a useful, if still contestable, understanding of it.

I mention at the outset that I am aware of risks of overbreadth and underbreadth in the use of the word "trauma." My use is influenced by the fourth edition of the *Diagnostic and Statistical Manual of Mental Disorders* and by Judith Herman, Jonathan Shay, Bessel van der Kolk and Onno van der Hart, and others who talk about "trauma" in a wide range of groups.[3] What survivors of trauma have in common, on my account, is the experience of utter helplessness in the face of overwhelming, life-threatening violence of human origin (such as child abuse, rape, war, torture, the Holocaust). This use poses a serious danger of overbreadth, however: Why include in the same discussion such radically different forms of trauma as surviving a single incident of rape and surviving the Holocaust? These events are incommensurable. The single rape is not as traumatic as—nor is it traumatic in the same ways as—the many horrific events experienced by individuals during the Holocaust. Nor is a single rape (as opposed to genocidal mass rape) accompanied by destruction of family, home, and community, as was experienced by Jewish survivors of the Holocaust. But there are similarities in what the survivors experience in the aftermath of violence, and similarities in the role narrative can play in the survivors' recovery. Nonetheless, it is politically, historically, and morally problematic to talk about such a diverse group of "survivors," and we must remain mindful of the crucial differences among survivors of different kinds. In this chapter, I focus most on the case of rape trauma.

There is also, in my use of the term "trauma," a risk of underbreadth: Why exclude trauma not of human origin, that is, trauma not intentionally inflicted? Although accidents and natural disasters can be traumatic, I do not discuss them here, because I think they affect the survivor's sense of self in a somewhat different way. They do not, typically, lead to a sense of betrayal by and inability to trust one's fellow human beings.[4]

What follows is divided into two sections. The first focuses on the role of narrative in studying trauma. I leave the term "narrative" vague because I want the term to encompass verbal and nonverbal (such as painted or physically enacted) accounts. A narrative tells the story of an event over time, situated within a larger temporal framework, though it need not be chronologically unidirectional. I consider Binjamin Wilkomirski's *Fragments: Memories of a Wartime Childhood* a survivor's narrative, even though it shifts back and forth in time.[5] Unlike passively experienced trauamatic memories, a narrative requires a narrator, an agent who makes choices about what to tell and how to tell it.

I argue, in this first section, that understanding trauma requires one to take first-person narratives seriously as an essential epistemological tool. (This approach may be obvious to many readers, but it goes against two millenia of philosophical teaching. In my training as a philosopher, I was taught to shun the literary and suggestive particularity of narrative for the ostensibly precise and universal persuasiveness of argument.) Here I also discuss epistemological and political pitfalls of the use of first-person narratives and suggest ways of attempting to avoid these hazards.

The second section discusses the role of narratives in recovery from trauma and analyzes the performative aspect of speech acts in recovering from trauma. Under the right conditions, *saying* something about traumatic memory *does* something to it: defuses it, renders it less intrusive, less disruptive, and transforms it into narrative memory that can be integrated into a self in the process of being rebuilt. I also look at the role of cultural memory in the experiencing of trauma and in the construction of trauma narratives as well as at limits of linguistic narratives in rebuilding a self undone by trauma. Other forms of action (such as learning self-defense) may be needed to facilitate recovery. These, too, may be viewed as telling a story, a nonverbal embodied narrative, in which the narrator has greater imaginative and physical control over the plot. It is not simply a retelling or a reenactment but a reworking and revising of the story, which resubjectifies the survivor, reviving her from the helplessness and objectification of the traumatic event.

THE EPISTEMOLOGICAL SIGNIFICANCE
OF NARRATIVE IN UNDERSTANDING TRAUMA

As a philosopher working on trauma, I have had to work my way through and defend myself against considerable bias within the discipline of philosophy against the particular, the concrete, the personal, and the narrative as useful in arriving at knowledge.[6] An excellent illustration of this disciplinary bias comes from Bertrand Russell's *The Problems of Philosophy*, a text that still frequently appears in anthologies used in courses introducing students to philosophy. In the main introductory philosophy text used at Dartmouth, it appears under the heading, "What Is Philosophy?":

The free intellect will see as God might see, without a *here* and *now*, without hopes and fears, without the trammels of customary beliefs and traditional prejudices, calmly, dispassionately, in the sole and exclusive desire of knowledge—knowledge as impersonal, as purely contemplative, as it is possible for man to attain. Hence also the free intellect will value more the abstract and universal knowledge into which the accidents of private history do not enter, than the knowledge brought by the senses, and dependent, as such knowledge must be, upon an exclusive and personal point of view and a body whose sense-organs distort as much as they reveal.[7]

What doesn't appear in introductory philosophy textbooks is the following from Nietzsche: "Gradually it has become clear to me what every great philosophy so far has been: namely the personal confession of its author and a kind of involuntary and unconscious memoir."[8]

Russell's *Problems of Philosophy* was one of the first philosophy texts I read. It has taken me nearly twenty years to see the appeal of Nietzsche's view of philosophy as disguised autobiographical narrative. I was aware that for centuries philosophers had written in the first-person singular, but "serious" ones, such as Descartes, did so as part of an argumentative strategy to be employed by any reader to establish, ultimately, the same universal truths. They weren't really talking about themselves. As we so often tell beginning students of philosophy who write "I feel that" or "I think that," such self-descriptions have no place in "serious" philosophical argumentation. What the reader (the professor) wants to know is not what this particular author happens to feel or think and why, but rather what reasons any rational person has to accept the position in question. Those "accidents of private history," disparaged by Russell, must be put out of one's mind if one is to "see as God might see, without a *here* and *now*."

Now, of course, Russell, like Nietzsche, was an atheist, and so it is a bit of a mystery why he thought human beings could accomplish feats of this sort which, when attributed to God, made the idea of such a being incredible. But many, perhaps most, mainstream analytic philosophers writing today share Russell's view and consider the search for timeless, acontextual truths to be the sine qua non of the philosophical enterprise.

However, some philosophers—even some trained as I was in the analytic tradition (Anglo-American, not psychoanalytic)—have come to reject this view. Many feminist philosophers agree with Virginia Held that "the philosophical tradition that has purported to present the view of the essentially and universally human has, masked by this claim, presented instead a view that is masculine, white, and Western."[9] Having acquainted ourselves with feminist theorizing as

carried out in other disciplines, we are finding the traditional philosophical obsession with the impersonal and acontextual increasingly
indefensible. As we find that the "accidents of private history," especially those connected with gender, race, ethnicity, religion, sexuality,
and class, are not only worth thinking about but are also inevitably
(if invisibly) present in much of philosophy, we are beginning to write
in the first person, not out of self-indulgence but from intellectual
necessity.

Feminist ethics, in accepting subjective accounts as legitimate
means of advancing knowledge, has made it more academically acceptable to write in the personal voice. In questioning the dichotomy
between the personal and the political, insisting on the relevance of
particular women's actual experiences, feminist methodology can
reveal the bias in the exclusion of rape and other forms of sexual violence from the traditional concerns of ethics. As Held observes,
whereas "traditional moral theory is frequently built on what a person might be thought to hold from the point of view of a hypothetical ideal observer, or a hypothetical purely rational being," feminist
ethics relies on the actual experiences of concrete individuals, paying special attention to the formerly neglected experiences of women
and other marginalized groups (1993, 34). Feminist theorists increasingly look to first-person accounts to gain imaginative access to others' experiences (in stark contrast to Ross Harrison, who asserted in
one of the rare philosophical articles on rape in the mid-1980s, that
"there is no problem imagining what it is like to be a victim"[10]). Such
access facilitates empathy with others, valued by many feminist theorists as a method of moral understanding needed to complement
more detached analytical reasoning.

The "accident of private history" that forced me to think about the
"personal" as philosophical was a near-fatal sexual assault and attempted murder on 4 July 1990 outside of Grenoble, France, in which
I was beaten, raped, strangled, and left for dead at the bottom of a
ravine. Unlike Descartes, who had "to demolish everything completely and start again right from the foundations" in order to find any
knowledge "that was stable and likely to last,"[11] I had my world de-
molished for me. The fact that I could be walking down a quiet, sun-
lit country road at one moment and be battling a murderous attacker
the next undermined my most fundamental assumptions about the
world. After my hospitalization, I took a yearlong disability leave from

teaching and found myself, like Descartes, "quite alone," with "a clear stretch of free time" in which to rebuild my shattered system of beliefs (Descartes 1984, 13).

As I carried out this process of cognitive, as well as physical and emotional, recovery, I was dismayed to find very little of use to me written by philosophers. It occurred to me that the fact that rape was not considered a properly philosophical subject, although war was, resulted not only from the paucity of women in the profession but also from disciplinary bias against thinking about the "personal," against writing in narrative form. Personal experiences of men have been neglected in philosophical analysis as well. The study of the ethics of war has dealt with questions of strategy and justice as viewed from the outside, not with wartime *experiences* of soldiers or with the aftermath of their trauma.[12]

In philosophy, first-person narratives, especially ones written by those with perspectives previously excluded from the discipline, are necessary for several reasons. I'll discuss just three. Such narratives are necessary to expose previously hidden biases in the discipline's subject matter and methodology, to facilitate understanding of and empathy with those different from ourselves, and to lay on the table our own biases as scholars.

First-person narratives can expose gender and other biases inherent in much traditional moral, legal, and political philosophy. They can serve to bear witness, to bring professional attention to injustices suffered by previously neglected or discounted groups. Such narratives can provide a basis for empathy with those different from ourselves, which, as Diana Meyers has argued, is crucial for an adequately inclusive understanding of certain moral, legal, and political issues.[13]

In other fields as well, first-person accounts can facilitate understanding cultural attitudes and practices different from our own, as anthropologist Renato Rosaldo demonstrates in "Grief and a Head-hunter's Rage."[14] In that chapter, Rosaldo, who had previously published a book on head-hunting among the Ilongot (in the Philippines), describes how the experience of rage after the death of his wife, Michelle Rosaldo, gave him new insight into the rage Ilongot older men felt in bereavement. Before his own encounter with grief, Rosaldo writes, he "brushed aside" Ilongot accounts of "the rage in bereavement that could impel men to headhunt." He says he probably "naively equated grief with sadness." Only after "being repositioned" by his own "devastating loss" could he begin to grasp that "Ilongot older men mean precisely what they say when they describe the anger in bereavement as the source of their desire to cut off human heads" (1989, 3). This is not to say that he fully comprehended or condoned the past head-hunting behavior of the Ilongots, but it became less foreign to him. His first-person narrative, likewise, makes the practice less foreign to us, his readers. As he explains, his "use of personal experience serves as a vehicle for making the quality and intensity of the rage in Ilongot grief more readily accessible to readers than certain more detached modes of composition" (1989, 11).

At other times, first-person narratives are used simply to put on the table one's perspectives and possible biases, which, of course, acknowledges that such things inevitably work their way into our research, however scrupulously "objective" we try to be. Susan Estrich begins her book *Real Rape* with an account of the rape she survived in 1974. To justify this radical and courageous introduction to a long-neglected legal subject, Estrich argues that if the rape wasn't her fault, if she's not ashamed, why shouldn't she mention it? "And so I mention it. I mention it in my classes. I describe it here. I do so in the interest of full disclosure. I like to think that I am an informed and intelligent student of rape. But I am not unbiased. I am no objective observer, if such a thing exists (which I doubt; I think the major difference between me and those who have written 'objectively' about the law of rape is that I admit my involvement and bias). In writing about rape, I am writing about my own life."[15]

As Held observes, feminists who doubt "that anyone can truly reflect the essentially and universally human, and [are] suspicious of those who presume to do so, . . . often ask that speakers openly acknowledge the backgrounds from which they speak so that their hearers can better understand the contexts of their experiences" (1993, 19). In *Feminist Morality: Transforming Culture, Society, and Politics*, Held overcomes her own "psychological inclination" and philosophical training and describes her personal and intellectual background, acknowledging explicitly that the feminist views presented in her book are not reflective of a wider range of feminist thinking, but rather emerge from her own "philosophical background and experience" (1993, 19–21). Likewise, in *Moral Prejudices: Essays on Ethics*, Annette Baier includes a discussion of her development in the profession as a feminist philosopher as well as a series of anecdotes about her experiences as a woman in a world in which trusting certain men can be dangerous. In her defense of these unusual philosophical moves, she acknowledges, "I know, however, that I will not convince many of my fellow moral philosophers" of their appropriateness, given that "the impersonal style has become nearly a sacred tradition in moral philosophy."[16] But to her credit she is not dissuaded by comments such as the one proffered by a "respected older mentor" after she gave a talk employing such anecdotes about trust: " 'This may all be great fun, but is it real professional work?' " (1994, 328 n. 20).

The above theorists who employ the personal voice all recognize a fundamental characteristic of feminist theory, which is that it takes women's experiences seriously. Likewise, trauma theory takes survivors' experiences seriously. And we cannot know what these are a priori. We need to tell our stories, making sure to listen to those of others, especially when they're at odds with ours.

First-person narratives in feminist philosophy and in trauma theory may seem to be of the same genre as Descartes's *Meditations*, but in spite of having superficially similar narrative structures, they differ radically in their intellectual aims. Feminists and trauma theorists writing of their own experiences do not claim, as did Descartes, that any rational person carrying out the same line of abstract reasoning will reach the same impersonal conclusions. Rather, we are suggesting that anyone in these particular circumstances, with this kind of socialization, with these options and limitations may (may, not must) view the world in this way. If first-person narratives are to help serve as an antidote to the obliteration of difference in theory, they must avoid the risk of overgeneralization.

Theorizing in the personal voice is not without its hazards, as the above discussion of the importance of acknowledging one's biases points out, but I think that with care these hazards can be largely avoided by those writing and reading such narratives. At the very least, they can be noted. They include: the dilemma of speaking only for oneself versus speaking, without warrant, on behalf of a larger group; taking statements of experience or remembered experiences at face value, as foundational; generating (unjustified) counternarratives of victimization; and perpetuating stereotypes about one's group.

The theorist who uses her own narrative of trauma or of victimization in her scholarship faces the dilemma, on one hand, of speaking only for herself, giving into self-indulgence or speaking about experiences so idiosyncratic that her narrative is of no use to others, or, on the other hand, of presuming to speak for all members of a group to which she belongs (all trauma survivors, all rape survivors, all white, female, North American, middle-class rape survivors). However carefully the group is delineated, she risks overgeneralizing (and undergeneralizing). Although a survivor experiences, remembers, and narrates trauma as a member of at least one group, such a narrative should not be taken, in isolation, as standard for victimized members of that group. Furthermore, we need to rethink our (all or nothing) assumptions about identity, acknowledging the complexities of our multiple identities.[17]

The hazard of presuming to speak for all members of a group, such as all women (as white, middle-class academic feminists have been all too prone to do), can be avoided to some extent by making clear the background from which one writes and refraining from overgeneralizing in one's conclusions. Through my participation in a survivors' support group as well as in the antirape movement I discovered the many ways in which my race (white) and class (middle), in addition to my academic preoccupations, had distanced me from the concerns of many other victims of sexual violence. Although all of us in the support group (in center-city Philadelphia) had been raped, and we shared the symptoms of post-traumatic stress disorder, these symptoms had a more devastating effect on some of us than on others because of our different backgrounds and present circumstances. I wondered whether I would ever function well enough to resume my teaching and research, while others worried about finding housing for themselves and their children, or about getting off drugs, or dealing with a racist legal system that takes black rape victims less seriously than white ones, or about supporting themselves (since they'd worked the night shift and were now too afraid to take public transportation to work after dark). We all struggled to get from one day to the next, but our struggles were not the same. It is important to bear in mind that we need not speak *for* other survivors of trauma in order to speak *with* them.

A second pitfall is to take experiences and narrated memories of subjective experiences at face value, as given or foundational. As Andreas Huyssen notes, "The past is not simply there in memory, but it must be articulated to become memory. The fissure that opens up between experiencing an event and remembering it in representation is unavoidable."[18] Much recent psychological literature on memory stresses the construction that goes on in memory and argues against the "snapshot" (or "videotape" or "flashbulb") model of memory.[19] The tendency to take certain memories—traumatic memories—as simply given and retained as snapshots exists in trauma theory when traumatic memories are viewed as bodily, fragmented, sensory, intrusive, recurrent, uncontrollable, in contrast with narrative memories, which are viewed as linguistic, more coherent, more under control. Yet, traumatic memory, like narrative memory, is articulated, selective, even malleable, even though it may not be under the survivor's conscious control.

Furthermore, I would add to Huyssen's observation of the gap between experience and memory that there is, in addition, a gap between the event (which may be described in countless ways) and the experience of it. Here I reject a naive realist view of perception and of experience generally, a view that may be unwittingly evoked by those trauma theorists who emphasize the "snapshot" character of traumatic memory. (Yet not even snapshots capture "the given" as it is, without distortion and selection.)[20] Events are experienced by means of representations—sensory perceptions, bodily sensations, and linguistic classification (even if only as "something terrifying")—and these are all influenced by the perceived cultural meanings of the events. As Maurice Halbwachs notes, "It is in society that people acquire their memories."[21] I would add that this is so even when people are alone at the time the memories are acquired. "It is also in society that they recall, recognize, and localize their memories" (Halbwachs 1992, 38) and again, I would add, even when they are alone during the process.

How one experiences a trauma, for example, depends on how one (often unconsciously) categorizes the event: is it life-threatening, is it human-inflicted, is it inescapable? These categorizations determine whether one feels fear, anger, hopelessness, and other seemingly unmediated emotions. How an experience is categorized depends on available models and metaphors. While I experienced my assault as a rape-in-progress, I attempted to enact a range of rape-avoidance scripts. When, after the first murder attempt, I experienced the assault as torture-resulting-in-murder, I recalled stories of Holocaust victims and heard my assailant speaking in what I later described as a "gruff, gestapo-like voice." Since I was not familiar with a literature of generic attempted-murder victim narratives, I framed my experience in terms of a genre with which I was familiar. I do not advocate such appropriation of others' trauma narratives, however, as I am aware of the risks of misappropriation, especially of the Holocaust archetype. But inevitably events are experienced and later narrated through available archetypes. These, then, must be subjected to critical analysis.[22]

I recall first experiencing my assault as an incomprehensible random event, surely a nightmare. It reversed the epistemological crisis provoked by Descartes's question, "What if I'm dreaming?" Instead, I asked myself in desperation, "What if I'm awake?" When the sexual nature of the assault became apparent, I experienced it as a rape ("oh, so that's what this is") and tried to recall all I'd heard about what one is supposed to do in such a situation. When, after I "woke up," subsequent to being strangled into unconsciousness, I realized that I was being treated as a corpse (my assailant was dragging me by my feet to a creek bed at the bottom of a steep ravine), I redescribed the event as "a murder-in-progress." Each new categorization affected my perception of my assailant and my strategies of defense. And each inflects how I remember and would now describe the event: "I felt a sudden blow from behind, like being hit by a car"; "I was a victim of gender-motivated sexual violence"; "I survived a near-fatal murder attempt."

In light of these ways in which I experienced the traumatic event, I am puzzled by literary theorist Cathy Caruth's discussion of trauma as an "unclaimed" or "missed experience."[23] She writes that trauma is the result of "the lack of preparedness to take in a stimulus that comes too quickly. It is not simply, that is, the literal threatening of bodily life, but the fact that the threat is recognized as such by the mind *one moment too late*. The shock of the mind's relation to the threat of death is thus not the direct experience of the threat, but precisely the *missing* of this experience, the fact that, not being experienced *in time*, it has not yet been fully known" (1996, 62). There is a slippage, in Caruth's discussion, from a noting of the lack of preparedness for the threat of death to a claim that the experience of the threat of death is missing, which may be true in the case of some survivors. But research on trauma indicates that, at least in the case of a single traumatic event, the event is experienced at the time and remembered from that time, although the full emotional impact of the trauma takes time to absorb and work through (Herman 1992; Shay 1994; van der Kolk and van der Hart 1995).

The anthropologist Elizabeth Tonkin notes that "the contents or evoked messages of memory are . . . ineluctably social insofar as they are acquired in the social world and can be coded in symbol systems which are culturally familiar."[24] The same can be said of experiences themselves. Historian Joan Scott rightly rejects the "appeal to experience as uncontestable evidence and as an originary point of explanation—as a foundation upon which analysis is based."[25] Such an appeal to experience not only weakens "the critical thrust of histories of difference," as Scott notes, but it also fails to capture the experience of experience.

Naomi Scheman has argued that even psychological states such as emotions are social constructs, which is not to say that anyone consciously constructs them or that one can choose not to have them.[26] As Scott puts it, "Subjects are constituted discursively, experience is a linguistic event (it doesn't happen outside established meanings), but neither is it confined to a fixed order of meaning. Since discourse is by definition shared, experience is collective as well as individual" (1992, 34). It is important to note the parenthetical comment she makes after stating that "experience is a linguistic event." She writes: "It doesn't happen outside established meanings." She is not implying, as some postmodernist theorists are uncharitably accused of thinking, that experiences such as rape or torture don't really happen, are all in the head, all in the culture, or all in the terms used to describe them. Events happen. But they can be described in countless ways, and they are experienced under some descriptions and not others.

To say that events are experienced only under descriptions (or, more broadly, representations) is to say more than that the experience must be viewed in context. Just as the experience is not simply given, neither is the context. Literary theorist Jonathan Culler's critique of the concept of context is useful here: "The notion of context frequently oversimplifies rather than enriches discussion, since the opposition between an act [or experience, I would add] and its context seems to presume that the context is given and determines the meaning of the act. We know, of course, that things are not so simple: context is not fundamentally different from what it contextualizes; context is not given but produced; what belongs to a context is determined by interpretive strategies; contexts are just as much in need of elucidation as events; and the meaning of a context is determined by events."[27]

Keeping in mind these caveats against taking the experience, its context, or its memory as given, we can avoid a third hazard of first-person narratives of trauma and victimization, which is the tendency to generate competing narratives of victimization, not all of which are justified. Legal theorist Martha Minow points out that "victim talk" tends to provoke counter-"victim talk" (note the recent rhetoric of the "angry white male victim" of affirmative action), and not all these narratives can be taken at face value, since they are often at odds with one another. She acknowledges that "individualized stories are essential to avoid the dehumanizing abstractions that allow people to forget or trivialize the suffering of others." But she warns that "there is a risk that emphasizing individual stories and stressing feelings can undermine critical evaluation and analysis of contradictory claims."[28] Once victims' stories are accepted as unassailable, unjustified reverse-victimization claims are harder to contradict, and ultimately no victimization claim can be taken seriously. The solution is not to silence (or ignore) all victimization claims but to evaluate them and attempt to overcome the difficulties of understanding experiences of those who are different from ourselves. Since perceptions of nondominant groups are commonly considered "biased" insofar as they depart from the norm, special efforts are required to evaluate them fairly. In order to do this, we need "to insist upon connecting personal stories with larger understandings of social structures within which those stories arise" (Minow 1993, 1437).

First-person narratives—of trauma or of other experiences of victimization—cannot be taken simply at face value. Consider, for example, the self-blame common among survivors of rape. No testimony is incorrigible. If a claim of victimization is made on behalf of a group, or because of one's membership in a group, the past and present victimization of the group in question needs to be critically examined. "Personal" testimonies must be framed by longer historical accounts and broader social and political ones.

It is also important, however, to avoid the trap of considering only discrete historical events to be traumatic. Historian Pamela Ballinger, for example, asserts that "war veterans and survivors of the Holocaust and the A-bomb" are distinguished from "survivors of incest and other abuse" by the fact that "in the case of abuse victims, no overarching historical 'event' (particularly that of state-sponsored violence . . .) exists within which individual memories may participate or contest. Rather, the event of abuse took place privately. Its recollection, however, is facilitated by a broad social environment obsessed with memory and in which groups may jockey for benefits through appeal to collective histories."[29] The moral relevance of such spatiotemporal considerations is never made clear, however. What Ballinger considers "private," that is, sexual abuse as opposed to collective violence, can be viewed instead as gender-motivated violence against women, which is perpetrated against women collectively, albeit not all at once and in the same place. The fact that rape occurs all the time, in places all over the world, may render it less noticeable as a collective trauma but does not make it an exclusively "individual" trauma.

When a traumatic event is viewed as "individual" or "private," it is viewed as politically insignificant, an isolated event best forgotten. (In contrast, there can also be political pressure to remember traumas, such as rapes, that are made part of a nation's story of victimization.)[30] I experienced, before and after my assailant's trial, considerable pressure to forget. During a pretrial trip to France, I went to Grenoble to look over legal documents and discuss the case with my lawyer. I also met with the *avocat général*, who had possession of my dossier and, with some reluctance, agreed to show it to me. It included depositions, police records, medical reports, psychiatric evaluations, and photos of my bruised, swollen face and battered body, my assailant's scratched face, neck, and genitals and his muddied clothes, the disturbed underbrush by the roadside, my belt found in the woods, and footprints in the mud at the bottom of the ravine. After our discussion of how the case would most likely proceed, as I was about to leave his office, the *avocat général* stunned me with these parting words of advice: "When the trial is over, you must forget that this ever happened." I protested that forgetting such a traumatic event is not an easy thing for a victim to do. He then looked at me sternly and said, "But, *madame,* you must make an effort." As if this had been simply an isolated event, of concern only to me.

A fourth hazard of narrating trauma, insightfully discussed by political theorist Wendy Brown in *States of Injury,* is to perpetuate one's self-definition as victim and others' stereotypes of one's group as weak and helpless (1995, 52–76). I lack space here to reply to her challenging critique of victim-based identity politics as a tool for liberation but will say simply that it is *only* by remembering and narrating the

past—telling our stories and listening to others'—that we can participate in an ongoing, active construction of a narrative, not one that
confines us to a limiting past, but one that forms a background for the
present from which an imagined future can emerge.

THE ROLE OF NARRATIVE
IN RECOVERING FROM TRAUMA

I have been discussing the epistemological significance of narrative
in understanding trauma and victimization and will now examine the
psychological significance of narrative in recovering from trauma.
Although in this section I mainly discuss the constructive use of
narrative in recovering from trauma, I note that in the therapeutic
context as well as in the scholarly domain the employment of first-
person narratives is not without hazards. One hazard from the therapeutic standpoint, as noted below, is to take the narrative uncritically,
at face value, which can lead to unwarranted self-blaming. Another
is to confuse the epistemological role of narrative in understanding
trauma with the therapeutic role of narrative. To be epistemologically
useful, first-person narratives must be scrutinized critically. In incorporating a first-person narrative into my discussion of trauma, I am
doing scholarship, not therapy with an imagined audience, and I expect this scholarship to be treated as critically as any. My intent here
is to deflect the objection that narratives of victimization in scholarship are "not fair" (that is, not fair game for criticism).[31]
    The undoing of the self in trauma involves a radical disruption of
memory, a severing of past from present, and, typically, an inability
to envision a future. And yet trauma survivors often eventually find
ways to reconstruct themselves and carry on with reconfigured lives.
In this reconstruction, trauma narratives—what might be called
"speech acts of memory"—play an important role. Working through,
or remastering, traumatic memory (in the case of human-inflicted
trauma) involves a shift from being the object or medium of someone else's (the perpetrator's) speech to being the subject of one's own.
The act of bearing witness to the trauma facilitates this shift, not
only by transforming traumatic memory into a more or less coherent narrative, which can then be worked into the survivor's sense of
self and view of the world, but also by reintegrating the survivor into

a community, reestablishing connections essential to selfhood. The study of trauma, I suggest, provides support for a view of the self as fundamentally relational—able to be constructed, destroyed, and rebuilt through relations to others.

The study of trauma also supports the view of memory as multiform and often in flux. Memories of traumatic events can be themselves traumatic—uncontrollable, intrusive, and frequently somatic. They are experienced by the survivor as inflicted, not chosen—as flashbacks to the events themselves. (That they are experienced in this way does not, however, give them epistemologically privileged status, as snapshots of how things "really were.") In contrast, narrating memories to others who are strong and empathic enough to be able to listen enables survivors to gain control over traces left by the trauma. Narrative memory is not passively endured; rather, it is an act on the part of the narrator, a speech act that defuses traumatic memory, giving shape and a temporal order to the events recalled, establishing more control over their recalling, and helping the survivor to remake a self.

In order to recover, a trauma survivor needs to be able to establish greater control over traumatic memories and other intrusive symptoms of post-traumatic stress disorder, recover a sense of mastery over her environment (within reasonable limits), and be reconnected with humanity. Whether these achievements occur depends to a large extent on other people. By constructing and telling a narrative of the trauma endured, and with the help of understanding listeners, the survivor begins not only to integrate the traumatic episode into a life with a before and an after but also to gain control over the occurrence of intrusive memories.

It is a curious feature of trauma narratives that in the right circumstances *saying* something about a traumatic memory *does* something to it. A useful (although not complete) analogy can be drawn between trauma testimonies and performative utterances as described by J. L. Austin. Performative utterances are defined by Austin, in part, as those such that "the uttering of the sentence is, or is a part of, the doing of an action, which . . . would not *normally* be described as, or as 'just', saying something."[32] In the case of trauma testimonies, the action could be described as transforming traumatic memory into narrative memory, or as recovering or remaking the self. In the case of both performative utterances and trauma testimonies, cultural norms or conventions, as well as uptake on the part of some other individual(s), are required in order for the speech act to be successful ("felicitous," as Austin puts it).

There is also an important disanalogy, however, between performative utterances and trauma testimonies. According to Austin, performative utterances "do not 'describe' or 'report' or constate anything at all, are not 'true or false'" (1962, 5). This claim is controversial, however: one might argue that some performative utterances, such as "I do," do describe something and may be taken to be true or false. In any case, trauma testimonies do purport to describe events that actually occurred.

Claims of memory—of the form "I remember that p"—are ambiguous, however. In one sense of "remembering" (which might more appropriately be called "seeming to remember"), such claims are about a present act of consciousness and can be true regardless of any correspondence to any past experience or state of affairs. In another sense, one can correctly be said to remember only things that were once experienced. It may be that the performative, healing aspect of trauma testimonies is distinct from their functioning as reports of historical fact. That is, the same utterance could be (at least) two kinds of speech act: one of bearing witness (describing events as they occurred) and one of narrating (and thus transforming) traumatic memories. The latter might have a performative aspect not shared by the former. One speech act might succeed, even if the other fails. The description might succeed in describing the world as it was, even if the performative fails because of infelicitous conditions. Or vice versa. This controversial conjecture is too complex to explore here, but it is relevant to the collision between the roles of testimony in clinical settings and in courts of law in the "recovered memory" debates.

Although there are many varieties of trauma narrative, the form discussed most widely in the literature on trauma is that of a survivor telling her story to another person, often a therapist. Most psychologists writing about trauma hold that one has to tell one's trauma narrative to an empathic other in order for the telling to be therapeutic. Dori Laub writes, "Only when the survivor knows he is being heard will he stop to hear—and listen to—himself" (Felman and Laub 1992, 71).

But some survivors are helped by telling their stories to imagined others—to potential readers, for example, or to others kept alive in a photograph (Felman and Laub 1992, 86–87). Narrating a trauma involves externalizing it, which can be done in a variety of ways. Writing in a journal can help externalize a trauma by temporarily splitting the self into an active (narrating) subject and a more passive (described) object. This process can help resubjectify a self objectified by trauma; it also can enable the survivor to gain greater empathy with herself.

Writing in others' imagined voices, as Charlotte Delbo has done in *Auschwitz and After,* can be another way of externalizing and hearing not only their narratives but also the writer's own.[33] Hearing other survivors' actual narratives in the context of group therapy can also be healing in ways that go beyond the capacity of individual therapy. It not only can enable a survivor to feel empathy for her traumatized self (by first feeling it for another who experienced a similar trauma) but also make possible appropriate emotions, such as anger, that she was not able to feel on her own behalf. By first feeling empathy with other survivors and getting angry with their tormentors, she is better able to get angry with her own. Hearing others' narratives can also help trauma survivors to move beyond unjustified self-blame. (Well, if she clearly wasn't to blame for her assault, why should I blame myself for mine?)

Arguably, the most serious harm of trauma is loss of control. Researchers on trauma have defined it as a state of complete helplessness in the face of an overwhelming force. Herman says the trauma victim "is rendered helpless by overwhelming force. . . . Traumatic events overwhelm the ordinary systems of care that give people a sense of control, connection, and meaning" (Herman 1992, 33). The most daunting task faced by the trauma survivor is to regain a sense of control over her or his life, and not all survivors employ the same strategies to regain that control. As Michele Fine has pointed out, some refrain from taking control by going to the police or seeking the help of a social worker, since they may have reasons to doubt the efficacy of such approaches. She observes: "Taking control is undoubtedly a significant psychological experience; knowing that one can effect change in one's environment makes a difference. How individuals accomplish this, however, does vary by economic and social circumstance, gender, and perhaps personal style." From my readings and my experiences, I have gathered that the attempt to regain control by means of self-blame is common to many survivors of different races and classes.[34]

Trauma survivors (rape survivors, in particular, because they are frequently blamed for their assaults) are faced with an especially intractable double bind: they need to know there's something they can do to avoid being similarly traumatized in the future, but if there *is* such a thing, then they blame themselves for not knowing it (or doing it) at the time. They are faced with a choice between regaining control by accepting (at least some) responsibility—and hence blame—for the trauma, or feeling overwhelmed by helplessness. Whereas many have misunderstood, for example, rape victims' self-blaming as merely a self-destructive response to rape, arising out of low self-esteem, feelings of shame, or female masochism and fueled by society's desire to blame the victim, it can also be seen as an adaptive survival strategy if the victim has no other way of regaining a sense of control. At the same time, the fact that victims (especially rape victims) so readily blame themselves for what happened is another reason for not taking victims' narrative at face value.

The need for control reinforces, and is reinforced by, a fundamental assumption most of us share, which is our belief that we live in a just world in which nothing that is both terrible and undeserved will happen to us.[35] Even though many of us recognize the delusory quality of such a belief, our desire to make sense of our experiences, including our random bad fortune, often swamps our better judgment. Social psychologists have observed that not only do others tend to blame and derogate victims of crime and disasters of various kinds, but victims tend to blame and derogate themselves even when it should be obvious that they could not have brought on their misfortune. A striking example is the study done by Rubin and Peplau of fifty-eight draft-eligible young men who were informed by the 1971 lottery of their likelihood for being drafted into the armed forces (Lerner 1980, 140). They completed questionnaires designed to measure self-esteem before and after hearing the results of the lottery. Those with bad draft rankings showed lowered self-esteem; those with good ones showed enhanced self-esteem. Of course, depression can also lower self-esteem, and the subjects with bad luck were probably instantly depressed by the news.

One might think it would be easier (it certainly would be more appropriate) for victims of violence to blame their assailants. But a further reason for the prevalence of self-blame among rape survivors, in addition to the need for control and the belief in a just world, is the difficulty so many have in getting angry with their assailants. I have met many rape survivors and have been stunned by how few are able to feel anger toward their assailants. It was not until after I had taken a self-defense course that I was able to get angry with the man who almost killed me. These observations led me to speculate that experiencing anger toward one's attacker is so difficult because it requires imagining oneself in proximity to him, a prospect that is too terrifying if one is still feeling powerless with respect to him.

The difficulty of directing anger toward their attackers exacerbates trauma victims' tendency to blame themselves in order to feel more in control of their fate. Although self-blame can help victims regain a feeling of control, not all varieties of self-blame do. Psychologist Ronnie Janoff-Bulman has distinguished between behavioral self-blame, which attributes victimization to modifiable past behavior, and characterological self-blame, which attributes it to unalterable (and undesirable) character traits. She found that behavioral self-blame facilitates recovery by giving victims a sense of control, whereas characterological self-blame leaves victims feeling vulnerable and leads to a greater incidence of depression.[36] This finding isn't surprising, since we tend to think that our behavior is under our control, whereas our characters, to a large extent, are not. They are, on the contrary, what control us. Characterological self-blame also usually contributes to the loss of self-esteem already suffered by victims who have been subjected to degrading treatment by their assailants. The exception may be the victim who is able to blame the assault on traits of a "former self," traits no longer possessed by a "current self."[37]

Behavioral self-blame, on the contrary, appears to lessen depression and facilitate recovery. Indeed, those victims who find themselves unable to engage in behavioral self-blame are left with feelings of extreme helplessness that can make recovery more difficult. Patricia A. Resick notes that "two studies have found that rape victims who appraised the situation as 'safe' prior to the assault had greater fear and depressive reactions than women who perceived themselves to be in a dangerous situation prior to the assault."[38] If there was nothing victims could have done to prevent the attack, such as avoiding certain dangerous settings or situations, there is nothing they could do to prevent a similar attack in the future. This conclusion helps to explain the observation that trauma survivors who did not anticipate the trauma (and thus could not have done anything to prevent it) have a more difficult time recovering, other things being equal, than those who saw what was coming and experienced anxiety ahead of time. But even though behavioral self-blame can serve an adaptive function, it is a costly survival strategy for the victim, and it is not only fueled by but also contributes to society's erroneous and dangerous victim-blaming attitudes. Although this form of self-blame gives the victim the sense that she could avoid being assaulted again in the future by avoiding whatever "blameworthy" behavior "brought it on" in the past, it also leads to self-berating for her past "mistakes" and to unfair, and ultimately futile, self-imposed restrictions on her behavior in the future.

But given that the alternative to self-blame appears to be feeling helpless, which is harder to bear, how can self-blame be avoided? One way for rape survivors, in particular, to break out of the double bind of self-blame or helplessness is to take a self-defense course. Although learning self-defense does not guarantee that they will never be victimized again, it greatly increases their options for fending off assault[39] and enables them to feel in control of their lives without having to blame themselves or to restrict their behavior in ways never expected of men. And, perhaps even more important, it makes it easier for victims to put the blame where it belongs: on their assailants. This result is facilitated by the ability to feel appropriate anger toward the attacker once the terror induced by helplessness subsides. One group of researchers who studied women students who took a self-defense class "saw them discover that feeling angry was an alternative to feeling fearful or helpless. Learning to become angry with someone else rather than feeling frightened or helpless may enable the students to assume responsibility for the solution without blaming themselves for the problem."[40]

Of course, self-defense instruction is not a panacea. It does not eliminate the problem of violence and might even contribute to the common misperception of gender-motivated violence as an individual rather than a collective trauma. At best, it can give some people a greater chance of avoiding being victimized, most likely by deflecting the assailant's attention onto other targets. As C. H. Sparks and Bat-Ami Bar On have argued, self-defense tactics are "stopgap measures which fail to link an attack against one victim with attacks on others."And, as they point out, "knowledge that one can fight if attacked is also a very different kind of security from enjoying a certainty that one will not be attacked at all."[41]

I have been discussing here simply the role of self-defense in helping a trauma survivor to carry on in the aftermath of a violent assault. My discussion of self-defense training points to one limitation of purely linguistic narratives in enabling recovery from trauma. It may be that in some cases a kind of physical remastering of the trauma is necessary. In learning self-defense maneuvers and then imaginatively reenacting the traumatic event—with the ability to change the ending—in space as well as in the imagination, a survivor can gain even more control over traumatic memories. As Janet notes, "Memory is an action: essentially it is the action of telling a story" (1984, 2:272). In recovering from trauma, a survivor may be helped not only by telling the story but also by being able to rewrite the plot and then enact it.

NOTES

This chapter was completed at the School of Social Science at the Institute for Advanced Study in Princeton, N.J., where I spent 1997–1998 on a grant sponsored by the National Endowment for the Humanities. For helpful responses when I presented this as a talk at the Cornell University Society for the Humanities in March 1998, I am grateful to members of the audience, fellows of the Society for the Humanities, and, especially, Dominick LaCapra. I am also indebted to Atina Grossmann, Jodi Halpern, Margot Livesey, and Thomas Trezise for insightful comments on earlier drafts. Finally, I thank Mieke Bal and Joan W. Scott, for challenging discussions of some of the ideas in this chapter and for drawing my attention to numerous useful references, and Claudia Card, for helping to bring this writing into its final form, in numerous ways above and beyond the call of editorial duty.

1. Dori Laub, "An Event Without a Witness: Truth, Testimony and Survival," in *Testimony: Crises of Witnessing in Literature, Psychoanalysis, and History,* ed. Shoshana Felman and Dori Laub (New York: Routledge, 1992), p. 78.

2. See Sigmund Freud, "Remembering, Repeating and Working-Through," in *The Standard Edition of the Complete Psychological Works of Sigmund Freud* (hereafter SE), trans. under general editorship of James Strachey in collaboration with Anna Freud, assisted by Alix Strachey and Alan Tyson, 24 vols. (London: Hogarth, 1953–1974), vol. 12 (1958 [1914]), pp. 145–56; Freud, "Mourning and Melancholia," in SE, vol. 14 (1957 [1917]), pp. 238–58; Freud, *Beyond the Pleasure Principle,* in SE, vol. 18 (1955 [1920]), pp. 3–64; Pierre Janet, *Les médications psychologiques.* 3 vols. (1919–1925; reprint, Paris: Société Pierre Janet, 1984).

3. *Diagnostic and Statistical Manual of Mental Disorders,* 4th ed. (Washington, D.C.: American Psychiatric Association, 1994), pp. 424–29; Judith Lewis Herman, *Trauma and Recovery* (New York: Basic Books, 1992); Jonathan Shay, *Achilles in Vietnam: Combat Trauma and the Undoing of Character* (New York: Atheneum, 1994); Bessel van der Kolk and Onno van der Hart, "The Intrusive Past: the Flexibility of Memory and the Engraving of Trauma," in *Trauma: Explorations in Memory,* ed. Cathy Caruth (Baltimore: Johns Hopkins University Press, 1995), pp. 158–182. "Trauma" here, in contrast with my use of the term, also refers to traumatic events not of human origin. My use of "trauma" is closer to Freud's implicit use in "traumatic neurosis" (defined by Laplanche and Pontalis as the "type of neurosis in which the appearance of symptoms follows upon an emotional shock generally associated with a situation where the subject has felt his life to be in danger") than it is to his use in "trauma (psychical)" (defined by Laplanche and Pontalis as "an event in the subject's life defined by its intensity, by the subject's incapacity to respond adequately, and by the upheaval and long-lasting effects that it brings about in the psychical organisation"); J. Laplanche and J.-B. Pontalis, *The Language of Psychoanalysis,* trans. Donald Nicholson-Smith (New York: W. W. Norton, 1973), pp. 470 and 465.

4. I do, however, accept that psychic trauma has physical effects and that physical trauma has psychic effects. For discussion of this issue, see Susan J. Brison, "Speech, Harm, and the Mind-Body Problem in First Amendment Jurisprudence," *Legal Theory* 4 (1998): 39–61.

5. Binjamin Wilkomirski, *Fragments: Memories of a Wartime Childhood,* trans. Carol Brown Janeway (New York: Schocken Books, 1996).

6. The following discussion of philosophical bias against first-person narratives draws on my "On the Personal As Philosophical," *APA Newsletter on Feminism and Philosophy* 95.1 (1995): 37–40. I thank Eva F. Kittay and Diana T. Meyers (who edited that issue) and two anonymous reviewers for their comments. The earliest work in feminist philosophy of which I am aware that employs and defends the personal voice is Claudia Card, "Feminist Ethical Theory: A Lesbian Perspective" (unpublished manuscript), presented as a lecture in 1978 at the University of Minnesota and to the Feminist Inquiry Seminar at Dartmouth College.

7. Bertrand Russell, *The Problems of Philosophy* (New York: Oxford University Press, 1969), p. 160.

8. Friedrich Nietzsche, *Beyond Good and Evil,* trans. Walter Kaufmann (New York: Vintage, 1966), p. 13. In invoking Nietzsche's view of the autobiographical aspect of philosophy, I do not intend to endorse his other philosophical positions.

9. Virginia Held, *Feminist Morality: Transforming Culture, Society, and Politics* (Chicago: University of Chicago Press, 1993), p. 19.

10. Ross Harrison, "Rape—A Case Study in Political Philosophy," in *Rape: An Historical and Cultural Enquiry,* ed. Sylvana Tomaselli and Ray Porter (New York: Basil Blackwell, 1986), p. 51.

11. René Descartes, *Meditations,* in *The Philosophical Writings of Descartes,* vol. 2, trans. John Cottingham, Robert Stoothoff, and Dugald Murdoch (New York: Cambridge University Press, 1984), p. 13.

12. As Claudia Card has pointed out to me, there was not even a body of abstract philosophical literature on rape (E. M. Curley, "Excusing Rape," *Phi-*

losophy and Public Affairs 5 (1976): 325–60, was an exception) prior to articles by Susan Griffin, Carolyn M. Shafer and Marilyn Frye, Pamela Foa, and Susan Rae Peterson in *Feminism and Philosophy*, ed. Mary Vetterling-Braggin, Frederick Elliston, and Jane English (Totowa, N.J.: Littlefield, Adams, 1977). Published the same year was Lorenne Clark and Debra Lewis, *Rape: The Price of Coercive Sexuality* (Toronto: Women's Press, 1977). Now there are several anthologies of philosophical writings on rape (including first-person narratives) and a growing literature from other disciplines. See, for example, the first-person scholarship on rape by anthropologist Cathy Winkler, including "Rape As Social Murder," *Anthropology Today* 7, 3 (1991): 12–14, and "Ethnography of the Ethnographer" (with Penelope J. Hanke), in *Fieldwork Under Fire: Contemporary Studies of Violence and Survival*, ed. Carolyn Nordstrom and Antonius C. G. M. Robben (Berkeley: University of California Press, 1994), pp. 154–84.

13. Diana Meyers, "Social Exclusion, Moral Reflection, and Rights," *Law and Philosophy* 12, 2 (May 1993): 125–26.

14. Renato Rosaldo, *Culture and Truth: The Remaking of Social Analysis* (Boston: Beacon Press, 1989), pp. 1–21.

15. Susan Estrich, *Real Rape* (Cambridge: Harvard University Press, 1987), pp. 1–3.

16. Annette C. Baier, *Moral Prejudices: Essays on Ethics* (Cambridge: Harvard University Press, 1994), p. 194.

17. For insightful discussions of the use of "we" in group identity politics, see Marianna Torgovnick, "The Politics of the 'We,'" in *Eloquent Obsessions: Writing Cultural Criticism*, ed. M. Torgovnick (Durham, N.C.: Duke University Press, 1994), pp. 260–77, and Wendy Brown, *States of Injury* (Princeton, N.J.: Princeton University Press, 1995).

18. Andreas Huyssen, *Twilight Memories: Marking Time in a Culture of Amnesia* (New York: Routledge, 1995), p. 3.

19. See the recovered memory therapy debates, especially Ian Hacking, *Rewriting the Soul: Multiple Personality and the Sciences of Memory* (Princeton, N.J.: Princeton University Press, 1995); Elizabeth Loftus and K. Ketcham, *The Myth of Repressed Memories: False Memories and Allegations of Sexual Abuse* (New York: St. Martin's Press, 1994); and Lenore Terr, *Unchained Memories* (New York: Basic Books, 1995).

20. See Nelson Goodman, *Languages of Art* (Indianapolis: Hackett, 1976), pp. 14–16.

21. Maurice Halbwachs, *On Collective Memory*, ed. and trans. Lewis A. Coser (Chicago: University of Chicago Press, 1992), p. 38.

22. For insightful discussion of the misappropriation of Holocaust narratives, see James E. Young, *Writing and Rewriting the Holocaust: Narrative and the Consequences of Interpretation* (Bloomington: Indiana University Press, 1988), especially pp. 83–133.

23. Cathy Caruth, *Unclaimed Experiences* (Baltimore: Johns Hopkins University Press, 1996).

24. Elizabeth Tonkin, *Narrating Our Pasts: The Social Construction of Oral History* (New York: Cambridge University Press, 1992), p. 112.

25. Joan W. Scott, "'Experience,'" in *Feminists Theorize the Political*, ed. Judith Butler and Joan W. Scott (New York: Routledge, 1992), p. 24.

26. Naomi Scheman, "Individualism and the Objects of Psychology," in

Discovering Reality: Feminist Perspectives on Epistemology, Metaphysics, Methodology, and Philosophy of Science, ed. Sandra Harding and Merrill B. Hintikka (Boston: Reidel, 1983), pp. 225–44.

27. Jonathan Culler, *Framing the Sign: Criticism and Its Institutions* (Norman: University of Oklahoma Press, 1988), p. xiv.

28. Martha Minow, "Surviving Victim Talk," *UCLA Law Review* 40 (1993): 1435. Another common example of "victim-talk" generating counter-"victim-talk" is domestic violence litigation in which each partner may claim to be the victim (Claudia Card, correspondence).

29. Pamela Ballinger, "The Culture of Survivors: Post-Traumatic Stress Disorder and Traumatic Memory," *History and Memory* 10, 1 (Spring 1988): 121–22. For an excellent defense of the opposing view—that rape is a form of collective violence against women—see Claudia Card, "Rape As a Terrorist Institution," in *Violence, Terrorism, and Justice,* ed. R. G. Frey and Christopher W. Morris (Cambridge, Eng.: Cambridge University Press, 1991), pp. 296–319.

30. See Atina Grossmann, "A Question of Silence: The Rape of German Women by Occupation Soldiers," in *West Germany Under Construction: Politics, Society, and Culture in the Adenauer Era,* ed. Robert G. Moeller (Ann Arbor: University of Michigan Press, 1997), pp. 33–52.

31. For a similar—and, I believe, similarly misguided—objection to so-called "victim art," see dance critic Arlene Croce's explanation of her refusal to attend and review Bill T. Jones's *Still/Here* in "Discussing the Undiscussable," *New Yorker,* 24 December 1994/2 January 1995, 54–60. For insightful analysis of the Croce article, see Elizabeth V. Spelman, *Fruits of Sorrow: Framing Our Attention to Suffering* (Boston: Beacon, 1997), pp. 133–56.

32. J. L. Austin, *How to Do Things with Words* (Cambridge: Harvard University Press, 1962), p. 5.

33. Charlotte Delbo, *Auschwitz and After,* trans. Rosette C. Lamont (New Haven: Yale University Press, 1995).

34. Michele Fine, "Coping with Rape: Critical Perspectives on Consciousness," in *Disruptive Voices,* ed. M. Fine (Ann Arbor: University of Michigan Press, 1992), p. 73.

35. See Melvin J. Lerner, *The Belief in a Just World: A Fundamental Delusion* (New York: Plenum, 1980).

36. Ronnie Janoff-Bulman, "Characterological Versus Behavioral Self-Blame: Inquiries into Depression and Rape," *Journal of Personality and Social Psychology* 37, 10 (1979): 1798–1809.

37. In "Self-Blame in Victims of Violence," *Journal of Social Issues,* 39, 2 (1983): 150, Dale T. Miller and Carol A. Porter suggest that this splitting of the self may be a way of coping,

38. Patricia A. Resick, "The Psychological Impact of Rape," *Journal of Interpersonal Violence* 8, 2 (June 1993): 223–55. For the studies she cites, see E. Frank and B. D. Stewart, "Depressive Symptoms in Rape Victims: A Revisit," *Journal of Affective Disorders* 1 (1984): 77–85, and K. L. Schepple and P. B. Bart, "Through Women's Eyes: Defining Danger in the Wake of Sexual Assault," *Journal of Social Issues* 39, 2 (1983): 63–81.

39. See Pauline B. Bart and Patricia H. O'Brien, "Stopping Rape: Effective Avoidance Strategies," *Signs* 10 (Autumn 1984): 83–101.

40. Louise H. Kidder, Joanne L. Boell, and Marilyn M. Moyer, "Rights

Consciousness and Victimization Prevention: Personal Defense and Assertiveness Training," *Journal of Social Issues* 39, 2 (1983): 153–68.

41. C. H. Sparks and B.-A. Bar On, "A Social Change Approach to the Prevention of Sexual Violence Against Women," *Work in Progress,* series no. 83-08 (Wellesley, Mass.: Stone Center for Developmental Services and Studies, Wellesley College, 1985), p. 3.

11 / *Pornographic Subordination:*
How Pornography Silences Women

LYNNE TIRRELL

Catharine MacKinnon opens *Only Words* with a challenge to her reader: "Imagine that for hundreds of years your most formative traumas, your daily suffering and pain, the abuse you live through, the terror you live with are unspeakable—not the basis of literature."[1] With this opening, MacKinnon gives pride of place to her commitment to the importance of women's being able to name, describe, and protest our experience. She raises the question of literature here, but her concern is really the law and particularly the law as it protects pornography. My concern is not to address whether legal reform is appropriate; my goal is to help to make sense of MacKinnon's claim that pornography silences women. I urge that we think about the interpretive frameworks that pornography establishes and promotes, particularly their power over ourselves and others around us, and that we try to be creative in combating these forces—whether the law steps in or not. MacKinnon would like to see the law prevent some men (and sympathizing women) from nearly monopolistic control over defining women as particular kinds of sexual beings. Such prevention would open the possibility that perhaps, once the voices of today's pornographers are quieted, other voices could be heard. MacKinnon's project of silencing pornographers is only half the story. We must also be constructing our own interpretations of women and sexuality. We must be thinking of what we *want* to be saying, and we must begin to say it.

The claim that pornography silences women is like other silencing claims; it seems so exaggerated that it is generally dismissed. Weakly interpreted, the claim reminds us of the terrible fact that women die every year in the process of making pornography and that these women neither foresaw their deaths nor consented to them. MacKinnon's point is stronger. She is urging that the very existence of pornography as we know it today, a multibillion-dollar-a-year industry with very wide-ranging influence, serves to silence all women as agents and undermines our ability to define ourselves and live our lives outside of its cultural matrix.[2] Its general conflation of sex with male dominance and female subordination is totalizing; everything comes within the sphere it has appropriated for itself. So, we have two interdependent tasks: we must break down the totalizing power of pornography, and we must construct our own cultural matrices within which we can acknowledge our dignity and live healthier, happier lives.

This problem of gaining the authority to name our experience is a theme throughout late twentieth-century feminist work; it is a general problem for oppressed people, not specific to women's oppression. Because oppression silences, fighting oppression requires developing voices, languages, and cultural and interpretive matrices for the articulation of our experiences. It is difficult for the oppressed to name their experiences and describe their worlds, for oppression puts them in a double bind. If they tell how things seem to them, they will be viewed as either complicit or crazy. James Baldwin, and more recently Nathan McCall, both express gratitude to Richard Wright for his controversial novel *Native Son*, which Wright almost did not write for fear of the disdain of the black middle class and the glee of racist whites.[3] Bigger Thomas is a frightening protagonist. Still, many African American men found his presence in literature liberating. Baldwin said, "Growing up in a certain kind of poverty is growing up in a certain kind of silence," adding that the basic elements of your life are unnamable because "no one corroborates it. Reality becomes unreal because no one experiences it but you."

Similarly, Catharine MacKinnon argues that the claim that pornography is a form of speech, "an expression of ideas, a discussion, a debate, a discourse," ultimately teaches women that "language does not belong to you, that you cannot use it to say what you know, that knowledge is not what you learn from your life, that information is not made out of your experience. You learn that thinking about what happened to you does not count as 'thinking' but doing it apparently does. You learn that your reality subsists somewhere beneath the socially real" (OW, 6). Richard Wright's *Native Son* was a faithful portrayal of a way of life, a condition of life, that had been invisible to and invalidated by the world, especially the reading world, until he wrote it. Depicting Bigger Thomas was a brave and radical act, which Baldwin did not see as retarding the chances for black liberation despite the concerns of the black middle class and the joys of white racists. Baldwin explains why it is so important to gain the ability to speak for oneself, to depict and describe one's world; he says: "Life was made bearable by Richard Wright's testimony. When circumstances are made real by another's testimony, it becomes possible to envision change."[4]

ABSOLUTISM

The power of our words and images to make things real by naming them is the heart of the issues concerning hate speech and pornography. Words and images do have the power to make something seem real, and sometimes seeming is the first step toward being. This power works both sides of the street. As MacKinnon notes, "Elevation and denigration are all accomplished through meaningful symbols and communicative acts in which saying it is doing it" (OW, 13).[5] The worry is that the normative force of the derogatory categories is so strong that uttering them moves beyond the realm of mere discourse and into the realm of coercive action.

Antipornography feminists and antihate speech activists tend to be absolutist about the interpretation of the images or expressions that constitute harmful modes of discourse. They tend to hold that the derogatory words and images have one interpretation, that it is harmful, and that it is produced in and serves to reinforce a context of oppression and exploitation. Absolutists maintain that derogatory words or images have no redeeming value, for they cannot be used in nonderogatory ways. Absolutists think that the community's only power is to eradicate the terms. Richard Delgado, for example, claims that racist derogatory terms "are badges of degradation even when used between friends; these words have no other connotation."[6] No matter who says these words, when, where, and why, the terms each have one meaning and one function—degradation. Similarly, MacKinnon claims that pornographic images ultimately say and do just one thing: they subordinate women through sex. Contexts may mediate other discourses, but MacKinnon proclaims that "pornography is largely its own context" (OW, 108).

Absolutists are right that our expressions, through the use of words and pictures, have an ontological power that must not be overlooked. Words and images have the power to shape reality. Absolutists are also right to emphasize that saying words and presenting images count as acts or deeds, but unfortunately they tend to offer too simplistic an account of what those deeds are. This oversimplification of the linguistic, conceptual, and ontological force of these derogatory terms and subordinating images is what grounds the Absolutist's practical political program. Once the oversimplification is exposed, we can see and respect the tremendous complexity of what we can do with our words and images, even these nasty ones.

Absolutists generally appeal to the power of the broader social context to explain the derogating force of the words or images; this force is what severely restricts the interpretation of the expression. For example, in *Words That Wound* Mari Matsuda says, "Racist speech is particularly harmful because it is a mechanism of subordination, reinforcing a historically vertical relationship" (1993, 36). Pornography maintains gender hierarchy; there can be no doubt that these expressions occur in a context in which there is "a historically vertical relationship" and that pornography is instrumental in maintaining women's subordination. MacKinnon reverses Matsuda's order of explanation; she sees sexist oppression as the result of pornography, arguing that social "inequality is substantially created and enforced—that is, done—through words and images. Social hierarchy cannot and does not exist without being embodied in meanings and expressed in communication" (OW, 13). Pornography, according to MacKinnon, is not a problem just because it says that women are subordinate, for there are "many ways to say what pornography says, in the sense of its content." The achievement of pornography is what's unique, since "nothing else does what pornography does" (OW, 15).

Elsewhere, MacKinnon explains that "what pornography *does* goes beyond its content: it eroticizes hierarchy, it sexualizes inequality. It makes dominance and submission into sex. . . . [Pornography] institutionalizes the sexuality of male supremacy, fusing the eroticization of dominance and submission with the social construction of male and female."[7] So pornography is not defined by sexual explicitness but rather by its fusion of sexuality with male dominance and female submission. This fusion goes some way toward effecting the subordination. MacKinnon and Dworkin's Model Ordinance defines pornography as "the graphic sexually explicit *subordination* of women through pictures and / or words" (OW, 121 n. 32) and specifies a variety of contents through which such subordination may be achieved. Most people reading their definition of pornography focus on the list of contents and think that one can read backward: if "women are presented as dehumanized," then it is pornography; if "women are presented as sexual objects who enjoy sexual humiliation or pain," then it is pornography, and so on. But these "contents" are not sufficient for a set of words or images to be pornography; somehow the picture has to get from being about subordination to being itself subordinating. It is crucial that MacKinnon and Dworkin emphasize the subordinating power of the depiction, which leaves open the possibility that not all graphic sexually explicit depictions of women's subordination will be pornographic. I am not sure this is a possibility that the ordinance is really supposed to leave open, but I suggest later that MacKinnon *must* leave it open in order to promote women's testimony about our lives.

THE CASE: *BOWMAN V. HELLER*

Now I ask you to consider a sexual harassment case involving pornography that is currently on appeal in Massachusetts. This case helps to illustrate a direct use of pornography to undermine a woman's credibility, but it also suggests a provisional answer to how pornography silences women more generally.

In late October 1987, David Heller cut some pictures out of a pornographic magazine and pasted the face of his coworker Sylvia Bowman over the models' faces. Heller then photocopied the pictures, distributing them first to five colleagues he thought would enjoy the "joke"; ultimately, they passed throughout the Massachusetts Department of Public Welfare, where both he and Sylvia Bowman worked. Heller took the image of Bowman's face from postcards she was using to campaign for president of the union, thereby linking his created image with her campaign. Sylvia Bowman did not see the photocopies until after she had lost the union election; later, she sued Heller for sexual harassment. She won, and he has appealed, with Alan Dershowitz at his side. Dershowitz, claiming to abhor what Heller did, argues that the lower court's decision violates Heller's right to free speech. David Heller says that the photo collages were "a harmless prank" and "a childish satire"; he still doesn't get it about the harm he did to Sylvia Bowman.

Sylvia Bowman heard about the pictures the day they first hit the office, but she decided, with the help of her campaign manager, John Stockman (who had seen them), not to view them while she was actively campaigning. She was warned that they would be devastating. When the campaign was over but before the results were known, Bowman met Stockman at a luncheonette during a break, at which time he handed her a sealed envelope with the pictures and advised her not to look until she was home. When Stockman left, Bowman looked; her shock was so intense that she doesn't remember what she did next. One witness said she thought that Sylvia Bowman was having a heart attack or a stroke; her psychologist has testified that Bowman is now suffering from post-traumatic stress disorder.[8]

One amicus brief argues that Heller "interfered with Bowman's ability to freely and effectively participate in her workplace. As a result . . . Bowman instead found herself the object of sexual remarks, ridicule, and derision. Bowman found it increasingly difficult to attend work-related activities and eventually could not go back to work at all."[9]

Little in this story fits the standard paradigm of hate speech. No one hurled a face-to-face epithet at another person, no one expressed anger, there was no violence and no direct or explicit threat of violence. And yet, there are important similarities between the standard model of hate speech and the less acute but more chronic and perhaps more insidious cases that the Bowman case exemplifies. One key similarity is that when we put the perpetrator's behavior into a broader social context, we can see how it serves to reinforce patterns of oppression, exploitation, and discrimination. Derogatory words and images have the power that they do because they support and are supported by a host of other sorts of social practices, from discriminatory employment practices to the redlining of neighborhoods to unequal access to education, and so on.

The pattern of the *Bowman v. Heller* case is quite typical of what has come to be at issue in discussions about whether freedom of speech (particularly men's) should be restricted in this arena because of the harm pornography does (particularly to women). This case blatantly exemplifies a pattern typical of the way many men and women react to pornographic images. David Heller thinks it is fun and "a harmless prank" to superimpose Bowman's face on the bodies of pornographically posed women; Sylvia Bowman feels assaulted by such images. That this happened so publicly is somewhat unusual, but neither Bowman nor Heller has stepped outside of their traditionally gendered identities for their parts in this drama. Heller is the adolescent boy, thrilled that sex is a game that's rigged in his favor. Bowman is the good woman who must distance herself from these images and the women within them—this is woman-as-sex and that's not the kind of woman she is. Bowman is positioned as the chaste woman who has been maligned. These identities are not exhaustive, of course, and they may even be stances enacted because this drama is playing itself out in the courtroom. For Bowman, in the context of the court, it would cost dearly to identify in any way with the women who are victimized in the making of pornography or to identify with those who see such sexual explicitness as liberatory.

David Heller's photo collages began with pornographic magazines; he saw the women in these magazines, and he imagined Sylvia Bowman as these women. The result was, in his eyes, "absurd." Women pictured in pornography have faces of their own, but in those contexts their faces are not of much consequence and are often obscured. Their pose, their exposure, their body as a thing for male consumption, is what matters. In fact, it is all too common for men to mentally put other women's faces on these images, and the faces they superimpose tend to be familiar. It also goes the other way around: men impose and superimpose these images on women's bodies. Robert Jensen reports, for example, that a man "who was convicted of molesting two 6-year-old girls and said he had also raped teenage girls, explained how he would masturbate at home to pornography while thinking of the young girls who rode the bus he drove and then watch the girls on the bus while fantasizing about the pornography."[10] We don't know how often this happens, but it puts us all in the position of Sylvia Bowman—not having opened the envelope yet and knowing the time has come when we cannot ignore it any longer.

In the eyes of the law, the issues surrounding *Bowman v. Heller* concern sexual harassment and freedom of speech. Heller was certainly being expressive when he made his nasty pictures, but he was not necessarily declaring or stating or asserting anything at all. Creating and presenting an image is not the same as saying a sentence or shouting a slogan. In this case, the creation of the image is more like the shouting of an epithet, in that it is a basic linking of a person with an expressive unit and the conceptual and behavioral network with which it is associated. If this interpretation is right, then the central action of *Bowman v. Heller* should be understood as like the paradigmatic hate speech case, except that it didn't first happen face to face.

．When David Heller created and circulated the pictures of Sylvia Bowman, he used images in a way that is very much like name-calling. Sociologist Irving Allen points out that name-calling "is a technique by which outgroups are defined as legitimate targets of aggression and is an effort to control outgroups by neutralizing their efforts to gain resources and influence values."[11] Think about the effect of Heller's composites on Bowman: like other forms of derogation, the pictures served to mark Bowman as a member of an out-group, they rationalized other forms of sexist treatment from other men in Bowman's office, and they reinforced psychological oppression.[12] They put Bowman in her place, as a woman.

The central cases of hate speech are generally taken to be those in which the speaker seems hateful and the words are clearly used as weapons.Yet the same reductive classification also occurs in cases in which there is no obvious anger, in which the words or images have become so normal that they are nearly invisible, cases in which we don't give them a second thought. Even in such cases, the individual is reduced to the derogated category. Taking the metaphor of words as weapons seriously, keep in mind that some weapons work like guns, exploding in a violent moment, whereas others work more like Agent Orange, strategically and somewhat indirectly, taking their biggest toll over time.The law is most interested in the incendiary nature of face-to-face name-calling. But an exclusive focus on these cases yields a very different understanding than one that also attends to speech acts like "You know Sylvia, the so-and-so." Such casual third-person uses may be more pervasive and ultimately more powerful, for they insidiously reinforce the mode of discourse along with its conceptual framework and its social ontology.

Such uses presuppose that it is okay to divide the world into those who are so-and-sos and those who are not, that being a so-and-so is a relevant feature of a person's identity, that so-and-so's are different from and less than not-so-and-so's, and that they deserve worse treatment and certainly less respect. Generally, in using a term, one makes an implicit commitment to the viability and value of the expression and the network of meanings with which it is associated. Even casual third-person uses reinforce the mode of discourse and its associated conceptual framework—the stereotypes associated with the terms. Perhaps most important, such uses tend to reinforce belief that the terms actually refer to distinct ways of human being.

In the Bowman case, we see a vivid illustration of the way that a particular conception of women's sexuality is used both to silence one woman and to teach her (and us) about what it is (or ought to be, by the pornocrat's lights) to be a woman. It is interesting that Sylvia Bowman was not initially the intended audience. Heller created the image to ruin Bowman's chances of becoming union president; the images were made for third parties, not for Bowman. The question of the effect on Bowman seems not to have been at issue for Heller. The images were meant to neutralize her power in the workplace through ridiculing her to others behind her back. This third-person use of the images was crucial to their efficacy.

Heller claims that by creating and showing the pornographic pictures he was ridiculing Bowman; Alan Dershowitz claims that Heller was just saying that she is a woman (and so should not be elected). Although the trial court sealed its evidence, the Boston Globe reported that the images both depicted women masturbating, one holding a banana.[13] The image of Bowman's face came from her campaign postcard. Think for a moment about campaign portraits. Such portraits generally show the candidate looking at the camera and smiling, a direct gaze. Putting such a direct-gazing smiling face on top of the masturbating model says much more than that Sylvia Bowman is a woman. To see that this is so, suppose instead that Heller had taken a photo from a 1950s Ladies' Home Journal of a woman in an apron taking cookies out of an oven and pasted Bowman's face on it—Sylvia Bowman as Donna Reed. Both involve stereotypes that fail to fit Bowman, but one image is explicitly sexual, while the other is glaringly not.

Sylvia Bowman says she felt humiliated by what David Heller did to her. If Dershowitz wants to argue that Heller's photo collages are equivalent to saying, "Don't vote for her—she's a woman," he must explain why Bowman wouldn't have felt humiliated if Heller had actually stood up and said this sentence. Such a statement probably would have made her angry and probably would not have cost her many votes. But the pictures are not reducible to such a sentence. What was expressed and done with these images? My view is that Heller not only reminded Sylvia Bowman (and others) that she is a woman, but he chose a particular arena, an arena of explicit male control of women as sexual beings, to make the point that she is supposed to be a thing for male consumption. He also reminded her (and others) that she doesn't measure up on this scale—that's one way in which he thinks he is ridiculing her. In reminding her that she is a sexual thing to be consumed and that she not only can be viewed this way but now has been viewed this way by many people she knows and whose respect she values, Heller exposes "the public lie that women are respected persons."[14]

In creating these pictures, Heller underscores MacKinnon's point that for women "the values of pornography are the values that rule our lives" (1987, 133) and that central to these values is male supremacy. Bowman, an activist, portrayed as gruff, acerbic, and certainly aggressive in campaigning for the presidency of her union local, must be made to remember that she is ultimately subordinate to any and every man in the office. In making the pictures, Heller sets himself up as Bowman's "revealer": he speaks with self-proclaimed and socially (if covertly) endorsed authority about who Sylvia Bowman is. Creating these pictures is an expression of Heller's power as male; here's MacKinnon, in *Feminism Unmodified:* Male power makes authoritative a way of seeing and treating women, so that when a man looks at a pornographic picture—pornographic meaning that the woman is defined as to be acted upon, a sexual object, a sexual thing—the *viewing* is an act, an act of male supremacy" (1987, 130). Heller isn't just caught *looking*—he is, like a god, caught *creating.* Not only is he acting by looking, but he is controlling what he sees. She may be masturbating, but he made her do it. And now, when her coworkers see her campaign postcard, with its smiling cameo head and direct gaze, they will think they know what she is smiling about—they will associate that image of Sylvia Bowman's head with the pornographically posed bodies—and that mental connection will continually erode their respect for her.

Absolutists are right about at least one thing: *Derogatory terms and images are part of the process of naturalizing the domination and subordination that characterize oppression.* Sylvia Bowman was "put in her place" by Heller's photo collages; she was told, through the images and the impact of the images on her coworkers, that no matter what her social and economic contribution to the world, she was ultimately just a woman, a thing to be stripped and viewed and had, an object of male consumption and predation. Bowman's boss told her that he found the pictures "stimulating." Others agreed with Heller that it was ridiculous to think of Bowman as sexual. Either way, Sylvia Bowman feels that she cannot go back to work. Derogatory terms have the power to shape our social ontology, our social ways of being, because they are prescriptions parading as descriptions, giving people a proclaimed reality to live down to. Because that so-called "reality" is constituted by rigid stereotypes, the person labeled by the term cannot simply shrug off certain aspects of the stereotype: what doesn't fit does damage.

The apparently rigid connection between the word or image and its associated stereotype seems to support the absolutist's one-image-one interpretation view. But this view is too narrow, too fixed, and too rigid to be true. Thinking of terms or images as having one meaning is a neat way to do theory, but it leads to false views: here it leads us to think of language as somehow fixed and settled, a set of tools each with one function. It leads us to focus on contents rather than contexts. Reality intrudes on such a theory.

RECLAIMERS

There is another side to this story, however, a side that I am only going to briefly mention, although I think it is very important. *Reclaimers* differ from Absolutists in thinking that derogatory words or images may have some redeeming value and that they may sometimes be used in nonderogatory ways. Holding that communities can control the meanings of their own words and images, Reclaimers think that we can and should try to change the meanings of these terms of subordination. Attempting a sort of linguistic aikido, some members of the groups against which these terms have been used have been trying, with varying degrees of success, to reclaim the derogatory terms and turn them into terms of endearment, or at least terms of in-group reference that differ significantly in meaning from the original terms used by the dominant group. Some African Americans say that they can use "nigger" as a term of endearment, some lesbians use "dyke" as a term of pride, some disabled people join Reynolds Price in preferring the term "gimp," and many gay men and lesbians have adopted and promoted the term "queer."

Such reclamations attempt to change the meanings of these terms through subversive uses within the subcommunity. Reclaimers want to disarm the harmful power of these terms and images by internal reorganization—by changing their meanings—rather than by external sanctions. What is taboo gains power, so the Reclaimer does not want to strengthen the taboos against these terms. Instead, the Reclaimer asks us to recognize the subcommunity's jurisdiction over the meaning of its own self-referring labels and images. If the community succeeds in changing the norms governing the meaning and use of their terms, they'll have changed the very power of the term. (Antipornography feminists tend to be Absolutists about the interpretations of the images they see in pornography, whereas anticensorship feminists tend to be more like Reclaimers in that they argue that pornography can sometimes be liberatory for women.)

The Reclaimer's position highlights the fact that meaning not only requires whatever preestablished potential meanings a term can have—its culturally supported contents, as it were—but also the active interpretation of the interplay between those potential contents and the context in which they occur. What is innocent in one context may be damnable in another and vice-versa. When a makeup artist doing an actor's face says, "You have the most remarkable cheekbones," we see no reason for concern. On the other hand, a dean uttering this same sentence to a job candidate during an interview does something very different with the same words. Context may make the difference between whether an utterance is a threat or a promise, whether it is an act of aggression or a dramatic demonstration, whether it is an appropriate observation or an act of discrimination. Keeping context in mind, it is not hard to see the Reclaimer's point that whether a term is derogatory on a particular occasion of use may well depend upon who says it, under what circumstances, and why. Perhaps whether a sexually explicit image is subordinating will also depend upon features of its context.

Unfortunately, our current context is saturated with pornography. MacKinnon argues that "the more pornography there is, the more it sets *de facto* community standards. . . . In other words, inequality is allowed to set community standards for the treatment of women" (OW, 88). Attention to hate speech and pornography highlights the norms that are built into our language and the categories it contains and reinforces; in particular such attention highlights how riddled these norms are with inequality, even today. The danger is that once the daily injustices become taken for granted, naturalized, we then assume that there is a metaphysical basis for our social differences, and this cycle becomes self-perpetuating. At root, the problem is that these derogatory terms and images have the power to prescribe and enforce a social reality that is morally unjust.

On Heller's behalf, Alan Dershowitz argues that "even if the photocopies were 'nothing more than a reduction of Bowman to a sexual object and an attack on her as a woman, rather than as a political candidate,' . . . Heller, had he so chosen, would have been perfectly entitled, as a matter of constitutional right, to urge others to vote against Bowman *precisely because* she was a woman, or, indeed, an 'ugly', 'obese' or 'old' woman."[15] Dershowitz admits that the intent of these images is "to ridicule" Bowman, which is accomplished in part by making her just like the women in the magazines (what a whore) and also by highlighting how little she is like them—old, fat, coarse, and ugly, according to the prosecution (they are saying she is a worthless whore). By putting Bowman on this scale of sexual desirability, a scale clearly weighted against sixty-something heavyset women, Heller attempts to make her appear "ridiculous." The trial court found that the collages "communicated to" Bowman that "despite her long commitment to both her work and union activity, she could quite easily be reduced to nothing more than a naked woman, spread-eagled and exposed" (*Bowman* brief, 8). Who among us is immune to such reductive treatment?

Catharine MacKinnon seeks to remind us that the assault of pornography is an assault on our credibility. It is an interpretive matrix that women like to forget or to treat as peripheral to our experiences, but it is not peripheral to the ways that many men view women and to the ways in which they undermine our credibility in our work and other projects. MacKinnon wants the content of our lives, as we see it, including our most heinous moments, to be sayable, to be said. Within current social practices, these daily horrors of women's lives are unsayable: "You cannot tell anyone. When you try to speak of these things, you are told it did not happen, you imagined it, you wanted it, you enjoyed it. Books say this. No books say what happened to you. Law says this. No law imagines what happened to you, the way it happened. You live your whole life surrounded by this cultural echo of nothing where your screams and your words should be" (OW, 3).

What MacKinnon wants to be sayable is not just a set of neutral descriptions of our experiences, not merely "he touched me here and did this and said that," but also statements and judgments about those more neutrally described events. She wants to build what philosophers call "thick" descriptive terms into the content category—rape, incest, and so forth—not just basic or "thin" terms, like descriptions of physical movements. But seeing certain movements *as* rape requires an interpretive framework that many people lack. This familiar philosophical point appears in many apolitical contexts; it is, for example, Nelson Goodman's point about realism being relative to systems of interpretation.[16]

Goodman argues that we call an artwork realistic because its mode of representation closely matches our everyday interpretive practices; it is easy to interpret it using the same skills we use to interpret what we see all around us. Realists do not challenge our habits of seeing. In a misogynist society, pornography is realist in this sense. It does not challenge the basic interpretive frameworks that construct women as sexual objects. Particularly relevant to this is Sandy Bartky's view that feminists "are no more aware of different things than other people; they are aware of the same things differently."[17] The interpretive framework is what gives life to the distinction between content and point of view. Once one sees a woman as a person, then one will see certain acts as rape and build that interpretation into the object. It is this interpreted reality, this "thick" version of reality, that MacKinnon wants said and sayable.

Against the view that the cure for bad speech is more speech, a view that would support the reclamation project, MacKinnon says that "so long as pornography exists in the way it does, there will not be more speech by women. Pornography strips and devastates women of credibility, from our accounts of sexual assault to our everyday reality of sexual subordination. We are stripped of authority and reduced and devalued and silenced" (1987, 193). We may speak, but we are speaking a language that is not generally understood. Inferences we would draw, which we would expect others to draw, are left

undrawn without a shared alternative framework. MacKinnon is
claiming that pornography has such powerful control of the interpretive framework that even when women speak the horrors of our
lives, these events are not perceived as horrible but rather as erotic,
as a turn-on. She says that "in a world made by pornography, testimony about sexual harassment is live oral pornography starring the
victim" (OW, 67), which may be why the trial court sealed Heller's
photo collages. MacKinnon suggests that it is impossible to evade
the framework of pornography, that this framework undermines
women's credibility as speakers, and that our "thick" judgments of
the events that have so shaped our lives not only do not make sense
but cannot be heard to even gain consideration. Pornography silences
through its totalization.

A PROBLEM

MacKinnon's position against pornography is troubled by a conflicting set of claims that ultimately undermines her goal of promoting
women's semantic authority. MacKinnon's goal is to promote for
women the freedom to describe and depict our experience *as* we
experience it. Yet she claims that women's *experience* is pornographic (the reality depicted in pornography has become the reality
of our lives; we really are raped, battered, objectified, and so forth,
and this reality is interpreted—even by women—as sex).[18] Because
pornography has had such a powerful effect on our social ontology—
it made men men and women women—it makes sexism sexy. Mac-
Kinnon sees it as having so shaped our gendered identities that
"woman" is a pornographic construct as we know it.

Pornography is a totalizing discourse—it covers everything, and
once it is explicitly brought to bear on someone, as it was on Sylvia
Bowman, its impact cannot be undone. From this MacKinnon concludes that pornographic images (pictures and words) should be pro-
hibited in order to allow women the freedom to articulate our own
experiences as our own, and not be pornographed when we do. But if
MacKinnon is right that women's experiences are pornographic, then
to speak them is to make more pornography. Banning the content,
even banning the complex content of pornography, will just result in

the further silencing of women's testimony about our experiences in a heterosexual misogynist society.

And so we come to the question, can we really speak ourselves outside of pornography as long as pornography continues to exist? MacKinnon suggests that we cannot and that this is one good reason to attack pornography head-on. On the other hand, most feminists can read Linda Marchiano's *Ordeal* without putting it within the pornographic interpretive matrix; it doesn't turn us on.[19] We tend to read it as an account of the crimes Marchiano was subjected to when she starred in *Deep Throat*. We find in the book testimony of a survivor's struggle to cope, which shows that although pornography is powerful, it is not totalizing.

The critical matrix of pornography is a major force in women's oppression, and MacKinnon's work helps to show us why. I think that she is right about a lot of things for which she does not get enough credit, but what is missing from her writings, although perhaps not from her advocacy work more generally, is an explicit appreciation of the way that feminist countercultures have made possible lives and realities that were formerly impossible and only raggedly lived. This mutual reinforcement of women by women is one of the achievements of women's consciousness-raising groups in the 1960s and 1970s, and it is still going on today. A woman does not need to believe that everyone has ears for her story before she can tell it—she just needs a few someones.[20] As long as some folks are participating in the mutually influencing dialogue that marks community, then the story can be told and preserved.

MacKinnon's position on silencing suggests that all our stories are perverted by the context of pornography from the moment they are even thought, much less told. I wonder how much that position is conditioned by her thinking about the law and the context of trying to get other lawyers and judges, mostly men, mostly white, mostly saturated with pornography, to take women and our experiences seriously, to even believe that we exist as we know that we do. And when I wonder this, I wish she could think a little bit more the way Marilyn Frye was thinking when she said a few years ago, in response to a somewhat hostile question, that she really is not so much interested in dismantling patriarchy as in seeing what kind of world women could create, that she hopes that in the process of creating such a world, well, maybe patriarchy would just crumble from lack of interest.[21] Women have already begun the process of speaking themselves outside of pornography and outside of patriarchy more generally. These insistent voices are the "more-speech cure": it is time to pay more attention to these important voices.

NOTES

I would like to thank Chico D. Colvard for research assistance on this chapter.

1. Catharine A. MacKinnon, *Only Words* (Cambridge: Harvard University Press, 1993), p. 3; hereafter OW.

2. See Gail Dines, Robert Jensen, and Ann Russo, *Pornography: The Production and Consumption of Inequality* (New York: Routledge, 1998).

3. Richard Wright, "How 'Bigger' Was Born," in *Black Voices: An Anthology of Afro-American Literature*, ed. Abraham Chapman (New York: Penguin, 1968), pp. 551–53; Nathan McCall, *Makes Me Wanna Holler* (New York: Random House, 1992), pp. 117, 158–60.

4. Cited by Margaret Spillane, in "The Culture of Narcissism," in *Culture Wars: Documents from Recent Controversies in the Arts*, ed. Richard Bolton (New York: New Press, 1992), p. 304.

5. MacKinnon, *Only Words*, p.13. She lists all performatives: signs saying "Whites Only" or "Help Wanted—Male" or speech acts such as "You're fired."

6. Richard Delgado, "Words That Wound: A Tort Action for Racial Insults, Epithets, and Name-Calling," in *Words That Wound: Critical Race Theory, Assaultive Speech, and the First Amendment*, ed. Mari J. Matsuda, Charles R. Lawrence III, Richard Delgado, and Kimberlé Williams Crenshaw (Boulder, Colo.: Westview, 1993), p. 107; see also pp. 94 and 109–10. As I have argued, the expressive commitment of the term is at issue, not the connotation; see Lynne Tirrell, "Derogatory Terms: Racism, Sexism, and the Inferential Role Theory of Meaning," in *Feminism and Philosophy of Language*, ed. Kelly Oliver and Christina Hendricks (Albany: State University of New York Press, 1998). Delgado's use of "connotation" here and elsewhere in his article is the ordinary language use, so I take him to mean something like "attitudes conveyed or associated with the expression."

7. Catharine A. MacKinnon, *Feminism Unmodified* (Cambridge: Harvard University Press, 1987), p. 172.

8. Brief of the appellee Sylvia Smith Bowman, at *Bowman v. Commissioner of the Department of Public Welfare, et al.* 420 Mass. 517 (1995) SJC-06726, pp. 7–9.

9. Brief amicus curiae of the Lawyers' Committee for Civil Rights Under the Law of the Boston Bar Association, the Asian Lawyers' Association of Massachusetts, the Massachusetts Black Lawyers Association, and the National Conference of Black Lawyers, in support of plaintiff—appellee (Sylvia Smith Bowman), at *Bowman v. Commissioner of the Department of Public Welfare, et al.* 420 Mass. 517 (1995) SJC-06726, p. 6.

10. Robert Jensen, "Pornography and the Limits of Experimental Re-

search," in *Gender, Race, and Class in Media*, ed. Gail Dines and Jean M. Humez (Thousand Oaks, Calif.: Sage Publications, 1995), 298–306.

11. Irving Lewis Allen, *The Language of Ethnic Conflict: Social Organization and Lexical Culture* (New York: Columbia University Press, 1983), p. 15.

12. For more on psychological oppression, see Franz Fanon, *Black Skin, White Masks* (New York: Grove Press, 1967), and Sandra Lee Bartky, "On Psychological Oppression," in *Femininity and Domination: Studies in the Phenomenology of Oppression* (New York: Routledge, 1990), pp. 22–32.

13. Kimberly Blanton, "'Free Speech' new defense in cases of harassment," *Boston Globe*, 7 August 1994, pp. 1, 24.

14. Carolyn Shafer and Marilyn Frye, "On Rape and Respect," in *Women and Values*, 1st ed., ed. Marilyn Pearsall (Belmont, Calif.: Wadsworth, 1986), pp. 188–96.

15. Brief for the appellant David Heller, at *Bowman v. Commissioner of the Department of Public Welfare, et al.* 420 Mass. 517 (1995) SJC-06726, p. 30.

16. Nelson Goodman, *Languages of Art* (Indianapolis: Hackett, 1976), pp. 3–44. For more on this, see Lynne Tirrell, "Aesthetic Derogation," in *Aesthetics and Ethics: Essays at the Intersection*, ed. Jerrold Levinson (Cambridge, Eng.: Cambridge University Press, 1998), pp. 283–314.

17. Sandra L. Bartky, "Toward a Phenomenology of Feminist Consciousness," in *Femininity and Domination: Studies in the Phenomenology of Oppression* (New York: Routledge, 1990), p. 14.

18. Monique Wittig argues that "woman" itself is a derogatory term, because it is what it is, means what it means, only in contrast and in comparison with "man," so, "woman" means "slave to man" (*The Straight Mind* [Boston: Beacon Press, 1992], pp. 9–18).

19. Linda Lovelace, with Mike McGrady, *Ordeal* (New York: Berkley Books, 1981); "Linda Lovelace" is a pseudonym for Linda Marchiano.

20. On the importance of community for the making of meaning, see Lynne Tirrell, "Definition and Power: Toward Authority Without Privilege," *Hypatia* 8, 4 (Fall 1993): 1–34.

21. Marilyn Frye, comments during the discussion period after presenting a paper on recent feminist treatments of essentialism to the Women's Studies Program and the Philosophy Department at the University of North Carolina at Chapel Hill, spring 1992.

12 / *Speech That Harms: The Case of Lesbian Families*

JOAN C. CALLAHAN

In March 1998 the Social Security Administration sent me a letter with this information:

> If you die this year, you need 30 credits for your survivors to get benefits. Your record shows you have enough. If they met all other requirements, monthly benefit amounts would be about:
>
> | | |
> |---|---:|
> | For your child | $695 |
> | For your spouse who is caring for your child | $695 |
> | When your spouse reaches full retirement age | $930 |
> | For all of your family members, if others also qualify (more children, for example) | $1,715 |
>
> We may also be able to pay your spouse or eligible children a one-time death benefit of $255.[1]

How interesting, I thought. My partner and I have been together since 1988. Her biological son from a previous marriage was a year and half old then. He's twelve now, and I am the only second parent he knows. If either of us were a man, my partner and I could marry. But we're not, and we can't. And, therefore, the very substantial benefits outlined in this letter are inaccessible to my life partner and the child we have been raising together for over a decade. If I die, this money will go to a heterosexual couple and their children, even though *my* work has earned these benefits and *my* income has been taxed all of my working life to make these benefits available.

In this chapter I argue that one important step the state should take toward meeting its obligation to ensure equal protection from harm for all of its innocent citizens is to make what I call "subordinating speech" subject to tort action. My argument pertains to all gender minorities and by extension to other subordinated groups. Feminism and feminist ethics are concerned about *all* forms of social subordination.[2] At the same time, I want to emphasize that this is not an abstract question for me. I come to this discussion from my lived position within a lesbian family. In a society that is sexist, homophobic, and racist, lesbians get a double or triple whammy, depending on our racial or ethnic social locations.

Feminist analyses need to consider the special impact of social practices on women who resist heterosexist mandates, including mandates built into laws governing marriage. Since lesbians as a group are economically worse off than gay men as a group, social practices that disadvantage sexual minorities have a proportionately greater negative impact on lesbians. When children are part of these alternative families, lesbian families are, typically, worse off than the families of gay men. And there are far more lesbian families with children than families with children headed by gay men. Finally, the cultural combination of sexism and homophobia creates a sensitive moral issue for women generally, since heterosexual married women often benefit at costs to lesbians. There are, then, a number of reasons for feminist ethics to pay special attention to the impact of social practices on lesbians and our families.

The example of social security benefits is just one among hundreds of benefits that the state provides to heterosexuals and withholds from gender minorities.[3] In this chapter, I want to address these injustices in terms of the normalization of systematic injustice. In particular, I want to focus on the normalization of injustice against gender minorities and how that normalization is nurtured by speech that degrades and subordinates gender minorities.[4] I argue that this sort of speech should be subject to tort action.[5] In order to make this position plausible, I need to discuss the objections that are commonly brought against restricting so-called hate speech. This requires addressing several distinctions and arguments, namely, the distinctions between offense and harm, speech and conduct, the public and the private, and government action and government inaction, and the arguments that regulating any subordinating speech will lead to too much speech regulation (the slippery slope or wedge objection), attempting to regulate subordinating speech will have a "chilling effect" on speech, liberal neutrality requires that we cannot regulate speech on the basis of its content, and most subordinating speech fails the "fighting words" test for unprotected speech.

I argue that subordinating speech is more than "merely" offensive—it is directly and indirectly substantially harmful; subordinating speech is conduct and, as harmful conduct, a form of conduct rightly addressed by law; the distinction between the private action of individuals and the public action of government cannot do the conceptual or moral work it is expected to do in this context; government inaction on subordinating speech has the moral status of very important action; we can stop on the slippery slope—a subordinating speech tort can be appropriately circumscribed; some "free" speech ought to be "chilled"; so-called liberal neutrality is not neutral in its effects; and the abandoned first prong of the "fighting words" doctrine (which pertains to injurious speech) should be put on its own legal feet as a separate doctrine.

Throughout, I understand "subordinating speech" to be largely what others commonly call "hate speech" or "abusive speech," but I include speech *about* as well as speech *addressed to* members of target groups. I use the term "subordinating speech" to help keep the focus on the real effects of this kind of behavior. That is, certain forms of speech have the indirect but powerful effect of helping to keep members of certain groups in subordinate social positions, some of those positions marked by interlocking sets of subordinating attitudes and practices. This subordination is itself harmful as well as unjust. I begin with the distinction between offense and harm.

OFFENSE AND HARM

Nadine Strossen, director of the American Civil Liberties Union, typifies use of the distinction between offense and harm in the civil libertarian arguments against regulating subordinating speech.[6] In discussing the neo-Nazi march in Skokie, Illinois, in the late 1970s,[7] Strossen says: "The essentials of a Skokie-type setting are that *offensive* speech occurs in a public place and the event is announced in advance. Hence, the *offensive* speech can be either avoided or countered by opposing speech. Traditional civil libertarians recognize that this speech causes psychic pain. We nonetheless agree with the

decision of the Seventh Circuit in Skokie that this pain is a necessary price for a system of free expression" (1997, 292; emphases
added.[8] Strossen does three things here: she classifies the neo-Nazi
demonstration as speech, she classifies the speech in question as
offensive, and she is willing to allow the purported good of free
speech to outweigh the burden of "psychic pain" caused by subordinating speech. I take up her first point in the next section. Here, I
consider the second and third: the construction of hate speech as
"offensive," and the civil libertarian's willingness to allow a tradeoff
between unencumbered speech and the "psychic pain" of targets of
subordinating speech.

The first point to notice here is that there is a hidden qualifier of
"offensive"—the speech in question is constructed as *merely* offensive, which is just to say that it does not constitute a harm. The second point to notice is that even though Strossen recognizes the fact
of "psychic pain" caused by subordinating speech, she does not treat
this as a genuine harm.

The construction of subordinating speech as offensive but not
harmful is crucially important to the civil libertarian argument, since
once it is agreed that something, let's call it X, causes genuine harm,
X becomes a legitimate candidate for state interference. If X is merely
offensive, it is very hard to justify state interference with X, particularly when interfering with X is thought to be inimical to fundamental societal values, such as individual liberty, which (at least
partially) grounds the right to free speech. The argument goes like
this: Since people might be offended by all sorts of things that people say, we cannot start regulating offensive speech. Citing the
Supreme Court, Strossen captures the argument: "Noting that we are
'often . . . subject to *objectionable* speech,' the Court has ruled that
in public places, we bear the burden of averting our attention from
expression we find *offensive.*[9] Otherwise, the Court explained, 'a
majority could silence dissidents simply as a matter of *personal pre-
dilections*'" (1997, 293, quoting first *Rowman v. United States Post
Office Dept.* 397 U.S. 728, 738 [1970], and then *Cohen v. California,*
21; [emphases added]). These characterizations by the Court do two
things: they limit the negative effects of subordinating speech to
mere offense, and they make the offense "taken" highly subjective.
What are we to make of this distinction between offense and harm
as it works in the civil libertarian argument?

First, I find the offense/harm distinction reminiscent of the ordinary/extraordinary means distinction that purportedly gets applied in medical cases where a decision needs to be made about appropriate care for someone who is terminally ill. In these cases, it sounds as if some real distinction is first discerned and then deployed to help decide what medical treatments are morally required. But what is really going on is that a decision is already being made, in classifying treatment as "extraordinary," about what treatment is appropriate in a given case. A treatment thought to promise a patient no real benefit is labeled "extraordinary," and once so labeled, there is (by definition of "extraordinary") no obligation to administer it. Notice what happens: a value judgment (that any benefits of the treatment are not sufficient to require the treatment) is presented as an empirical (medical) judgment (that treatment would be extraordinary), which is then invoked to justify a value judgment (withholding treatment is justifiable).

It is, I submit, the same with the offense/harm distinction. If people act in ways that affect others negatively, people who think the state should not interfere with those behaviors label those behaviors (merely) "offensive" and label "harmful" only behaviors they think appropriately regulated by the state. Thus, like the so-called ordinary/extraordinary means distinction, a value judgment precedes the categorization of an action as (merely) offensive or (genuinely) harmful, and then the offense/harm distinction is invoked to justify allowing the behavior or to justify state interference with it.[10] Once this progression is clear, it is also clear that the critical question is whether there are good reasons to classify a certain kind of behavior as a candidate for state proscription or regulation. The offense/harm language shrouds this critical question. We want to know whether the state's protecting people from certain forms of speech can be justified. To argue yes is to argue that the forms of speech in question should be classified as seriously harmful, that is, as having the effect of seriously setting back important interests.[11]

My concern here is with harms that result from deeply entrenched, continuing social centrisms. The centrism in focus in this chapter is heterosexism, and those subordinated are gender minorities. The interests at stake range from economic interests to interests in having a robust sense of self-worth to interests in being treated as full citizens. The exclusion of the families of gender minorities from Social

Security benefits is a genuine and substantial material harm; the beatings, killings, and suicides associated with (real or perceived) sexual orientation are real harms to their victims. If anything counts as harms, these do. Consequently, a social environment that tolerates (or worse, encourages) a construction of gender minorities as appropriately excluded by the state from the concern shown heterosexuals is itself seriously harmful to gender minorities. Insofar as subordinating speech contributes to such a social environment, it is seriously harmful to gender minorities, and the state has a clear obligation to try to prevent that harm and to redress that harm when it occurs.

The Social Security example helps to clarify what is so galling about the claim made repeatedly and used to justify discriminatory laws, namely, that gender minorities want "special rights." It is completely obvious that special rights are granted to *heterosexuals,* who are given the right to marry and, thereby, the right to legal enforcement of their claims to goods such as Social Security benefits for their partners and children.

The "special rights" rhetoric is deliberately constructed to conserve existing discriminatory practices. Insofar as this rhetoric achieves its goal, it is substantially harmful to gender minorities. Like more blatant insults, it is harmful in two ways. It is directly harmful to us every time we confront this construction, since it is completely transparent to us that the rhetoric is invented to help ensure that we will continue to be deprived of rights and goods that are readily available to heterosexuals and are rigorously protected by the state. Whenever we confront this rhetoric we are reminded that we are not full citizens. It is indirectly harmful insofar as it succeeds in helping to maintain that status. Mari Matsuda makes the point about direct harm in the context of race: "As much as one may try to resist a piece of hate propaganda, the effect on one's self-esteem and sense of personal security is devastating. . . . However irrational racist speech may be, it hits right at the emotional place where we feel the most pain. The aloneness comes not only from the hate message itself, but also from the government response of tolerance. . . . the victim becomes a stateless person. Target-group members must either identify with a community that promotes racist speech or admit that the community does not include them."[12]

This result is far more than "mere" nonharmful offense or the assumed tolerable "psychic pain" that civil libertarians such as

Strossen are willing to allow. The propaganda places its target group members outside the community of full citizens, which harms directly by dealing a crushing blow to self-esteem every time a target-group individual hears, reads, or otherwise experiences subordinating speech and harms indirectly by contributing to a social construction of target-group members as less than full citizens, which is then instantiated in custom and policy. Strossen and the Supreme Court are quick to say that the burdens of subordinating speech are worth their costs. But notice that these burdens are borne by those of us who are already excluded from full citizenship; the payment is exacted of those with the least in the way of civil resources. Strossen and the Court fail to address this injustice of placing the costs of "keeping the marketplace of ideas open" on the shoulders of the targets of harmful speech.[13]

A recent event illustrates this distribution of the burden of the costs of free speech. In Jasper, Texas, James Byrd, a forty-nine-year-old black man, was beaten, chained by the ankles to the back of a pickup truck, and dragged for more than two miles. His head and right arm were torn off in the dragging. Byrd's mutilated body was found just outside Jasper on 7 June 1998. Three white men, linked to white supremacist groups, were charged with the hideous murder. Although it has denied any connection with the murder, the Ku Klux Klan wasted no time in securing a permit to hold a rally in Jasper on 27 June 1998. In this case, just who are the "we" Strossen assumes when she writes of bearing the costs of free speech?

Finally, it is important to understand that the direct and indirect harms of subordinating speech are only possible in the case of members of groups that are socially subordinated. It is important to understand this fact when the question comes around to setting policy, since it provides the needed limit on what speech should not be protected. That is, the social location of target groups as subordinate to dominant groups is what accounts for both the direct and indirect harm at issue here. On the individual level, social subordination allows for the absorption or internalization of the message by those targeted (Matsuda et al. 1993, 26); on the social level, it fosters the perpetuation of institutionalized, legally sanctioned social subordination.

Not long ago, I was eating alone in a fast-food restaurant not far from my campus. Across the aisle four young people began a snide conversation about some "faggot" they know. I was barely able to finish my meal. Not only did the talk degrade me, it scared me, because it was so clear that these kids felt so smugly superior to the "faggot" centering their discussion. As Charles Lawrence points out, what is so frightening and demoralizing about incidents of subordinating speech is that "they are not the isolated unpopular speech of a dissident few. . . . These incidents are manifestations of an ubiquitous and deeply ingrained cultural belief system, an American way of life" (Matsuda et al. 1993, 74).[14]

In appealing to the distinction between offense and harm, then, civil libertarians begin by assuming what cannot be plausibly argued, namely, that the negative effects of subordinating speech are not the sort of genuinely injurious effects that are properly the purview of state regulation. But this matter must be argued; it is not enough to simply presume it. The distinction assumed here between offense and harm begs the question by cordoning off speech as nonharmful. There is no reason to accept this stipulation, and there are excellent reasons to reject it.

This cordoning off points to a further distinction in the civil libertarian's linguistic toolbox, namely, the distinction between speech and conduct.

SPEECH AND CONDUCT

In criticizing Charles Lawrence's case for hate-speech regulation, Strossen serves again as an example, this time in deploying the commonly made distinction between speech and conduct: "Although Professor's Lawrence's specific proposed code appears relatively modest, his supporting rationales depend on nothing less immodest than the abrogation of the traditional distinction . . . between speech and conduct" (1997, 290, 303). Now, simply invoking a traditional distinction is not an argument, no matter how much indignation is brought to the invocation. Further, this distinction is extremely puzzling, since speech is unquestionably a form of human action or conduct. Few activities are more characteristically human than speech. Many theorists argue that speech (broadly construed, as systems of symbolic signs) is what distinguishes human beings from the rest of nature. Finally, civil libertarians themselves routinely collapse the distinction between speech and conduct. Recall that Strossen takes the neo-Nazi demonstration in the Skokie case to count as speech. And the KKK permit to rally in Jasper is justified on the basis of free speech, whether or not a word is said or displayed. Insofar as the distinction between speech and conduct attempts to completely detach speech and conduct, the distinction fails.

On the other hand, there obviously is a conceptual distinction between speech and conduct. That is, conduct is a category that includes speech as an instance. Some speech is verbal; some consists in other uses of symbols. This difference is why it makes sense to classify a demonstration with or without words as speech. Once speech and conduct are understood this way, however, the civil libertarian appeal to that distinction transparently begs the question. The real question is whether speech is a form of conduct that should not be regulated by the state. How might one argue this position?

The civil libertarian might contend that speech, by its very nature, cannot be harmful in the ways that other conduct is harmful—the "sticks and stones might break my bones, but words will never hurt me" position.[15] But I have argued that subordinating speech is genuinely and substantially harmful, directly and indirectly. If the civil libertarian wants to hold that the direct effects on individual self-esteem and the systematic exclusion of gender minorities from goods and rights readily available to heterosexuals should not count as harms, then the burden is squarely on her to show why this is so. That burden has not been met.

Another, very different kind of argument for cordoning off speech from other forms of conduct might allow that the effects of subordinating speech are genuinely harmful and that speech is a form of conduct, but deny that these are harms the state should be in the business of trying to prevent, and that speech is a form of conduct that the state should be in the business of trying to control. Arguments such as these generally lean on assumptions about unwanted but unavoidable effects that would be caused by any state regulation of speech, which is the slippery slope or wedge argument.

THE SLIPPERY SLOPE ARGUMENT

Nadine Strossen again provides an example for us in her criticism of Charles Lawrence, who allows that his particular proposal on the regulation of racist speech applies as well to homophobic hate speech. Strossen says "Thus, Professor Lawrence himself demonstrates that traditional civil libertarians are hardly paranoic when we fear that any specific, seemingly modest proposal to regulate speech may in fact represent the proverbial 'thin edge of the wedge' for initiating broader regulations" (1997, 290).[16]

First, I note without comment the insidious implication here: that it might be all right to regulate racist speech, but regulation must not extend to homophobic speech. Second, the argument offered is more confusing than it might appear. There are two forms of slippery slope or thin-edge-of-the wedge argument—a logical form and an empirical form.

The logical form of the wedge argument holds that there are no logical stops between A and Z, and therefore A is logically or morally equivalent to Z. This form of the wedge is constantly used in the abortion debate, when it is argued that we cannot find a bright line between the time when a very young human being is a person and when it is not. The human being at fifteen is obviously a person with the full range of fundamental rights, including the right not to be killed for reasons less than self-defense. And this statement is true of the human being at fourteen and a half and at fourteen and so on. The argument presses back by small steps to the infant, the fetus, the embryo, bringing us to conception as the only point where we can clearly distinguish between different kinds of beings (eggs and sperm versus conceptuses) and to the conclusion that once a human being is conceived, it must be recognized as having the full range of moral rights we recognize grown persons to have. This form of the wedge argument, then, holds that because there are no clear logical lines that can be drawn, there is no morally justifiable place to stop on the "slippery slope" once we begin to descend. If we hold that any mature human being is a person with the full range of basic rights, including the right not to be killed for reasons less than self-defense, the argument tells us that we are logically committed to recognizing brand-new human conceptuses as persons having those same rights. Alternatively, if we deny those rights to human conceptuses, we have no logical ground for not denying them to mature human beings, and we are committed to permitting all sorts of other killings of human beings for reasons less than self-defense.[17]

The empirical version of the wedge argument allows that there are logical stops between A and Z. But once we start with A, we can but will not stop until we get to Z. This version of the wedge argument is employed in the physician-assisted suicide debate, where it is argued that once we start allowing physician-assisted suicide, that concession will lead to allowing physician-committed euthanasia on request (voluntary euthanasia), which will lead to euthanasia without request (involuntary euthanasia). So, even though we can draw conceptual distinctions here, the claim is that practice will overrun distinctions and doctors will end up killing "undesirables." Therefore, it is argued, we must not allow physician-assisted suicide.

When civil libertarians such as Strossen talk about the "thin edge of the wedge," are they using the logical or empirical version of this argument? In the context of subordinating speech, the logical version of the wedge argument would involve claiming that we cannot make logical distinctions among forms of speech. The empirical version of the wedge argument would involve claiming that even though we can make logical distinctions among forms of speech, we will not be able to control ourselves—we'll careen down the slippery slope, whether we like it or not.

The empirical version of the slippery slope is, in general, not a very compelling argument. It projects a kind of doomsday scenario that cries out for empirical support. My starting to walk west in Lexington, Kentucky, in no way entails that I'll drown in the Pacific ocean. I can stop, and the crucial question for this form of the argument pertains to the reasons for holding that I won't stop. This places the burden of justification on the proponent of the empirical wedge, who needs to show just why we should believe that any regulation of subordinating speech will lead to unacceptable regulation of speech more generally. This burden has not been carried by the civil libertarian, and with an appropriately circumscribed policy there is no reason to believe that it could be carried by the civil libertarian. Before closing, I'll sketch the main contours such a policy might have. For now, however, the point is just that if she is using the empirical version of the wedge argument, the civil libertarian needs to bring forward compelling empirical evidence for the belief that what she fears will happen will indeed happen.

Further, even if this burden can be met, the civil libertarian must convince us that what she fears will happen should not happen. But this burden is not carried either. Reconsider Strossen's complaint against Lawrence. Why should we accept with Strossen that since regulating racist speech might lead to regulating homophobic speech, we should not regulate racist speech?

On the other hand, if the civil libertarian is using the logical version of the wedge argument, she needs to make clear why we cannot distinguish among the forms of speech that are relevant. As I have argued, the concern here is about forms of speech that injure directly and indirectly. Those injuries are only possible for members of groups in certain social locations. Speech that does not directly assault members of these groups or that does not contribute to the normalization of the social subordination of these groups would not be a candidate for tort action. We might have some disagreements about whether particular instances of speech are to be considered subordinating for the purpose of tort action, but we have such disagreements in the law all the time. The fact that we can disagree does not entail or otherwise indicate that we are unable to make meaningful and very useful distinctions that serve the purpose of doing away with the very substantial harms of social subordination. Thus, if the civil libertarian is using a logical wedge argument here, the burden is on her to show that we cannot make the logical distinctions necessary to protect a robust system of free expression. Again, this burden has not been carried, and there is no reason to think that it can be carried.

The civil libertarian, however, raises another concern, which is slightly different from either the logical or the empirical wedge argument. This concern might be understood as allowing that subordinating speech is harmful in the ways I have indicated, including the indirect harms of normalizing social subordination. But, the objection says, if we are going to include the indirect harms of social subordination as harms rightly proscribed by the state, the state must prohibit all subordinating speech, even such speech in private places, and this prohibition would involve too much state interference with individual lives. Further, according to this objection, proponents of state interference with subordinating speech confuse private discriminatory action with discriminatory action by the state. Both of these prongs of the objection presume an important moral distinction between state action and state inaction.

THE PUBLIC AND THE PRIVATE, INDIVIDUAL VERSUS
STATE ACTION, STATE ACTION AND INACTION

Once again, Nadine Strossen's critique of Charles Lawrence provides an example for us, this time of the civil libertarian's appeal to a distinction between the public and the private: "The rationales that Professor Lawrence advances for the regulations he endorses are so open-ended that, if accepted, they would appear to warrant the prohibition of all racist speech, and thereby would cut to the core of our system of free expression. . . . his supporting rationales depend on nothing less immodest than the abrogation of the traditional distinction . . . between state action and private action" (1997, 290). There really are two prongs to this objection, which are joined by an assumption. One prong contends that if we allow that there are harms produced by subordinating speech and that the state should try to prevent these harms, the state will need to interfere egregiously with the private lives of citizens. Thus, this prong holds that there would be a collapse of the public and the private, which would destroy completely our system of free expression and compromise unacceptably our right to privacy. The second prong contends that theorists such as Lawrence confuse the private actions of individuals with the public actions of the state; that is, if John Q. Public uses subordinating speech, that is a private action, which is just not equivalent to state action. The assumption linking these two prongs is that state inaction in the face of individual action is not equivalent to state action.

In regard to the first prong, it is true that if the state is obligated to prevent the harms associated with subordinating speech, it should seek to do so no matter where that speech occurs, including people's living rooms. But regulating speech in people's living rooms, it is argued, is absurd. It is concluded that respect for privacy requires that the state leave speech alone. This argument, however, is not compelling.

First, there are already all sorts of injurious conduct that are not protected by privacy. Second, if concern for privacy is sufficient to preclude policy meant to prevent subordinating speech, it should also be sufficient to preclude our laws against slanderous speech, since slanderous claims can be made in living rooms, too. Finally, laws prohibiting sodomy remain on the books of many states. It is difficult to imagine policies set up to prevent the harms of subordinating speech that could have comparable potential for inviting state interference with private lives. Yet we hear no public outcry on this issue. Nor do we see civil libertarians systematically working on the local and federal levels to ensure that the choice of intimate partners is equally protected for all citizens. Like so many other things, privacy is an acute concern when it involves heterosexuals but not when it involves gender minorities. Once again, then, the burden is on the civil libertarian to show why attempting to prevent subordinating speech is more worrisome from the perspective of acceptable free expression and privacy than state prohibitions on many other forms of conduct.

The second prong of this objection is that theorists such as Lawrence confound individual and state action. But there is no conceptual confusion here. The state protects individuals against the harmful activities of other individuals all the time. We have already seen that the "sticks and stones" position is false—the words of individuals, like their fists, can and sometimes do harm. The state's job is to act to prohibit such individual actions. Thus, proponents of positions like the one I am suggesting are not confusing individual and state action.

The assumption linking the two prongs of this objection is that state inaction must be distinguished from state action. Two points need to be made here. The first recalls the Social Security benefits example with which I began. There could hardly be a clearer example of the state's participation in discrimination. Not only does the state permit individuals to harm others in socially subordinate positions, but it also actively participates in harming those in subordinate positions. Other examples include, at the federal level, the recent Defense of Marriage Act (which explicitly permits states to limit marriage to heterosexuals) and the rash of recent state laws that explicitly so limit marriage, all of which plainly constitutes aggressively discriminatory action by the state.

Even where states have not explicitly excluded gender minorities from benefits and protections, the state discriminates against us. The rights and goods attaching to the civil institution of marriage compose just one set of exclusions. Even when the state merely "stands by," it acts. As I write this chapter in June 1998, all but ten of the United States permit discrimination on the bases of sexual orientation and gender presentation in such crucial areas as employment and housing.[18] When individuals or corporate agents (the state included) have obligations of protection, failure to protect has the moral status of action. When the state fails to act on these exclusions, that failure has the moral status of action, just as a parent's intentional failure to feed one of his children has the moral status of action.[19]

Thus, the state discriminates against me *directly* and obviously when it taxes me and then deprives me of access to the resources that have been taken from me but are made available to heterosexuals and also when it ensures by explicit law that my life partner and I will not have access to the institution (marriage) that would secure my right to those resources. And the state discriminates against me *indirectly* by refusing to come forward on my behalf if I am denied employment or housing or services merely because I am not a heterosexual.

Take a moment to try to imagine a world in which gay men and lesbians are in the majority and hold the various kinds of power currently held by heterosexuals in our world. Imagine that people in that world can be fired or refused a lease for an apartment simply because they are heterosexual. And imagine that gay people in that world, who have control of the government, tax straight people and then make the proceeds from those taxes exclusively available to gay people. In such a world, straight people would surely be outraged and object that the state, which does and allows these things, treats them unjustly. And they would be right, just as surely as a white minority would be right about the injustice of analogous treatment were it to occur in a comparably discriminatory state run by people of color. The civil libertarian argument, then, fails again insofar as it leans on distinctions between public and private, individual and state action, and state action and inaction.

The kinds of popular distinctions and arguments we have seen so far are accompanied by more technical arguments pertaining to First Amendment law. The two chief technical arguments involve the so-called fighting words doctrine and the doctrine that speech may not be regulated on the basis of its content. Let me take the content argument first.

THE FIRST TECHNICAL ARGUMENT: LIBERAL "NEUTRALITY" AND CONTENT- OR VIEWPOINT-BASED SPEECH

As before, Strossen provides an example, this time of the content-neutrality argument: "Any speech regulations would be invalid if

they discriminated on the basis of a speaker's viewpoint. Viewpoint-based discrimination constitutes the most egregious form of censorship and almost always violates the First Amendment" (1997, 294). As usual, there is important rhetoric here in addition to the explicit argument. Notice, for example, the use of "discrimination" and "censorship." These terms are loaded, and Strossen's argument trades on their normative and emotive force. We all know that discrimination and censorship are bad things and certainly things the state should not be engaged in. Here we have rhetoric reminiscent of the question-begging offense / harm and speech / conduct rhetoric examined earlier. The rhetoric is deployed but never justified.

In addition to Strossen's rhetoric, it needs to be noticed that underlying this argument is a commitment to what is assumed without argument to be neutrality. This is the familiar doctrine of liberal neutrality, which holds that the state must remain neutral on matters such as individuals' conceptions of the good life for themselves and individuals' intellectual positions. But liberal neutrality is a myth, a dangerous myth, since appeals to so-called liberal neutrality almost invariably serve the status quo in the end and shroud injustices at every turn.[20] In just this way, so-called liberal neutrality fails to be neutral. Consider again the costs of maintaining a system of unencumbered speech. As we have already seen, the state's remaining "neutral" on subordinating speech places the costs of "free speech" squarely on the shoulders of those of us who are already otherwise disadvantaged by a system of so-called liberal neutrality. When there are differentials of power in a system, "neutrality" almost always tends to favor those in power.

Addressing the explicit argument here, the claim that the state ought to remain neutral on the content of speech fails to recognize that the state's remaining neutral serves existing differentials in social location. Insofar as the state fails to address subordinating speech, it allows the continued normalization of the harms of subordinating speech. The doctrine of liberal neutrality as incarnated in the argument against content-based regulation of speech, then, is clearly not neutral in its effects. In short, "neutrality" often fails to yield real equality.[21] In the case of subordinating speech, the doctrine of content neutrality clearly places a disparate burden on those in subordinate social locations while, at the same time, contributing to the continuation of a system that includes those subordinate social locations.[22]

THE SECOND TECHNICAL ARGUMENT:
FIGHTING WORDS

The second technical First Amendment argument appeals to the doctrine of fighting words. In *Chaplinsky v. New Hampshire* (1942), the Supreme Court held that certain "fighting words" are not protected by the First Amendment. Included in the decision were words "which by their very utterance inflict injury or tend to incite an immediate breach of the peace" (315 U.S. 358, 1942). But subsequent decisions have narrowed the fighting words doctrine to the second of these disjuncts. Strossen leans on this version: "In *Gooding v. Wilson* [1972], the Court substantially narrowed *Chaplinsky*'s definition of fighting words. . . . In *Gooding*, as well as in every subsequent fighting words case, the Court disregarded the dictum in which the first prong of *Chaplinsky*'s definition was set forth and treated only those words that 'tend to incite an immediate breach of the peace' as fighting words" (1997, 295–96; *Gooding v. Wilson*, 405 U.S. 518 [1972]).

Now, it is true that the Supreme Court has narrowed the fighting words doctrine to the second prong ("tend to incite an immediate breach of the peace") in *Chaplinsky*. But it does not follow that the first prong (words "which by their very utterance inflict injury") in *Chaplinsky* should not be adopted on its own terms. Indeed, I suggest that speech that by its very utterance inflicts the harms I have already discussed should not be protected by the First Amendment. Instead of reincorporating this prong into the so-called fighting words doctrine, I suggest we let it stand on its own doctrinal feet. We might call it the "subordinating speech" doctrine.

THE SUBORDINATING SPEECH DOCTRINE

Civil libertarians commonly claim that the regulation of hate speech will "chill" free speech (for example, Strossen 1997, 297–98). But it is not as obvious as the civil libertarian assumes that this is an overwhelming problem. I have already argued that the harms inflicted by subordinating speech are very particular insofar as they pertain to groups that are in socially subordinate locations. These socially subordinate locations make members of these groups vulnerable to the direct harms of subordinating speech, a vulnerability that is not shared outside these social locations. So, for example, it is precisely because gay men and lesbians do not have access to the rights and goods the state ensures for heterosexuals that we are, unlike heterosexuals, in a position to be directly harmed by subordinating speech. The same social reality makes subordinating speech targeting gender minorities indirectly harmful, for such speech nurtures the continued normalization of discrimination against us. The consideration of social location, then, tightly circumscribes who counts as a target of unprotected subordinating speech. If speech that subordinates us is "chilled," that is a good thing, not a bad thing. My argument, then, cuts both ways. The social location of certain groups qualifies some speech targeting members of those groups as subordinating speech, and this sort of speech itself contributes to the continuing subordination of its targets.

If subordinating speech is not protected, how should it be sanctioned? This is a question of institutional design, and answering it adequately would be a whole separate project. I can, however, offer some suggestions about the contours of a policy on subordinating speech.

Richard Delgado has proposed that we recognize a tort for racial insults. Since I find his replies to the objections against such a tort to be convincing, I'll not rehearse them here.[23] A more general tort for subordinating speech would encompass racial insults. Delgado requires that actionable racist speech be directed at a plaintiff and that the defendant intends to insult. I find these restrictions too narrow.

For example, in the recent legislative session here in Kentucky, there was a sustained debate over whether to make explicit law to preclude same-gender marriage. The hatred of gender minorities that infused comments by a number of legislators in the floor debate was overwhelming. We (same-gender couples) were labeled sinners and analogized to animals. In this case, the legislators were addressing one another. But as we, the targets of this speech, watched the debate in disbelief, the direct and indirect harms of subordinating speech were very clearly accomplished.

I follow Delgado's proposal, then, but with some modifications (Matsuda et al. 1993, 109). In order to prevail in an action for subordinating speech, I suggest that the plaintiff needs to be a member of a socially subordinated group; show that the defendant's language was addressed to him or her or about him or her as a member of such a group; show that the defendant's speech is degrading to members of this group; and show that a reasonable person would understand that the defendant's speech is degrading to members of this group. I take "degrading" here quite literally as referring to speech that grades its targets lower than the relevant dominant groups. I would add to this list that the scope of liability for such speech should be shared by corporate agents when appropriate. Thus, for example, the political parties of those Kentucky senators and representatives, as well as the Commonwealth itself, would appropriately share in the liability for the subordinating speech of their legislators.[24]

Scales and forms of compensation would have to be set, of course. The fact that the details need to be worked out is no more valid an objection to a new tort of subordinating speech than it would be to any other proposal of a new tort.

CONCLUSION

The child I coparent has just finished his first year of middle school. It's been a harrowing experience for all of us. His mother and I have made it a practice from the beginning to "come out" (as lesbian parents) to his teachers, and his mother has made it her custom to spend at least one full morning a week working at his school ever since he was in nursery school. Until this year, things were fine. But this year the insult of choice among children (specifically, boys) at his middle school is "faggot," and our son has been harassed continually (by boys) about having two moms. Despite our meeting several times with his principal, the school year concluded with both of these problems remaining unaddressed. We're all relieved that summer is here, but it was a very difficult year for our son. There were days when he was reluctant to go to school, and we remain uncertain how much his academic work itself was affected by his discomfort at school.

This is just one example of the normalization of homophobia. Our children grow up believing that gender minorities are properly the object of scorn, and even their schoolteachers and principals do not correct this assumption. At twelve, this child knows all too well the costs of being a target of hate speech and the costs to him of the failure of his teachers and principal to protect him. The principal's excuse for doing nothing is that sexual orientation is not a legally protected category. By its inaction, then, the state provides this principal with an excuse to turn away from those who should be able to rely on him, children with gender minority parents and children who themselves will turn out to be gender minorities.

It is no exaggeration to say that systemic homophobia is killing our kids. Roughly 30 percent of gay teenagers report attempting suicide, and roughly 40 percent of all attempted teen suicides are connected to real or perceived homosexual orientation. And the majority of suicide attempts requiring medical intervention are similarly connected to sexual orientation. It remains unclear how many accomplished teenaged suicides can be laid at the feet of homophobia.[25]

Further, fear of being perceived as homosexual has led to murder. Consider the case of Michael Carneal, a fifteen-year-old boy whose 1 December 1997 shooting spree left three of his fellow students dead and five wounded. Carneal says he was continually called "gay, gattof, nerd, geek, and was threatened with [other] violence." He claims he originally intended only to threaten his peers to stop their taunting but changed his mind when he started "thinking about all the things they'd done to me . . . all the names they called me."[26] As this book goes to press, the United States is still reeling from the hideous murder of Matthew Shepard, a gay University of Wyoming student who, on 8 October 1998, was savagely beaten and left to die, tied like a scarecrow to a fence outside Laramie, Wyoming. Shepard was barely alive when he was found, and he died several days later. He was lured to his death by Aaron James McKinney and Russell Henderson with the help of their girlfriends, Kristen Leann Price and Chasity Vera Pasley. Price said her boyfriend, McKinney, and Henderson were embarrassed because Shepard made a pass at them at a bar. "He said that he was gay and wanted to get with Aaron and Russ," Price told ABC's *20/20*. Her friends killed Shepard "to teach him a lesson not to come on to straight people," she said. When Matthew Shepard was buried on 16 October 1998, the funeral was picketed by antigay demonstrators carrying signs saying "God Hates Fags" and "No Fags in Heaven."[27] Again, just who are the "we" who bear the costs of such speech?

When we face such realities squarely, civil libertarian appeals to mere offense, slippery slopes, and fighting words stand out as irresponsible pedantry. Protecting innocent citizens from harm by others is the first obligation of the just state. It is long past time for the state to come forward to protect its gender minorities, and it is long past time for those in the dominant groups to join in insisting on this protection.[28]

NOTES

Thanks to Claudia Card for extremely helpful comments on an earlier draft of this chapter.

1. From a letter to me from the Social Security Administration, dated 5 March 1998.

2. On what I take a characteristically feminist perspective to include, see Joan C. Callahan and Dorothy E. Roberts, "A Feminist Social Justice Approach to Reproduction-Assisting Technologies: A Case Study on the Limits of Liberal Theory," *Kentucky Law Journal* 84, 4 (1996): 1197–1234, and "Editor's Introduction," in *Reproduction, Ethics, and the Law: Feminist Perspectives*, ed. Joan C. Callahan (Bloomington: Indiana University Press, 1995).

3. For rights and benefits that come with marriage, see these Web pages: http://www.freedomtomarry.org/benefits.html and http://www.buddybuddy.com.mar.list.html.

4. To be precise, we could distinguish between "sexual minorities" (as including lesbians, gay men, and bisexual individuals) and "gender minorities" (as including transsexual and transgendered individuals). For efficiency's sake, I adopt "gender minorities" here to cover both groups.

5. A tort is a wrongful action not involving breach of contract that results in harm to another for which the injured party is entitled to compensation. My intent is to suggest a policy that will use the teaching power of the law to articulate societal disapproval of this sort of speech and that will effectively discourage this sort of speech without putting the otherwise full liberty of wrongdoers at stake, which criminal penalties would do.

6. Nadine Strossen, "Regulating Racist Speech on Campus: A Modest Proposal?" *Duke Law Journal* 1990 (June 1990): 484, excerpted in *Hate Speech on Campus: Cases, Case Studies, and Commentary*, ed. Milton Heumann and Thomas W. Church (Boston: Northeastern University Press, 1997), pp. 289–309; hereafter, page numbers refer to the latter volume.

7. In 1977–78, an American neo-Nazi group gained permission to hold a march in Skokie, Illinois, a largely Jewish community with a number of Holocaust survivors. The argument was made that a permit should not be granted, since the residents of Skokie should be protected from "such personally odious expressions." The argument was rejected. See, e.g., *Collin v. Smith* 578 F2d. 1197, 1205–1207 (7th Cir.), cert. denies, 439 U.S. 916 (1978), and *Village of Skokie v. National Socialist Party*, 69 Ill. 2d 605, 373 N.E.2d 21, 23–25 (1978).

8. Samuel Walker provides another example: "The issue before us is whether offensive words, about or directed towards historically victimized groups, should be subject to criminal penalties" (*Hate Speech: The History of an American Controversy* [Lincoln: University of Nebraska Press, 1994], p. 1).

9. See, for example, *Erznoznik v. Jacksonville,* 422 U.S. 205, 210 (1975), and *Cohen v. California,* 403 U.S. 15, 21 (1971).

10. James Rachels clarifies this problem with the ordinary/extraordinary means distinction in "More Impertinent Distinctions and a Defense of Active Euthanasia," in *Biomedical Ethics,* ed. Thomas A. Mappes and Jane S. Zembaty (New York: McGraw-Hill, 1981), pp. 355–59.

11. For more on harm, see Joan C. Callahan, "On Harming the Dead," *Ethics* 97, 2 (1987): 341–52; "Paternalism and Voluntariness," *Canadian Journal of Philosophy* 16, 2 (1986): 199–219; and "Liberty, Beneficence, and Involuntary Confinement," *Journal of Medicine and Philosophy* 9, 3 (1984): 261–93. On harms as setbacks to interests, see Joel Feinberg, *The Moral Limits of the Criminal Law,* vol. 1, *Harm to Others* (New York: Oxford University Press, 1984), chapt. 1.

12. Mari J. Matsuda, "Public Response to Racist Speech: Considering the Victim's Story," in Mari J. Matsuda, Charles R. Lawrence III, Richard Delgado, and Kimberlé Williams Crenshaw, *Words That Wound: Critical Race Theory, Assaultive Speech, and the First Amendment* (Boulder, Colo.: Westview, 1993), p. 25.

13. Diana Tietjens Meyers, "Rights in Collision: A Non-Punitive, Compensatory Remedy for Abusive Speech," *Law and Philosophy* 14, 2 (May 1995): 226. See also Charles Lawrence, "If He Hollers Let Him Go: Regulating Hate Speech on Campus," in Matsuda et al., *Words That Wound,* p. 80, and Frederick Schauer, "Uncoupling Free Speech," *Columbia Law Review* 92 (1992): 1321–57.

14. Meyers makes the point this way: "Indeed, if it weren't for the climate of racism, sexism, homophobia, and ethnocentrism in the United States, discriminatory verbal or pictorial abuse would not be so seriously harmful" ("Rights in Collision," p. 222).

15. On how words can be much more harmful than sticks and stones, see Frederick Schauer, "The Phenomenology of Speech and Harm," *Ethics* 103, 4 (July 1993): 635–53.

16. See also Strossen: "To attempt to craft free speech exceptions only for racist speech would create a significant risk of a slide down the proverbial 'slippery slope'" (*Hate Speech on Campus,* p. 302).

17. Joan C. Callahan, "The Fetus and Fundamental Rights," in *The Ethics of Abortion,* ed. Robert M. Baird and Stuart E. Rosenbaum (New York: Prometheus, 1993), pp. 249–62.

18. A recent improvement is that on 28 May 1998 President Bill Clinton added sexual orientation for the first time as a protected category under a wide-ranging Executive Order to prevent job discrimination in the federal government (Executive Order 11478, Equal Employment Opportunity in the Federal Government). He said it would provide a uniform policy for the federal government, and he urged Congress to pass a long-pending bill, the Employment Non-Discrimination Act (ENDA), to extend protection from job discrimination to all American workers in both the public and private sectors. ENDA has languished in Congress since the mid-1970s. See http://www.religioustolerance.org/hom_empl.htm for an articulation of the current version of ENDA as well the history of the act.

19. On the moral status of acts and omissions, see Joan C. Callahan, "Acts, Omissions, and Euthanasia," *Public Affairs Quarterly* 2, 2 (1988): 21–36.

20. Problems with so-called liberal neutrality are legion and have been addressed numerous times in numerous ways by critical legal theorists, critical race theorists, and feminists (among others). See Callahan and Roberts, "A Feminist Social Justice Approach," as well as Joan C. Callahan, "Procreative Liberty: Whose Procreation, Whose Liberty?" *Stanford Law and Policy Review* 6, 2 (1995): 121–25, critical note on John Robertson's *Children of Choice: Freedom and the New Reproductive Technologies* (Princeton, N.J.: Princeton University Press, 1994).

21. See Nadine Taub and Wendy Williams, "Will Equality Require More Than Assimilation, Accommodation, or Separation from the Existing Social Structure?" *Rutgers Law Review/Civil Rights Developments* 37 (1985): 825.

22. The Supreme Court has recognized a similar point in the context of employment. In *Griggs v. Duke Power Co.,* 401 U.S. 424, 431 (1971), the Court makes clear that an employment practice that is facially neutral but in fact favors one group over another is illegal, independent of the intent of participants: "The objective of Congress in the enactment of Title VII is plain from the language of the statute. It was to achieve equality of employment opportunities and remove barriers that have operated in the past to favor an identifiable group of white employees over other employees. Under the Act, practices, procedures, or tests neutral on their face, and even neutral in terms of intent, cannot be maintained if they operate to 'freeze' the status quo of prior discriminatory employment practices" (*Griggs v. Duke Power Co.,* 401 U.S. 424 431 [1971]. See also *Albemarle Paper Co. v. Moody,* 422 U.S. 405 (1975).

23. Richard Delgado, "Words That Wound: A Tort Action for Racial Insults, Epithets, and Name Calling," in Matsuda et al., *Words That Wound,* pp. 89–110.

24. Cf. Meyers's suggestion ("Rights in Collision," p. 228ff.) that universities be held liable for compensation to targets of hate speech on campuses.

25. For continually updated information see the Gay, Lesbian, and Straight Education Network, on the Web at
http://www.glstn.org/pages/sections/
and the Suicide Problems page at
http://www.virtualcity.com/youthsuicide/index.htm.

26. "Gay Taunts Led Teen to Shoot," *News Planet,* 30 June 1998, http://www.planetout.com/newsplanet/article.html?1998/06/30/3.

27. "God Hates Fags" is the name of an internet site. For pictures on that site of the picketing of gay men's funerals, including Matthew Shepard's, see http://www.godhatesfags.com/gold.jpg
and hhtp://www.godhatesfags.com/shepard_funeral.jpg.

28. Inexpressible thanks to Kentucky Representative Kathy Stein, who has done just this, with remarkable courage and eloquence.

Part Four
Love and Respect

13 / *Feminist Sex at Century's End: On Justice and Joy*

CHRIS J. CUOMO

This chapter rethinks aspects of the feminist sex "wars" through an expansive conception of feminist ethics. Rather than debate the particulars regarding sexual inclinations and choices, I argue that feminist ethics should attend to the unconscious, including its potential for such life-affirming experiences as sexual pleasure. I also argue, contrary to Drucilla Cornell, that feminist ethics should not shy away from normative and critical questions. I believe feminist ethics should promote both justice and joy. I therefore advocate a radical, critical openness to the plurality of feminist positions, motivations, commitments, and priorities regarding sex.

My theory emerges from frustration and optimism. The frustration is about chasms that hinder fruitful and engaging feminist ethical projects, both practically and theoretically. I find these chasms to be obstacles to understanding and movement in ongoing dramas regarding the politics of sexuality in feminist and lesbian communities. Similar obstacles are also evident in feminist philosophers' lack of attention to each other's work, especially when this lack parallels loyalties to boundaries held in place by established male traditions—such as the boundary between Continental and analytic philosophy.[1] For example, recent feminist work on Levinas and "the ethical" includes little discussion of feminist ethical theory, a philosophical field in which critical issues include the deconstruction of the atomistic and ahistorical "moral agent," the inseparability of norms from contexts, and resistance to replicating oppressive assumptions and oppressive forms of being.[2]

I write in the hope that such obstacles are not inevitable, and with optimism about what might emerge from a more engaged interchange. There are theoretically and politically significant reasons for the lack of cross-pollination among different approaches to feminism and ethics. Indeed, variations among approaches to ethics correspond to varied beliefs concerning knowledge, being, and meaning. These differences are rich sites for feminist investigation. But gaps in theoretical and political approaches are not benign when they confine the scope of theoretical and ethico-political work, or when they contribute to a climate in which professional and philosophical differences matter more than the promise of what those of us who are disloyal to civilization might build together. The normative edge of *feminism*—a term that presupposes that some states of affairs are preferable to others—implies enough agreement that those interested in what feminism might say about ethics ought to be interested in each others' perspectives and work. A minimalist conception of feminist politics on which we can agree could make the tensions I discuss manageable, even if they indicate deep metaphysical disagreement. Minimal agreement on feminist values and practices, on the importance of justice and improving the lives of the oppressed, and on there being limits to what we can know about ethical agency and meaning is a starting point for feminist politics across difference.

The first obstacle I address is a tendency, which I'll call "libertarian," to reject any attempt to articulate norms.[3] This rejection is expressed among some feminist thinkers as a disdain for rules, moralizing, and judgmental positions on the ground that norms are inherently constraining and therefore harmful. Libertarian feminists typically represent themselves as renegades within feminism, as standing counter to "feminist law" and against the inclination of other feminists to explore and engage meanings of right and wrong, good and bad. I argue below that Drucilla Cornell's conception of "ethical feminism" is an example illustrating that even feminists who are interested in theory-building regarding ethics sometimes take a paradoxically libertarian stance.

It is not surprising that most work in feminist moral philosophy is not written by libertarian feminists. Instead, feminist moral philosophers tend to promote a feminism, which I'll call "conscious," concerned primarily with addressing oppression. Conscious feminism does not avoid normativity but is built on the assumption that feminist norms can and should be sought, consciously and intentionally. But the presupposition that ethics is predominantly a conscious matter is a second obstacle that stands in the way of more satisfying feminist ethical projects. That is, when we restrict our attentions to fully conscious ethical matters, we cannot theorize ethics as shaped by factors beyond conscious control and awareness.[4]

I wish to argue, contrary to libertarian feminism, that the articulation of ethical norms and values ought to remain central to feminism, but also, contrary to conscious feminism, that our discussions of ethics ought to be informed by critical thinking about less accessible, less conscious, aspects of ethical being. Although I do not take up which theory of the unconscious is most accurate and most useful for feminist ethics, I briefly consider suggestions made by others regarding how we should understand the psyche.

In what follows, I draw upon my own experiences and evolving reflections concerning sexuality and sexual ethics in lesbian/queer communities. My aim is to understand what has appeared to be an impasse in feminist understanding and theorizing about norms, judgments, and the role of the unconscious in ethical life and to point toward a more inclusive and challenging course.

ETHICS AS JUSTICE AND JOY

I begin with some claims about ethics. These claims are ideals, although they are not analytic or exhaustive. They are meant to give the reader a sense of what I mean by "ethics" and "feminist ethics."

1. *Somehow, we are ethical beings.* We (who sense ourselves as ethical) care about others and are moved by the interests of others. Caring is woven thoroughly into our being and, hence, our values and deliberations. We have fundamentally dependent and social natures but also a sense of ourselves as isolated and independent. Despite the latter, our commitments to others, and to our projects together, create a framework in which others' well-being remains necessary to our conception of the good.

2. *Ethics should promote joy.* Ethical principles, practical wisdom, affective responsiveness, and character and virtue help us live good lives, lives in which we are able to explore our possibilities, seek happiness, joy, and contentment, and in which our being with others is more like communion and less like war.

As ethical beings we move toward relationships and communities characterized by cooperation, honesty, and fulfillment of many sorts of life potential, which includes unique potential for pleasure, joy, and knowledge but also the possibility of emotional, physical, and creative brilliance. Philosophical ethics pursues understanding of the ground on which we value and promote health, integrity, and other aspects of flourishing.

3. *Ethics should promote justice.* Ethics helps us identify, address, and work to reduce harm and injustice. Ethics helps us articulate and negotiate personal and communal goals and limits in terms of respect, doing the right thing, and being fair. Values and evaluations can help us find alternatives to ways of being and social structures that are directly or indirectly exclusionary, harmful, or oppressive. Ethics is useful for renouncing the notion that those who are white, male, rich, or straight are inherently more deserving of good lives or of the deeply significant freedoms and material resources needed to pursue flourishing. Ethics allows us to name injustice and figure out how to respond in its presence. Because the work of naming injustice is historical as well as immediate, ethics must be somewhat backward-looking.

4. *Ethics should attend to the psyche.* Ethics must attend to the unconscious aspects of the psyche in which we become subjects and in which we therefore become gendered, raced, sexual, and ethical. Any ethical position that takes as its starting point resistance to long-standing injustice and deep harm must be aware that such histories shape identities and psychologies.[5] Unconscious drives and motives develop within oppression and so are not entirely accessible, transparent, or trustworthy. Likewise, the joyful aspects of life that help stoke ethical being often occur in its unconscious layers. Ethics must also attend to the fact that persons are complicated, rarely simply oppressors or simply oppressed. Ethics must therefore see itself and practices, experiences, and identities as multiplicitous and complex.[6]

5. *Ethics should be forward-looking.* Ethical responses within exceedingly oppressive contexts include visions and aspirations of more liberated forms of being and relating. Commitments to forward-looking ethical projects lead us to engage experiences and desires critically but also to see them as possible sources of information and inspiration. Ethics helps maintain hope.

Feminist ethics should promote both justice and joy. But justice and joy can indicate very different projects—one normative, the other exploratory. We need protection and vigilance in the face of racism, misogyny, and other forms of harm. We also need evaluations of and recommendations for conscious choices and actions. But joy and other fundamental affective (and less clearly chosen) aspects of being are part of what makes fighting oppression worthwhile. Such responses enable us to gain insight regarding freedom, even in the midst of oppression. Even physical ecstasy might be a rich source of self-respect and loving regard for others who are capable of pleasure.

Joy is a complex emotion. It is a feeling or experience of deep pleasure, with a higher-order sense of oneself as pleased. Joy includes not only pleasure but also the awareness of that pleasure as profoundly satisfying. Such awareness might include contentment with life or situation; awe at one's capacity for connection, ecstasy or contentment; wonder or delight for a world in which such feelings are possible; gratitude for what one is feeling; relief from the hardships or pain from which one is somewhat free in a joyful moment; or just a general sense of well-being, one's own or that of others. Joy is ethically significant because it is more than a feeling. It reminds us what we love, with whom we are bound, what we can do, and why we fight. It brings us to a rock-bottom knowledge that, despite it all, life can be good.

In practical moral life, we experience tensions between the avoidance of evil and the pursuit of joyful living; between a thirst for justice (the eradication of injustice, oppression, and the influence of the master) and drives toward contentment (the experience of life as fundamentally worthwhile, the ability to partake in the diverse pleasures available to us as individuals and in connection with others). A tension between a thirst for justice and a drive toward joy runs parallel to disagreements in the history of philosophy concerning the role of ethics in human life and communities and, hence, concerning what questions ethical theorists ought to consider. This tension may be an element of disagreements cast variously as between consequentialist and deontological perspectives, between evaluations of actions and evaluations of character, between rules and values, and between justice and care. I focus here on the tension between justice and joy because I believe it also captures aspects of some crucial feminist debates.

Feminist philosophy has not yet attended to the moral significance of joy and other affirmations of living. In fact, ethical theory in general rarely includes consideration of the affective sources of ethical care and motivation. Perhaps this lack of philosophical interest is due in part to the fact that joy has been assimilated to happiness, and ethical concern with happiness is easily reduced to traditional liberal utilitarian arguments. My discussion of joy is neither a utilitarian argument for happiness as summum bonum nor an argument for the unqualified freedom to pursue happiness. Rather, I am interested in joy as something more specific than happiness, as one of many sources of ethical being (other sources include moral knowledge, motivation, and a proclivity to be oriented toward Others in ways that are not harmful and destructive).

How might feminists integrate concern with fighting injustice and oppression with the desire to further happiness, flourishing, and joy? What should we do, and how should we *be,* when justice and joy appear to conflict? These questions are bewitchingly complex in feminist thinking about sex.

FEMINIST SEX

The centrality of sexuality in some versions of feminism indicates the interests and perspectives of those with the privilege of determining the boundaries and emphases of feminist politics.[7] Feminism's perennial interest in sexuality is also a product of the interrelationships of sex/gender and sexuality, of (some) women's sense of a need to have more control over sexuality, and of our keen desire for sex about which we feel really good. Feminist frenzy around sex is also a product of the sexiness of exposing what we are encouraged (ambiguously) to keep under wraps. In certain versions of feminism, so much seems to hang on sex, as though discovering the truth about it and its relation to other forms of power will foster a fundamental freedom. This view of sex is built on optimistic assumptions about the control anyone can have over her own embodied and social responses. In fact, erotic responses and desires are products of cultural and personal fantasies about sexual engagement, many of which keep women focused on men. How could moral and political projects that aim to increase and transform women's power *not* be concerned with the intricacies of sex?

Feminist interest in sex has never been univocal. Alongside the fact that sexuality always sits within a nexus of racial and class formations, personal histories, political positions, and other aspects of identity make it impossible to characterize any one opinion as *the* feminist position on sex. It was probably inevitable that the libertarian feminist response to sexual repression would confront the conscious rejection of domination head-on in the feminist "wars" regarding the ethics of sadomasochism, pornography, prostitution, and sex with men. It is tempting to describe those debates as between two fundamentally different sets of priorities. In the literature, libertarian positions that aimed to free women and lesbians from moralism and repression pitted themselves against conscious stances on violence against women. What emerged could be characterized as a contest regarding "status" as victims at the hands of other feminists: You (sadomasochists) are hurting us (good feminists) with your violent sexual expression and practice (read: you are eroticizing the injustice that we are fighting). You (prudes) are hurting us (free thinkers) with your criticism and lack of tolerance (read: you are trying to deny us a precious source of joy).

In libertarian arguments, there was a mistaken assumption that breaking laws (whether of heteropatriarchy or of "correct" feminism) was sufficient to constitute a radical departure from oppressive norms. I agree with Bat-Ami Bar On that the libertarian position assumed a liberal conception of individual agency and social change that betrayed its radical intentions, and that it is not radical to hold that experiences and feelings are exempt from critical engagement or to eschew all forms of ethical judgment.[8] More important, libertarian feminists generally failed to provide a nuanced articulation of *why* certain freedoms and pleasures matter, and how they are relevant to feminist perspectives or feminist ethics.[9] On the other hand, conscious positions generally did not attempt to address certain realities of sexuality—its messiness, diversity, detachment from choice, and permeation by power, fear, passion, and uncompromising desire. Although pleasure should not be realized at the expense of others' physical or emotional well-being, the sticky business of sex makes the causal connections of harm and intention particularly difficult to trace. Social, sexual beings hurt and nurture each other through sex, in simple and complicated ways. What counts as harm is relative, and harm might not even justify curtailing sexual knowledge, expression, or liberty. In the end, conscious feminists refused to explore the resistant potential in the contradictory pleasures of female sexual exploration.

The feudlike impasse in feminist thinking about sex and ethics was created in part by the fact that those who prioritize pleasure did not want to hear about rules, judgments, and oppression, and those centrally concerned with justice and the conscious means of eliminating oppression did not acknowledge the unconscious layers of sexual being. Even more generally, we were not tuned in to the fact that although drives and desires are not easily or realistically accommodated by talk of choice and agency, they are a large part of what creates the texture and motivation of ethical life.

The heat that characterized feminist conflicts over sexuality has certainly subsided. We might hypothesize that its dwindling has resulted from the mainstreaming of lesbian chic and niche marketing or from an increased need to address the threat of the radical right in the United States. Perhaps the move away from characterizing gender and sexuality as uncomplicated by race and class makes it less likely that feminists will analyze sexuality as either simply "empowering" or "oppressive" of all women. In any case, some feminists clearly feel that a truce was reached and that they decided to peacefully coexist with, or quietly avoid, those with whom they disagree regarding the ethics of sexuality. My own sense is that the poles have actually shifted (some may have even dissolved) and that a loose consensus regarding the power and importance of sexual pleasure and exploration is now present in many feminist lesbian/queer communities. Perhaps we are in the process of attending to the psyche and its potential for experiences that feed the soul at the same time that we are building feminist, antiracist ethics and forms of life.

A MIGRATION STORY

My feminist politics have always been interwoven with sexual choices, reflections, desires, and identity. My passage from straight-radical campus feminist to bisexual urban activist to lesbian academic, from the mid-1980s to the early 1990s, from New York to the Midwest, was largely about my desire to enact feminist values—to "give free reign" to desires previously repressed and to "choose ways of being" that were not oppressive to myself and others. Immediately, these ethical desires found sexual expression (though, of course, the question of whether the ethics were driving the sex or the opposite was true is still up for grabs). I saw the ways that I came to do love, intimacy, nakedness, bodily writhing, and exploration as ways of choosing the many faces of female power and beauty and of rejecting sexist oppression and white supremacy. This is how I thought, wrote, and spoke about lesbian and feminist sex. Through much of this migration, my conception of "acting on values" was that it was a conscious critical endeavor, fueled by a concern to minimize the influences and vestiges of racist heteropatriarchy in my life and my culture. And I was utterly turned on by the women and dykes around me.

As for what I *did:* When I spray-painted a mainstreet porn shop with other radical lesbians, the excitement of organizing the action was augmented by our flirtations and the sexiness of our renegade performances. I agitated against sadomasochism and for women-only spaces, among girlfriends who I thought so hot they'd melt the buckle on my fanny pack. In bed, where I hung out a lot, my girlfriend and I sometimes dressed up in drag; I wasn't sure what to think about liking her fingers in me (though I felt less ambiguous about how much I liked fucking her); I got a thrill when she talked dirty in the language of heteropatriarchy, and I felt glad and happy all of the time that I was with a woman and not a man. I read and wrote erotic stories with purely prurient interest. With friends, lovers, and fellow activists I thought and talked about sex, which we nearly always took to be an inherently good part of our lives and about which we nearly always felt comfortable giving opinions and passing tenuous judgments. Despite the fact that at the time I was quite certainly "against" sadomasochism and pornography, my sexuality, as the above makes obvious, was replete with complicating contradictions.

Now, at the turn of the century, with a body that has begun to feel itself aging and with an overwhelming sense that most of the people I encounter are profoundly unhappy and unfulfilled, I am aware that without the intensity of joy and other rich affective experiences, our ethical commitments to ourselves and others are empty, dull, and uninspired. I find that I am less judgmental about my own and others' choices and desires. Yet I am also still interested in seeing what feminism has to offer those of us who are deeply attached to the importance of both sex and ethics, both joy and justice. Almost unknowingly, I have moved from a concern with working to eliminate oppression and harm to a more constructive interest in creating/discovering experiences, forms of communication, and expressions of being that forget oppression, resist its force and trajectory, and diminish its seemingly thorough reach. I think of this progression as a shift toward an ethic of flourishing. As far as sexuality goes—and where doesn't it go, really—I believe this ethic includes a moral commitment to joy.

The shifts in and around me have led me to rethink chasms of disagreement among feminists, including disagreement about the political significance of sex and the relevant matter of ethics. While I do not seek a metatheory for understanding or eliminating these chasms, I am optimistic that we can—that indeed we have already begun to—move beyond them, as surely as our own positions change and evolve. Certainly some differences among us are irreconcilable or indicative of differences that should not be bridged with the relatively simple "common ground" approach that I recommend here. Still, unimagined contributions to feminist ethics, strategies, and communities might emerge from a more engaged interchange among feminist positions with hope both for justice and for joy.

I've already mentioned two problems that have helped block understanding in feminist fights about ethics in general and about sex in particular. The first is a libertarian tendency to want to avoid normativity and critical judgments altogether. The second is the neglect in feminist ethics of the unconscious as a factor in moral life. Both of these obfuscating approaches to ethics are illustrated in the following example.

In the late eighties, I attended a lesbian and gay studies student conference. One panel stands out in my memory. It included papers on lesbian sadomasochism and bar culture and was commented upon by a stylish white dyke who looked cool and tough. She summed up the papers enthusiastically, for a suitably interested audience, remarking on the varieties of lesbian outlaw practices. I, too, felt drawn to theorizing lesbians as outlaws. But in the midst of writing a dissertation on feminist ethics, I also craved an investigation of what about outlaw status and identity is politically and ethically important, especially for lesbians. If regimes of power and law are oppressive, positioning oneself against them would be good. But being an outlaw, even in relation to deadly regimes, is not intrinsically good. Rather, some outlaw identities and practices are better than others, and some are just pissing in a river. I raised my hand and asked the dykes on the panel why they thought being a lesbian outlaw is a good thing.

I don't remember what other panelists said, but the stylish commentator returned to the podium, puffing up with all her big dyke pride, and said that being an outlaw was important *because it turned her on.* I wanted an ethico-political answer, a statement from which I could generalize. But she was describing the good solely in terms of her lesbo-sexual feelings. I was unsatisfied. I thought that getting turned on, while certainly political, was insufficient to recommend forms of lesbian being as counterhegemonic to phallocratic, racist, and heterosexual domination. I suppose she in turn thought my question obtuse.

Where else could this exchange have gone? While I know hardly anything about the stylish commentator, it is perhaps overdetermined that some mutual understanding was lurking beneath our apparent difference: we were both white academics, we called ourselves "lesbian," we were both interested in lived politics and how these relate to theoretical questions at the intersection of feminism and post-structuralism. But given even these commonalities, it would be inaccurate to characterize our disagreement as one-dimensional. It would also be wrong to characterize our disagreement as indicative of the most pressing issue in feminist politics. Nonetheless, I believe it does indicate a direction for feminist thinking about sex, and for working across difference, that did not seem available to us then and there.

Is getting turned on relevant to ethics? Should it be relevant to feminist ethics? Clearly, unless one is a hedonist, pleasure, excitement, and ecstasy cannot serve as ethical barometers, indicating the good or right. But if these experiences are significant in awakening and motivating in us a sense of ethics and commitments to flourishing, then we should pay careful attention to them and hence to the complex and chaotic workings of the psyche. Pleasure is not trivial, and it is not a neutral "response," an instance of which can be evaluated as either consistent with or opposed to feminist values. Rather, it is part of the complicated weave of ethical agency and selfhood. The role of pleasure and joy might be crucial to the creative embodiment of the ethical. Even if it is crucial for only some of us, feminists should take to heart the ethical significance of joy and other affirmations of life.

LESBIAN "SEX" IN FEMINIST PHILOSOPHY

Some philosophers in the lesbian and feminist tradition that has nurtured my thinking have argued that lesbians don't really have "sex." "Sex," they argue, is defined by heteropatriarchal systems of domination and is lived in terms of male power.[10] Although I do not dispute these empirically accurate criticisms, I cling to the powerful presence of sex in my own life and in lesbian and queer relationships and communities.

Sex has many meanings. Sex depends on exclusions and boundary-marking, all informed by norms of gender. Where we touch, who we touch, how we talk or write or move, how we feel when we do the things we do, all denote sexual spaces and interactions. Gender, race, age, relation, and physical and historical particularities all determine which intimate interactions are taken to be sexual. Sex also functions in resistant spaces, including the bodies, psyches, and relationships of resistors. In the lesbian/queer communities in which I exist, "sex" refers to a realm of physical intimacy and response, including pleasure, orgasms and extraordinary touch, and communication. It often refers to genital sensation, making out, nakedness, and dress up. It refers to bodies coming together, in space or in the imagination, and sharing information about desire—about what turns them on, what alights in them intense pleasure and excitement. And although sex is usually taken to refer to genital or orgasmic contact, it is not reducible to those or to any of the other features I have mentioned.

The realities of lesbians and sex are not exhausted by what is found between the covers of *Susie Sexpert's Lesbian Sex World*.[11] But by and large, lesbians, femmes and butches, gay girls, female queers, dykes, tortilleras, and bulldaggers think of themselves as having sex, as beings who are unapologetically sexual. Even if lesbians *do* things (and each other) differently, most of us tend to think of the doings as sex. If current lesbian literature, popular culture, and consumer habits are any indication, homoerotically inclined females are heavily invested in having and enjoying sex. Claims that lesbians don't have sex fail to capture the extent to which what we do is as informed by taboo, history, scent, drive, development, and lust as are the body-to-body interactions of the rest of the world. Concerning sex in this sense, the political response of most lesbians in the 1990s appears to be not "We Shall Overcome" but rather "They Can't Take That Away from Me."

The so-called sex radicals of the eighties helped bring sex out of the American cultural closet and in fact made sex fashionable in lesbian-identified communities. Although lesbian and feminist cultures seem to have gravitated toward explicitly sex-positive attitudes, it does not follow that *all* consequences are good. In capitalism, "fashion" means sales, and female-focused sexuality now gets niche-marketed to urban middle-class lesbians, along with rainbow-striped dog collars, corporate-controlled music by women artists, and sport-utility vehicles. Predictably, the versions of sex sold through gay-friendly capitalism tend to rely on and promote racist, patriarchal, and able-bodied conceptions of female embodiment and desire.

Anthony Weston, an environmental ethicist, has argued that during the "originary moments" in which a value system (or, we might say, a discourse) is undergoing a dramatic, expansive shift, we ought to encourage and accommodate a proliferation of new concepts, practices, principles, and values put forth by those who aim toward more liberatory ethics.[12] If, at the end of the twentieth century, we might characterize feminist explorations of sex as an originary moment, then there might be potential in feminist approaches that explicitly express feminist values in ways that are sex-positive. In this extended originary moment regarding feminist sex, we might see desire as not simply given, or "Natural," while also acknowledging that we have less control over desire than some feminists would like to think.[13] But because some contexts are freer than others, we might work to create spaces in which to explore and pursue what inspires and delights us without simply creating new markets for capitalism.

WHY WE STILL NEED NORMS

Though I've been focusing on ethics and sex, a more general point can be made about feminist ethics. That is, feminist explorations of the ethical relevance of joy and other emotions and unconscious responses need not reject normative ethical theory, judgments, and principles. Rather, ethical projects should be tempered by more explicit, more realistic, and tentative theories of the psyche. Interrogations of the deep sources and sites of ethical life need not lead us to reject ethics or ethical theory. If we are moved in ways that are not completely conscious, then taking joy to heart requires attention to the role of the unconscious in ethical life.

Feminist Contentions: A Philosophical Exchange, a book that exhibits and addresses key debates in feminist philosophy, contains a wide-ranging and complex exchange among Judith Butler, Nancy Fraser, Seyla Benhabib, and Drucilla Cornell. In addition to predictable dialogues regarding feminism and postmodernism, a number of the "contentions" at hand cluster around questions of normativity and the "good" that is promoted or assumed by feminism. A central struggle develops between Cornell's conception of an antinormative "ethical feminism" and the more explicitly invested, theoretically weighty ethical norms endorsed by Fraser and Benhabib. Because Cornell's stated rejection of ethical norms and theories is so thorough, her position provides a helpful reference point for considering the logic and limits of antinormative feminist positions on sexuality. At the same time, her loyalty to psychoanalytic theory exhibits both the dangers and attractions of an ethical approach that takes seriously the often unconscious and inarticulable power of desire, drives, and emotions in shaping us as sexual and ethical beings.

In "What Is Ethical Feminism?" Cornell argues for a feminism grounded in an attitude that she calls "the ethical," defined as "the aspiration to a nonviolent relationship to the Other and to otherness in the widest possible sense." Although she sees this aspiration as entailing attention to "what kind of person we become," she distinguishes it from *morality,* which she takes to be a system "that absolutely governs the 'right way to behave.'" Instead, she holds that "the ethical is not a system of behavioral rules, nor a system of positive standards by which to justify disapproval of others. It is, rather, an attitude towards what is other to oneself."[14]

Cornell's critique of ethical theory is threefold. She claims that ethical theory tends to be intolerant and moralizing, that nothing about ethics should be taken as absolute, and that normative and universal ethical theory cannot address what it means to take responsibility for what is unconscious. Although Cornell admits that all feminists make judgments, she believes we should be suspicious of any attempt to present judgments as integrated in a moral system. She asserts that the systematization of ethics excludes the crucial feminist task of continually reimagining our own standards of right and wrong. But although Cornell derides any determinable, theoretical reflections on morality, she also states that it is ultimately *for ethical reasons* that we should not construct ethical theories, because such attempts are likely to become moralistic and intolerant of difference. These worries about intolerance and moralizing echo libertarian feminists' claims that judgments regarding sexuality are repressive, damaging, and a waste of feminist attentions. Putting aside for a moment the question of whether such an antinormative normativity is even coherent, what should we make of this distaste for moralizing?

Feminist rejection of moralizing makes sense if "rejecting" norms or rules is an expression of an anarchist, resistant impulse that is necessary in feminism. An accompanying worry is that normative claims are too prescriptive—indicating that there is one way of thinking, doing, or being that is the only right/good/feminist way. In her categorical rejection of ethical theorizing, Cornell's moralizing models are Catharine MacKinnon and reformist feminists who eschew radical sexual politics. She appears ignorant of the volume of work in feminist ethics that rejects purity and is critical of liberal conceptions of the self and rationality. Values and evaluations of feminist ethics *are* normative (not just descriptive), but they need not be absolute, universal, unified, or exclusive. Within philosophy, feminist ethics has razed moral edifices that assume, falsely, that ethical agents are reducible to rational robots and that ethics equals rule-following, and it has favored constructing ethical theories that are sensitive to context, difference, particularity, and connection.

Resistance to rules implies normative evaluations. Cornell's critique presupposes norms beyond those she acknowledges as required by the ethical. For example, her statement that intolerance is unethical, or that "apotropaic," evil-mitigating gestures are crucial for feminist practice, cannot be made solely on the basis of "the ethical," as she conceives it. Likewise, Cornell is mistaken that her version of "the ethical" demands that "we deconstruct the claim that we share an identity as women and that the differences between us are secondary," because her conception of the ethical is not specific enough to do so.[15] Rather, difference is a starting point for feminism because of commitments to represent women, race, sexuality, and gender as accurately as possible and to avoid silencing or otherwise harming women who are likely to disappear under the mirage of a shared identity. Cornell reduces ethics to worries about intolerance and the limits of masculinist traditions, but she neglects to balance the merits and dangers of specific claims about how we ought to be and how we ought to be together. What feminist ethics needs is not to reject norms but to develop normative ethical theory that is situated, psychologically sophisticated, and open to revision.

Cornell is also concerned that ethical theory presents norms as absolute and beyond debate. But presenting a system of apparently consistent and justifiable ethics need not imply that values, judgments, or principles are final or unrevisable. In fact, feminist ethics often achieves systematization through contingencies, articulating values that are contextual, socially situated, interested, and partial. It is certainly true that "the ethical imagination" is expressed as much in art and poetry as argumentative prose. Yet our understandings about who we are, what we care about, and who we might become are also deepened through searches for patterns of consistency and coherence in feminist ethical imaginings and beings.

Cornell's most worthwhile question is "How can we take responsibility for what is unconscious?" Related questions include: How is the ethical relation informed by the psychical fantasy of Woman? How can feminists struggle to make unconscious patterns conscious if we cannot be certain when we are succeeding or being authentic? How does the Other, and the Other in ourselves, call us to responsibility? How does the ethical demand our own transformation?[16] Because these questions are crucial, feminist ethics would benefit from critical engagements with theories of the unconscious and with scientific inquiries concerning the development of identity, including the interwoven, relative formations of gender, race, class, and sexuality. The work of Cornell and other feminist psychoanalytic thinkers might help prompt feminist ethics that is unafraid to explore the psychological depth of our forms of life.

But such cross-pollinations will not occur without mutually respectful, pragmatic engagement across differences. Cornell implies that without explicitly employing a theory of the unconscious, feminists are engaged in superficial research that is destined to replicate reality. A theory of unconscious motivation and the construction of social fantasy, she claims, "must be the basis of any critical research program."[17] But this claim is reductionist. If Cornell is right that "reality is shaped by unconscious fantasies that severely restrict our field of vision and political imagination," then she is right that the question of how we can best broaden our fields of vision and imagination is crucial. However, it is also begging the question for many different intellectual and political approaches. Reimagining our forms of life and of love is certainly part of the work of feminist ethics. We need to know more about the unconscious in order to theorize accurately our moral possibilities. But no amount of pondering the workings of the unconscious will amount to resistance or to justice.

Analysis is no certain route to political transformation. As Benhabib and Fraser make clear in *Feminist Contentions*, feminist struggles are not reducible to struggles to make unconscious patterns conscious, and struggles to change conscious and unconscious patterns are not reducible to a search for an accurate account of the unconscious.[18] Indeed, our attempts to achieve transformation, and to diversify and explode cultural understandings of Woman, are consciously strategized, discussed, and pursued. We should not become so preoccupied with judgment, with theorizing the psyche, or with working out the details of ethical life that we forget to inspire and notice change.

"IF I CAN'T DANCE . . ."

Feminist ethics should not be a war between justice and joy. If we give up the belief that ethics is an entirely conscious matter and the belief that any formulation of norms or judgments is a threat to liberty, it becomes possible to forge ethical possibilities that are both resistant and creative and to nurture joy alongside our righteous rage. The project of feminist ethics is therefore a matter of building cultures—not dreamy feminist utopias where consensus and uniformity rule, but varied spaces, practices, identities, and communities in which resistant rhythms might continue to develop. We don't dance to forget the revolution. In the music, the movement, the looks on others' faces when they are illuminated with joy, when we notice and enjoy the fact that we are in tune, the world is good.

NOTES

I would like to thank Claudia Card for superb editing and Vicky Davion for helpful advice. This chapter is dedicated to the memory of Linda Weiner Morris, whose friendship brought me joy.

1. I would venture that the main reason we are not reading each other's work, or reading it with care, is political in the local sense. The professional designators that mark what is and is not worth considering (of which the Continental/analytic divide is merely one) are fairly rigid. Admittedly, no one can keep up with the volume of new books, journals, and articles in "feminist theory" published each year. Decisions about hiring, promotion, and tenure often rest on the extent to which our work relates to some phallocratic tradition. It is easy to see why feminist academics are selective about what they read beyond their spheres of expertise. But let's face it: feminist scholars must read outside of our narrow spheres.

2. See, for example, Tina Chanter, *Ethics and Eros: Irigaray Rewrites the Philosophers* (New York: Routledge Press, 1995), and Cynthia Willett, *Maternal Ethics and Other Slave Moralities* (New York: Routledge Press, 1995). Both books are innovative, informative, and highly engaging. Yet their lack of attention to work in feminist ethics is disappointing.

3. Obviously, this position entails a deep contradiction (to be "against" norms is to imply a norm). My focus here is not on the contradiction but on the substantive worries beneath this stance.

4. Notable exceptions to this trend in feminist ethics include Claudia Card, *The Unnatural Lottery: Character and Moral Luck* (Philadelphia: Temple University Press, 1996), and Diana Tietjens Meyers, *Subjection and Subjectivity: Psychoanalytic Feminism and Moral Philosophy* (New York: Routledge, 1994).

5. Cheryl Hall argues that feminist ethics needs a "theory of the psyche" in "Politics, Ethics, and the 'Uses of the Erotic': Why Feminist Theorists Need to Think About the Psyche," in *Daring to Be Good: Essays in Feminist Ethico-Politics*, ed. Bat-Ami Bar On and Ann Ferguson (New York: Routledge, 1998), Although Hall and I disagree about the kinds of feminist philosophies of mind that will be most helpful, I think our projects are quite compatible.

6. The ontology I have in mind here is inspired by the work of María Lugones; see especially "Purity, Impurity, and Separation," *Signs* 19, 2 (1994): 458–79 and "Playfulness, 'World'-Travelling, and Loving Perception," in *Lesbian Philosophies and Cultures*, ed. Jeffner Allen (Albany: State University of New York Press, 1990), pp. 159–80.

7. Katie King provides a useful story of how sexuality came to be a central theme in U.S. feminism in *Theory in Its Feminist Travels: Conversations in U.S. Women's Movements* (Bloomington: Indiana University Press, 1994).

8. Bat-Ami Bar On, "The Feminist Sexuality Debates and the Transformation of the Political," in *Adventures in Lesbian Philosophy*, ed. Claudia Card (Bloomington: Indiana University Press, 1994).

9. Libertarian positions generally defended freedoms in traditional liberal terms instead of articulating radical, feminist, or other ethico-political exploration of the significance of sexual pleasure and exploration.

10. Examples include Claudia Card, *The Unnatural Lottery: Character and Moral Luck* (Philadelphia: Temple University Press, 1996), pp. 140–62; Marilyn Frye, "Lesbian Sex," in *Lesbian Philosophies and Cultures*, pp. 301–15; Sarah Hoagland, *Lesbian Ethics: Toward New Value* (Palo Alto, Calif.: Institute for Lesbian Studies, 1988); and Joyce Trebilcot, *Dyke Ideas: Process, Politics, Daily Life* (Albany: State University of New York Press, 1994).

11. Susie Bright, *Susie Sexpert's Lesbian Sex World* (San Francisco: Cleis Press, 1990).

12. Anthony Weston, "Enabling Environmental Practice," *Environmental Ethics,* 14, 4 (Winter 1992): 325–38.

13. For insightful discussion of feminism, psychology, and the politics of desire, see Sandra Lee Bartky, "Feminine Masochism and the Politics of Personal Transformation," in *Femininity and Domination: Studies in the Phenomenology of Oppression* (New York: Routledge, 1990).

14. Drucilla Cornell, "What Is Ethical Feminism?" in Seyla Benhabib, Judith Butler, Drucilla Cornell, and Nancy Fraser, *Feminist Contentions: A Philosophical Exchange* (New York: Routledge, 1995), p. 78.

15. Ibid., p. 85.

16. Ibid., p. 84.

17. Cornell, "Rethinking the Time of Feminism," in *Feminist Contentions,* p. 146.

18. Seyla Benhabib, "Subjectivity, Historiography, and Politics: Reflections on the Feminism/Postmodernism Exchange," and Nancy Fraser, "Pragmatism, Feminism, and the Linguistic Turn," in *Feminist Contentions.*

14 / *Liberalism and the Ethics of Care*

VIRGINIA HELD

Although some feminists are liberal feminists, the basic presuppositions of liberal political theory are often seen as conflicting with much feminist theorizing. I examine the conflicts between liberalism and such feminist projects as developing an ethics of care, thinking of persons as relational, and conceptualizing society and its institutions in the light of the values of care and caring activities. I argue against various liberal critiques of these feminist projects and for the further development of the feminist thinking they involve. I conclude that care is a value of no less importance than justice, and that it is highly relevant to "public" as well as "private" contexts.

CARE AND CITIZENS

Those of us who defend a feminist ethic of care and feminist views of persons and societies as relational frequently encounter the criticism that such views cannot, or should not, apply at levels beyond the personal. The ethic of care, we hear, fails to treat people as adult individuals. Adult citizens, our critics claim, usually don't care about strangers, don't want to be expected to care for them, and don't want to be cared for by them. Liberal theories are designed to address standard adult situations. They demand respect for individuals and assurances of autonomy, and they specify what justice requires between independent individuals. Adult individuals, these critics hold, don't want to be seen for moral purposes as enmeshed in relationships they did not choose, such as being the son of certain parents or a person brought up with a certain religious heritage; rather, they see themselves as individual, rational moral agents, and they expect to be so regarded for moral purposes. They recognize obligations to respect others' rights. But caring is something they see as limited to particular relations of family, lovers, or friends and as largely irrelevant to political institutions and even to moral theory. They fear that if we conceptualize citizens in terms of their personal connections, we threaten their autonomy and risk treating them paternalistically. Thus Ann Cudd writes, "Care is not what most normal adults need or want from most others in society" (1995, 612).

These criticisms of care ethics fail to note that the feminist views in question are often presented as a corrective, to question the expansion of liberal individualism into the whole of morality, rather than to deny that political liberalism has any value. In developing a view of morality different from an expanded liberal individualism, feminists interested in an ethic of care consider whether there may be value in thinking about the political realm also from a care perspective rather than solely from the familiar perspective of liberalism. This is only the beginning, not the end, of the care ethics exploration.

When, for instance, I suggest that in trying to understand social relations between persons we should think about how they would look if we used as a model the relation between a mothering-person and child instead of the more usual model of contracts between self-interested strangers, my point is to suggest the alternative model as an exercise of the imagination. Missing this point, critics have found it offensive to think of citizens as either children or parents rather than as autonomous adults with no special obligations to care for other citizens (Held 1993, 213).

I wish to claim not that there is no room for standard liberal individual autonomy but that liberal ideology increasingly leaves no room for anything else. There must be room for much more than liberal individualism for either individuals or societies to flourish.

Ann Cudd rejects being thought of as a child because "I am not a child" (1995, 612). This misses the point. When we think of ourselves as very young or very old, highly dependent on others, seriously ill or under heavy medication, or ignorant of the relevant factors on which policy is decided, it might be more suitable to imagine how we would wish to be treated by those who would care about us *if we were* children than to imagine what we and others would choose from the even more remote and inappropriate position of the fully independent and effectively equal rational agent (Card 1995). How would we have wanted our parents to treat us? How could they have avoided inflicting some of the humiliations and harms we experienced even though we *could* not then be equally autonomous rational agents? Are some of the values appropriate in such contexts values we could also foster in relations between the bureaucracies of the welfare state and its beneficiaries?

A comparable thought experiment applies to those of us who are adult and for the moment relatively capable of independence, as we consider how to treat fellow members of society or humanity. What can we learn from being engaged in practices of care that might be relevant *if* we cared about others in a way that was less encompassing than parental care but not so different as to approach the emotional indifference apparently assumed by liberal theories? Sara Ruddick emphasizes how the experience of mothering, or "fathering" (if we understanding it not in its traditional sense but as referring to activities similar to those of mothering), is highly relevant to fostering peace in the world. Others may show how those thoughtfully involved in the work of bringing up children or caring for the dependent may design better public institutions for child care, education, health care, welfare, and the like—not just better in terms of efficiency but in embodying the relevant values. Political institutions that have the task of governing activities in which the value of care is more obviously relevant may also be greatly improved by considering their design from the perspective of mother/child relations rather than only from the perspective of the liberal rational contractor.

CRITIQUES OF THE ETHICS OF CARE

The most influential liberal theorists and their leading communitarian critics have, as Susan Okin (1989) demonstrates, paid virtually no attention to feminist arguments. A well-known liberal theorist who has taken the ethics of care sufficiently seriously to criticize it is Brian Barry. Devoting much of chapter 10 of his *Justice as Impartiality* (1995) to the feminist critique of impartiality, he attributes the feminist critique to misunderstandings. Unfortunately, he fails himself to understand much of what characterizes feminist ethics and the ethics of care.

Thoroughly disparaging Lawrence Kohlberg, the psychologist of moral development criticized by Carol Gilligan, Barry faults Kohlberg's abilities as a philosopher and blames him for the confusions that Barry believes are responsible for the feminist critique of impartiality. Barry, however, misinterprets Kohlberg: contrary to Barry's account, Kohlberg did not specify the "right answers" to the dilemmas with which he presented his experimental subjects and then score them as moral reasoners according to such answers. The scoring depended on the *kinds* of reasons supplied by the moral reasoners under study in reaching their answers—whether their reasons were general, universal principles, for instance, or whether they were particular loyalties. More important, much of what feminist moral philosophers have written about feminist morality and the ethics of care has little to do with Kohlberg but does have much to do with the kind of justice as impartiality that Barry defends.

Barry advocates what he calls second-order impartiality, which requires of the moral and legal rules of a society that they be "capable of attaining the . . . assent of all" taken as free and equal individuals (1995, 191). This does not require, he maintains, universal first-order impartiality, according to which we cannot be partial to our own children and spouses. As long as we can all accept a set of impartial rules, he notes, these rules can permit us to give special consideration to our families and friends.

Barry admits that most second-order impartialist theories, such as John Rawls's theory of justice, are designed for judging institutions in a nearly just society and are of little use for prescribing actions under currently existing conditions, especially when such actions would be performed in the context of seriously unjust institutions. He neglects to recognize that a merit of an ethic of care is that it carries no such limitation. Barry allows that there can be second-order impartiality theories that endorse the morality of breaking some bad laws instead of waiting for them to be changed. His arguments for impartiality are in many ways an improvement over the arguments others have offered. But he sides with impartialists generally in holding that justice, in his case justice as second-order impartiality, always has priority over considerations of care. For Barry, care should be the basis of choice only where the requirements of justice have already been fulfilled. He argues that there can be no genuine conflicts between this kind of justice and care: they deal with different matters.

This interpretation does not address the arguments of defenders of the ethics of care who question rather than accept the priority of justice as impartiality (even second-order), yet do not reject impartiality altogether. These advocates of care deny that we are simply talking about different matters: we are both talking about morality, and we disagree about it. The issue is often which would be better, the approach of justice or the approach of care? This question can arise in public as well as in personal contexts, and we may wonder whether we should treat persons as if the liberal assumptions of impartial justice apply to them. I disagree with Barry that we should always prioritize justice as impartiality and relegate care to the status of an optional extra for personal contexts (Baier 1994). Sometimes the points of view of care and of justice provide different moral recommendations and evaluations on the same issues. When they do, we must choose between them. At any rate, we may not be able to follow both.

Some feminists, of course, have defended liberal contractarianism, arguing that contractual views ought to be extended beyond the political sphere to assure women's equality in the family (Hampton 1993; Okin 1989). These liberal feminists are critical of and largely reject the ethics of care. Feminists defending the ethics of care agree that, of course, women are to be treated as equals but deny that justice and equality are the only or even the primary moral considerations in the family, and not only in the family but often elsewhere as well. They deny that a morality built on liberal individualism can be adequate to all these contexts.

Other feminists reject the contrast between care and justice or their conceptualizations as distinct points of view (Card 1990; Ruddick 1995). But the liberal critique of the ethics of care does assume that there is a contrast and that justice always has priority. It is to this position, the priority of justice, that this chapter is primarily addressed.

THE CRITIQUE OF LIBERALISM

Criticism of the liberal, contractual model of social relations takes at least two forms: a charge of inaccuracy and an evaluative criticism. The charge of inaccuracy claims that the contractual model distorts reality by leaving out vast areas of human experience that it claims to apply to but in reality cannot cover. Contractualists may respond by saying that they intend to cover only relations between strangers and not relations of love and affection. This response, however, does not take account of the facts that such dominant moral theories as utilitarianism and Kantian ethics are built on the stranger model of social relations and that morality is standardly understood to cover all situations. Rational choice theory and moral theories built on it are even more explicit in accepting liberal, contractualist assumptions about social relations (for example, Gauthier 1986). But even if the liberal view is carefully confined to the political, the response fails to deal with assumptions made in conceptualizing the relevant assemblage of strangers. It fails to address the appropriateness, implications, and effects of treating just any social relations as if they were between autonomous, self-interested strangers.

The second kind of criticism of the contractual model is evaluative. It suggests that even if, in advanced capitalist societies, relations between persons have indeed become more like contractual relations between self-interested strangers, this is not morally a good model for relations between persons. Moreover, applying a contractual model to more and more situations, the way rational choice theory does, promotes the wrong kind of social development—anomie and walled enclaves for the affluent, for instance. To encourage morally better social relations, this critique holds, we should limit rather than expand the use of the liberal, contractual model, both in our institutions and practices and in the ways we think about social issues.

Turning first to the charge of inaccuracy, let's consider the liberal image of the individual citizen. Liberals suggest that we should choose principles for the design of our political institutions that would be acceptable to us as free, equal, rational, and fully impartial persons. Principles and institutions thus recommended will be those to which we could contractually agree for furthering the rational pursuit of our individual interests. Within these principles and institutions we will pursue our economic interests. Doing so will produce industries in which we can choose to be employed, and it will yield products we can choose to consume. Within the constraints of the laws recommended by our political principles and made and enforced through our political institutions, we can develop whatever ties of sociality and affection we wish. How plausible is it to conceptualize citizens and thus persons in this familiar way?

A glaring deficiency of the liberal image of the individual citizen is that it abstracts from an interconnected social reality, taking the ideal circumstances of an adult, independent head of a household as paradigmatic and ignoring all the rest. It overlooks the social relations of an economy that makes its members (including heads of households) highly interdependent. Members of any national economy are deeply dependent on each other, and they are increasingly dependent on others around the globe. The liberal view overlooks the facts that citizens have all been helpless infants, totally dependent on others for years of affectionate care, and that those who have cared for them have often been dependent on still others for support while their labor was expended in such care. It overlooks that at any given time a large percentage of any country's population are children, and an increasingly large percentage are the frail elderly. Nearly all persons have periods of their lives in which they are seriously ill. Much of the time, what persons need and want are thus not the services that autonomous, self-interested individuals can buy or insure themselves for; they need and want the relational care that escapes the model of the aggregate of free and equal individuals agreeing to the terms of a social contract.

To the extent that we are economically interdependent, we need and want public policies and arrangements that will enable us to provide care to those we care about (who need not be limited to our immediate "loved ones") and that will enable us to receive care when we need it. These are just as important aims as having policies and arrangements that will advance our independently determined economic self-interest. If a contractual model were applied directly to situations of economic interdependence, it would treat the economically powerless and the economically powerful as if they were equally autonomous, obscuring the conditions conducive to exploitation and deprivation.

The contractual model is demeaning when applied to domains of experience where care is the primary value. If parents care for children now only so that their children will care for them when they are aged, and both children and parents understand the terms of this bargain, the relation of parent and child is deprived of the valuing of both for their own sakes and for the sake of the relation of caring between them. If apparent friends maintain their practices of meeting, conversing, exchanging gifts, or visits or intimacies only because each believes it will serve his or her own interests to do so, we would probably judge such "friendships" to be superficial at best. And if a person who is ill or otherwise dependent is cared for by people who are only going through the motions of doing what they are paid to do, we know that this care is not the best.

Many liberals contend that the contractual model is intended to apply only to the political rather than to the personal sphere (for example, Rawls 1993). But then where do the health care and the child care industries belong? They are certainly not within the domain of the private or familial as conceptualized by the forefathers of contemporary liberalism. Industrial economies have never fit satisfactorily into the traditional liberal framework of public and private, structured as they are by public decisions and capable as they are, in turn, of shaping political outcomes. Robert Dahl, for instance, wrote already in 1970 that to think of the contemporary corporation as private is "an absurdity," and this statement is even truer at the end of the twentieth century. Still, to see human relations in the marketplace as contractual and based on rational self-interest does not clash grossly with our experience of them.

Health care and child care, however, are more problematic. Should they be regarded as among the arrangements and services for which free, equal, rational, autonomous persons contract? To do so seems questionable, for before any of us can actually become the kind of person liberalism imagines, we have already received many years of child care that has been more than what merely contracted services can provide. Children do not become autonomous rational agents without having been cared for and valued for their own sakes. People born disabled or ill may never become the rational contractors of liberal theory. When people become ill or dependent on others' care, they may be too far removed from the assumptions of the contractual model for it to apply to them. Moreover, all who provide care for others without earning wages for their services forgo what they could otherwise use that labor capacity to earn and hence are often deprived of resources they need and want. Yet it would clearly be a mistake to think of children, the disabled, the ill, and all those who care for them as beyond the reach of moral guidelines and the practices ordering public life. An implication is that the terms of liberal discourse are less suitable for thinking about the whole of society and large parts of it than they are thought to be by liberals who dismiss the political significance of the ethics of care. If the terms of liberal discourse are too limited, it may be fruitful to try the experiment of thinking in terms of values discernible most clearly in the domains of family and friends and to consider extending those values to other domains.

When, for instance, managed health care becomes more and more driven by market considerations, questions certainly can be and are being raised about the appropriateness of the liberal contractual model for this domain. The value of care, understood best in a context of family and friends, can be sought for this domain of social activity, which ought to provide what members of a political community need when they are medically vulnerable. Whether we are providers or recipients of care in the household, the care that has value for us is largely overlooked by the liberal contractual model. Perhaps we should seek values comparable to this care in the services provided by public arrangements and institutions for health care.

What, now, about the effects of treating the political and public domains as if they could be adequately captured by the liberal assumptions in question, while we recognize their distance from actual reality? Liberals believe this approach will promote the justice required by principles that would be agreed to by hypothetical rational agents in contractual relations. But critics of liberal individualism draw different conclusions. Because the liberal model assumes indifference to the welfare of others, employing this model leads to a narrowing of the gap between model and reality and to the wider acceptance of the assumption of indifference as standard and appropriate—not only as assumption but as description and guide. It promotes only calculated self-interest and moral indifference in place of the caring and concern that citizens often have for fellow citizens (albeit less intense than for family and friends), that members of smaller communities still more often have for each other, and that most persons could have for other persons, even in foreign places and distant lands. The liberal critic of care ethics may prefer such indifference to paternalistic interference, but a discussion of the issues involved here will show that the liberal is wrong to suppose that these are the only alternatives. The defender of care ethics can show that paternalistic interference is not the only alternative to calculated self-interest: mothering care can include promoting the competent but not disconnected autonomy of the child and can be sensitive to the importance of avoiding paternalism. Taking the point of view of the child can contribute to this sensitivity.

Annette Baier has discussed how adopting the assumptions of liberalism contributes to making actual indifference to others more pervasive. She writes: "Liberal morality, if unsupplemented, may *unfit* people to be anything other than what its justifying theories suppose them to be, ones who have no interest in each others' interests" (1994, 29). The young Korean philosopher Ranjoo Herr has examined how an adequate conception of autonomy can be seen as compatible with an ethic of care. Any plausible moral position, she holds, should be based on autonomy: one should be guided by a self-prescribed morality rather than by standards imposed from without. An ethic of care should thus be chosen autonomously out of personal conviction, as a result of critical reflection on one's life (Herr 1998). Jean Keller shows even more clearly how autonomy as self-governance is compatible with, not antagonistic to, care ethics.

Thinking of persons as relational does not mean that we cannot make autonomous choices to reject social ties that we formed in growing up; feminists have much experience with such rejections. It means we can conceptualize those choices as taking place within social relations that partially constitute us as what we are. We maintain some relations, revise others, and create new ones, but we do not see these as the choices of independent individuals acting in the world as though social ties did not exist prior to our creating them (Meyers 1997). Jean Keller writes that "whatever shape feminist ethics ends up taking, it will incorporate a relational model of moral agency. That is, the insight that the moral agent is an 'encumbered self,' who is always embedded in relations with flesh-and-blood others and is partly constituted by these relations, is here to stay" (1997, 152). Such a self can still, she shows, choose autonomously.

Further, an aim of an ethic of care is to promote the responsible autonomy of the cared for. Conceptions of autonomy within care can then be much more satisfactory for thinking about large domains of activity, including public activity, than are liberal contractualist conceptions of individual autonomy.

THE DILEMMA OF LIBERAL MORALITY

Thinking of society's members, then, as if they were fully independent, free, and equal rational agents obscures and distorts the condition of vast numbers of them at the very least and has the effect of making it more difficult to address the social and political issues that would be seen as relevant and appropriate if these conditions were more accurately portrayed and kept in view. As Eva Kittay writes, liberalism has "constructed an equality for heads of households . . . and then counted the head of a household as an *individual* who is independent and who can act on his own behalf" (1995, 11). She argues that this portrayal creates a distorted view, enabling the privileged to imagine that dependencies do not exist. The illusion that political society is composed of free, equal, independent individuals who can choose to associate with one another obscures the reality that social cooperation is required as a precondition of autonomy. It thus obscures the realities that we are all completely dependent on the care of others for significant parts of our lives and that many of us are what Kittay calls "dependency workers" on whom those dependent for care must rely. Dependency workers are even less independent than other workers in industrial economies, because they are routinely unpaid or ill paid and are thus fully or substantially dependent on others for basic necessities.

There is a considerable literature on whether the social contract at the level of either theory or practice can even get started (let alone sustain itself) without assuming a social cohesion or trust or civic friendship on which it is parasitic (Baier 1994; Held 1984; Schwarzenbach 1996). If the view is correct that contractual relations require some deeper level of social cohesion or trust or concern, an ethic of care may be an excellent source of insight for understanding the relevant factors in such cohesion or trust. Looking at the closest ties, how they are developed, and how trust is cultivated within them may be instructive. A thin version of such social cohesion may provide a framework within which fellow citizens can trust each other for certain purposes, perhaps seeing each other as self-interested economic agents who can contractually agree to various rules for organizing their interactions, or as independent rational contractors agreeing to a limited set of political principles and institutions. But we should never lose sight of how society is vastly more than its economy and its political system. We need moral principles and practices to guide us in this wider or deeper domain as well as in the more limited areas of market and politics.

Instead, over several centuries of traditional ethics, the assumptions and conceptions of political liberalism have been pushed outward to other domains, with the result that even morality intended to apply at the most inclusive levels of whole societies and the most affectional levels of family and friends has been constructed on assumptions and conceptions shared by political liberalism. The image of the rational contractor then becomes ubiquitous, and recommendations based on it are thought of as suitable guidance for moral decisions in any context.

This morality, however, runs into obvious difficulties in many domains. To conceptualize relations between mothers and children as based on a rational contract is bizarre. To suppose that a Kantian morality can serve well for the context of the family is highly problematic when we move beyond questions of the minimal respect owed to each person: we don't, for instance, play with our children out of respect for the moral law, and yet giving our children a morally good upbringing involves a great deal of playing with them. Or consider a very different context, the international one: it makes little sense to try to account, on the individualistic grounds of liberal theory, for "national identity" or whatever it is that enables a political entity to be an entity within which liberal norms can be accepted. Social ties that enable persons to identify themselves as members and to recognize others as fellow members of a community or nation are presupposed by the norms of any political entity. And to move beyond merely local or national norms to something more like global ones, some sense of care and concern for or solidarity with other inhabitants of the globe will be needed.

Because of the deficiencies of liberal morality in contexts such as those of families and groups, one of two directions tends to be pursued by liberal theorists. Either liberal morality is pressed onto informal, personal, and collective domains regardless of its difficulties therein. Or the human bonds of families, friends, groups, and nations are relegated to the status of the "merely sentimental" or the "instinctual," "natural," "emotional," and "irrational," as opposed to the rational and the moral (Held 1993). They are then regarded as lying outside morality and are left unexamined from the moral point of view in a region to be empirically described but about which morality is thought to have nothing to say. Thus, either liberal morality is pressed onto domains other than that of the already existing state, in which case it is an unsatisfactory morality, or it is not applied at all to such domains, and morality—which has been equated with liberal morality—is imagined to have nothing to contribute in such domains. This result is clearly also unsatisfactory; mothers understand that the problems they confront in bringing up children are much of the time *moral* problems, and we can understand that we ought to deal with the *moral* aspects of how nations draw their boundaries and decide on their membership.

We need better moralities than the traditional ones. If in constructing them, an ethic of care seems adequate for various regions of experience, we might usefully think about applying it to other regions.

THE ACCEPTANCE OF LIMITED LIBERALISM

Those who argue for the importance of an ethic of care usually share a commitment to many of the achievements of liberalism in their appropriate domains: political institutions democratically constituted and systems of fundamental rights upheld by an independent judiciary.

An example of this can be seen in feminist treatments of rights. At first, many feminists in thinking about rights were struck by how fully rights reflect masculine interests and how much the very concept of a "right" seemed to clash with the approach of an ethic of care. Nel Noddings, speaking from the perspective of the ethic of care (to the development of which she contributed), warned of "the destructive role of rules and principles" of which rights are reflections: If we "come to rely almost completely on external rules [we] become detached from the very heart of morality: the sensibility that calls forth caring" (1984, 47). Annette Baier wrote that "rights have usually been for the 'privileged,' and the 'justice perspective' and the legal sense that goes with it are shadowed by their patriarchal past" (1994, 25–26). Feminist legal theorist Catharine MacKinnon wrote: "In the liberal state, the rule of law—neutral, abstract, elevated, pervasive—both institutionalizes the power of men over women and institutionalizes power in its male form. . . . [M]ale forms of power over women are affirmatively embodied as individual rights in law. . . . abstract rights authorize the male experience of the world" (1989, 238–48). And sociologist Carol Smart urged feminists not to focus on rights or the gaining of equal rights for women because of the "congruence" she thought exists between law and "masculine culture" and because law "disqualifies women's experience" and women's knowledge (1989, 2).

Despite these apparent rejections of the liberal focus on the centrality of rights, however, most feminists—even when influenced by the ethic of care—have also come to accept the necessity of rights for feminist aims. The potential of rights claims to bring about social change is clear. Reformulating conceptions of equal rights, women have argued successfully for pregnancy leave, child care provisions, and more equitable pension arrangements. Rights to freedom from sexual harassment have made the climate of many workplaces less hostile to women. Rights have been of the utmost importance for decreasing racial discrimination and attaining the most basic protections for women globally. Patricia Williams writes: "Although rights may not be ends in themselves, rights rhetoric has been and continues to be an effective form of discourse for blacks" (1991, 149). Even Martha Minow, deploring the ways rights have ignored relationships, is moving toward "a conception of rights in relationships" that can counter oppressive forms of public and private power; she wants to "rescue" rights, not abandon them (1990, 306).

When liberal conceptions are confined to their appropriate domain of the legal-political institutions of society and the contested issues within them, feminists generally are willing to employ these conceptions. But they have argued that liberal conceptions do not serve us well in our much wider experiences as human persons in a large variety of relationships.

CARE AND JUSTICE

Much of the interest feminists have had in the ethics of care has been to establish care as having as much importance for morality as liberal justice (Held 1995). For those who are convinced that justice and care are comparably important and that neither can be reduced to the other, the debate can then concern the relations between justice and care. Is justice primary and care an essential supplement? Are they alternative frameworks of interpretation within which any moral problem can be considered? Is care the more fundamental value within which domains of justice should be developed? How should either or both be reconceptualized in the light of feminist understandings?

I am coming to the view that care and its related considerations are the wider framework—or network—within which room should be made for justice, utility, and the virtues. This perspective does not mean that all other values, points of view, or the institutions or practices they recommend can be reduced to aspects of care. Reduction does not seem the right approach (Held 1996; B. Williams, 1985). But within caring relations of a personal kind we can make room for insisting that we treat others justly, as equals. Within a moderate and extended version of caring for other persons as human beings and fellow members of society or the globe, we can make room for entering into contractual relations on the basis of rational self-interest and for accepting the political institutions such relations recommend. We cannot dispense with the network of caring relations, but neither will it deal well with all moral problems.

Within a caring personal relationship, there can certainly be competition, as when friends play tennis and each tries to win. But if the pursuit of self-interest is given priority across the whole of their interactions, they will not long be friends. A society, in a comparable way, can have a limited range of interactions based on rational self-interest and contractual restraints. But if these are the only kinds of interactions there are, the society will not long cohere. Something like "civic friendship" is needed (Aristotle 1985; Schwarzenbach 1996).

I find care the most basic moral value. Without the actual practice of care, there cannot be human life at all, because human beings require it to survive. But unless we recognize the value of such care, we fail morally to evaluate this most basic practice without which human life is impossible. Perhaps we can think of this value as the most comprehensive, because, although there can be life without justice, there cannot be life without the care that has value. The caring concern each of us has for some others that enables life to go on can then be extended to a caring moral concern for all other persons that makes a satisfactory morality possible (Benhabib 1992; Habermas 1995). Within a network of caring relations we can require justice and equality, fairness and rights. To understand their implications it may be appropriate, within political domains, to imagine persons as abstract, independent rational agents contracting with each other as equals and to see what rights they would then have. But we should never forget that these ways of thinking are suitable only for limited domains, not for the whole of morality. Although justice and equality should be required in the family, in the sense that each member should be treated fairly and their rights should be respected, good family relationships go far beyond this requirement. And good social relations that can sustain political systems require a level of caring concern for all members that is wider and deeper than justice and rights can provide.

It is sometimes claimed that liberal political principles are needed exactly when relations of affection or of special ties are absent (Vallentyne 1991; Rawls 1971; Cudd 1995). But unless we have sufficient motives to care about our fellow human beings and to value this caring, we will not care whether their rights are respected or not, especially in the case of people who are too weak to make serious trouble for us, as the history of domination, exploitation, and indifference makes evident.

Some who argue for an ethic of care, especially its earliest advocates, want clearly to distinguish *caring* from a vague *caring about,* fearing that if the distinction is not maintained the essential features of what an activity such as caring for a small child is like will be lost. Thus Nel Noddings wrote that the "caring about" that is involved in our giving money for famine relief is not genuine *caring,* because caring is an interactive relation in which each party recognizes the other as a particular person; it involves personal engagment (1984, 18, 112).

But others—including myself—think the value of caring that can be seen most clearly in such activities as mothering is just what must be extended, in less intense but not entirely different forms, to fellow members of societies and the world. Thus Joan Tronto notes that "caring seems to suffer a fatal moral flaw if we allow it to be circumscribed by deciding that we shall only care for those closest to us" (1993, 183). A feminist approach to caring, she argues, "needs to begin by broadening our understanding of what caring for others means, both in terms of the moral questions it raises and in terms of the need to restructure broader social and political institutions if caring for others is to be made a more central part of the everyday lives of everyone in society" (1993, 184), not just of the women and other devalued groups who have traditionally done the bulk of the work of caring. "The need to rethink appropriate forms for caring," she writes, "raises the broadest questions about the shape of social and political institutions in our society" (1993, 185). And, we can add, not just within "our society" in the sense of our nation or our own community but at the global level as well (Robinson 1999).

Along comparable lines, Neena Das writes about caring for distant others. "Caring for distant or numerous others," she argues, "is not only a legitimate *option* that one can make part of a caring practice," but rather something that exerts a moral pull on us. "When we come to know of others in dire situations such as chronic famine, chronic poverty, or war, it has a compelling force. This call on our moral selves should not go unheeded" (1996, 13–14). The practice of caring, like any practice, is enabled by a sociohistorical context: hence, "if caring is embedded in social inequities, there has to be a response to this larger context" (Das 1996, 14).

To many feminists, then, thinking about the social world in terms of caring is entirely appropriate, although a very different way of thinking than the way of liberal individualism. It is different in at least its epistemology (Held 1993; Walker 1989), in its way of conceptualizing persons (Held 1993; Keller 1997; Meyers 1997), and in its understanding of public and private (Held 1993; Tronto 1993).

CARE AND THE ECONOMY

I close by considering a domain in which we can contrast a liberal morality with a set of recommendations that an ethic of care might yield. I choose the domain of the economy. The economy should perhaps be the domain par excellence for liberalism, because liberal theory was first developed for the economic domain, liberalism is largely built on the model of economic man, and rational choice theory and liberal theories of justice are based on assumptions underlying thinking about the economic domain. But is it clear that liberalism offers a more suitable approach to evaluating economic activity than an ethic of care might offer?

First, we know that a modern economy is greatly dependent on governmental policies for its well-being: governments can stimulate economic activity or stifle it, provide a climate of stability in which economic activity can flourish or fail miserably to do so. Governmental taxation, spending, and trade policies deeply affect a society's economic health. A government for which care is an important value and framework of interpretation would approach many of the issues involved in government's relation to the economy differently from one for which care is seen as a merely private value. It would favor an economy that promoted caring connections between persons rather than only individual satisfaction and the pursuit of self-interest through competition. It would often favor limiting rather than expanding markets.

Among the issues that liberal theory does not handle well are those concerning what should be out of the market and what should be in it. Debates concerning this issue are proceeding in the United States with respect to many activities. Advocates of the market want more and more activities *in* the market where they will have to meet criteria of efficiency and will be affected by what are claimed to be the benefits of competition. Opponents say that it is inappropriate to have these activities in the market, because they aim at different values than market values and should do so in different ways than the market provides. Health care, for instance, is being pushed more and more into the market—and subjected to what some see as dangerous market pressures (Ginsburg 1996). Advocates of the market often want more and more child care and education to be in the market, while opponents resist this trend. Culture, including the gathering and presentation of news, has become almost exclusively determined by market forces, yet it is doubtful that such practices are compatible with democracy and the health of society (Held 1996). Market enthusiasts seek to privatize more and more public park management and to reduce pollution through market incentives, but their plans often lose sight of distinct environmental values.

Liberalism may offer a strong sense of rights and the view that basic political rights are not for sale. For instance, we cannot—at least overtly—sell our rights to vote or our rights to a fair trial, and we cannot literally sell ourselves into slavery. But most of what is required to maintain the life to which we have a right, such as obtaining the food and shelter we need to live, is left to the market. The culture that shapes our values and our lives is left to market forces. We sell our labor to buy food and shelter, and in the United States not even welfare for those unable to sell their labor has been recognized as a right. One *can* argue within a liberal framework for positive rights—for enablements or access to basic necessities, for instance—that should be asssured regardless of market outcomes (Held 1984). Liberal theory thus can provide arguments with which to criticize existing arrangements concerning access to basic necessities. But it would still leave unsettled most issues concerning what should be in or out of the market.

If children have a right to education, for instance, should it be provided by a system of public schools that teach, among other things, civic values and social cooperation? Or should it be provided by a system of vouchers that parents can use as they wish in an educational marketplace? Even if publicly funded child care were recognized as some kind of right (difficult to imagine in the United States but *conceivable* in liberal theory), we would still have the question of whether the right should be honored by tax credits and payments that parents could spend in a market for child care. Or should it be assured through a system of public child care fostering the view that the society cares about and for all of its children? Similar questions arise for health care.

From the point of view of liberal justice, we get few answers. One can *imagine* the market for education, child care, health care, culture, and wilderness experiences being fair, and one can *imagine* provisions to enable all who enter such markets to do so in ways that conform to liberal principles of justice. But this is hardly all we need to say. From the point of view of an ethic of care, we can say that fairness is not the only consideration. In the case of such activities as education, child care, health care, culture, and safeguarding the environment, there are very good, if not always overriding, arguments that these activities should not be only or primarily in the market— even if the market is fair—because the market is ill-equipped to pursue many values, including those of mutually shared caring concern.

An especially compelling case can be made with respect to what many call "contract pregnancy" or "surrogate motherhood." On the basis of an ethic of care, it has been persuasively argued that this activity should not be interpreted in the terms of contracts and markets, where the issues have been about the enforceability of such contracts (Guichon 1997; Shanley 1993). To the extent that law becomes involved, the activity should be covered by family law rather than by contract law (Guichon 1997). Arguments against the market are especially persuasive here: creating a child should not be seen as producing a commodity; gestation is not the sort of service that should be marketable. Arguments along comparable lines can be offered for many other activities (Anderson 1993; Held 1984, 1996). Where the boundaries of an economy should be, what should be in the market and what should not be, will look very different depending on whether or not we recognize care as a central consideration.

The possibilities should not be precluded that economies themselves might be guided by concerns of care much more than at present. But even if activity within an economy is not influenced by the values of caring, the people who can affect the reach of the market and governmental policies that have an impact on it and regulate it certainly could and should be influenced by the values of caring. Looking at public issues such as those touched on here from the perspective of an ethic of care would greatly improve our choices regarding economic activity and social relations.

REFERENCES

Earlier versions of this chapter were presented at Dalhousie University (Halifax, Nova Scotia), the University of Toronto Law School, Union College (New York), the University of Turku (Finland), and Kutztown University (Pennsylvania). I am grateful for many interesting comments on these occasions and especially to Richmond Campbell, Felmon Davis, Jennifer Nedelsky, and Susan Sherwin. And I wish to thank Claudia Card for many valuable suggestions and editorial improvements.

Anderson, Elizabeth. 1993. *Value in Ethics and Economics.* Cambridge: Harvard University Press.

Aristotle. 1985. *Nicomachean Ethics.* Trans. T. Irwin. Indianapolis: Hackett.

Baier, Annette. 1994. *Moral Prejudices: Essays on Ethics.* Cambridge: Harvard University Press.

Barry, Brian. 1995. *Justice As Impartiality.* Oxford: Oxford University Press.

Benhabib, Seyla. 1992. *Situating the Self.* New York: Routledge.

Card, Claudia. 1990. "Gender and Moral Luck." In *Identity, Character, and Morality: Essays in Moral Psychology,* ed. Owen Flanagan and Amelie Oksenberg Rorty. Cambridge, Mass.: MIT Press.

———. 1995. Review of Virginia Held, *Feminist Morality* (1993). *Ethics* 105, 4: 938–40.

Cudd, Ann. 1995. Review of Virginia Held, *Feminist Morality* (1993). *Philosophical Review* 104, 4: 611–13.

Dahl, Robert A. 1970. *After the Revolution.* New Haven: Yale University Press.

Das, Neena. 1996. "Beyond the Interpersonal and the Particular in Care Thinking." Unpublished.

Gauthier, David. 1986. *Morals by Agreement.* Oxford: Clarendon Press.

Ginsburg, Carl. 1996. "The Patient As Profit Center: Hospital Inc. Comes to Town." *Nation* 263, 16: 18–22.

Guichon, Juliet Ruth. 1997. "An Examination and Critique of the Contract Model of Legal Regulation of Preconception Arrangements." Ph.D. diss., University of Toronto Faculty of Law.

Habermas, Jurgen. 1995. *Moral Consciousness and Communicative Action.* Trans. C. Lenhardt and S. Nicholsen. Cambridge, Mass.: MIT Press.

Hampton, Jean. 1993. "Feminist Contractarianism." In *A Mind of One's Own: Feminist Essays on Reason and Objectivity,* ed. Louise Antony and Charlotte Witt. Boulder, Colo.: Westview.

Held, Virginia. 1984. *Rights and Goods: Justifying Social Action.* New York: Free Press.

_____. 1993. *Feminist Morality: Transforming Culture, Society, and Politics.* Chicago: University of Chicago Press.

_____. 1996. "Justice and Utility: Who Cares?" *Philosophic Exchange 1995–1996.* Proceedings of the Center for Philosophical Exchange, no. 26. Brockport: State University of New York.

_____. 1998. "Media Culture and Democracy." In *Demokratischer Experimentalismus,* ed. Hauke Brunkhorst. Frankfurt: Surkamp Verlag.

_____, ed. 1995. *Justice and Care: Essential Readings in Feminist Ethics.* Boulder, Colo.: Westview.

Herr, Ranjoo. 1998. "The Concept of Autonomy and Care Ethics." Unpublished.

Keller, Jean. 1997. "Autonomy, Relationality, and Feminist Ethics." *Hypatia* 12, 2: 152–65.

Kittay, Eva Feder. 1995. "Taking Dependency Seriously." *Hypatia* 10, 1: 8–29.

MacKinnon, Catharine A. 1989. *Toward a Feminist Theory of the State.* Cambridge: Harvard University Press.

Meyers, Diana Tietjens, ed. 1997. *Feminists Rethink the Self.* Boulder, Colo.: Westview.

Minow, Martha. 1990. *Making All the Difference: Inclusion, Exclusion, and American Law.* Ithaca, N.Y.: Cornell University Press.

Noddings, Nel. 1984. *Caring: A Feminine Approach to Ethics and Moral Education.* Berkeley: University of California Press.

Okin, Susan Moller. 1989. *Justice, Gender, and the Family.* New York: Basic Books.

Rawls, John. 1971. *A Theory of Justice.* Cambridge: Harvard University Press.

_____. 1993. *Political Liberalism.* New York: Columbia University Press.

Robinson, Fiona. 1999. *Globalizing Care.* Boulder, Colo.: Westview.

Ruddick, Sara. 1989. *Maternal Thinking: Toward a Politics of Peace.* Boston: Beacon.

_____. 1995. "Injustice in Families: Assault and Domination." In *Justice and Care: Essential Readings in Feminist Ethics,* ed. Virginia Held. Boulder, Colo.: Westview.

Schwarzenbach, Sibyl. 1996. "On Civic Friendship." *Ethics* 107, 1: 97–128.
Shanley, Mary Lyndon. 1993. "'Surrogate Mothering' and Women's Freedom: A Critique of Contracts for Human Reproduction." *Signs* 18, 3: 618–39.
Smart, Carol. 1989. *Feminism and the Power of Law.* London: Routledge.
Tronto, Joan. 1989. "Women and Caring: What Can Feminists Learn About Morality from Caring?" In *Gender/Body/Knowledge*, ed. Alison M. Jaggar and Susan R. Bordo. New Brunswick, N.J.: Rutgers University Press.
———. 1993. *Moral Boundaries: A Political Argument for an Ethic of Care.* New York: Routledge.
Vallentyne, Peter, ed. 1991. *Contractarianism and Rational Choice.* New York: Cambridge University Press.
Walker, Margaret Urban. 1989. "Moral Understandings: Alternative 'Epistemology' for a Feminist Ethics." *Hypatia* 4, 2: 15–28.
Williams, Bernard. 1985. *Ethics and the Limits of Philosophy.* Cambridge: Harvard University Press.
Williams, Patricia. 1991. *The Alchemy of Race and Rights.* Cambridge: Harvard University Press.

15 / *Getting to the Bottom of Things*

SHARON BISHOP

> I'm not talking of problems. I'm saying that we've
> never sat down seriously together and tried to get
> to the bottom of anything.
> > Nora to Torvald in Ibsen, *A Doll's House*[1]

In recent years, moral theory has been under attack from various
quarters, many of which—although hardly all—are explicitly feminist. It is now common to encounter arguments that classical theories, especially utilitarianism and Kantianism, drive out the claims
of particular attachments by virtue of their excessive regard for impartiality. The hostility toward classical theory seems grounded in
doubts about its program of finding a supreme principle or set of
ranked principles that are final and, in turn, impose the standards of
rationality on practical life. Such procedures presume to describe how
agents ought to guide their daily lives by establishing principles that
give the same results for everyone in any morally significant situation. Most contemporary critics of this long established tradition believe that this effort to ground moral principle in a general theory of
rationality—one marked by an insistence on objectivity, impartiality, and universality—can be passed on to the deliberative processes
of agents only by obscuring the particulars of their own lives.

Attempts to come to terms with these criticisms have been many
and varied. They include the strategies of limiting moral theory to a
rather narrow range of phenomena, replacing objectivity with new
forms of relativism, and making care and concern more dominant
than impartial justice in the moral life. As a result there is significant
controversy about the role of morality in deliberative processes and
about what sense it makes to regard moral considerations as final.[2]

Although I appreciate the spirit of much of the recent criticism of classical and modern moral theory, I am doubtful about many of the solutions that are offered. In the pages that follow, my intention is to explore as naturally (that is, as atheoretically) as possible a case of moral deliberation and agency. The purpose of this investigation is to follow lines of thought and commitment with an eye to whether these criticisms require such drastic solutions as replacing impartial judgment with care and concern or rejecting the idea that morality is objective or final. My intent is to see when and how objective justification becomes important in moral living. This chapter will not resolve traditional problems about the philosophical status of moral claims, nor will it contribute to resolving conflicts between Kantian and utilitarian theorists. What it can offer is a contribution to a shifting understanding of the role of objectivity and justification in moral deliberation.

As a first step, I turn to a case of moral deliberation in literature, Ibsen's *A Doll's House* and Nora's decision to leave her husband and children. I choose this case because Ibsen's play is familiar and easily accessible. It presents a decision in a type of case that is recurrent and that many people are familiar with either as a partner or a child who has had to deal with the effects of the decision. As a result, quite a few people have a good bit of knowledge about what is involved in decisions in actual cases of this nature. The advantage of the play over real life is that the terms of the decision are spelled out in some detail, and anyone who reads or sees the play can go back over the terms in order to rethink them and attend to their realism and plausibility.

Nora's decision comes at the end of the play at the point when she understands her husband, herself, and the dynamics of their family life for the first time. That is, she comes to know what her family life has really been like in contrast to how it has appeared to her. In the course of her conversation with her husband, it is clear that a number of considerations weigh on her. She opens the discussion by saying to her husband, Torvald, that in the eight years of their marriage, they have never talked seriously about anything. And when her husband puts her off with a question about whether he should have involved her in problems or worries that he says she couldn't help with, she responds that she isn't talking about business. Her complaint is that they have never seriously tried "to get to the bottom of anything."

This comment is different from anything she has said before. To this point in the play, she has bantered with friends and her husband, she has been serious with friends about particulars of their experience and hers, and she has begged and cajoled her husband. What she has not been is reflective about the qualities of her life or about what is important in life. Her comment here implies that there is something that "getting to the bottom of things" amounts to and that it is something to be serious about. It is also something that is not readily apparent, or at least not always, since it may require that two adult people take time and some pains to understand it.

However, it is evident that by this time Nora has reached on her own some serious conclusions about her family life that she is prepared to put forward as explaining and justifying her decision to leave. It is worth looking at these in some detail. First, she has been wronged by her father and then by her husband. Neither has understood her, and each has treated her as a doll, a plaything. She herself has taken part in her role as plaything by developing the same tastes as her husband and by begging or doing tricks for what she wanted. She has never put forward her own wants or ideas because she has had none that she could call her own. Nora is chided by Torvald for being unfair and ungrateful. When asked whether she has been happy, she replies that she has not been happy, only merry or lighthearted. Ibsen has given merriment and lightheartedness an important part in the play, but they only demonstrate Nora's serious concerns. By themselves they cannot be valued for what they bring to lives. Nora now knows that she must learn to become something other than what she was in the marriage. But she tells her husband that he is not the person to teach her.

When Torvald reminds her of her duties to husband and children, she responds that she has equally sacred duties. She calls them duties to herself. What she has in mind is that she is a human being before being a wife and mother, and that fact is something that has a very serious claim on her attention. Whatever it is she believes, it is serious enough to counter what the majority says, what she has found in books, what her religion says, what the laws says. She can no longer rely on any of these. She cannot count on her religion because, in fact, she does not know what it says, only what her minister has told her it says. The law isn't what she had thought. She had believed that it was fair, but she learns that it would take exception to her as a married woman borrowing money in her own name. She had forged her dying father's signature out of concern not to worry him and to get the money she believed necessary for her husband's health, perhaps his survival. Finally, when he says that the only possible reason for all this is that she no longer loves him, she agrees.

What made her lose her love for him is telling. It was just that evening when she had been waiting for a miracle that would fulfill her fantasy about what kind of man she was married to. In her imagination, he had been one who would, having found out what she had done, take all the blame on himself. She had been preparing herself to take her own life to prevent her husband from doing this. However, when he is frightened that she is about to be exposed, he does not worry about her but about how it will reflect on him. When the danger is past, he wants to go back to things as they were before, to have her as his doll or, at best, his pet.

Apparently, in seeing this complex of things, Nora has seen through to "the bottom of things" in her family life. And she is absolutely clear about this realization and about what she will do. She sees it as what she must do. Her clarity about what her life has been can be supported by detailed descriptions of events in their daily lives and conversational exchanges between her and her husband. It really has been the case that she has been treated as a doll and a plaything with no ability to take on serious responsibilities. And it is true that she has herself played a role in creating and maintaining this state. Whether that is because she wanted to or because she was expected to, she no longer knows. What seems significant here is that she is guided by the way she believes things really are and that she, and we who see or read the play, can see that things really are as she sees them. It is the concrete manifestations of these wrongs and mistaken values that carry her and our convictions about the moral qualities of what has happened to her in daily life with her husband.

Knowledge of these concrete qualities of daily life provide a model for a role for objectivity in the moral regulation of life. What Nora and we need to be objective about are the concrete ways that she and humans generally are hurt and compromised, the specific ways values are achieved, and the seriousness or importance of these concerns.

Although it is easy to see her decision as principled, there is no evidence that she thinks this is a decision that everyone in her circumstances ought to make, as some readings of the philosophic traditions would require. Nor is it necessary to attribute that to her. It is sufficient that she is able to be convinced and convincing that the situation is dire enough to warrant what she does. For that, her decision has to be one that anyone would be permitted to make. But also, she would need to regard her decision as reasonable or required in the circumstances. Whichever way she sees it, she acts in the conviction that her move is worthwhile. And she has assembled concrete judgments about the values exemplified in her actual life that underwrite her judgments.

It is not that she must be able to articulate the grounds for her decision in this way. But it must be that her sense of what she's doing can be explained in this way. The issue of whether her decision is morally regulated turns on whether her decision and act are best explained by reference to her perceptions of what has gone wrong and her understanding of the different set of values she is reaching for. Whether she is, in fact, justified turns on whether the situation has the concrete features she claims and whether the values she is aiming for better express ideals of a moral life.[3]

Part of what values and moral principles do in this situation is describe general features of concrete wrongs. Our moral understanding of what happens in concrete situations is advanced and deepened by our understanding of the general nature of the various wrongs involved in these lives. Seeing her treated as a plaything, we see the wrongness and cruelty involved in treating anyone as a toy. Seeing her treated as a doll, we see the special wrongness of treating women as playthings. Seeing her become a toy, we see the ways this kind of treatment corrupts its victims, and we see more about why this kind of treatment is wrong. The result is that our confidence in the wrongness of treating people as less than complete human beings is reconfirmed.

The general principle that people ought to be treated and respected as human beings with a full range of human capacities and powers receives support from the wrongs we and Nora see in this particular situation. But the principle, in turn, helps us understand the general nature of the wrongs done to her and the importance of shifting our lives and institutions so that they exemplify the principle. This principle helps to pick out wrongs that anyone ought to avoid, which is different from Nora's decision that she ought to leave her husband, a decision not everyone would have to make. Thus there appears to be an asymmetry between certain principled decisions, on one hand, and principles that set out wrongs or prohibitions, on the other. No doubt the principle that human beings should be treated and respected as complete human beings requires support and explanation that is separate from its reciprocating support in concrete situations like this one. However, that would be a different task, one that links to conceptual issues that are not readily apparent in ordinary deliberation. What is of interest here is the interplay between general principles or values and concrete wrongs with a clear claim on being objectively visible.[4]

By following Nora's daily life and her decision, we are in a position to say more about the values involved and the general features of the changes that would be required if these two people were to have lives that were morally satisfactory. These values and changes are identifiable by the way things have gone wrong and by Nora's developing an understanding of them. Because of what we have seen in the play and what Nora says about her life, we know that she will have to do something about becoming a more complete human being who can think reliably for herself, who knows how to maintain her own tastes and ideas even when significant figures in her life oppose her views, and who knows how to help her children get to the bottom of things. Torvald, it is clear, will have to be able to see her as more than a wife, mother, and plaything. He will have to be able to see her as a complete human being with her own views that may differ from his. He will also have to stop caring so much about what others think about him and about her, and he will have to attend more to what is really important.

If this is a plausible way to describe the individual tasks that would shift the moral character of each in the required direction, several things about these tasks are worth noting. For one thing, they are tasks that require a change in what these people care about. They will be changes that affect how they act and how they talk to others. In effect, they will be changes in character that affect how they move forward in life. At the end, Nora has already changed a great deal that she cares about. What had been important to her was having a carefree life and pleasing her husband. This latter desire is presented by Ibsen partly as an ideal that she has adopted and enjoyed and partly as a necessary strategy for survival that requires her to be secretive and manipulative. The result is that we get glimpses of an ideal of life that may have a place for comfortable and carefree bliss, but along with it we have a clear picture of the distorted values their current life exemplifies.

Torvald's changes are ahead of him. But they can be described at least in general terms. He must, as we already saw, stop caring so much about the opinions of others. He must begin to care about Nora as a human being. What is impossible at this point, both for us as observers and for them as agents, is to state with any degree of precision what this change would require in the lives of each. These implications would have to be worked out in their daily lives and in the serious conversations that Nora would want. Their successes and failures would be apparent in the concrete interchanges of their daily lives.

The inability to say more precisely what these changes are is connected to broad facts about human reflective capacities. Among these is the fact that the future is open in ways that are not always predictable. It is not now known what circumstances will confront them as individuals or as a couple, and, so, it cannot be known what qualities of character they will most need, or how they could treat one another as full human beings in these yet unknown circumstances. More important, value underdetermines action and policy, and the meaning and significance of events in people's lives are not fixed by facts about the world. That is, the inability to know what the changed life would be like is not merely due to the absence of information but is endemic to the process of developing meaningful ways of living. This is true whether the value to be realized is, as it has come to be for Nora, the full humanity of herself and at least those close to her or, as Torvald's was, honor in the community. Ways of life that express and meet these ideals are partly found and partly invented, which Nora suggests in the play when she says that the transformation of herself and Torvald would be a miracle. It is not just that Torvald's changes are unlikely but that the transformation would be in some way mysterious, that is, not fully transparent to human reason, something that might or might not be invented as a meaningful way for these two to have, as she puts it, "a true marriage."[5]

A second feature of the tasks that lie before them is that they must be guided by having "gotten to the bottom of things," that is, by working out what is significant or important for human beings, which is not the same as what is dutiful, required, or obligatory. It is clear in Ibsen's play that wrongs are things that must be responded to or changed, so duties and requirements based on them are important. But it is also clear from the play that too much can be made of duty, that it can be injurious. It can be used to dominate and assert mastery at a devastating cost to innocent pleasures and human growth. There is no general formula for how to avoid these extremes, but the play provides a clear warning that duty is a powerful tool and, like most tools, can be used to destroy as well as to build or correct.

Likewise what is important is not the same as what is good or beneficial. These concepts have little role in the play, but their most evident role is in Nora's acts before the play opens. She borrows money for her husband's good so that he can recover his health. And she protects her dying father from worry by forging his signature on a loan document. These actions, clearly important, are presented as the only serious acts for which Nora has taken responsibility. But these are acts that also conflict with her so-called duties as a wife and a citizen. No general solution is presented to problems arising from conflict between duty and good. But there is clear indication that under these conditions, doing good trumps duty, and something can be said about why this should be so in these circumstances. The law doesn't allow Nora to borrow in her own name. And her husband is foolishly stubborn about taking care of his own health and about taking on debt.

But in addition to the categories of duty and good and the tension between them, there is a further category, which deals with questions of what counts for human beings, what matters to them. This category does not seem to be captured either by the notions of duty or by the idea of what is good as that is seen in the play. In the play, we learn about what does and does not matter and about what does not matter much. One thing we learn or are reminded of is that being a plaything is incompatible with what matters humanly. True, early in the play Nora's being a doll is in fact something that counts for them both. But she and we come to see it as incompatible with her humanity and with Torvald's ability to respect and appreciate the woman he is closest to. In seeing these things, we are reminded of

both the value of living a human life in ways that allow open assertion of legitimate powers and the distorting powers of ways of life
that deny this truth.

We also see other things that matter to these people. Friendships
are among them. An important family friend is dying. How he faces
death is important to him, and it affects what Nora and Torvald may
do if they are to respect their friend. The health and comfort of loved
ones matters. A loved one's health may be worth forging a document,
maybe even a lie to a person one loves. How one loves counts. Whatever has been the basis of Nora and Torvald's love, there are reasonable doubts about whether it is worth continuing their relationship.
How mothers love their children is important. As Nora has come to
understand, they need to be wise enough to know how to treat their
children as human beings and to teach them what is of genuine significance in human life. In short, a variety of things are of importance
in the lives of these people.

What becomes clear about these things that matter is that they
make claims on the people for whom they matter, and in doing that
they also make claims on others. Thus, these people must see the
things that matter in a certain light. They must see them as worth
their while and at least worth the forebearance of others. Not that
everyone must take each of these things to matter, but each of them
is something that is reasonable for anyone to take as important in a
whole life. Other people may put together packages of things that
matter that differ in many respects from this one. They may leave
out or weigh differently aspects of the things that matter to Nora, or
they may include different things altogether. But in seeing something
as worth one's devotion in this way, one must see it as something reasonable for an embodied human to devote herself to and as something worth devotion in these circumstances. Both of these demands
require claims to objectivity.

To this point, I have suggested that moral regulation of a decision
like Nora's is grounded in a complex of considerations about which
objective claims are made. But Ibsen's play also reminds us how easy
it is to lose track of what really matters. Torvald consistently turns
away from what is humanly important. He is remote from his children. He treats his wife alternately as a doll and as a daughter. Even

his erotic attachment follows these lines. He is incapable of being present for a friend who is dying. His primary notion of things that matter consists of money, the law, and his reputation. While these things do matter, in Torvald their mattering is distorted.

He is inflexible about money and will not go into debt for the sake of his own health. He is also stingy about the use of money for the small pleasures and joys in life. He is rigid about the law and insensitive to the difficulties other people have in making a life and providing for their families. He cares more about the appearance of impropriety than he does about what has mattered to his wife. Nora, too, has lost track of what matters, because of her dominating interest in keeping intact a carefree, pleasing home. In the process, she has lived a guilty secret and allowed herself to live a distorting idea of womanhood. Both the play and our attention to the complexities of moral living make clear the different lines that losing track of what really matters can take.

The reminder that it is easy to lose track of the things that matter brings into focus the fact that moral living requires more than our sensitivity to concrete wrongs and our understanding of their general features. It also requires an array of qualities of character and independence of judgment. In part, Nora and Torvald lose track of what is valuable, because of their own needs and insecurities, just as other humans do. But social, legal, and moral conventions are also things that make any of us lose track. Nora's experience of being wronged and her general grasp of human life and value enable her to develop the independence of judgment required for the moral regulation of her life.

The above discussion has focused on what claims to objectivity are about and on what they do. But it is also important to see what they do not have to do. Claims to objectivity do not need to resolve a conflict between competing demands in such a way that one party is to blame for the wrongs and the other party is the one wronged. But they do provide grounds for thoughts about issues of where blame lies, who is most wronged, and what the nature of that wrong is. That they do provide such grounds may, in turn, lead the parties to become fixed on issues of blame and thus become stuck in the roles of wrongdoer and victim of wrongdoing.

In this play, and in the moral regulation of life generally, judgments about value that lay a claim to objectivity have a different and important role. They ground Nora's sense of what she's about. Knowing about them, she comes to know what she stands for and how she is prepared to proceed. She decides that she can't go on with Torvald, but that she is going forward in life. We know that to her this means that as she proceeds, she will be trying to get "to the bottom of things." A primary target for her is to learn how to be a woman who is a human subject in the fullest sense, one who has her own tastes and, more important, her own ideas about religion and about what's right. In the process, she's going to try to understand how the law could be so unresponsive to her ideas about what she as a woman had a right to do, to protect a dying father and save a husband's life. And she will try to learn how to be a mother who could be a parent to children who are human subjects.

As for Torvald, we know far less about what he is learning as his wife leaves him and about how he might go forward in life. But he is presented as a person who is always regulating his life in the light of what he thinks is right and proper. As Nora leaves, she frees him of all responsibility for helping her and denies him permission to write to her. So, he is not left with the option of transforming himself so that he could have "a true marriage" with her. In any case, we have no reason to think that he understands what their marriage really has been or what the practice of it has done to her. But if he comes to see that, then he will have the task of coming to terms with his role and responsibility in it. His coming to terms with these things may also be regulated morally. If so, it will involve his capacities for seeing the concrete wrongs and understanding the basis for their wrongness. Beyond that, it will put strains on his ability to accept guilt and act reparatively and on his ability to transform himself so that he can at last treat women as full human beings.

These transformations in both characters call at least as much on their affective moral capacities as on what they are able to see and to know. Torvald will need to acknowledge his role in their marriage and to appreciate what he has gained and she has lost. One way of thinking about these things is to prepare himself for a conversation with her at some distant time. Not that he needs to prepare himself for a real conversation, but the lines of development of his acknowledgment and appreciation follow lines that would prepare him for a conversation in which the parties could be moved by moral considerations. What he cannot do, if his transformation is regulated morally, is to ignore these things. Moral regulation requires that he attend to the fallout from his earlier way of life so that if he had the opportunity, he would be prepared to meet with Nora in a way that could be reparative.

Similarly, Nora's affective moral capacities have had a role in her power to act on her beliefs at this point in her life. Despite the fact that she will have an uncertain financial and material future, she is able to release herself and Torvald from responsibilities to each other. She also faces her inadequacies as a human being and articulates them for herself and her husband. Perhaps what makes this process tolerable is that she has found a way to use these judgments about herself to form a new project that is far more compelling than her earlier role to found a home and please a husband. She also has to overcome her attachment to her children in order to leave. And moral thought has a role here, if her leaving is regulated by her desire to act in the best interests of her children. It might be objected that she is simply using the claim about what would be better for them to answer the charge of abandoning her duty. This claim, however, at best only defends her action. It does not account for her ability to let her children go to the care of someone else. Something more is needed to underwrite the magnanimity involved in forgoing her own attachment for their sake. Her judgment about what would be best for them may function in this way. Needless to say, whether her judgment is correct is also open to discussion.

So far we have been following the lines of moral regulation in the family crisis portrayed in Ibsen's play. It is also important to keep in mind that a crisis like this one might be ruled in other ways that would not count as moral regulation. A woman could go mad or kill herself, or she could simply disappear. The crisis could be denied, and a couple could go on as before, as if nothing had happened. But in moral regulation, the parties must look for grounds for action that make the costs of change worthwhile and that will shape what they care about and take responsibility for.

Just as it is possible for the crisis to be ruled nonmorally, it is open for moral regulation to take another tack. There are different possibilities for Nora. She could, for example, work to transform her-self and, with her husband, to transform their marriage through the kinds of conversations they had never had. However unlikely it is that they might succeed, this is a possibility. At least, it is until she decides not to pursue it for what are, to her, the soundest reasons. Her decision to leave sets out what she is taking responsibility for, not what she thinks everyone ought to do. Other people in similar or even exactly the same circumstances might respond differently.

Others might find some way to remake a marriage and a relation-ship with a parent, as Maggie does in Henry James's novel *The Golden Bowl*.[6] No two crises, of course, are exactly similar, nor are any two people, and that may be part of why it is so difficult for some and so easy for others to say that "I and anyone else in my circum-stances ought to leave." But also relevant to anyone's decision is what they are capable of and willing to take responsibility for. The facts of Nora's circumstances and the values of morality will not uniquely determine what she should do. The facts and principles do not determine one and only one outcome. They provide understand-ings and grounds for character transformation, action, and rework-ings of relationships that have a claim to being both morally regulated and objective. That is, the grounds for change are recognizably moral, and they are based on the way things really are, including particu-larly the possibilities for these people at this time.

The capacities that make these actions and reworkings possible are parts of our moral repertoire. They are part of the interplay be-tween knowledge, imagination, and sensibility that regulates our relations to one another and carries our lives forward. When these reworkings are guided morally, they are regulated by the parties' assessments of what is worth their devotion and commitment. And in the real world, this assessment may include what it is reasonable to ask and expect of themselves and others.

Early in the play, for example, Nora is not presented as a charac-ter who has taken full responsibility for her actions in borrowing money for her husband's recovery and the forgery of her dead father's signature. In some sense she does not know enough to do that. She doesn't understand the full implications of the law's prohibition on her borrowing in her own name, and she doesn't appear to think that signing her father's name is problematic. She believes she has to hide what she has done, but that seems to be out of fear of her husband's reaction and the wish to maintain the fiction that he does not need to rely on her.

Had she understood the law and been able to face her husband's reactions, she might have been able to take full responsibility for her acts. Then she might have been able to borrow the money by signing her father's name and take the risk in full knowledge that if found out she would somehow have to bear the consequences. Her position might have been that this was a reasonable response to the known circumstances (including the fact of her inability to borrow in her own name), and she might have possessed the strength of character to carry it off no matter what the fallout. That is, she might have been able to bear the law and society's punishment without catastrophic damage to her equilibrium and the sense of what her life was about. It would be possible for her act to be morally regulated and to be seen that way. In the play, she is not presented this way. At the threat of exposure, she is guiltily anxious and terrified about being caught. She does not have confidence that she can carry on her life if the worst should happen, and she imagines suicide as a way out.

By the end, her knowledge is more complete and includes quite prominently the realization that she does not know about the world she lives in. Nor does she know what she thinks is right. But now she is in position to take responsibility for herself and for learning what is required for her to take on serious projects in the world. To this point, she has only been able to take on one task that she sees as serious, and that was to borrow money and pay it back. However, she has had to keep under wraps both this act and this unexpected aspect of her character. She has had to pretend to be frivolous, whimsical, and irresponsible about money. In fact, she has secretly saved from the budget for her own clothes, and she has found a way to make money by copying at night. Although the saving compromised her joy in fine things, she took satisfaction and pride in the accomplishment of taking care of her debt, something she did on her own.

As she prepares to leave, she has found answers to all the claims that Torvald brings forward in their conversation. And the project she is taking on is one that has its own significance, that is, the making of a full human being, which is presented as having a status worth her devotion and worth giving up what she had wished for her life. She also has answers for why she should not go on as wife and mother. These may be read as only attempts to justify her action in the face of her explicit commitment to marriage and the responsibilities she has as a mother, but such a reading underestimates the role of such reasons in an ongoing moral life. In the play, all discussion is brought to an end with her leaving. But in real life a person might have a later conversation with a former partner or with adult children. This possibility provides a heuristic for thinking about what constitutes adequate reasoning in situations that have serious consequences for oneself and others.

In these situations, an agent who deliberates morally will be aware of losses and hurts that characteristically come in the wake of decisions like this one. Good moral reasoning in such situations is, in part, the presence of considerations that would support the others' understanding and acceptance of the seriousness of the project. And moral character is, in part, being moved by these kinds of considerations. That is, moral agents have the capacity to be moved by their knowledge of the consequences to others as well as by the seriousness of their projects. And those who stand to be hurt need to have the capacities to appreciate the importance of others' projects and to accept disappointments and losses for important enough considerations. Theory cannot give precise directions about how to do this, but it can outline and advance understanding of the characteristics and importance of various moral considerations.

The above discussion has bearing on a case considered by Bernard Williams in his essay "Moral Luck." Williams presents a character based on Gauguin as someone who, like Nora, is moved by moral considerations and deliberates about whether to leave his family. This quasi-fictional Gauguin's reason for leaving is to devote himself to a life of realizing his gifts as a painter. Williams argues that at the time he makes his decision, Gauguin cannot be justified, since he cannot know whether he will be successful. Being successful is a matter of luck, both the external luck that an accident doesn't occur and the luck, internal to his project, that he has the gifts and that they do work out. Williams argues that Gauguin will be justified in his choice only if he succeeds; if he fails, he will have "no basis for the thought that he was justified in what he did. If he succeeds, he does have a basis for that thought" (1981, 23).

In part, Williams is interested in showing that luck plays a bigger role in moral life than it is allowed in the philosophic conception of morality that we have inherited from Kant and the utilitarians. In the inherited tradition, Williams argues, Gauguin would have to be justified at the time of his decision, and Williams thinks he cannot be. He concludes that the difficulty with this conception of morality is that it treats moral considerations as final, that is, as overriding all other values. As a result, it leaves inadequate room for personal attachments and projects.

Williams is worried that morality, as conceived in these traditions, makes moral life too demanding. He seems to think that if we take these traditions seriously, we will inevitably or characteristically be led to view morality as imposing a heavy and ubiquitous burden of responsibility. This assumption leads him to claim that "we have in fact deep and persistent reasons for being grateful" that the world we inhabit is not one in which morality is universally respected (1981, 23).

Although it is sympathetic with the wish to keep the heaviness and ubiquity of morality at bay, Williams's solution seems to involve an unacceptable cost. In rejecting the idea that moral considerations override all other values, he appears to favor a view in which moral, aesthetic, personal, and perhaps other values compete for our attention in deliberation, with no general limits on how to resolve conflicts between these competing values. It is this last demotion of morality that is worrisome, because it seems to leave us without the kinds of considerations that are important in regulating changes in individual lives and institutions. In particular, we are apparently left without the means to critique oppressive institutions and to justify actions that make possible serious projects but involve harm to others. These tasks are some of the most important for moral regulation.

If we return to Williams's case and follow it out more fully, we may be able to see whether his solution is required. Gauguin deliberates about which set of commitments he will devote himself to living out—those to his wife and children, which will, let us suppose, include his having a set of commitments to his life as businessman, or, giving those up, realizing his talents as a painter? From this position he can't, of course, know that he will succeed or even that he has the talent and discipline to succeed. Much could happen that is beyond his control; from where he sits, all he can do is commit himself to the kind of effort he believes is required to develop his talent. But if his deliberative process is adequate to the seriousness of this choice, he needs to think hard about his chances for success, about what he knows about his talents and his capacities for commitment to the work to develop them. He needs as well to think about the commitments he is considering giving up and what that means to himself and his family. If, however, he makes a serious effort to think through what he is doing and its effects on others, it is hard to see why he *does* have enough for a grounded thought that he is justified or, at least, that his project is within the bounds of morality.

Let us imagine that he leaves, spends some significant number of years painting, and then returns to confront his family again. What does his grounded thought that he was justified do for him and his family? Supposing he is given an opportunity to have a conversation with them about his decision and his life, we might see a number of things happen. But one thing we would expect is for him to begin telling his family about the importance of his project and in what ways it was something worth his devotion. It is also true, as Williams notes, that his wife and children have grounds for reproaching him. But he does have something to offer them by way of helping them understand the importance of his project and why he made the choice he did. Who knows what will happen in this conversation? Many things are possible, but there are, broadly speaking, two primary ways for it to go. One, his wife and children may be unmoved by his words, presence, or explanations. They may not regard these things as coming anywhere close to mitigating their abandonment, and they may remain rejecting and unforgiving. Or, two, they may be more or less moved by his efforts to explain his life.

Note that his success or failure does not play an essential role in the conversation, although it may be affected by whether he has returned a success or a failure. But these factors are not necessary to his family's acceptance or rejection. In fact, it is not unlikely that his "you see I was successful, and so, I was justified" is at least as likely to lead to their rejection of him as to their understanding and acceptance. The claim that he was justified is all too likely to mean that their suffering does not have a status that can compete with his project and its success. Or, they may see it as some kind of attempt to defend or excuse him. What they will want to know is what kind of project could have been worthy of their husband-and-father's devotion in the light of what they have had to do without. It is less the success or failure of this project than its significance that does the work in this context. More than his success, it is his ability to acknowledge their loss and to acknowledge that they are important that grounds and aids in their acceptance of his choice. Something similar seems true for third parties as well. Those of us who stand outside this family, hear the story, and take it to involve serious losses (whichever way Gauguin lives his life) will also be interested in how to understand the parties and particularly the project that led that character to leave his family.

Looking ahead in this way, we can begin to see his decision as a turning point about what he is taking responsibility for. The way in which he does this will say a lot about his character and moral capacities. It is important that he does consider the pull of his promises and the difficulties his children and wife might face. A person in this situation, far from having the job of showing how aesthetic or some other values trump moral ones in this case, has the responsibility of showing how the seriousness of his project has a moral dimension that could ground acceptance of losses.

If the point of morality is to enable people to live together and prosper under a regulatory system that is not based on might or on the unequal status of persons, then it is hard to see how it could not impose considerations that are final. That is what it would mean to accept the system. When individuals regulate their relations morally, they must in a broad way address each other by appealing to considerations each could accept. What they cannot do is "pull rank" on one another or simply impose their will. On the other hand, moral regulation may not provide a unique and definite resolution that it is reasonable to regard as the correct one. In a world of many conflicting and competing sources of claims, the best that can be hoped for is some solution that addresses the interests of each by offering the kinds of considerations that would be reasonable to accept. Clearly, these sometimes may not be accepted. In such cases, we may have conditions in which moral regulation is not possible. And that is not something to be grateful for.

NOTES

1. Henrik Ibsen, *Eleven Plays of Henrik Ibsen* (New York: Modern Library, n.d.), p. 85.

2. Examples of critics I have in mind are Bernard Williams in many essays, but particularly in "Moral Luck," in *Moral Luck: Philosophical Papers 1973–80* (Cambridge, Eng.: Cambridge University Press, 1981), Carol Gilligan, *In a Different Voice* (Cambridge: Harvard University Press, 1982), and Marilyn Friedman, *What Are Friends For?* (Ithaca, N.Y.: Cornell University Press, 1993).

3. There is a difficult issue here that is outside the bounds of this chapter. Ideals of moral life have to meet two criteria. One is that they have to be her ideals; they must be what she understands and sets for herself. Second, they must meet some standard of reasonableness. For example, reasonable moral ideals cannot be formulated around frivolous or pointless human activities, nor can they be based on the human desire to dominate and subdue others or to elevate oneself above others. How to characterize a standard of reasonableness for moral ideals is a complex philosophical project.

4. The principle that people should be treated and respected as complete human beings does seem to be a part of Nora's developing moral ideal. My claim is that for her to be justified in holding it, there must be considerations available to show that the ideal is reasonable. That does not entail that it must be an aspect of every reasonable moral ideal.

5. See David Wiggins, "Truth, Invention, and the Meaning of Life," in *Needs, Values, Truth,* 2d ed. (Oxford: Blackwell, 1991), for an argument that both invention and discovery have a role in human activities that are treated as meaningful.

6. Henry James, *The Golden Bowl* (New York: Scribner's, 1904).

16 / *Ways to Think About Dying*

JEAN P. RUMSEY

> There's going to be a departure, I'll be there, I won't miss it;
> it won't be me, I won't say anything. . . .
> All is noise, unending suck of black sopping peat, surge of
> giant ferns, heathery gulfs of quiet where the wind drowns,
> my life and its old jingles . . . and what I'm doing, all-important,
> breathing in and out and saying, with words like smoke, I can't
> go, I can't stay, let's see what happens next. (Beckett 1967)

I should here like to emphasize the "thinking" element of the title of this chapter.[1] My concern is primarily with questions of how we are to think about death and dying rather than with their existential dimensions. Certain philosophical and cultural preconceptions underlie, and may occlude, our thinking on this topic. Primary among these preconceptions are abstract individualism; the conception of death as an event, dichotomous with life, rather than dying as a process occurring through time within life; and denial of the realities of how we die. The "death with dignity" perspective is one example of denial. Herbert Hendin, in a recent *Hastings Center Report*, charges that "death with dignity" is sometimes used as a "marketing technique" in case histories that promote the normalization of euthanasia and assisted suicide (1995, 19). That this perspective is often unrealistic is shown by Assaya Pascalev in her study of dying in intensive care units. She details the way in which aggressive medical procedures turn death into "a continual process of discrete medical victories and losses through which the patient as a person vanishes" (1996, 32). There is often no person left for whom to predicate either dignity or its loss.

My primary task here is to establish the self as relational, not atomistic, and to develop important implications of that viewpoint for both theory and practice. On this view one must conceive of dying as a process through time, involving not only the one dying but also those with whom she has been interconnected in life and may remain connected in death. This perspective opens up questions of "re-membering" the living—reintegrating the self after a death—as well as those of remembering the dead.

A difficulty of inquiring into death and dying is its paradoxical nature. Herbert Fingarette points out that from an objective point of view it is certain that I will die, but from a subjective point of view it is certain that I will not (1996, 7). Thus Albert Camus finds death absurd: "In reality there is no experience of death. It is possible to speak of the experience of others' deaths. It is a substitute, an illusion, and it never quite convinces us. . . . From the inert body on which a slap makes no mark the soul has disappeared. This elementary and definitive aspect of the adventure constitutes the absurd feeling" (1955, 21).

Fingarette concludes that because the subject itself is paradoxical, we must be willing and able to live with multiple perspectives and sometimes conflicting beliefs. He sees this as the pivotal lesson of the story of Job, in which the truth finally revealed to the sufferer was that his complaint from the single perspective of justice is "laughably inadequate" (1996, 88). A final example of conflicting perspectives, captured in these lines by David Ignatow, is that we die both together and alone:

> No such luck. No one will jump into
> my grave. You keep reading this
> with curiosity. We are in the world, dying together,
> but scanning these words
> you see me die alone. (1991, 58)

Let us turn our attention to the cultural context of this phenomenon near the end of this twentieth century in our own society.

THE CULTURAL CONTEXT:
PRACTICES AND HABITS OF THOUGHT

> I obey traffic signals. I am
> cordial to strangers, I answer my

mail promptly. I keep a balanced
checking account. Why can't I
live forever? (Ignatow 1991, 22)

We may add from the folk tradition: "When I am dead, and laid in grave / And all my bones are rotten / By this may I remembered be / When I should be forgotten" (Opie and Opie 1959, 32). Children are often able to see through our Western cultural denial of death. As evidence, Iona Opie and Peter Opie found variations of the folk rhyme above in 1736, 1825, and in schoolbooks of the 1950s (by ten- to twelve-year-olds). And readers of this chapter may remember variations on this durable grade school verse: "Whenever you see the hearse go by / And think to yourself that you're gonna die / Be merry, my friends, be merry. Your eyes fall in and your hair falls out / And your brains come tumbling down your snout / Be merry, my friends, be merry" (Opie and Opie 1959, 33). Clearly, children who delight in such lines have not yet been properly assimilated into our death-denying culture.

Philippe Aries has chronicled the history of death in the West from the "Good Death" of the past to today's "Hidden Death." He calls our modern Western conception of death "Forbidden Death." In this paradigm, death must be concealed not only from the dying person but also from her family and from public view (Aries 1974). In his 1984 work, *The Silent World of Doctor and Patient*, psychoanalyst Jay Katz indicted physicians for their part in maintaining this silence, which, he argued, is tantamount to the abandoning of patients. It is the rare patient who can break that silence, as did the Nobel prizewinner Luigi Pirandello near his death in 1936. When his physician stood over his deathbed, trying to cheer him with white lies about his condition, Pirandello is said to have responded "No need to be so scared of words, doctor. This is called dying" (Slater and Solomita 1980, 48). Euphemisms and practices hide death, such as expiration certificates rather than death certificates at a prominent Chicago hospital during the fifties, the use of a hearse that often resembles an ordinary limousine, and the practice, even after conventional funerals, of not allowing the mourners to see the coffin lowered into the ground.

Aries points out that the initiative for organizing rituals that would give the dying process meaning, as well as give opportunities for the living to communicate with the one dying, "has passed from the family, as much an outsider as the dying person, to the doctor and the hospital team. They are the masters of death—of the moment as well as of the circumstances" (1974, 89). His claims are supported by recent figures which show that since the 1960s, death has become medicalized in the United States, with 80 percent of deaths taking place in hospitals rather than in homes. Aries argues that under this conception the strong emotions that death calls forth must be avoided both in the hospital and in society: "One does not have the right to become emotional other than in private, that is to say, secretly" (1974, 88–89). This constraint contributes to the norm of the "good patient"—one who is quiet and tractable, causing no trouble to her caretakers or fellow patients.

Even if we disagree with the acceptance norm above, many of us would probably agree with Daniel Callahan's call for physicians to make death more peaceful by expecting, preparing for, and accepting death themselves, by refraining from practices of "technologically attenuating" death, and by doing better palliative care (1993, 30). However, Eric Krakauer, writing from a resident's perspective, seriously doubts the likelihood of such changes given currently entrenched patterns of thought and practice. The scientific, objective view of the world and ourselves, he argues, is fundamental to modern Western thought: "To truly give up the will to ultimate power over nature, and thus over death . . . would be to call into question the absolute legitimacy of the modern objective mode of thinking" (Spiro, Curnen, and Wandel 1996, 29). Changing to a less domineering attitude toward nature and death would demand a reexamination of the entire Western intellectual tradition.

If the physician or medical team commands even the time of death, death is no longer simply a "natural" happening, but a happening that is somewhat under human control (note the parallel with induced labor in childbirth). David W. Moller, a sociologist, worries that as a culture we have nearly convinced ourselves that death is not a natural part of the life cycle. He finds twentieth-century thinking about death dominated by denial, avoidance, fear, and loneliness, whereas in the past, "the regular involvement of death in everyday life enabled humans to mitigate the ordeal of death and tame its sting in a public and communal way" (1996, 237). In contrast, modern medicine is characterized by technological dominance, bureaucracy, emotional neutrality and the view of death as an adversary, all in-hospitable to human needs for shared cultural norms and for rituals marking the end of a life.

Moller also finds denial of death's reality in the hospice movement, quoting Sandal Stoddard, who writes that persons are "helped to live fully in an atmosphere of loving kindness and grace until the time has come for them to die a natural death" (Stoddard 1978, 3). Like Hendin, Moller suggests that hospice patients are being "force-fed" a death-with-dignity philosophy that has become a "new (bureaucratic) form of managing dying patients" (1996, 43).

If ritual comforts the dying and the bereaved, Bert Keizer, formerly a physician in the Netherlands, observes that no rituals have been developed for euthanasia because euthanasia is a rare (and often controversial) occurrence in history. He says he has learned to find his way "through riteless regions" by keeping a mental list of all the things to be done and methodically instructing the other participants: "I'll be there at half-past six, then I'll give you a hand and say my farewell, then I'll call your son, and while he is with you, I'll go get the nurse . . . etc. Hoping in this way to knot myself a rope bridge across the abyss"(1994, 81).

David Moller also argues that seemingly opposed orientations toward death—the open-awareness, death-acceptance stance and the closed-awareness, death-avoidance stance—both powerfully affirm the American value of individualism and related cultural values of autonomy and separateness (1996, 238–39). He is especially concerned that the acceptance view dismisses the harsh realities of death, creating for dying patients unrealistic expectations that mandate concealment of its wretchedness. Thus "the sting of death is removed from public visibility and remanded to the private world of dying individuals and their loved ones" (Moller 1996, 239). The emerging concept of a negotiated death, worked out through active participation by the patient, family, nurses, physicians, and lawyers, is yet another way in which death is individualized in our culture. Thus individualism serves the broader social community by hiding death but intensifies the grief experience of the surviving individuals through their social isolation and the narrowing of the grieving community. Moller believes that voluntary communities such as the Compassionate Friends, a community of parental mourners, can help ease the burden of an otherwise fragmented, isolated experience (1996, 241).

It remains only to consider the individualism in our habits of thought. Annette Baier reports that the term "individualism" is a relative latecomer to the English language and that it was coined by Alexis de Tocqueville in the nineteenth century. He defined individualism as a disposition of each member of the community to sever himself from the mass of his fellow creatures and to draw apart with his family and friends. The Oxford English Dictionary cites more recent senses: a "self-centered feeling or conduct as a principle, a mode of life in which the individual pursues his own ends or follows his own ideas, feelings and independent individual actions or thought, egoism." Baier comments that this definition includes both de Tocqueville's intended near-egoism, "plus the independence of thought and action that gives us our concept of sturdy individualism as a virtue" (Schott 1997, 301). Baier recognizes the moral importance of this virtue but feels that methodological individualism as a way of thinking is limiting and stultifying, at odds with realities of human interdependence and concomitant needs for cooperation. Similarly, although independence of thought and action are of great value for individuals and society, this independence can take on a negative value when interpreted as independence *from* others rather than *for* self-direction—as I have argued elsewhere that Kant did in his *Anthropology* (Schott 1997, 132; Kant 1974, 135).

Another critic of individualism, Caroline Whitbeck, argues that its model of persons is adequate only to transactions among peers in a market society but is not adequate to model the vulnerability of the sick, the young, and the poor: "What happens when individuals are too young or too sick to compete and contract with other peers is largely ignored and unpresentable in terms of the atomic model of persons. . . . Individualism ignores both the interdependence of people and their historical character" (Gould 1983, 58). Hilde Lindemann Nelson and James Lindemann Nelson call our attention to the abstractness of the model of "autonomous self-interested entities interacting contractually in pursuit of their own goods. These individuals, untouched by any particular language, culture, or socialization, seem woefully inadequate to the facts of biological existence" (Holmes and Purdy 1992, 42).

A significant contemporary book, *The Metaphysics of Death* (1993), edited by John Martin Fischer, exemplifies individualist assumptions in abstract thought. Fischer tells us in the introduction that "the focus will be on the main basic and abstract problems concerning the nature of death: Can death be a bad thing for the individual who dies? What is the nature of the evil of death, if it is an evil? If death can harm a person, who is the subject of the harm, and when does the harm occur? If death can be a bad thing for a person, would immortality be good?" (1993, 3). These questions focus on one generic individual, abstracted from context. The philosopher-turned-physician Bert Keizer tells us of his reevaluation of Wittgenstein's famous answer to the question of whether death is a bad thing for the individual who dies. Wittgenstein wrote: "Death is not an event in life. We do not live to experience death. Our life has no end in just the way in which our visual field has no limits" (1961, 147). Keizer replies: "I remember how relieved I felt when first reading these words of Wittgenstein's. But after you have stood at the gravesides of others a few times, you find it hardly consoling, this circumstance that you don't have to attend your own funeral. For one of the greater miseries of life is that others die" (1994, 19).

Thomas Nagel's well-known essay "Death," included in Fischer's anthology, raises further questions about the limitations of abstract individualist modes of thinking. He questions whether, in general, it is a bad thing to die. He assumes that since life, like most goods, can be multiplied by time, more is better than less, and argues that the added quantities need not be temporally contiguous. Because of this potentiality, reasonable people would, he claims, be attracted to long-term suspended animation or freezing. Although he admits that there are some disadvantages (family and friends may have died in the meantime; the language may have changed; the comforts of social, geographical, and cultural familiarity would be lacking), he maintains that these "inconveniences" would not keep the individual's additional existence from being advantageous (Fischer 1993, 62–63). In Clifford Simiak's science fiction classic *City*, Sara, unhappy with her work and life, decides to take "the Sleep" for a few hundred years, but only because the Temple administrators have told her that when she awakens she will be adjusted (to whatever life is like in whatever era she awakes) "almost as if you belonged, even from the first" (1952, 158). Without such a miracle, life after a long period of suspended animation would smack of exile, whose burdens Socrates described so well, and which the justices in *Furman v. Georgia* (408 U.S. [1972]) argued would be more inhumane than capital punishment.

William Joseph Gavin warns of what might happen when we sever the self's tenuous connection with its environment: "The self is embodied, and grows or dies, through interaction with its contexts—cultural and otherwise. Loss of open or challenging or inviting contexts will ultimately result in loss of self, that is, death" (1995, 133). This warning embodies a social conception of the self, which I believe to be more adequate as a basis for our understanding of death and dying than the individualist conceptions just examined.

THE RELATIONAL SELF:
FROM ISOLATION TO AFFILIATION

According to Virginia Held, the nature of the self is one of three basic moral concepts that is being transformed in our time.[2] She finds pathological the traditional view of the self as an inner citadel with strong walls to protect one's autonomy. She forwards a different conception of autonomy, secured by creating and sustaining relationships of empathy and mutuality with others (Held 1993, 60, 63). Many working on this project of transformation are feminist philosophers: Virginia Held (1993), Annette Baier (1985), Caroline Whitbeck (Gould 1983), Marilyn Friedman (1993), Margaret Walker (1992), Claudia Card (1991), María Lugones (1987), and others. However, the project also has strong roots in mainstream philosophy through such thinkers as Nicolai Hartmann, George Herbert Mead, William James, and, more recently, Charles Taylor. Hartmann holds that the concept of an isolated consciousness of self exists only in philosophical theory, not in reality: "From infancy a human being stands within the context of human personalities, grows into it, and in it develops and builds up his whole moral consciousness. The elemental interwovenness of the 'I' and the 'thou' is not to be disintegrated. This unity—however enigmatic—can constitute the only starting-point of theory" (1932, 127).

Hartmann's contemporary George Herbert Mead presented a concept of the self as an ongoing social process involving interactions among self and others. The self, he maintains, does not exist prior to this process but is, in his metaphor, "an eddy in the social current and so still part of the current. . . . the raw materials out of which this particular individual is born would not be a self but for his relationships to others in the community of which he is a part" (1934, 200).[3]

Charles Taylor employs Mead's concept of the significant other to explain how the self is created by, and constituted by, our dialogical relations with others: "We define our identity always in dialogue with, sometimes in struggle against, the things our significant others want to see in us. Even after we outgrow some of these others—our parents, for instance—and they disappear from our lives, the conversation with them continues within us as long as we live" (1995, 229).

Taylor's metaphor of "outgrowing" significant others has a certain plausibility, and yet, I will argue, it may be misleading. For building our identity is not entirely like the biological processes of growth and decay; it is a human process involving choice of which relationships to continue and which to break off. If, for example, I become very close to a pacifist friend, we may decide to sever relations with a hawkish friend from my past. If I become close to someone who loves Italian opera, the person with whom I used to enjoy country music may be dropped. Chance and reflection may overturn some of these choices, but Taylor's basic point remains: "If some of the things I value most are accessible to me only in relation to the person I love, then she becomes part of my identity" (1995, 23).

Furthermore, a new relationship may make radical changes in one's life. Susan Brison, a victim of rape, which made her a more cautious person, writes of the slow healing that eventuated in her willingness to have a child. The child himself caused changes in her: "He is the embodiment of my life's new narrative, and I am more autonomous by virtue of being so intermingled with him. Having him has also enabled me to rebuild my trust in the world around us. He is so trusting that he stands with outstretched arms wobbling, until he falls, stiff-limbed, forward, backward, certain the universe will catch him. So far, it has, and when I tell myself it always will, the part of me that he's become believes it" (Meyers 1997, 32). And yet, there is no knowing what will recall to her the part of her that was traumatized by the rapist.

Events and persons from the past come bidden or unbidden, welcome or not. Lucille Clifton's (dead) mother appeared to her in the hospital room where she lay ill with cancer:

enter my mother
wearing a peaked hat.
her cape billows
her broom sweeps the nurses away,
she is flying, the witch of the ward, my mother
pulls me up by the scruff of the spine
incanting Live Live Live! (Clifton 1987, 55)

In his short story "Dawn," Elie Wiesel shows how moments of crisis may bring together selves from one's entire past. Elisha, aged eighteen, is recruited into a terrorist movement and faces his first assignment, avenging the death of one David ben Moshe. Pacing his room at midnight, he finds visitors pouring in—all those who had contributed to making him the person he is today, his permanent identity. There were childhood friends, relatives, comrades, and others who had suffered with him at Buchenwald and Auschwitz. A small boy who reminds Elisha of himself explains that they've all come to see Elisha turn into a murderer—a natural curiosity for those so closely connected to him (Wiesel 1972, 166).

These stories tell us that there is in Taylor's statement an important implication for our understanding of this relational concept of the self as applied to issues of death and dying. We may remain in dialogue with those of our dead who have been important to us to varying extents throughout our lives. The degree to which this dialogue is understood and practiced varies with cultures and with individuals. Some persons may prefer dialogue with the living (and surely not all Native American poets commune with both grandmothers before they begin to write, as does the Navajo poet Joy Harjo). But notice the warning here: both the voices of my parents, whom I thought I'd outgrown, or the rapist, from whose damage I'd thought myself healed, or any person I have chosen to exclude from my "better" or "real" self might enter my consciousness, unbidden, as long as I live.

Let us turn next to the work of feminist philosophers in transforming concepts of the self. Some call it the "social self," some the "relational self." Some use both terms. But there is general agreement that it is a self constituted by its relationship with others, one in which concern for other persons is fundamental, and a conception into which the classic dichotomy between egoism and altruism does not quite fit. In ordinary language the bereaved often say, "I don't know how I can go on—he [or she] was a part of me." What does it mean to say "he/she was a part of me"?

Caroline Whitbeck holds that a feminist ontology based on a self-other *relation* is significantly different from an ontology based on the self-other *opposition* underlying much Western thought (Gould 1983, 64). Bell hooks articulates a similar view. Discarding an oppositional construct of the self, hooks states: "I evolved the way of knowing I had learned from unschooled southern black folks. We learned that the self existed in relation, was dependent for its being on the lives and experiences of everyone, the self not as signifier of one 'I', but the coming together of many 'I's." Hooks contends that the concept of self in relation means that "we would know the voices that speak in and to us from the past—from our living and from our dead" (hooks 1989, 30–31).

It should be noted here that the voices that speak within us are not necessarily familial or even personal. Such leaders as Mahatma Gandhi, Mother Theresa, and Martin Luther King Jr. may be more central to a person's identity than those around one. A young minister in Minneapolis, the Reverend Alika Galloway, replied in this way to a question about why her sermons often included quotations from Sojourner Truth: "The ability to pierce through walls of suffering, disbelief and isolation with truthful, powerful, spiritual theological words is a hallmark of womanism and Sojourner Truth, and I am deeply engraved with both. She is imprinted on me" (1997). Thus there is a significant element of choice in the construction of one's identity, although, as in the example of the woman scarred by rape, there is also a large element of moral luck.

There is widespread feminist agreement with Caroline Whitbeck's definition of a person as "an historical being whose history is fundamentally a history of relationships to other people, developed in a practice of the (mutual) realization of people" (Gould 1983, 65). Forms of this practice, she claims, are mainly considered women's work, unnoticed by the dominant culture. Among these are child rearing, the education of children and adolescents, care of the dying and nursing of the sick, and "a variety of spiritual practices related to daily life" (Gould 1983, 65). Although this work is invisible and undervalued in our culture, it is some of the most important work in which human beings can engage. Its value is not simply for those in need of care or bringing up or aid in dying, but also for those doing the work. Sara Ruddick demonstrates in her analysis of the practice of mothering how important virtues are developed and that they contribute to the good life not only for the individual and those close to her but also for the broader society (1989).

What does the relational self imply for our understanding of death and dying? First, death is not simply a process undergone by the dying individual. It is undergone—differently—also by those intimate with that individual. A death, like a birth, is, as Sara Ruddick holds, "also a social experience, engaging the intense feelings and often the demanding care of the living" (1989, 213). Her comparison of death with birth is echoed in the metaphor with which Timothy Quill titles his 1996 book on assisted suicide, *A Midwife Through the Dying Process,* and by Therese Schroeder-Sheker, a music thanatologist who has learned to use music as it was used in medieval monastic infirmaries to "unbind" pain and assist monks who were about to die. She calls her work "midwifery, but on the other end" (1991, 83–84).

Although it is one person who dies, others are intimately involved with and affected by that death. A survivor may feel a heavy responsibility to the dead, to finish incomplete projects or support causes close to that person's heart. Saint Augustine describes his sense of responsibility in feeling that his dead friend was precariously preserved in him: "I felt that my soul and his soul were 'one soul in two bodies': and therefore was my life a horror to me, because I would not live halved. And therefore perchance I feared to die, lest he whom I had much loved, should die wholly" (Dinnage 1990, 10). A contemporary philosopher recounts his experience on the death of his daughter, aged sixteen. They had worked together through the process of her dying by talking about death, sharing their anger and fears, and examining philosophical questions about death. The father reported that his daughter "maintained (or perhaps she only pretended to maintain) that her death would not be such a very bad thing for her—for she would be 'out of it' once it took place. . . . She claimed that death would be worse for me, since I would be left behind to suffer its aftereffects." (Feldman 1994, vii). And indeed, he reported that after her death he "found it impossible to think coherently about anything."

Similarly, Gerda Lerner speaks of the difficulties of comprehending that her husband had really died: "The fact of his death, his absence, is incontrovertible. I 'know' it in many different ways and with many different modes of perception. Yet, to this day, I still do not 'know' it in the way I know other facts. It shifts, it wavers—sometimes it is as true as a rock; sometimes it is as true as a bad dream. I imagine it must be that way for the dying until that final stage when they really 'know'—then they let go" (1985, 58). María Lugones's concept of "world-travel" gives us a helpful way in which to read these experiences: the bereaved were, for a time, visitors to or temporary prisoners of the "world" of their dead (1987). Iris Murdoch makes this metaphor explicit: the bereaved are "thrown into the world of the dead," from which they gradually return in time (1992, 500–501).

What are the implications of this relational conception of the self for moral theory and for understanding specifically moral issues in death and dying? Clearly, on this view moral theory would focus not on relations between autonomous adults, not on the isolated individual agent, but on the agent in community, in her cultural and historical situation. Margaret Walker holds that we must reject the "theoretical-juridical" model of mainstream Western ethical thought, because "its preoccupation with equality and autonomy, uniformity and impartiality, rules and reciprocity fits relations of nonintimate equals and transactions of contracts among peers" (1992, 24). Thus it has little to say about the unequal relationships of those who care for particular others, and it neglects the importance of intimate human relationships in favor of abstract problem solving. In its stead she suggests an alternative conception, which she calls "expressive-collaborative," which conceives of morality as "a socially embodied medium of mutual understanding and adjustment between persons in certain terms, particularly those that define those persons' identities, relationships, and values" (1992, 24, 32).

Primary resources of this sort of theory would be shared moral vocabularies, communication skills, knowledge of one's own moral values, the ability to understand the moral values of others, and the will to attempt mutual adjustment on the basis of that understanding. Most important are virtues, which Walker describes both in the traditional Aristotelian way and as complex interpersonal skills. Indeed, her alternative moral theory has much in common with Aristotle's: the human agent as essentially social, shared moral norms, the importance of attending to particulars, and the integration of reason and emotions. It appears that she objects primarily to modern Western ethical theory, which, as Annette Baier observes, "has concentrated on the morality of fairly cool relationships between those who are deemed to be roughly equal in power to determine the rules and institute sanctions against rule breakers" (1995, 116).

In order to understand moral issues in death and dying, I believe that some theory such as Margaret Walker's, based as it is on a relational conception of the self, a recognition of human inequalities, and a positive conception of the function of morality, will be most nearly adequate. Support for this view is found in recent challenges in medical ethics journals to "principle-based ethics," recommending instead virtue ethics, the ethics of caring, or casuistry, which focuses on particulars. In the domain of death and dying, much work needs to be done on virtues (for which Aristotle's *Nicomachean Ethics* can be helpful). For instance, the reader might be surprised, as I was, to discover that Nel Noddings, a primary exponent of a care ethic, does not consider the self-sacrifice of those who care for a hopelessly comatose parent to be virtuous. Rather, she argues that their suffering is unconscionable, using it as evidence for her support of euthanasia. Although she does not couch this argument in Aristotelian terms, she clearly considers it a case in which an unreflective excess of the virtue of caring has turned into a vice (1989, 138).

We may also inquire into how this relational conception of the self influences one's view of one's own death. I agree with the British philosopher Derek Parfit that accepting this conception takes some of the sting out of this prospect. Parfit writes that on changing to a relational view, he became less depressed at the prospect of his own death. When he conceived of life atomistically, he states, "I seemed imprisoned in myself. My life seemed like a glass tunnel, through which I was moving faster every year, and at the end of which there was darkness. When I changed my view, the walls of my glass tunnel disappeared. I now live in the open air. There is still a difference between my life and the lives of other people. But the difference is less. Other people are closer. I am less concerned about the rest of my own life, and more concerned about the lives of others" (1984, 281). Coincidentally, the publication date of his book connects his thought with George Orwell's *1984*, in which one of the techniques of the dictator is vaporization: removing all evidence that a citizen had ever existed.

I turn next to the question of how the community can best live through the deaths of those close to them, remember their dead, and rebuild their selves after this loss.

MOURNING: REMEMBERING THE DEAD
AND RE-MEMBERING THE LIVING

Perhaps, after all, death is a subject best left to poets, musicians, stonecutters, and storytellers. What these lines of Adrienne Rich's poem "Living Memory" convey about the relationship of the living and the dead does not translate well into ordinary prose:

> All we can read is life. Death is invisible. . . .
> The granite bulkhead
> Incised with names, the quilt of names, were made
> By the living, for the living. . . .
> When Selma threw
> her husband's ashes into the Hudson
> and they blew back on her and us, her friends
> it was life. Our blood raced in that gritty wind. (1989, 49–50)

Shakespeare's Sonnet Sixty-Five is an explicit effort to preserve his love in art:

> O fearful meditation; where, alack,
> Shall time's best jewel from Time's chest lie hid?
> Or what strong hand can hold his swift foot back?
> Or who his spoil or beauty can forbid?
> O none, unless this miracle have might
> That in black ink my love may still shine bright. (Booth 1977, 59)

These examples from the enormous worldwide archives of memorial poetry are written, and many other sorts of artworks are created, in order that the living may come to terms with their dead.

Many scholars are concerned about the absence of commonly accepted rituals and practices at death. Paul Rosenblatt holds that failure to engage in such rituals "can leave people at sea about how the death occurred, who or what the deceased is, how to relate to others, how to think of self and much more." He adds that in our own society physicians, generally poor ritual specialists, have been entrusted to preside over death (Parkes 1977, 31). Yet, for mourning work to be effective, it must be communal. He deplores the fact that many Westerners think of grieving as an individual process, noting that even grief therapy is often individually focused (Parkes 1977, 43). Timothy Quill recounts the death of Rob, an AIDS patient, whose partner invited a friend with experience in Native American ritual to the bedside. "The poking, prodding, and monitoring that usually characterizes death in twentieth-century America was replaced by chanting, drumming, and praying. For a brief moment the medical floor was transported to a time, a place, and a culture where death was accepted and sometimes even welcomed. Robb . . . peacefully slipped into a coma and died, with drums receding in the background" (Quill 1996, 46). Dr. Quill credits the leadership and activism of HIV-infected patients with helping the doctor-patient relationship to change from an authoritarian model to one based more on partnership and collaboration.

Claude Levi-Strauss once compared successful mourning work to a contract with the dead. In return for being respectfully remembered, the dead agree to stay in their own place and share a concern for the interests of the living. In this way the survivors establish peace and continuity with the dead, forgiving them for their terrible absence, being forgiven by them for continuing life (Dinnage 1990, 8–9). But as in life, successful contracts are best made with persons one can trust. Professor Kwasi Wiredu tells us that among the Yoruba the death of a virtuous person who has led a full and productive life is not strictly an occasion for mourning: "The Akans would attend the funeral of such a person in white, instead of the customary black, brown, or red," and the Yoruba would speak of celebration rather than lamentation. Such a person joins the ancestors in a serene afterlife whose primary concern is beneficial interaction with the community of the living (Wiredu and Gyekye 1992, 147). However, an individual who suffers an inappropriate death will trouble the living, who may not even give him a proper funeral ceremony. In the view of the Akans of Ghana, Wiredu says, "a person whose life is cut short by an accident or an 'unclean' disease or any other untoward circumstance does not gain immediate access to the country of the dead but becomes a neighborhood ghost, haunting the living" (1992, 147).

In our own society, untended, untimely, or unlucky deaths often arouse our guilt, offend our sense of justice, and leave us sleepless, even though a literal belief in ghosts is not widespread. Attention to the facts of deaths, such as those through domestic violence, famine, or war, may mobilize resistance to the persons, practices, or ideologies responsible for those deaths. Collective memorials, such as the Vietnam War Memorial or the AIDS Quilt, are an important way of respecting and attending to those deaths. Political action is another way. In "Gender, Death, and Resistance," Jean Franco praises the Mothers of the Plaza de Mayo for enabling their country to "establish a dialogue with its dead" (1991, 78).

Such communal mourning work—listening to and telling stories, sifting and winnowing memories, fashioning artworks or joining in quiet vigil with others—is among the most important work we do. Listening to the stories of the dying is one of the primary functions of hospice workers. Primo Levi wrote that the strongest need of survivors of Auschwitz was for others to hear their stories. He suffered a recurrent nightmare in which nobody would listen to him. "Why," he asks,"is the pain of every day translated so constantly into our dreams, in the ever-repeated scene of the unlistened-to story?" (Levi 1993, 60)

This attention to the dying softens our culture's sharp opposition between living and dying, self and others. We, the living, visit the worlds of our dead and work on projects that they cared about in life, or at the very least we heap rocks on memorial cairns. Similarly, they visit us from time to time, for they are a part of who we are, though they happen to have died.

I conclude with a look at mourning rituals from rural Greece and from our own culture. The essential purpose of rural Greek rituals, according to Loring Danforth, is to mediate the opposition between life and death by showing that death is an integral part of life (Danforth and Tsiaras 1982). Funeral laments sustain the belief in interaction between the living and the dead, for they are phrased as conversations with the dead. "Wake up, Uncle. Wake up and hear the songs. Uncle, what can we give you to take to Anna [who had died earlier]?" (Danforth and Tsiaras 1982, 127). Jill Dubisch, an anthropologist working in the same area, tells us that "mourning provides a limninal period during which the deceased continue to have ties to the material world. Women bring food and flowers to the graves, light the oil lamps, keep the grave sites neat, and generally tend to the needs of the dead" (1989, 190). Ritual events are carefully structured in time; the forty-day service releases distant kin from the obligations of mourning and is followed by yearly services that mark slow changes drawing the close survivors away from the death world. The end of the mourning period (usually five years) is marked by the exhumation of the bones and their consignment to the village ossuary (and thus to the collective care of the community).

Such rituals allow for the periods of craziness that often afflict those who have suffered deep loss, giving them culturally sanctioned time in which to return to the land of the living. This practice is diametrically opposed to current practice in the United States, according to which the bereaved are urged to resume their ordinary lives within weeks or even days after the death.

And yet, even in the culture of the United States, Toni Morrison describes in her novel *Sula* a disorderly funeral service at which the women shrieked over the bier and at the lip of the open grave. Her protagonist Nel was at first greatly offended by their behavior. But then she suffered a separation of her own, when her husband deserted her, and she changed her view on the ceremony: "What she had regarded since as unbecoming behavior seemed fitting to her now; [the women] were screaming at the neck of God, his giant nape, the vast back-of-the-head that he had turned on them in death. But it seemed to her now that it was not a fist-shaking grief they were keening but rather a simple obligation to say something, do something, feel something about the dead. They could not let that heart-smashing event pass unrecorded, unidentified" (Morrison 1973, 107). Both the measured Greek rituals and the wild disorder of this American funeral affirm the interrelationships of humans one with another and the reality of loss. They give weight to the view that we are social selves, constituted by our relationships with others. They give meaning to the otherwise puzzling metaphor, "a part of me died with her."

NOTES

I thank Claudia Card, Sara Ruddick, and Donna Decker for direction and encouragement; Joy Kroeger-Mappes and Uma Narayan for written comments, and audiences from the Midwest Society for Women in Philosophy for helpful responses to predecessors of this chapter. I also thank the center for Advanced Feminist Studies at the University of Minnesota and Clarion University of Pennsylvania for support.

1. I refer readers who seek substantive answers to questions about dying to Herbert Fingarette's recent book, *Death: Philosophical Soundings* (1996). My purposes in the present chapter are much more limited than those of Professor Fingarette.

2. The other two basic moral concepts that are being transformed are the relationship between reason and emotion and the distinction between public and private, both of which have an important bearing on issues in death and dying.

3. Linda Gilbert presents a theory of the social self by drawing on Mead's work and developing the concept of the "plural subject": the fusion of two egos, based on a special holistic commitment, one to the other, making wholes out of disparate, unified parts and facilitating not only shared projects but those of each member. She sees this fusion not as rare, as in great love affairs, but as a basic, everyday modus operandus that helps us to coordinate decisions and discover shared standards of conduct (Gilbert 1996).

REFERENCES

Aries, Philippe. 1974. *Western Attitudes Toward Death.* Trans. Patricia M. Ranum. Baltimore: Johns Hopkins University Press.
Baier, Annette. 1985. *Postures of the Mind.* Minneapolis: University of Minnesota Press.
———. 1995. *Moral Prejudices.* Cambridge: Harvard University Press.
Beckett, Samuel. 1967. *Stories and Texts for Nothing.* New York: Grove Press.
Booth, Stephen. 1977. *Shakespeare's Sonnets.* New Haven: Yale University Press.
Callahan, Daniel. 1993. "Pursuing a Peaceful Death." *Hastings Center Reports* (July–August).
Camus, Albert. 1955. *The Myth of Sisyphus and Other Essays.* Trans. Justin O'Brien. New York: Penguin.
Card, Claudia, ed. 1991. *Feminist Ethics.* Lawrence: University Press of Kansas.
Clifton, Lucille. 1987. *Next.* Brockport, N.Y.: BOA Editions.
Danforth, Loring, and Alexander Tsiaras. 1982. *The Death Rituals of Ancient Greece.* Princeton, N.J.: Princeton University Press.
De Tocqueville, Alexis. 1967. *Democracy in America.* vol. 2. Trans. Henry Reeve. New York: Schocken.
Dinnage, Rosemary. 1990. *The Ruffian on the Stair.* New York: Viking.
Dubisch, Jill. 1989. "Death and Social Change in Greece." *Anthropology Quarterly* 62, 4: 189–99.
Emmanuel, Linda. 1995. "Re-examining Death." *Hastings Center Report* 25, 4: 27–35.
Feldman, Fred. 1994. *Confrontations with the Reaper.* Oxford: Oxford University Press.
Fingarette, Herbert. 1996. *Death: Philosophical Soundings.* Chicago: Open Court.

Fischer, John Martin, ed. 1993. *The Metaphysics of Death.* Stanford, Calif.: Stanford University Press.

Franco, Jean. 1991. "Gender, Death, and Resistance." *Chicago Review* (April): 59–78.

Friedman, Marilyn. 1993. *What Are Friends For? Feminist Perspectives on Personal Relationships and Moral Theory.* Ithaca: Cornell University Press.

Furman v. Georgia 408 U.S. (1972).

Galloway, Alika. 1997. "New Minister." *Minneapolis Women's Press,* September 17–30.

Gavin, Wiliam Joseph. 1995. *Cuttin' the Body Loose: Historical, Biological, and Personal Approaches to Death and Dying.* Philadelphia: Temple University Press.

Gilbert, Linda. 1996. *Living Together: Rationality, Sociality, and Obligation.* Lanham, Md.: Rowman and Littlefield.

Gould, Carol, ed. 1983. *Beyond Domination.* Totowa, N.J.: Rowman and Allanheld.

Hanen, Marsha, and Kai Nielsen, eds. 1987. *Science, Morality, and Feminist Theory.* Calgary: University of Calgary Press.

Hartmann, Nicolai. 1932. *Ethics.* Vol. 3. London: Allen and Unwin.

Held, Virginia. 1993. *Feminist Morality: Transforming Culture, Society, and Politics.* Chicago: University of Chicago Press.

———. 1995. *Justice and Care: Essential Readings in Feminist Ethics.* Boulder, Colo.: Westview.

Hendin, Herbert. 1995. "Selling Death with Dignity." *Hastings Center Report* 25, 3: 19–23.

Holmes, Helen Bequaert, and Laura W. Purdy, eds. 1992. *Feminist Perspectives in Medical Ethics.* Bloomington: Indiana University Press.

hooks, bell. 1989. *Talking Back.* Boston: South End Press.

Ignatow, David. 1991. *Shadowing the Ground.* Hanover, N.H.: University Press of New England.

Kant, Immanuel. 1974. *Anthropology from a Practical Point of View.* Trans. Mary J. Gregor. The Hague: Martinus Nijhoff.

Katz, Jay. 1984. *The Silent World of Doctor and Patient.* New York: Free Press.

Keizer, Bert. 1994. *Dancing with Mr. D.* New York: Nan A. Talese.

Leder, Drew, ed. 1992. *The Body in Medical Thought and Practice.* Dordrecht: Klewer.

Lerner, Gerda. 1985. *A Death of One's Own.* Madison: University of Wisconsin Press.

Levi, Primo. 1993. *Survival in Auschwitz: The Nazi Assault on Humanity.* Trans. Stuart Woolf. New York: Macmillan.

Lugones, María. 1987. "Playfulness, 'World'-Traveling, and Loving Perception." *Hypatia* 2, 2: 3–19.

Mead, George Herbert. 1934. *Mind, Self, and Society.* Chicago: University of Chicago Press.

Meyer, Michael. 1995. "Dignity, Death, and Modern Virtue." *American Philosophical Quarterly* 32, 1 (January): 45–55.

Meyers, Diana, ed. 1997. *Feminists Rethink the Self.* Boulder, Colo.: Westview.

Moller, David W. 1996. *Confronting Death.* New York: Oxford University Press.

Morrison, Toni. 1993. *Sula.* New York: Knopf.

Murdoch, Iris. 1992. *Metaphysics As a Guide to Morals.* London: Penguin Books.

Noddings, Nel. 1989. *Women and Evil.* Berkeley: University of California Press.

Opie, Iona A., and Peter Opie, eds. 1959. *The Oxford Book of Children's Verse.* New York: Oxford University Press.

Parfit, Derek. 1984. *Reasons and Persons.* Oxford: Oxford University Press.

Parkes, Colin Murray, et al., eds. 1977. *Death and Bereavement Across Cultures.* London: Routledge.

Pascalev, Assaya. 1996. "Images of Death and Dying in the Intensive Care Unit." *Journal of Medical Humanities* 17, 4: 219–35.

Quill, Timothy. 1996. *A Midwife Through the Dying Process.* Baltimore: Johns Hopkins University Press.

Rich, Adrienne. 1989. *Time's Power: Poems 1985–88.* New York: W. W. Norton.

Ruddick, Sara. 1989. *Maternal Thinking.* Boston: Beacon Press.

Schott, Robin May. 1997. *Feminist Interpretations of Immanuel Kant.* University Park: Pennsylvania State University Press.

Schroeder-Sheker, Therese. 1991. "Musically Midwifing Death." *Utne Reader* (September–October): 83–84.

Simiak, Clifford. 1953. *City.* New York: Ace Books.

Slater, Scott, and Alec Solomita. 1980. *Exits.* New York: E. P. Dutton.

Spiro, Howard M., Mary G. McCrea Curnen, and Lee Palmer Wandel, eds. 1996. *Facing Death.* New Haven: Yale University Press.

Stoddard, Sandal. 1978. *The Hospice Movement.* New York: Vintage.

Taylor, Charles. 1995. *Philosophical Arguments.* Cambridge: Cambridge University Press.

Thomasma, David C., Thomasine Kushner, and Steve Heilig. 1996. "Physician-Aided Death: The Escalating Debate." *Cambridge Quarterly of Health Care Ethics* 5, 1: 1–131.

Walker, Margaret. 1989. "Moral Understandings: Alternative 'Epistemology' for a Feminist Ethics." *Hypatia* 4, 2: 15–28.

———. 1992. "Feminism, Ethics, and the Question of Theory." *Hypatia* 7, 3: 23–28.

Wiesel, Elie. 1972. *Night, Dawn, The Accident.* New York: Hill and Wang.

Wiredu, Kwasi, and Kwame Gyekye. 1992. *Person and Community: Ghanaian Philosophical Studies* Vol. I. Washington D.C.: Council for Research and Values in Philosophy.

Wittgenstein, Ludwig. 1961. *Tractatus Logico-Philosophicus.* Trans. D. F. Pears and B. F. McGuinness. London: Routledge and Kegan Paul.

The Contributors

JACQUELINE ANDERSON is professor in the Humanities Department at Olive-Harvey College. She serves as board president of the Lesbian Community Cancer Project and is a member of the steering committees of Chicago Black Lesbians and Gays, the Gay, Lesbian, Straight Education Network, the editorial board of the Institute of Lesbian Studies, the Mountain Moving Coffee House Collective, and the Midwest Society for Women in Philosophy, for which she has also served as executive secretary.

SANDRA LEE BARTKY is professor of philosophy and women's studies at the University of Illinois, Chicago. She teaches feminist theory, phenomenology, poststructuralism, and critical theory. She is the author of *Femininity and Domination: Essays in the Phenomenology of Oppression* (Routledge, 1990), which deals with such topics as female embodiment, beauty norms, sexual objectification, internalized oppression, and the exploitation of women's emotional labor. She has served on the American Philosophical Association's Committee on the Status of Women and is currently a member of the APA's Committee on the Status and Future of the Profession. In addition, she is a founder of the feminist philosophical journal *Hypatia* and the Society for Women in Philosophy, now an international network with three chapters in the United States and chapters in Canada, England, Germany, Norway, Argentina, and Mexico.

SHARON BISHOP is professor of philosophy at California State University, Los Angeles, where she teaches courses in ethics, political philosophy, and philosophical psychology. She is coeditor with Marjorie Weinzweig of *Philosophy and Women* (Wadsworth, 1979). Her teaching and research interests include feminist ethics and moral psychology.

SUSAN J. BRISON is associate professor of philosophy at Dartmouth College, where she also teaches in the women's studies program. She is the author of *Speech, Harm, and Conflicts of Rights* (Princeton University Press, forthcoming 1999), and coeditor of *Contemporary Perspectives on Constitutional Interpretation* (Westview, 1993). She is currently working on a book on trauma and memory.

CHESHIRE CALHOUN is associate professor of philosophy at Colby College, Waterville, Maine. She received her Ph.D. from the University of Texas at Austin in 1981, with a dissertation on morality and the emotions. She is coeditor with Robert Solomon of *What Is an Emotion? Classic Readings in Philosophical Psychology* (Oxford University Press, 1984) and author of many articles, including "Responsibility and Reproach," "Changing One's Heart" (on forgiveness), and "Standing for Something" (on integrity). She is at work on a book, provisionally titled "Centering Sexuality Politics," which develops the thesis that heterosexist domination is a separate axis of oppression not reducible to gender domination.

JOAN C. CALLAHAN is professor of philosophy and director of women's studies at the University of Kentucky, where she also is affiliated with the social theory program. She is the author of many articles and has published the following books: *Reproduction, Ethics, and the Law: Feminist Perspectives* (Indiana, 1995); *Menopause: A Midlife Passage* (Indiana, 1993); *Preventing Birth: Contemporary Methods and Related Moral Controversies,* with James W. Knight (University of Utah Press, 1989); and *Ethical Issues in Professional Life* (Oxford University Press, 1988). Her Webpage is http://www.uky.edu/~buddy/buddywelcome.html.

CLAUDIA CARD is professor of philosophy at the University of Wisconsin, with teaching affiliations in women's studies and environmental studies. She is the author of *Lesbian Choices* (Columbia University Press, 1995) and *The Unnatural Lottery: Character and Moral Luck* (Temple University Press, 1996) and editor of *Feminist Ethics* (University Press of Kansas, 1991) and *Adventures in Lesbian Philosophy* (Indiana University Press, 1994). She edits the Feminist

Ethics book series for the University Press of Kansas and chairs the American Philosophical Association's Committee on the Status of Lesbians, Gays, Bisexuals, and Transgendered People in the Profession. She is writing a book on evil.

CHRIS J. CUOMO is associate professor of philosophy and a member of the women's studies program at the University of Cincinnati. She is a community activist, author of *Feminism and Ecological Communities: An Ethic of Flourishing* (Routledge, 1998), and an active member of the Midwest Society of Women in Philosophy. She is currently coediting with Kim Hall a book on gender and whiteness (Rowman and Littlefield, forthcoming 1999).

VIRGINIA HELD is Distinguished Professor of Philosophy and professor of women's studies at Hunter College and the Graduate School of the City University of New York. She is the author of *Feminist Morality: Transforming Culture, Society, and Politics* (University of Chicago Press, 1993), *Rights and Goods: Justifying Social Action* (Free Press, 1984), and *The Public Interest and Individual Interests* (Basic Books, 1970), and editor of *Justice and Care: Essential Readings in Feminist Ethics* (Westview 1995) and *Property, Profits, and Economic Justice* (Wadsworth, 1980). She is one of the authors of *Women's Realities, Women's Choices* by the Hunter College Women's Studies Collective (Oxford University Press, 1995).

MARCIA L. HOMIAK is professor of philosophy at Occidental College, where she teaches courses in philosophy, women's studies, and ancient history. She is currently working on a book on Aristotle's moral theory, entitled "Virtue and the Limits of Reason."

AMBER L. KATHERINE teaches critical thinking and philosophy at Edgewood College in Madison, Wisconsin (akatherine@edgewood.edu), where she lives happily with her extended grrrl family. Her dissertation (Michigan State University 1996) is a philosophical investigation into issues raised by Audre Lorde's "An Open Letter to Mary Daly" of 1979. Each spring and fall she participates in meetings of the Midwest Society of Women in Philosophy. She is currently at work on a story entitled "Lucky Cosmos: A Gemini Project," which takes up issues of philosophical interest to those thinking on the feminist second/third wave cusp.

JEAN P. RUMSEY is associate professor of philosophy at Clarion University of Pennsylvania. Her articles on Kantian ethics, feminist ethics, and medical ethics, have appeared in the *Journal of Value Inquiry, Journal of the History of Philosophy,* and *Hypatia,* among others. Her research interests also include anthropology. She is currently involved in the University of Pittsburgh's Consortium for Medical Ethics in Western Pennsylvania.

ROBIN MAY SCHOTT has held positions as associate professor of philosophy at the University of Louisville and the University of Copenhagen. She is the author of *Cognition and Eros: A Critique of the Kantian Paradigm* (Beacon, 1988; Pennsylvania State University Press, 1993), coeditor of *Forplantning, Kon og Teknologi* (Reproduction, Gender, and Technology) (Copenhagen: Museum Tusculanums Forlag, 1995), and editor of *Feminist Interpretations of Immanuel Kant* (Pennsylvania State University Press, 1997). She has published many articles on feminist interpretations of the history of philosophy and on questions of nationalism, war, and women.

ANNA STUBBLEFIELD is assistant professor of philosophy at Temple University, where she is also a member of the women's studies program and the Institute for the Study of Literacy, Literature, and Culture. She works with a group of teenage women who are writing about their experiences of gender socialization. She is writing a book on the nature, meaning, and political significance of African American racial identity and its implications for the debate in political philosophy on assimilationism and pluralism.

LYNNE TIRRELL is associate professor of philosophy at the University of Massachusetts in Boston, where she also teaches in the women's studies program. Her articles on philosophy of language, aesthetics, feminist theory, and the politics of discourse have appeared in many journals, including the *Journal of Philosophy, Nous,* and *Hypatia.* She is at work on a book on the power of discourse as embodied in the practices that shape derogatory terms and images.

IRIS MARION YOUNG is professor of public and international affairs at the University of Pittsburgh, where she teaches ethics and political philosophy. Her most recent book is a collection of her essays entitled *Intersecting Voices: Dilemmas of Gender, Political Philosophy, and Policy* (Princeton University Press, 1997).

Index